D0140729

Trade and Civilisation in the Indian Ocean

Before the age of Industrial Revolution, the great Asian civilisations –
whether located in the Middle East, India, South-East Asia, or the Far
East – constituted areas not only of high culture but also of advanced
economic development. They were the First World of human societies.

This book examines one of the driving forces of that historical
period: the long chain of oceanic trade which stretched from the South
China Sea to the eastern Mediterranean, passing through a series of rich
urban emporia. It also looks at the natural complement of the seaborne
commerce, its counterpart in the caravan trade. In analytical terms, the
book emphasises the methods of multi-dimensional history by high-
lighting the intricate relationship between space, time and structure. Its
main achievement is to show how socially determined demand derived
from cultural habits and interpretations operated through the medium
of market forces and relative prices. It points out, for the first time, the
unique and limiting features of Asian commercial capitalism, and
shows how the contribution of Asian merchants was valued universally,
in reality if not legally and formally.

Professor Chaudhuri's book, based on more than twenty years'
research and reflection on pre-modern trade and civilisations, is a
landmark in the analysis and interpretation of Asia's historical position
and development.

NOV - - 2013

Plate 1. Map of the world, from J.H. van Linschoten, *His Discours of Voyages unto the Easte and West Indies*, 1598.

Trade and Civilisation in the Indian Ocean

An Economic History from the Rise of Islam to 1750

K.N. Chaudhuri

Professor of the Economic History of Asia,
School of Oriental and African Studies,
University of London

WILLIAMSBURG REGIONAL LIBRARY
7770 CROAKER ROAD
WILLIAMSBURG, VA 23188

 CAMBRIDGE
UNIVERSITY PRESS

CAMBRIDGE UNIVERSITY PRESS
Cambridge, New York, Melbourne, Madrid, Cape Town, Singapore, São Paulo

Cambridge University Press
The Edinburgh Building, Cambridge CB2 8RU, UK

Published in the United States of America by Cambridge University Press, New York

www.cambridge.org
Information on this title: www.cambridge.org/9780521242264

© Cambridge University Press 1985

This publication is in copyright. Subject to statutory exception
and to the provisions of relevant collective licensing agreements,
no reproduction of any part may take place without the written
permission of Cambridge University Press.

First published 1985
Eighth printing 2005

A catalogue record for this publication is available from the British Library

Library of Congress Catalogue Card Number: 84–12152

ISBN 978-0-521-24226-4 hardback
ISBN 978-0-521-28542-1 paperback

Transferred to digital printing 2008

Contents

Maps

Plates

Preface

To turn to a general historical study of past civilisations after sixteen years of documentary and archival research is not an easy decision. The completion of my work on the English East India Company in the summer of 1975 left me with considerable uncertainty about the future direction in which I should go. A huge amount of material which I had collected still awaited further investigation and analysis, especially on the social aspects of the early European presence in Asia. At the same time, the urge to escape for a while from the rigours of a long scholastic incarceration was very strong. Several factors encouraged me to move in the direction of the present study. In the spring of 1975 I met Fernand Braudel for the first time in Prato, during the Settima Settimana di Studi at the Francesco Datini Institute, of which he is the President. Braudel and his wife received me with kindness and expressed an interest in seeing my current research, still unpublished at that time. He himself was then working on the last two volumes of *Civilisation matérielle* with the active support of his wife, and it was evident that a vast historical canvas, a work of great inspiration, was slowly taking shape. The sessions of the Datini Institute that year were devoted to world monetary history from the thirteenth century to the eighteenth. As I listened to the large collection of detailed papers presented, it occurred to me that a single work dealing with the general theme of long-distance trade and the role of money in pre-modern societies might fill a lacuna that still existed in the historiography of early trade.

In the autumn and winter of the same year, I was able to spend six months travelling in India, the Middle East, and South East Asia, and to visit some of the ancient towns and cities which were once prominent in the caravan and maritime trade of the Indian Ocean. The contrasting images of those journeys still convey to my mind the impression of a world that has almost vanished from contemporary Western Europe, a world inhabited by mankind for several millennia. Only once, in 1979 while walking through the streets of Ciudad Rodrigo in Spain, did I feel that I was face to face with the still-living past. The road that runs from Delhi to Agra, and then to Ajmer, Jodhpur and Gujarat, follows the old caravan route, often marked by tall league-towers, as do also the roads from Tehran to Isfahan, Shiraz, Yazd, and Kirman. To travel along these roads is to experience at first hand the simultaneous existence of the harsh realities of the old civilisation, the *ancien régime*, and its finest achievements. The exquisite lake-side marble pavilions of the Mughal emperors at Ajmer are flanked by the view of the precipitous mountain fortress, the scene of many bloody massacres, and an uncompromising instrument of military power. The awesome landscape of North India is only marginally softened by its fertile cornfields; but there is nothing comparable in the wide expanse of rocks, sand, and dried-out salt lakes which make up the Iranian plateau. The only sign of life is the occasional flock of sheep, a desert breed accustomed to conditions of extreme aridity. The glittering golden-domed shrine of Qumm rises above the empty plains as a magnificent tribute to the ascetical devotion of Islam. The lake palace at Udaipur, built in the early eighteenth century, has the classic outlines of Mughal architecture from the period of Shah Jahan, though it was the residence of a Hindu prince. Its interior gardens, of ravishing beauty and elegance, recall the parterres of Mughal gardens, though transformed by Rajastani sensibilities. I saw the lake palace during a North Indian spring as the overhead sun was pushing the day temperature towards the 35°C range. A few weeks later I was in Isfahan. Snow had not yet melted on the surrounding mountains. In the courtyard of the Madrase Madar-i-Shah, the spring blossoms were just beginning to appear on the almond and cherry trees. The stately plane trees planted in that courtyard garden of perfect geometric proportions were still bare against the turquoise-tiled dome. In 1677 John Fryer travelled from Surat to Isfahan by sea and land. His descriptions recorded the impact made by the Iranian primate city on someone well-accustomed to the sights of large trading towns:

thus attended we were brought over a most Magnificent Bridge with Arches over our Heads, and on both sides Rails and Galleries to view the River, the cloisters whereof were Paved with broad Marble . . . which led us to a stately large Street, continued on the other side with equal Gallantry of Buildings and Trees, till we were carried under their Lofty-Ceiled and Stately-Erected *Buzzars* . . . which is, I confess, the surprizingest piece of Greatness in Honour of Commerce the whole World can boast of, our *Burses* being but Snaps of Buildings to these famous *Buzzers*. (Fryer, II, 240–1)

The difference between the Indian adaptation of Islamic artistic tradition and the purely Islamised Iran is clearly visible, and yet the contrast is nothing like as strong as in the case of civilisations one meets in South East Asia. The sight of whitewashed Buddhist temples with multi-coloured roofing tiles and ornate Chinese religious shrines is as evocative of the cultural watershed between the west and the east in the Indian Ocean as the landscape itself, with its deep, slow-moving rivers and flooded rice fields.

The visual impressions brought back from that period of Asian travel gradually strengthened my earlier idea of undertaking a general study of long-distance trade, markets, and merchants in the context of different societies and civilisations. However, after I had written three preliminary draft chapters the plan was modified as a result of a suggestion from Robin Derricourt and the Cambridge University Press that the study might be directed more specifically at the origin, development, and structure of Indian Ocean trade before 1800. The suggestion came at a time when new undergraduate courses were introduced examining the comparative features of the pre-modern economic system of Asia. I am grateful to the Syndics of the Press for accepting my draft proposals in outline and to Robin Derricourt for constant encouragement while progress on the work was held up by many other academic commitments. In terms of historical methodology, the present study is very different from my *Trading World of Asia and the English East India Company*. The latter was an attempt to analyse long-distance trade and commercial decision-making in terms of rigorous quantitative techniques. The series of statistics compiled from the original records demonstrates that pre-modern trade was not a matter of chance but incorporated systematic, rational processes as well. That conclusion is supported by this study also, with the additional discovery that cultural values and contrasting social habits contributed as much to pre-modern economic exchange as did purely economic factors. The present work attempts to examine this constant interaction between the rationality of commercial decisions, financial aspirations, and the larger elements of causality embedded in the human society and the environment.

A special word of thanks is due to M.A. Cook, who read the entire typescript and offered many helpful suggestions and criticisms. His vast knowledge of early Islamic sources and terms has been readily available to me, and I am grateful to him for bringing to my knowledge a number of interesting references. I must thank Gerald Hawting for checking my Roman transliteration of Arabic script, though I have not always followed orthodox conventions for their own sake. For assistance in Chinese history I have constantly turned to W.S. Atwell and benefited greatly from his detailed analysis of China's monetary economy. Roland Oliver's interest in the comparative history of civilisations was a steady source of encouragement and support. My pupils, both undergraduates and research students, have always sustained my work with their own studies and ideas. I remember with particular pleasure the response of my class in 1979, when I presented a lecture course on this subject for the first time. Finally, I should like to thank A.G. Hopkins, who made many useful suggestions for improving the final presentation of the main arguments.

London, January 1981

Abbreviations

IOR   India Office Records (the records division of The India Office Library and Records, The British Library)

PRO   Public Record Office

Introduction

The idea that the study of a civilisation might be named after a sea originated with Fernand Braudel. Arab geographers were aware a thousand years ago of the relationship between different oceans and the Bilad al-Islam. In our own times, Braudel remains one of a select group of French historians and geographers who have perceived, with rare clarity, the connection between the sea and the people who lived around its shores. For them the interaction between space, the passage of solar time, and the identity of civilisations constitutes one of the most important latent forces of history. Ten years' work and residence in an Islamic country (Algeria) bordering the Mediterranean, as Braudel himself has told us, no doubt sharpened his insight into and awareness of cultural and geographical unity (and by definition differences), the memory of which has gradually been lost over the last two centuries and has had to be recaptured through long and painstaking research in a dozen different archives.[1] The title of the present work is an inadequate acknowledgement of a profound intellectual debt owed to Fernand Braudel and a recognition of the trend in social and economic history set in motion by the publication in 1949 of *La Méditerranée et le monde méditerranéen à l'époque de Philippe II*. Since its first appearance a whole generation of European historians have learnt their craft from this great teacher at the Collège de France and the VIe Section, L'École Pratique des Hautes Études. The French power-house in Paris is even sending out its signals and energy to the historians of Asia, who have laboured for so long under the fierce tropical sun, shackled to one another by the relentless, unchanging discipline of a sacred school tradition.

In the preface to the English edition of *The Mediterranean*, Braudel claimed that from the time of its first completion and subsequent revision two major truths have remained unchallenged. "The first is the unity and coherence of the Mediterranean region. I retain the firm conviction", he wrote, "that the Turkish Mediterranean lived and breathed with the same rhythms as the Christian, that the whole sea shared a common destiny, a heavy one indeed, with identical problems and general trends if not identical consequences."[2] The historian of the Indian Ocean must ask himself whether a similar claim is valid for the countries bordering that vast ocean, and if so whether the period from the rise of Islam to the mid-eighteenth century has the same coherence as the reign of Philip II chosen by Braudel. Before an attempt is made to look at

1

the problem, an important fact needs restatement. Historians who have to struggle daily with primary archival material and its interpretation know that Braudel's work is incapable of direct imitation. It is the result of an inborn intuition, an understanding of the complex interplay of events and impersonal forces, which does not explicitly make clear its theoretical reasoning and rigorous logic. His methods and approach however are not beyond comprehension and even mastery.

Is it possible then to discover the unity and diversity of Indian Ocean civilisations through the study of long-distance trade, which of necessity takes place across geographical and cultural watersheds and which has a compelling temporal dimension? Cast in this way, the question enables us to see clearly that the triple analytical foundations of Braudel's historical logic – space, time, and structure – also support our study of Asian trade and the social systems associated with it. But comparative analysis always contains contradictions. The question of unity in the Mediterranean was underlined by Braudel in the following lines:

> To pass from the true Mediterranean, as defined by its climate, to that greater Mediterranean where its influence is felt, is to pass from a physical unit to that human unit with which this book is concerned. This human unit is not merely the result of nature, or more particularly of the waters of the Mediterranean. The sea is everything it is said to be: it provides unity, transport, the means of exchange and intercourse, if a man is prepared to make an effort and pay a price. But it has also been the great divider, the obstacle that had to be overcome . . . The Mediterranean has no unity but that created by the movements of men, the relationships they imply, and the routes they follow.[3]

There is no contradiction in this statement if we resort to the formal theory of causality as propounded by mathematicians of time.[4] In the philosophical conversation between the Buddhist teacher Nagasena and King Milinda (*c.* 155– 130 BC), both agreed that the fire which burned through the night was the same fire and yet the fire which burned early in the night was not the same as the fire which burned late.[5]

The Arab geographer al-Muqaddasi (*c.* 980) was perfectly aware of the geographical nuances of the Empire of Islam. The sun set on the extreme side of the territory of al-Maghreb, he observed, where it was seen to descend into the all-circling ocean. The peninsula of the Arabs was encompassed by the Sea of China from Egypt to 'Abbadan.[6] The Atlantic, the Mediterranean, and the Indian Ocean seemed to provide for the members of the faithful a physical cohesion that was already spiritually strong. But the key to al-Muqaddasi's thinking lies in the use of the phrase the "Sea of China". Muslim geographers were not ignorant of the military might of the rulers of Hindustan or the world of islands and sea in Indonesia. Yet the Indian Ocean derived its identity from an unspoken role assigned to the Celestial Empire. They could see, as we can, that the sea which washed the desolate beaches of Suez or the marshes around Basra provided an unbroken means of travel all the way to China, beyond which lay an unnavigable ocean, the Pacific. Islamic Near and Middle East, Hindu India, and China constituted zones of separate cultural identity. Geographical and economic ties between them strengthened an invisible sense of unity. The Indian Ocean as defined by climate also embraced another contrasting area far from the actual sea. The monsoon winds carrying rain-bearing clouds originated near the Equator and ran into the Himalayan barrier, where they stopped. But the north east monsoon during the winter months could be traced back to the high pressure forming in Central Asia. While the two seasonal monsoons held Asian food production in an iron clamp, Central Asia, with its pastures, deserts, cities, and caravan routes, was an indispensable backdrop to trans-regional economic activities.

The countries of the Indian Ocean did not share a common destiny during the period under review, as those of the Mediterranean may have done under Philip II. But there was a firm impression in the minds of contemporaries, sensed also by historians later, that the ocean had its own unity, a distinct sphere of influence. Means of travel, movements of peoples, economic exchange, climate, and historical forces created elements of cohesion. Religion, social systems, and cultural traditions, on the other hand, provided the contrasts. Historians of comparative civilisations must necessarily work with such dialectic tools. There are no positive numbers unless there are negative ones. The first set is verified by experience, the second only by a concept. In the historical context of Asia, as Charles Boone, the English Governor of Bombay, propounded in 1718 as an axiom of Indian statecraft, "if no Naval Force no Trade, if no Fear no Friendship".

His corporate masters in London were fully aware that the Society served by Boone and others was a Company of Trading Merchants and not Warriors.[7] The East India Company's officials in Asia could not purge their attitudes of a political ideology which had been in force from the time that the Portuguese conquistadores first arrived in the Indian Ocean. A commonly held ideology can, of course, give rise to a recognisable pattern, especially if the participants are maritime traders possessing the physical means of travel from one end of the Indian Ocean to the other. The rise of European sea-power and commercial expansion from the sixteenth century onwards provide only one example of the unifying influence of history. The astonishing success of Islam as a religion, a political empire, and a way of life was fully measurable in terms of our triple dimensions of time, space, and structure. From the mid-seventh century to the fifteenth, Islamic civilisation continued to expand towards the four points of the compass. From Alexandria to Canton, the Friday mosque symbolised its presence and raised an unanswerable question: how and why did it happen? The migration of nomads from Central Asia and the foundation of great military empires represented another catalytic force in Asian history;

and no one in the period of our study forgot the massive presence of Chinese civilisation and political power, expanding and receding through the ages like the rising and ebbing tides of the Indian Ocean. If Asian historians see a kind of chronological unity in the period from 650 to 1750, it is perhaps because they are aware of the course of Asian history during the two centuries from 1757 to 1947.

Is the "Indian Ocean" as a geographical space the same as Asia? The usage adopted in this study may confirm that impression. Both the Red Sea and the Persian Gulf are included in the list of seas of which the Indian Ocean is composed. Cartographers will find such liberty objectionable. Even the trans-Himalayan and T'ien Shan regions are discussed as if they were a natural complement to the Indian Ocean. The present line of argument can be justified once again by going back to the imagery emphasised by Braudel. He speaks of the Mediterranean as a physical unit and as a human unit. The frontiers of the two were not coterminous. Asia as a continent was an abstract concept, and during the period with which we are concerned people were unsure where Europe ended and Asia began. They were, of course, familiar with the difference between Muslims and Franks, between the people of Misr (Egypt) and those of Rum (Byzantium). From Constantinople to Andalusia, al-Muqaddasi commented, Christians were the feared masters of the northern Mediterranean and possessed the most accurate knowledge of its description, limits, and gulfs.[8] He was aware of the contradictions between the conventions of geography and those of everyday life, and the answer he gave to resolve them was perceptive. "If it were said", he wrote, "how is it possible that one and the same sea could be made into eight different seas? We reply that this is well-known to every one who undertakes a sea voyage."[9]

The caravan traders may have thought in the same way that they were travelling along a single continent divided by political frontiers, by secure and insecure zones, and by arid and fertile land. A historical study of long-distance trade enables us to see the underlying cohesion of the Indian Ocean and the contrasting nature of its different civilisations. Students of pre-modern Asia are often daunted by the formidable problem of comparative history. There are few studies which examine the historical past of the Indian Ocean countries before 1800 as a single subject. The tendency of history schools to divide themselves into regional branches has led to intense specialisation, adding greatly to our knowledge of finer details; but the task of integrating this knowledge into a general mosaic of interpretation is still incomplete. The purpose of this work is to begin a personal pilgrimage along that long road. Inter-regional trade conducted by sea and land symbolised at that time one of the most powerful features of social systems. If the pre-Industrial Revolution man was forced to live on bread or rice produced within walking distance, he was not altogether satisfied with clothing woven under his own roof. The daily necessities of life – clothing, pottery, tools, prophylactics, and even articles of food – assumed through the application of specialised skills and artistic imagination the status of valued, luxury objects. The process of exchanging such items incorporated many different forms, social customs, ritual usage, economic considerations, and above all, the problem of distance. Furthermore, long-distance trade as an international movement of goods and people provided a measure, even in our period, of the role of money and prices and of the state of the arts. It could not survive without universal agreement on the notion of safe-conduct, on a law of nations, and on the means to distribute the economic gains.

These themes provide our study with its subject matter. At the risk of stating the obvious, a few comments may be added on its structure and arrangement. Part I contains a discussion of the general problems (Chapter 1), followed by a description of the main historical events. The analytical logic is determined first by chronology – or, as the theorists would say, by the different components of time, long-term trends, cycles, and the random. But within each chapter runs another line of questions – to account for commercial events in relation to structures, whether these are identified in terms of space or of organisation. The arguments and ideas developed in Part I can be easily listed: the typology of single long-distance voyages mounted across the whole breadth of the Indian Ocean, methods of emporia trading, peaceful and armed trade, the individual partnerships of Asian merchants, and the bureaucratic operations of the Dutch and English East India Companies. Part II adopts a method of analysis which Fernand Braudel himself calls *la longue durée*. It will be readily seen that the chapters in this section are arranged by themes, though the logic of the actual sequence is not immediately apparent. It may also be asked what is *la longue durée* – a phrase and a concept that have aroused among historians of positivist inclinations much irritation and no little interest. Braudel himself defined it in the preface to his *Mediterranean* as "a history whose passage is almost imperceptible, that of man in his relationship to the environment, a history in which all change is slow, a history of constant repetition, ever-recurring cycles".[10] In another place, Braudel further elaborated his vision of time:

Among the different sorts of time that make up history, the long term thus presents itself as a troublesome, complicated, often entirely new character . . . it is in relation to such vast expanses of slow-moving history and to this infra-structure that the totality of history is to be rethought. Every one of the thousand levels, the thousand explosions of historical time, can be grasped if one starts with this concept of depth and semi-immobility; that is the centre around which everything revolves.[11]

In this study we have followed the broad direction of Braudel's definition of the various components of time; but no attempt has been made to develop a rigorous theory of historical change. The arrangement of Part II in particular relies on an identification of the environment, of the structural systems through which long-distance trade operated, and, finally, of the results or objects of the systems. Thus the two chapters on the sea and shipping analyse the physical domain of maritime trade, man's response to its mastery (as evident in knowledge of navigation and techniques of shipbuilding), and the slow-moving changes associated with them. Chapters 8 and 9, on land, commodities and markets, follow a similar logic, while in the final chapter we return to the problem of systems and structures created by man in his efforts to intensify economic exchange. The main historical movements are also retraced, to remind us of the relationship between *events* and *la longue durée*. It should be realised that the work can be read in many different sequences. For example, those who are interested in tracing the movements, the rationale, and the organisation of long-distance trade might take Chapters 1, 2, 5, 8, and 9 as a single unit. Similarly, trade as a process of economic exchange is discussed in Chapters 1, 9, and 10. Students of European expansion will find no difficulty in recognising the relevance of Chapters 3 and 4. The kind of history that is related in this study resembles in many ways the thinking and vision of early Arab architects: within the severe lines and the unitary plans will be found more than one obvious pattern.

PART I

General problems
and historical events

1

Trade and civilisation in the Indian Ocean: social, cultural, economic, and temporal dimensions

This study is concerned with the cultural and economic role of long-distance trade in an age when the technological breakthrough of the late eighteenth century had not as yet fundamentally changed the structure of Asian and European societies and state-systems. The period of history covered is long by any standard other than those of astronomers, geologists, historians of climate, and archaeologists. From the rise of Islam in the mid-seventh century to the beginning of European imperialism in the 1750s eleven centuries are spanned, a period during which the world saw the completion of an entire lifecycle for civilisation in general. In ecological terms alone, the old balance between human society and its environment was about to be replaced by a new order. The effects of the changes involved still continue to haunt us today, and there is no sign as yet of a possible equilibrium. For the period under study, the main historical movements stand out in bold relief. The diffusion of Islam as a religion and a way of life, if it marked the final break between the classical age and the new forces of expansion in much of the Mediterranean and the Near East, also created distinct zones of political tensions which ultimately checked its growth and destroyed the earlier sense of Arab intellectual triumph. The process of Christian *reconquista* in the Iberian peninsula was a forerunner in its chronological context of the great oceanic discoveries which the Spanish and Portuguese explorers were to initiate in the fifteenth century. These quickened the pace of seaborne trade and at the same time delivered a mortal blow not only to Muslim supremacy in the western Indian Ocean but also to the introspectiveness of India and China. Alone among the nations of Asia, the Japanese empire succeeded in keeping its frontiers closed to the outside world until it was ready to change its way of life from within. Of course, in the middle of the eighteenth century the Chinese empire still remained intact, as did also its political strength. Nor did the people of India contemplate as yet any real change to their social and cultural values. But neither the Chinese nor the Indian civilisation was able to isolate its economy from the unfolding effects of expanding world trade and industrial capitalism. Few observers would have believed, watching the international scene in the 1750s, that in a space of a hundred years the two great political and commercial nations of Asia would prove helpless in the face of foreign intervention which would actively change their economic destinies.

Map 1. The area of the Indian Ocean and trans-continental trade, 618–1750.

That the long millennium under review has a temporal unity we can take for granted without perhaps too much elaboration. The question is whether the historian, when handling such an extended period of history, is able to make any original contribution at all either to the analysis or to the narrative. The answer will surely depend on our ability to evaluate the significance of trade or economic exchange in civilisation and the way that time is an explicit component of human life. Long-distance trade has always occupied a large and important place in the study of history. However, the main focus of interest is generally on questions and problems that are easily interpreted by historians. Merchants and their social role provide a perennial subject for research, not merely because of the survival and volume of personal and business records, but also because of the way that the ruling elites and the politically powerful react to the activities, influence, and demands of those who are able to command a large amount of money. Pre-modern rulers, forced to depend on the economic surplus of agriculture, always suffered from the twin scourges of a shortage of ready cash and unending military expenditure. They knew only too well that ill-paid, mutinous soldiers were as much a threat to their power and authority as any known enemy outside. If the great merchants could be persuaded to become, partially at least, indirect paymasters of the army, so much the better. Persuasion could take the form of granting special privileges to the mercantile class in general, or more often of threats of violence to their personal safety and business property. Whether a ruler would take the short-term view of trade and its benefits or the long-term was conditioned by his financial needs and sense of desperation. In all the Asian civilisations with which we are concerned in this study, the merchant and his double, the banker, remained indispensable intermediaries in converting agricultural surplus into disposable state income.

Merchants are, by definition, generally obliged to travel. The organisation of trade, which reflected the scale of distances, revealed at the same time the mental world of the commercial community. Whether a great and wealthy merchant would actually accompany his goods to the overseas markets, use junior partners to fulfil that function, or follow the method of consigning the cargo to agents and friends abroad was decided by the institutional character of the market and its legal conventions. While most of the windows into the private lives and business decisions of medieval merchants are firmly shut, the chance discovery of a large body of papers belonging to the Jewish community of North Africa, who traded extensively in the eastern Mediterranean, the Red Sea, and the Indian Ocean (in the tenth and eleventh centuries), has suddenly opened for the detailed scrutiny of the historian the whole range of the considerations that influenced the activities of a group of pre-modern merchants. Members of the medieval Jewish community refrained from destroying documents bearing the name of God and "buried" their redundant papers in a "genizah" – the Hebrew name of a depository. The unique collection left by the merchants of Tunisia and Morocco, who had settled in Egypt during the period of the Fatimid rule, was found in the second half of the nineteenth century and brought to Europe. Their painstaking decipherment and collation in recent years represents a marvellous achievement in historical scholarship.

The geographical dimensions of long-distance trade are clearly visible in the correspondence of Cairo Genizah merchants. The presence of fellow-members of the community in towns as far apart as Qayrawan in Tunisia, Alexandria and Fustat in Egypt, and Aden at the entrance to the Red Sea facilitated the sale of goods by friends and associates resident there on behalf of the distant owners. In the year 1058–9, on the tenth day of Kislev (November– December), Abu Imran Musa b. Abi al-Hayy Khalifa wrote to Nahray b. Nissim at Fustat that he had returned from his journey to Syria and Palestine and suffered many hardships on the road, apart from having been repeatedly ill. He was distressed to learn of Nahray's losses during the current year, but this was no time for despair, especially this year when there was no one who had not suffered a loss. The news from Tripoli that the sultan there had imposed a fine on the community was another blow. The lapis lazuli belonging to the joint partnership could not be sold there; the money would be sent by land or sea when it fetched a price. The bundle of linen now being sent to Cairo should be sold in small lots of ten pieces. The carrier was already paid in full and was owed nothing.[1]

There are many similar letters in the Cairo Genizah documents. This particular correspondence refers to points that are full of analytical interest. The author was a travelling merchant as well as a user of the consignment system. He and his business partners were held together in a mutual bond of personal friendship, complete trust, and financial interest. In a community of such close-knit ties, the sanction against a defaulting member was the loss of his credit and reputation; a man who was not worthy of trust would quickly exhaust his fund of goodwill. There were certainly well-established conventions in commercial contracts in all the trading cities of the Mediterranean and the Indian Ocean. The legal corpus protected merchants when the contracts were concluded between inter-communal members, and the reputation of a port of trade turned on the fairness of its legal traditions. The fact that the sultan of Tripoli had levied a fine on the Jewish merchants of the city merely highlighted the opposite side of the coin that in most of the cities frequented by overseas merchants the local rulers granted a certain measure of juridical independence to them and made sure that the financial demands imposed on them remained within the bounds of tolerability. When a port of trade lost its reputation of fairness, it was only one step removed from commercial bankruptcy. Furthermore, the harsh behaviour of the ruling elites encouraged the officers and the crew of armed merchant ships to take the law into their own hands and either directly threaten the civic authorities or make reprisals on the local shipping. This was the remedy traditionally employed by the Dutch and English East India Companies against exactions and bad debts, and the pirate communities of the Indian Ocean could well have had a similar institutional origin. The exact reason why piracy becomes a communal activity at any historical period is still relatively unclear.

But there was no question even in our period of history of a political kingdom or an empire that took pride in its sense of sovereignty and the power of law enforcement allowing foreign merchants to suffer at the hands of pirates and robbers while they were within its sphere of jurisdiction. The Chinese

empire all through the ages suffered most from nomadic raids across its northern frontiers and from piratical attacks on the southern coastal villages and on
Chinese ships on the high sea. The result inevitably was a rigorous insistence
by the Celestial court on control of all forms of foreign trade and foreign
relations. It is not only the attitude of the Chinese ruling classes towards
"Barbarians" that explains the long survival of the tributary system of trade
under which the state took over many of the commercial functions normally
reserved for private merchants elsewhere; there was a rational logic behind it
as well. By keeping control of overseas trade in its own hands the Chinese
government attempted to institutionalise it on the same level as the rest of the
imperial administration. The tributary system of foreign trade was only partially successful, and private merchants always remained indispensable to
China's internal economy. When overseas voyages were periodically prohibited to them, the resolutions were by-passed either through present giving
or through the reluctance of the local mandarin class to damage the commercial economy of the coastal cities and regions. The system produced a
curious paradox. Chinese merchants who traded at foreign ports in defiance
of the imperial will were left without any diplomatic protection. In the seventeenth and eighteenth centuries, when the Dutch and Spanish authorities in the
East Indies treated the Chinese junk-owners harshly or even massacred the
Chinese inhabitants of Batavia or Manila, the imperial government in Peking
took no direct action in protest. An imperial court most conscious of its
sovereignty and the integrity of the political frontiers failed to subscribe to the
notion of a law of nations to protect its citizens abroad.

Other countries which participated actively in the seaborne trade of Asia
were far more sensitive to the reports of treatment received by merchants in
foreign ports and cities. Assaults by the local police or guards on visitors produced an outcry that was not confined to the overseas community alone. The
local merchants joined in the complaints. The concept of the reciprocity of
legal obligations and rights in so far as they applied to the travelling merchants
had developed early and remained in force to the end of our period. An
Egyptian document of the early fifteenth century makes it quite clear what
were the duties of the intendant of the domain, one of the highest officials,
towards merchants:

He will welcome the Karim merchants coming from the Yemen, seeking their goodwill, showing them courtesy, dealing with them justly, so that they may find a felicity
which they have not found in Arabia Felix [Yemen]; likewise the merchants who came
from the West . . . both Muslim and Frankish. Let him receive them kindly, and treat
them justly, for the profits . . . accruing from them . . . are very great.[2]

In 1744 the governor of the Mughal port of Surat, one of the greatest in India,
requested the English to respect the neutrality of the port in view of the naval
war between England and France. The East India Company's officials gave the

assurance. Three years later, when the governor died and his janissaries rioted in the city and even assaulted the members of the English Factory, the Company's Council pointed out that a city which lived by trade could not afford such lawlessness.[3]

Such incidents and violations of the accepted norms took place regularly. The rise and fall of different port-cities in the Indian Ocean were not altogether independent of political factors. Even under favourable circumstances Asian rulers were not always able to suppress pirates or to defend their merchants against attacks at sea. The strength and the efficiency of the navy belonging to an Indian Ocean power varied widely in response to strategic considerations and the value of seaborne trade to the rulers' income. China had strong war junks which were able to afford a considerable measure of defence to her seaports. The Indian subcontinent, on the other hand, with comparable coastlines and political institutions, remained always vulnerable to enemy attacks from the sea. The Indonesian chiefs possessed fast-moving war vessels, the prahus, and their reputation as sea-fighters was formidable. But against the heavily armed Portuguese carracks and galleons their craft proved inadequate. The Omani navy in the service of the sultans of Muscat in the seventeenth century had European-style ordnance on board and was not afraid to engage Western ships. No doubt detailed historical analysis of the circumstances which gave rise to these different maritime traditions would be able to suggest an explanation why certain nations of Asia valued sea-power more than the others. It cannot be taken as axiomatic that all Asian rulers undervalued ships as against cavalry. At the same time, we know that before the arrival of the Portuguese in the Indian Ocean in 1498 there had been no organised attempt by any political power to control the sea-lanes and the long-distance trade of Asia. The Iberians and their north European followers imported a Mediterranean style of warfare by land and sea into an area that had hitherto had quite a different tradition. The Indian Ocean as a whole and its different seas were not dominated by any particular nations or empires.

The reason for this failure to exploit the sea for trade and empire is not easily found unless we remember that the Spanish and Portuguese claims to the exclusive domination of the Atlantic and the Indian Ocean were as unique as the new geographical discoveries. The phenomenon that is in need of explaining is not the system of peaceful but that of armed trading. A comprehensive and convincing explanation has not been attempted as yet by historians.[4] In the Mediterranean, however, from Graeco-Roman times and perhaps even earlier periods of history, it was essential to exercise control over the vital sea-routes in order to control both economic resources and political settlements. Except in the Persian Gulf and the inland sea of the Indonesian islands, no such combination of geography, politics, economic factors, and historical experience was to be found in the Indian Ocean. When the Iberians developed long-distance armed merchant shipping, floating fortresses and warehouses, it became possible to extend the area of oceanic control from the home bases and to establish new bases in remote places. Advances in the technology of ship-building were an important factor here, though the Chinese junks were as large and powerful as the sixteenth-century European shipping. These vessels could easily have navigated the Atlantic and were capable of transporting a large number of armed men. But the Chinese empire and the successive politi-cal dynasties of the Indian subcontinent were fully occupied in upholding their political and economic power over unbroken *terra firma* and never seriously considered overseas colonial ventures as logical corollaries of seaborne trade. India of course had a crucial role in Indian Ocean commerce, not only in terms of geographical contours but also in terms of the overall volume and value of the commodities exchanged. The Indian lack of interest in sea-power in the pre-modern period remains distinctly enigmatic. The coastal rulers of South India and the Malabar occasionally emerged as sea-powers strong enough to demand toll money from passing ships and even to organise naval expeditions to the Indonesian archipelago. The large territorial kingdoms of India, with their capital cities far from the sea, showed no real interest in maritime mastery.

The conventions under which the long-distance trade of Asia grew and prospered before the period of European expansion are clearly visible, in spite of fragmentary historical evidence on the earlier centuries (seventh to tenth). In the distant past the main barrier to trade involving long voyages was neither the pirate nor the hungry prince but the most unpredictable tyrant of all, the sea itself. There is every reason to believe that prehistoric movements and migrations of people took place by both sea and land. The invention and use of the paddling and sailing canoe and various types of boats probably out-dated the discovery of the wheel, which was never used in pre-modern Africa. While the pack animal was the early means of transporting goods by land, the nautical skills necessary for seaborne trade were available to the coastal com-munities of the Indian Ocean. However, the possession of these skills was not a constant factor in time, and people who had once been accomplished theoretical navigators and long-distance sailors lost the art with the decline of their status as commercial carriers and intermediaries.[5] The Arab and Chinese geographical texts dating from the early centuries clearly speak of the hazards of the sea, the shipwrecks, storms, and landfalls, as things that had to be treated with respect if not fear. It is possible to discern two types of voyage in the complex of Indian Ocean trade. The first took place between the com-mercial cities of a fairly homogenous area such as the Red Sea and the Persian Gulf, united after the seventh century by the common bond of Islam. The sec-ond type was the long trans-regional trip to India, the Indonesian islands, and China. Bounded by the Pacific at one end and extending all the way to the Mediterranean at the other, it was this latter circuit of trade that constituted the foundation of pre-Columbian world economy in both the east and the west. In Asia commercial traffic was in the hands of highly skilled professional merchants, who operated as private individuals with little substantive state support. They enjoyed an unusual degree of political freedom in the trading emporia of the Indian Ocean, and the neutrality of the port-cities was closely connected with the movements of this group of merchants. While this was the general norm in trans-continental seaborne trade, the Asian ruling classes sometimes took part in shorter commercial voyages when opportunities for making profits were clearly visible. Ships were fitted out either in their names or often in partnership with a wealthy and prominent merchant.

In the Christian Mediterranean, with the rise of the Italian city–states, the institutional basis of world trade underwent a new development. The commercial rivalry between Genoa and Venice, erupting into open naval conflicts, and the Venetian encounters with the Muslim fleets fused together the interests of the merchants and the state. The Italian experience was reproduced later in Seville, Lisbon, Amsterdam, and London. Its transplanted seedlings were to be found everywhere in the Indian Ocean by the beginning of the sixteenth century.

Although the social position of the trading communities was never very high in any Asian country, the ruling elites were totally dependent on them for the fulfilment of two essential functions. It was impossible to create a market economy or to centralise the taxation system without the co-operation of the merchants. The pre-modern state apparatus did not have the necessary controlling mechanism to achieve such an end. Furthermore, rare and luxury commodities, which even seemingly primitive societies wished to possess, could be obtained only through trade. Historians on the whole have avoided analysing the fundamental factors which propel long-distance trade. The process of economic exchange and the determination of value are taken for granted. The assumption is that the desire for trade and the consequences following from it were responsible for many important historical events and movements. As a result of this neglect by historians, it is only economists who have attempted to provide an answer to the question why nations trade and why certain commodities are exchanged within a system of economic production. The first scientific theory of international trade was suggested by David Ricardo in the early nineteenth century, and its refined version still rests on his reasoning. The theory begins with the assumption that the possession of material goods is a contribution to welfare. When a unit of production has a structure of costs reflected in a lower price than what its competitors can charge that unit is efficient and its goods are exchanged against others produced under similar conditions of minimum cost. International trade is thus a matter of comparative price differences in different markets, and the division of labour on a world scale leads to a greater volume of output than would have been possible without specialisation. This explanation of long-distance trade may be valid for the period after the Industrial Revolution, but it is inadequate for the period under study.

Historians and indeed economists also know that relative prices are an important factor in demand without necessarily leading to changes in supply schedules. Pre-modern trade was primarily a function of three factors. Some areas or communities had a technological advantage which could not be diffused or copied elsewhere. Goods produced under such conditions were of course subject to the rationale of price considerations. Secondly, the geographical determinants of production were absolute in many cases, and certain commodities had unique sources of supply. Lastly, consumer tastes and social conventions played an important role in shaping the demand for high-valued luxury articles, though changes in socially determined demand were often a function of incomes and comparative prices. The impact of trade on human culture is well recognised by anthropologists and archaeologists;[6] it is also true that trade itself may be deeply influenced by cultural forms. Variations in historical attitudes towards precious metals, gold, and silver, are an excellent example of the double chain of causality between trade and society. International economic exchange was based on the index of value created by fixed units of gold and silver, and at the same time it was a conduit through which precious metals flowed from one region to another. No fundamental explanation other than the inherent quality of scarcity and visual attractiveness can be suggested for the human craving for these metals. Historians also know that the accumulation of gold and silver has been considered by nearly all civilisations as a process of social and material enrichment. The gradation of value, particularly the ratio between gold and silver, was not derived wholly from the relative scarcity of the two metals; it was also conditioned by the preference which some societies attached to monometallic currencies. Traditionally most countries of Asia honoured gold as the purest metal of all. In Hindu India ritual conventions allowed only gold and bronze to be made into temple regalia. It may be significant that the Arabic word "ashrafi" (derived from the expression "al-Malik al-Ashraf"), widely used as a regal epithet, came to be applied also to the gold coins of Egypt and India. Silver, if not actually polluting, had a lower standard of purity, and yet throughout the Middle East, India, and China silver coins in our period commanded the widest acceptance in daily transactions. The discovery and dispersal of hugh quantities of silver from American mines in the early sixteenth century suddenly injected into the system of world trade, including that of the Indian Ocean, a degree of purchasing power which pre-modern societies had not seen for a long time. The consequences for Asian economic and political development were far-reaching.

We can be certain that any country or geographical region that allowed gold and silver to establish a scale of values was susceptible to the operations of the price mechanism in its internal and external economy. But its power to attract precious metals through the medium of trade was dependent on technological factors and cultural norms. It is this constant interaction between strictly economic variables and collective mental states that makes a theoretical analysis of pre-modern commodity movements such a difficult task. The cultural dimensions of trade generally operate in two different directions. Certain articles possess a universal function in the societies that import and consume them, even when these societies are totally different in terms of forms and levels of civilisation. Other commodities, also exchanged through long-distance trade, convey meaning and information which are not identical in the case of the people who produced and consumed them locally and in that of those who purchased them at a great distance, through several commercial intermediaries.[7] A third variant may be added to the theoretical distinctions just made. When a new commodity is discovered in the course of oceanic or geographical explorations (coffee, tea, tobacco, maize, and potato can be cited as obvious examples), their acceptance is universal, though not cultural interpretation. In the Indian Ocean the exchange of gum resin used in the manufacture of incense derived entirely from universal ritual usage. Rare and highly prized incense such as myrrh was supplied from the Yemen, though lesser varieties of gum resin were also obtained in India and the Indonesian islands. The restricted sources of supply contrast strongly with the wide use of incense. In India and China religious worship and funerary rites were incomplete without its burning. Muslim and Christian practices were less specific, though the use of incense in the West was common enough. Sandalwood and various kinds of perfume were traded throughout the Indian Ocean and had a function in society similar to that of incense.

It can be argued that these are after all articles with a restricted range of application, and therefore that the possible asymmetry between the producing and consuming societies was at a minimum. The reasoning is not really valid. The capacity of a traded object to yield information does not depend on its functional characteristics but is derived from subjective meaning attached to it by the local and distant societies respectively. Take the example of cowries, a species of seashell found around the Maldive Islands of the Indian Ocean. For centuries the islanders led a remote existence based on coconut growing and fishing. Even the solid building material for their housing came from the sea in the form of coral encrustations recovered by divers at no little depth of water. However, from prehistoric periods cowries have been regarded as objects of symbolic meaning, though not all the cowries found in archaeological sites came from the Maldives. The possibility that the Maldive variety could be exchanged for the necessities of life – rice and cotton textiles – gave rise to an ancient and continuous trade between the islands and India. To the local community cowries became valuable only through the process of trade.

The recipient communities attached differing values and cultural significance to them, and the distance travelled by cowries was truly astonishing in our period. From India they were exported to East Africa and the Middle East, and through overland caravan trade or a series of bilateral tribal exchanges found their way to West Africa. Cowries obviously had a limited monetary value and were used as currency in parts of India and Africa. But they were also regarded as a prophylactic and much utilised as personal ornaments and animal decorations. The exact beliefs and symbolic significations must have differed from one society to another.[8]

While basic necessities of life exchanged in the Indian Ocean – such as salt, sugar, grains, and clothing – had the same use and meaning universally, even here consumer taste and social context were important. In 1682 the English East India Company sent a quantity of West Indian sugar to Persia directly from London because it was considered to be cheaper and finer than the Bengal sugar. The experiment was discontinued after it was found that the Iranians were unaccustomed to taking granulated sugar and preferred it in the form of "candy" or "lumps".[9] The use of broadcloth or European textiles in India and the Middle East was another striking example of cultural differences. There was a small but steady demand in these areas for heavy European woollen products. Whereas some of it came from the needs of the garment-makers, the bulk of the demand was concentrated in the industries supplying the army and the richer personal households. For the broadcloth was mainly used as floor coverings, as elephant and horse furniture, and for the manufacture of heavy ceremonial tents. The misconception in the minds of European exporters about the true nature of Asian demand for their products was responsible for a great deal of wasted effort. Just how strong ingrained ideas are even among merchants accustomed to constant foreign exposure can be seen from a directive given by the Directors of the East India Company to their officials in Bengal. The Company's Indian merchants in Calcutta were asked to appear before the English Council dressed in suits made from broadcloth in order to set a social example to other citizens of the town.[10] There was no apparent awareness that the humid and warm climate of Bengal might make the exercise totally impracticable. It is a fact that luxury objects emit non-decipherable signals when they are simply transplanted from the local environment to the remote in the course of long-distance trade. The symbolic meanings of shapes, designs, and colours in Chinese porcelain, silks, and rugs are not likely to have been understood by the non-Chinese; but there was no barrier to the appreciation of these objects as works of art and skilled craftsmanship. Fine cotton textiles exported from India were adapted over many centuries in their texture, patterns, and colours to suit the tastes of consumers in the Middle East, Indonesia, and even Japan. Strictly Indian designs and motifs in decoration were also applied to fabrics which were then exported to overseas markets. Buyers had become accustomed to the indigenous quality of the artistic expression. The two-way impact of trade is illustrated nowhere better than in the case of the Indian textile industry.

Habits associated with food and drink, clothing, and housing of course constitute the basis of culture systems and in the period before the Industrial Revolution largely determined the composition of long-distance trade. If a general distinction is to be made between pre- and post-Industrial Revolution trade, it would lie in the temporal rhythms. Technological considerations today have made international trade a vital feature of economic existence. Without an uninterrupted supply of fuel, raw materials, and food transported over many thousands of miles the world economy would collapse catastrophically. Pre-modern trade did not need this compelling continuity. The decentralised system of economic production made each region much more self-sufficient and reduced the influence of producers in long-distance trade. The ability of a particular society to generate a surplus over and above its own internal requirements, linked to the demands of the deficit areas, accounted for much of the pre-modern commercial exchange in the Indian Ocean. In theoretical terms this explanation is far removed from that suggested by Ricardo and the others; it comes closer to the historical reality. It should be noted at the same time that pre-modern trade was independent of temporal continuity only in so far as the latter was a necessary condition. In fact, trading caravans and voyages set out each year at their appointed seasons for age-old destinations. If they failed to arrive, there were scarcities, and perhaps even hardship where the transport of grains was involved, but not a general social disaster.

The great products of Asian civilisations – spices, silks, cotton textiles, porcelain and glass, jewellery and finely cut precious stones – all reflected the strength of social conventions in the regional markets. Raw materials for industries were exchanged in the maritime and overland trade of Asia, and there was a certain amount of demand for textile dyes, silk filaments, skins and hides, and for basic metals such as iron, copper, lead, and tin. Variations in consumer tastes, however baffling and inexplicable they are to historians, actually increased the flow of inter-regional trade and provided merchants with opportunities for high profits. Gastronomic traditions as they developed in the Indian subcontinent, Persia, and the Arab world held in high esteem the three finer spices of the Moluccas, cloves, nutmegs, and mace, and added the cinnamon of Ceylon to the list. In all these areas rice dishes prepared with some of the spices were considered indispensable to aristocratic tables and festive occasions. As rice could not be grown in arid land, it was exported from India to the Persian Gulf and the Red Sea, together with the spices brought from the Indonesian islands. The finer spices, however, did not move eastwards in the direction of China, though there was a large Chinese demand for black pepper grown both in Indonesia and on the Malabar coast of India. No real explanation is available as to why black pepper should be an accepted ingredient of Chinese food, but not cloves or nutmegs. The question can also be reversed. Why was Chinese food so much more varied and subtle than that anywhere else in Asia? The range of foodstuffs consumed in China was unparalleled and included exotic items which other Asian societies never dreamed of eating. Edible birds' nests and sea slugs brought from New Guinea and the Aru Islands in the Ceram Sea were sought-after delicacies which remained unappreciated by the non-Chinese.

The Indian Ocean was an area of social and cultural diversity rooted in four different civilisations: the Irano-Arabic, the Hindu, the Indonesian, and the Chinese. Seaborne trade, supplemented by the Central Asian caravan routes, created a strong sense of unity. The idea of a common geographical space defined by the exchange of ideas and material objects was quite strong, not only in the minds of merchants but also in those of political rulers and ordinary people. The writings of Arab geographers make it clear that, from the ninth and tenth centuries on, the world of Islam constituted more than an area of spiritual unification in which Muhammad was the Prophet of God. The political and religious frontiers of Islam ran across trade routes, kingdoms of non-believing princes, and natural boundaries made by deserts, mountains, and seas. Early Chinese historical works were aware of the eastern and western divisions of the Indian Ocean and the distinctive nature of the contacts between them created by foreign seafarers. The argument that the existence of a trans-continental trade, going all the way from China to the eastern Mediterranean, gave the countries of the Indian Ocean a historical unity is analogous to the argument that the empty canvas of the artist takes on meaning only when something is painted on it. Are there no other organic elements of unity which will satisfy the historian's innate craving for immutable truths? Perhaps an answer to the question can be found by looking at the problem from a different standpoint, that of time and the components of time which define the physical co-ordinates of space and objects seen against that space.

Mathematicians have divided chronological events into four categories: the stationary, the long-term, the cyclical, and the random. For the countries of the Indian Ocean, the stationary component of time is seen in the unchanging nature of the sea, its area and its depth, salinity and temperature, all of which contributed to the quality of the marine life and man's capacity to take a harvest from the sea. The coastlines of the Asian continent and the eastern shores of Africa also appear to have remained unchanging. The slow, long-term changes which took place in our millennium were mainly in the steady advance of coral reefs in some areas of the Indian Ocean and in the retreat of the sea around the riverine deltas. The growth of the coral gradually obstructed sea passages that had been open before and perhaps led to a changing pattern of navigation and trade routes. This was particularly true of the Red Sea, and was mentioned by the Arab navigator Ibn Majid.[11] The silting up

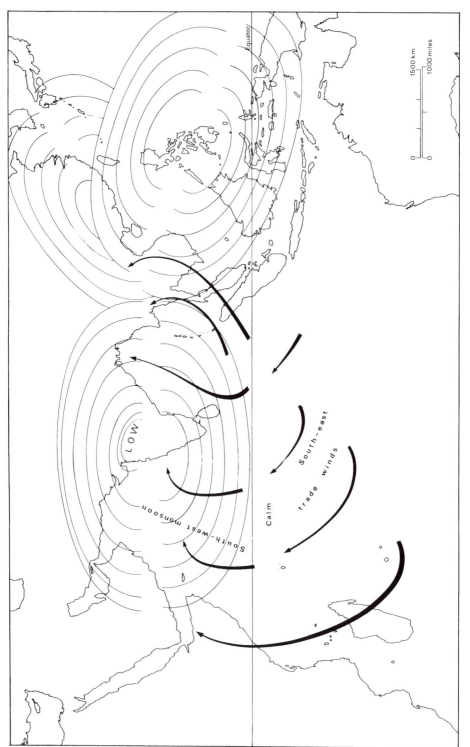

Map 2. Pressure and wind direction in the Indian Ocean from April to August.

of the deep-water channels at the mouths of the great rivers produced a different effect. All the major rivers of the Indian Ocean – the Euphrates–Tigris, the Indus, the Ganges, the Chao, the Mekong, the Hsi Kiang, and the Yangtze Kiang – were used by sailors and merchants to bridge the distance between sea-ports and landlocked cities. When navigation of the deltas and the upper reaches of the rivers became precarious, old, established ports and towns decayed and new ones better suited to trade became prosperous. If we take the two elements of time just outlined, we can see that the Indian Ocean was a single entity without any significant variations in its historical experience. But the most striking stationary component of time was the fact that people could sail from one end of the sea to the other until they reached the barrier of the Pacific, which remained practically closed to sailing-ships. Even the man-made obstacle to free navigation of the Indian Ocean – the Portuguese claim to domination, lasting less than a century – was no more than a small break in the profile of horizontal time.

There are other features of Indian Ocean civilisations which can be differentiated in terms of space and time. The influence of climate was pervasive. The wind-system known as the monsoons brought the whole area within the operation of a single global variable. The alternating bands of high and low pressure extending from the Equator to the Himalayas marked with great regularity the transition from good weather to periods of heavy rain and from light winds to strong ones reaching gale-force at times. The sailing season in the Indian Ocean was fixed with fine precision by the timing of the prevailing winds, which could be predicted with near-certainty by experienced sailors. The monsoons were a cyclical component of time. The solar year was the period of the single cycle, and the two equinoxes in March and September respectively separated the trough from the ridge. Although the wind system was a common element in Asian commercial interchange, it created distinctive geographic zones for cereal cultivation. The resultant food habits and the demand for commodities arising from the pattern of agriculture gave rise to the contours of both trade and civilisation. Asian society and agriculture were divided into two instantly recognisable blocs, the wheat and the rice cultures. The consumption of the two cereals had a multitude of other associations: the presence of deeply sunken wells, flooded fields, clustered mud-built villages, scattered homesteads with steeply sloping thatch roofs and bamboo-mat walls, and the appearance of meat or fish in the daily diet. The amount and incidence of rainfall accompanying the monsoon belts determined the geographical limits of wheat and rice growing. Wheat was a dry crop which needed selective irrigation if the winter rain was insufficient or irregular. It was the preferred food in the Middle East, North India, Central Asia, and the northern frontier districts of China. Various kinds of bread made from wheat flour revealed the national or ethnic identity of the baker and his customers. The huge flat loaves eaten by Turks, Persians, and Afghans were baked in large

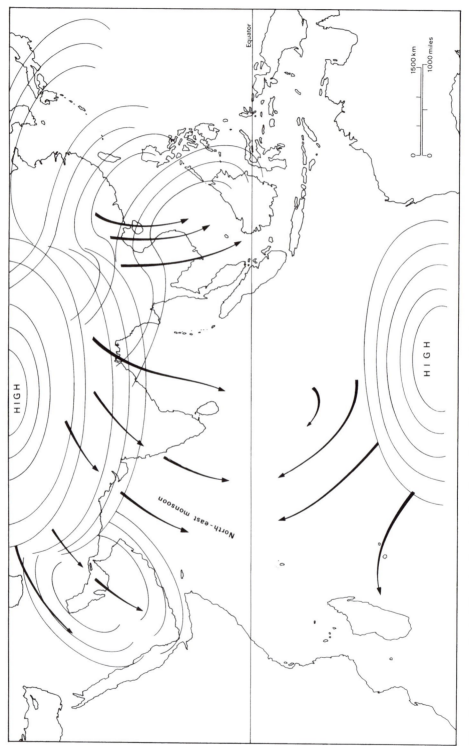

Map 3. Pressure and wind direction in the Indian Ocean from December to March.

North-east monsoon

HIGH

HIGH

Equator

1500 km

1000 miles

ovens, tell-tale signs of low winter temperatures and the presence of high mountains. In India bread was rolled thin and cooked over open wood fires or fried in oil. It was always freshly made and its appeal lasted less than the time it took to eat it.[12] The Chinese steamed dough served in the form of dumplings was a different matter altogether and would have astonished the Indian if not the Central Asian traveller.

That the differences in the art of bread-making were a subject of serious discussion concerning the comparative levels of civilisation we know from the writings of François Bernier, the French physician who lived in Delhi for a few years in the service of a Mughal courtier (1663–4). "There are many confectioners' shops in the town", Bernier informed his French readers, "but the sweetmeats are badly made, and full of dust and flies. Bakers also are numerous, but the ovens are unlike our own, and very defective. The bread, therefore, is neither well made nor properly baked. That sold in the Fort is tolerably good . . . never to be compared to the *pain de Gonesse* and other delicious kinds, to be met with in *Paris*."[13] After he had become familiar with Indian ways, Bernier admitted "It seldom happens that I find fault either with my meat or my bread." Whatever the defects of the bread sold in the bazaars of Delhi, it was made from flour; and all wheat-eaters were held together by the bondage of a common habit. The white flour might be mixed with brown or with the flour milled from millet: it tasted much the same. To a bread-eater other forms of carbohydrate were a dietary punishment. When Bernier described the legendary fertility of Bengal and its agriculture, comparing the latter to that of Egypt, he spoke with faint condescension of its inhabitants having to subsist on rice and seldom tasting bread.[14] In reality, the rice-eating people of Asia were fanatical in their adherence to food habits. It was not only bread that they rejected but also unaccustomed varieties of rice. The peasant farmers of eastern Bengal, Siam, and China ate coarse round-grained rice which the upper classes, used to the polished long-grained variety, would have found difficult to recognise as rice. Even livestock – pigs, chickens, and ducks – were given a special brown rice. Social gradations and gastronomic variations were much more marked in cooking rice than in making bread. The different habits and styles of cooking also reflected the farmers' skill in growing rice and in developing different strains. A Chinese work at the time of the Mongol conquest gives an evocative description of Hangchow's rice trade (1275):

our prefecture depends on a supply of rice from other parts of the country . . . The Hu-chou market, the Rice-market Bridge, and the Black Bridge are where the rice guilds are situated, and there all the merchants from other parts sell their grain. There are numerous varieties of rice, such as early rice, late rice, new-milled rice, winter-husked rice, first quality white rice, medium quality white rice, lotus-pink rice, yellow-eared rice, rice on the stalk, ordinary rice, glutinous rice, ordinary yellow rice, short-stalked rice, pink rice, yellow rice, and old rice.[15]

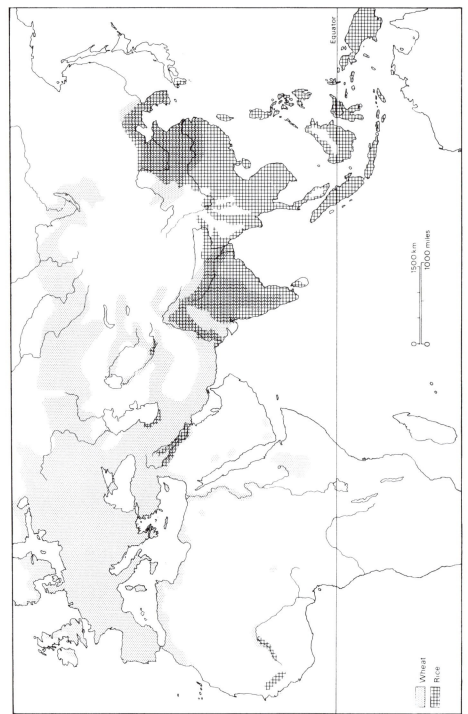

Map 4. The distribution of wheat and rice cultivation.

Equator

1500 km
1000 miles

Wheat
Rice

In what way can we relate the food habits of Asian people and the culti-vation patterns of wheat and rice to the Indian Ocean trade or to the problems of time and space? The monsoon and the supply of water gave rise to a regular cyclical rhythm in economic and social life in all those areas able to sustain a productive agriculture. It also drew the frontiers of cereal cultivation, which did not coincide with the political. The volume and the composition of Indian Ocean trade were conditioned to a great extent by the ability of the farmers to create a surplus not only in food crops but also commercially. A productive agriculture supported both the labour force employed in the manufacturing and service industries and the expenditures of the centralised bureaucratic empires of Asia. The lesser political kingdoms likewise drew heavily on the surplus in agricultural funds. The leading trade emporia of the Indian Ocean were often within or close to these smaller states. Urban centres by definition cannot exist without an adequate supply of food, water, and fuel. If the economic life of town or city is based on industrial production and long-distance trade, the nature of its specialisation is strongly determined by the character of local agriculture. The cultivation of rice in flooded fields was invariably an indication of large rainfalls and abundant water. In some areas, it was possible to take three rice crops from the land. The surplus food acceler-ated urban development in those civilisations which had a liking for city life. In others, it encouraged the growth of craft industries in rural areas. Both food and manufactured goods could be brought to the local market-towns in river boats.

Adam Smith, the father not only of modern economics but also of economic history, did not fail to see the linkages between agriculture, long-distance trade, and the division of labour in the context of Asian economies. He began his analysis with the practical observation that the enormous territorial extent of China, its vast population, its climatic diversity, and the productive capacity of the empire held together by easy water transport made "the home market of that country of so great extent, as to be alone sufficient to support very great manufactures, and to admit of very considerable subdivisions of labour". The Chinese, Smith thought, had little to learn from other nations in the tech-nology of pre-Industrial Revolution production, except perhaps from the Japanese. With greater foreign contacts the Chinese would easily learn, it was predicted, the art of using and constructing different machines. If the official policy of China in the past had been to encourage agriculture more than trade or industry, that of ancient Egypt and the Hindu government of "Indostan" was little different. While the internal market of the Nile valley was small, India was a much larger country with a far greater capacity for the consump-tion and manufacture of industrial goods. The extensive market created a strong relationship between agriculture and industry. As Smith put it, "Bengal, accordingly, the province of Indostan which commonly exports the greatest quantity of rice, has always been more remarkable for the exportation

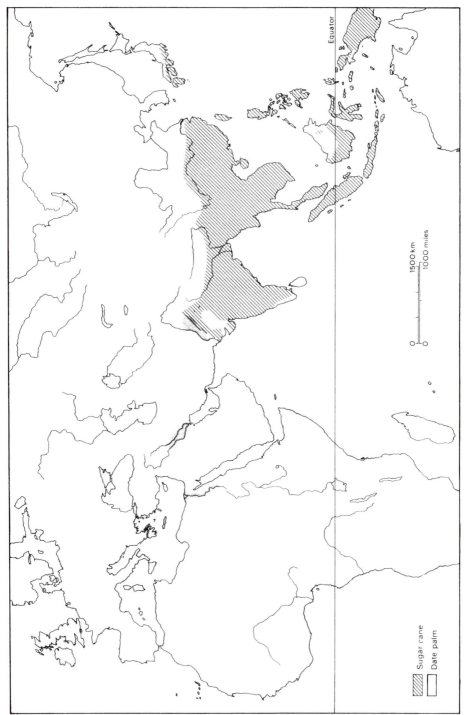

Equator

Sugar cane
Date palm

1500 km
1000 miles

Map 5. The distribution of sugar cane and date palm cultivation.

28

of a great variety of manufactures, than for that of its grain."[16] Historians are in the habit of going back to Smith's analysis as a way of lending authority to their own views. But Smith was an unusually perceptive observer of the structural changes which began to occur in the world economy from the middle of the eighteenth century; and his comments on the comparative productive systems in different countries demonstrate that contemporary awareness of those changes might have influenced their direction.

Rice was a valuable trading commodity in the Indian Ocean trade. It could be kept for several years, and old rice improved in taste. Wheat was susceptible to insect attack and was seldom transported by sea for any considerable distance because of the risk of spoilage. Wheat land was in the dry areas of Asia. Where major rivers, fed by mountain rains, melting snow, or glaciers, acted as commercial highways, wheat was brought to towns and cities by boat. In general, it was a load for the pack animals (camels and oxen) and heavy carts. Wheat land, the making of bread, and the caravan trade were connected together by an invisible net, woven by climatic, social, economic, and even political relationships. Centralised governments in the wheat- or millet-growing areas faced a perpetual hard struggle to bring the lesser chiefs or the independent-minded agricultural communities under a single authority. In the rice-growing lands, the control or destruction of the water channels, the dykes, or even the nursery beds of young seedling rice placed the terrible weapon of mass starvation in the hands of the war lords. The collective effort needed to plant and harvest rice and its favourable land:yield ratio forced centralised Asian governments to consider the welfare of cultivating villages much more than was the case with the extensive farming techniques associated with wheat and millet.

We have so far hinted rather than directly stated the functional co-axials of Asian food habits and the Indian Ocean trade. There are three attributes in man's daily life which lend identity to a social community: food, dress, and housing. Economic exchanges between one community and another, on the other hand, are as much stimulated by differences as by points of similarity or close identity. The argument is especially true of trade in precious or luxury objects. Works of art and high craftsmanship may differ in form and expression, but they also reflect the sensibilities of social groups. Such items are often collected or traded because of the unfamiliarity of the artistic tradition. All Asian civilisations bordering on the sea and stretching back to the far-away Himalayas and the T'ien Shan possessed distinctive cultures which rested on a foundation of daily necessities. The differences in food, clothing, and buildings and their implications for long-distance trade were instantly recognised not only by sailors and caravan traders who crossed the cultural watersheds but also by the ordinary people. A subtle expression of this awareness can be seen in the basilica of San Marco in Venice. The walls of the church are crowded with richly coloured and gilded paintings of classic European

Plate 2. Mughal miniature painting of an imaginary meeting between Emperor Jahangir and Shah Abbas of Persia, *c.* 1618.

themes, and then the eye suddenly catches a glimpse of a panel depicting a desert scene with a camel. The symbolic representation in the painting of Venetian trade with the Arab lands is more powerful than the surrounding scenes of sea battles with the Muslims. Chinese mandarins and emperors receiving Arab and Central Asian envoys would have taken note of their white robes decorated with gold brocade and the striking contrast in design, colour, and texture of their own silk ceremonial garments. It is a fact that the export of certain kinds of satin piece-goods from China was strictly controlled by the government; the regulations were an indication of the foreign demand for these goods and their exclusive position in Chinese society.[17] Jade, the most highly regarded material in Chinese art, was obtained only through long-distance caravan trade. The peaches, apricots, and apples of Samarkand graced the tables of the rich in India and Persia alike.

Cultural behaviour is a long-term or stationary component of time; but it is certain that the food and dress habits of the people of the Indian Ocean changed during the millennium of this study, if only because of the steady demographic advance. Trade and migration diffused the demand for and con-sumption of exotic products. Arabian coffee provides a spectacular example of the sudden emergence of a trade dependent on addictive habits which were also social. There is no reference to coffee drinking in Middle Eastern sources before the late fifteenth century, although it must have been known to the people of the Yemen earlier. After the sixteenth century, its consumption spread to Egypt and then rapidly to the rest of the Islamic world, in spite of its reputation in the eyes of the jurists as a narcotic.[18] In the late seventeenth cen-tury, Europeans carried coffee from the Yemenite port of Mocha to Amsterdam and London. By the next century coffee was being extensively grown in Java and the New World. Other crops from the American continent invaded Asia. The spread of tobacco, maize, and potatoes followed the lines of trans-oceanic trade.

In terms of time such changes were either a sudden break or a sideways movement; they can be classified nevertheless with stationary time. When new products entered the flow of international trade – as a result of price advan-tage, novelty of visual response, or just utility – the economic and social impact did not remain confined to consumers alone but spread out to pro-ducers also. Indian cotton textiles, both decorative and functional, were first imported into Europe as cheap substitutes for the finer and higher-priced linen and similar fabrics manufactured at home. From the second half of the seventeenth century, however, the imports began to assume mass proportions and became an important item for clothing in the West. By the end of the cen-tury domestic wool and silk weavers in most European countries affected by the increasing competition of the Indian products were agitating for tariff pro-tection or import restrictions, which were eventually granted. The protective legislation in Europe changed the composition of the Indian cotton exports but did not really succeed in reducing the total volume of trade. At the Indian end the rise of European demand, combined with the development of markets in West Africa, the Caribbean, and America, led to a considerable expansion of the textile industry.[19] The temporal transients created by the exchange of goods at the inter-regional level constantly interacted with the established parameters of technology, often setting off a chain-reaction. But the production cycles, as we have already seen, were regular and confined to the solar periodisation of time.

There was yet another component of time which critically affected long-distance trade. The random events of famines, wars, and storms at sea appeared unpredictable in the short-term view of the living witnesses. In the collective memory and expectation of society they were systematic within certain margins of error. People knew in the regions of uncertain rainfall that the dividing line between plenty and want, life and death, was very fine. But the famine itself could not be accurately predicted. A bumper harvest accelerated trade and stimulated demand. Commercial depressions invariably followed on from periods of dearth. Even areas of high agricultural productivity were not immune to the fluctuations of the climate. In Egypt the annual rise in the water level of the Nile was monitored with anxious precision. Too little water left the fields insufficiently irrigated. Flooding slow to recede delayed the sowing season or even caused it to be lost. In 973 the Fatimid caliph al-Mu'izz forbade the public news of the rise of the Nile before it had reached the safe level of sixteen arms or dhira (66.5 cm each arm) to prevent social and financial panic in the streets of Cairo.[20] Al-Muqaddasi, the famous Arab geographer, writing his work at about the same time, may have had this measure in mind when he pointed out that the very prosperity of the people of Misr made them constantly fear the periodic famines.[21] China was so frequently devastated by harvest failures that the government attempted to relieve public suffering by distributing grain from the "Ever Normal Granaries". In the northern provinces, the famine-stricken peasantry in desperate times even attempted to cross the dreaded Gobi desert in search of the means of survival.[22] Traders and merchants who depended on artisans for supplies of industrial goods faced financial ruin when famines drove away rural and urban population or dried up the flow of raw materials. One of the most graphic and harrowing accounts of an Indian famine and its effects on trade can be found in the papers of the English East India Company's factory in Surat during the 1630s. At the height of the famine in 1630, one letter after another describes the terrible mortality among weavers, spinners, all kinds of craftsmen, and the peasantry in Gujarat. There was a universal lament that what was once "the garden of the world" was now a complete wilderness. People fled from the province on foot and by sea in small boats; whole families, overcome by hunger and exhaustion, were found dead in scorched fields. Cloth-weaving towns which yielded fifteen bales of piece-goods daily were incapable of producing three; by the end of 1630 the letters reported a total standstill in cloth production and trade.[23]

Wars and the passage of large armies were as much feared as famines, and the random nature of these events, predictable only in their likelihood, made it difficult to think of systematic counter-measures to reduce their adverse consequences. It is sometimes assumed by historians that the Asian farmers were little affected by battles and political struggles. The stereotype image of the ploughman carrying on with his labours within sight of battlefields is a common one. In reality, wars inflicted terrible suffering on farmers and the inhabitants of towns. That merchants were seldom gainers by wars was a truth evident to all but the army contractors. In 1675, when the main financial and banking towns in western India suffered a severe shortage of money and loanable funds, the cause was ascribed to the widespread state of warfare then prevailing in the area.[24] The devastations caused by war lords and their armies in China are frequently mentioned as having led to permanent depopulation and shrinkage of cultivation.[25] Storms at sea, like harvest failures, were acts of God and were just as destructive to individual commercial fortunes. If the annual Red Sea fleet of the Surat merchants failed to arrive, the ensuing financial and liquidity crisis pulled down the large and the small members of the commercial community indiscriminately. The large amplitude of temporal variations (around the mean) was mainly caused by random factors which were always discounted by merchants and bankers in their internal calculations.

2

The rise of Islam and the pattern of pre-emporia trade in early Asia

In 618 Emperor Li Yüan succeeded to the Celestial throne after the murder of the last of the Sui, Yang Ti. The High Progenitor, as he was entitled later, and his son Li Shih-min, the Grand Ancestor, were the joint founders of the T'ang dynasty, one of the greatest in the long history of China. Four years later, on 16 July 622, in the far-distant and arid coastland of Arabia, Prophet Muhammad abandoned his birthplace and fled to the oasis town of Medina. It was from there that his followers were to prey on the caravans of the wealthy merchants of Mecca, on their way to the Mediterranean markets of Gaza and Busra (Bostra). For commerce and civilisation in the Indian Ocean, these separate and unconnected events mark out a fresh beginning, a new order. The two geographical divisions of the great sea, the western and the eastern, meeting together in the massive under-water volcanic cliffs of the Java seas, were now gradually brought closer in a long chain of trans-oceanic trade. The administrative unification and the economic achievements of T'ang China, while they were responsible for the creation of new consumer demands and social tastes for luxuries within the limits of the empire, also led in the Far East to the emergence of a larger zone of Chinese cultural influence. In spite of cyclical periods of civil war, political disintegration, and foreign invasion, the Celestial empire continued to act from the seventh century to the fifteenth as an area of economic high pressure, attracting to itself overland caravans, tributary missions from foreign princes, and large ocean-going vessels engaged in a two-way traffic. The Sinicisation of a large part of Asia and its people was as much connected with the political and military expansion of China as a general economic and social acceptance of her cultural values and standards of life.

The expansion and the new activities which became faintly evident in the rhythm of both caravan and trans-oceanic trade from the seventh century onwards in northern and southern China received a great deal of their impetus from the domestic aspirations and developments of the T'ang and Sung empires. However, in the West it was joined by the second and most powerful of the historical forces of the time, the rise of Islam and its expansion across the fertile lands of the Near East and South Asia. Movements of people by definition involve the exchange of ideas, economic systems, social usage, political institutions, and artistic traditions. The spread of Islam subsumed all these

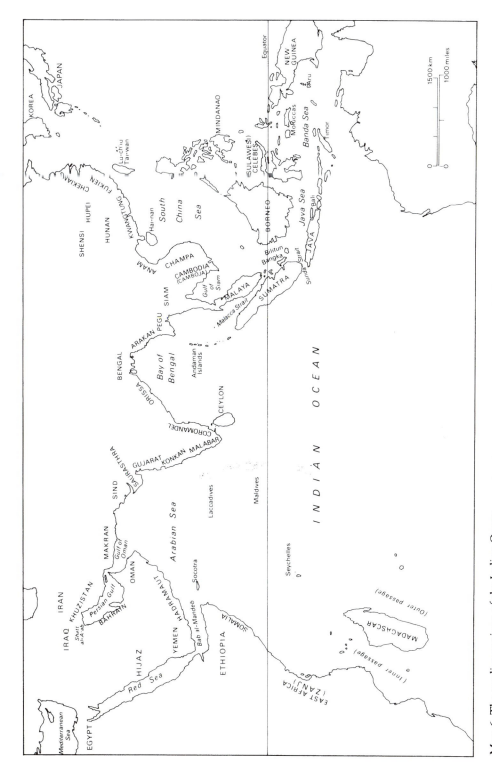

Map 6. The trading regions of the Indian Ocean.

35

things. It may be an exaggeration for lack of definite proof to state that the commerce of the Indian Ocean in the westward direction had entered a period of relative contraction during the later Roman empire with the weakening of a Mediterranean "world economy".[1] It is certainly true that the Arab conquests and rapid demographic diffusion and the political integration of Egypt, Syria, Iran, and North Africa created an enormously powerful zone of economic consumption. It was an expanding area that drew its commercial and fiscal strength from refashioning in the West the Mediterranean economy of antiquity and from harnessing the productive resources of the lands around the Indian Ocean in the East. Arab economic success in the early caliphate period was achieved with the aid of the skills possessed by the people of the ancient Near East. But the growth of great urban centres, a universal feature of Islam, and the new capital cities gave rise to an expanding demand for commodities of all kinds and for precious objects.[2] This in turn quickened the pace of long-distance trade. The revival of the sea and caravan routes across the famous international boundary lines, known to merchants since Hellenistic times, owed much to the ability of the Islamic rulers to protect their property and persons against violence. The laws of commercial contracts and the principles of juridical rights which evolved in the centuries following the foundation of Islam took into account a cardinal fact of pre-modern trade. Merchants who travelled by land and sea into the realms of foreign princes were prone to take their business elsewhere without the guarantee of a certain amount of commercial freedom secured by reciprocal political rights and obligations.

The civilisation of Asia and the geographical regions of the Indian Ocean, after the death of Muhammad (632), were characterised by two complementary and at times opposing forces at work. For almost a millennium there was a continued trans-regional movement of people from the desert and the steppe in the direction of settled land and prosperous urban areas. The dispersion and absorption of the desert Arabs throughout the Near East and the southern shores of the Mediterranean, and their early movements into East Africa and Sind, were accompanied by an overwhelming social, cultural, and political ascendancy of Arabic as a language of universal use. The unity and homogeneity of the Arab world under the Umayyad and Abbasid caliphates lasted for a long time. But eventually Turkish military expansion from Central Asia destroyed its cohesion. Much later, the violent irruptions of the Mongols in successive tidal waves not only overran the heartland of Islam but also subdued the Celestial empire itself. The newcomers, whether they were Turks or Mongols, were of course assimilated, in the east by the social and cultural traditions of China and in the west by those of the Arabs and Persians. As against the trans-regional migrations and the rise of associated state systems, there were purely local developments in Asia, the creation of regional economic and political units which intermingled with or resisted the larger forces according to particular ideology and accidental factors. The Fatimids came to Egypt from North Africa (969). Under their leadership and patronage the city of Fustat assumed a major role in the trans-continental trade of the Indian Ocean. Within China the steady movement of people from the north to the south continued, and the coastal towns and cities became important economic centres of distribution and maritime trade. Even the insular and inward-looking Hindu India kept up its earlier connections with the people and islands of South East Asia. In 1025, as the Tanjore inscription testifies, Rajendrachola organised from southern India the great punitive naval raid on the empire of Srivijaya in Sumatra.[3] A maritime expedition of this kind across the open sea must presuppose the possession of the necessary nautical skills in the art of shipbuilding and the techniques of navigation. It is inconceivable that a con-tinuous tradition of seafaring and seamanship across a dangerous ocean can ever have been maintained without economic reasons and incentives.

The strong cultural and religious ties that had existed between South East Asia, India, and Ceylon all through the Hindu and Buddhist periods were of course modified and enlarged when Islamic influence spread eastwards across the Indian Ocean. The most striking feature of the maritime expansion of Islam as a religion and a way of life was the geographical watershed it reached beyond the straits of Sunda and Malacca. Indian ritual and royal court tra-ditions had spread as far as ancient Siam and Cambodia. However, by the fourteenth century areas east of Java, Sumatra, and the Malayan peninsula were beginning to pass out of the gravitational pull of conflicting western Asian civilisations and were turning towards China. It was as if the pattern of the wind-system in the Indian Ocean, separating the trading voyages from the Red Sea to China into two distinct temporal zones, also determined how people should live. From the middle of the seventh century to the end of the fifteenth, the general direction and structure of the Indian Ocean trade are remarkably clear. There was a long line of trans-continental traffic, going all the way from south China to the eastern Mediterranean. The consuming and producing markets for this type of commerce were not only separated by vast distances but were also very dissimilar in their social and political values. The commodities exchanged therefore were such as could be easily integrated into a scale of economic and cultural utilities local to the area. The second typology of Indian Ocean trade incorporated shorter voyages and distances with flows of commodities going in the direction of regional markets. The patterns were as distinctive as in the case of the trans-continental movements. The relation-ship between distance and the organisation of trade underwent a significant change during the seven centuries from the period of Islamic expansion to the rise of Malacca as the leading commercial emporium of the Eastern Sea. Although the precise dates of the change cannot be established, it seems that up to the beginning of the tenth century or even later Arab ships and merchants had sailed all the way to China and back, calling at the intermediate ports

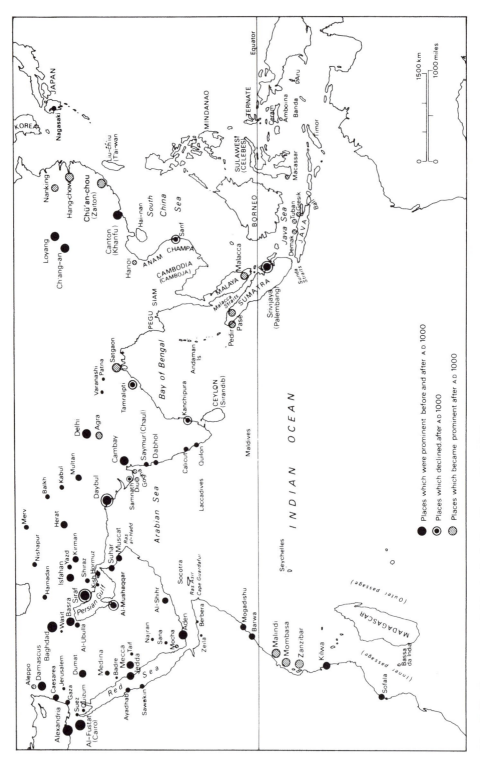

Map 7. Trading ports and cities in the Indian Ocean, 618–1500.

Places which were prominent before and after A.D. 1000

Places which declined after A.D. 1000

Places which became prominent after A.D. 1000

1500 km
1000 miles

JAPAN
KOREA
Nagasaki
Nanking
Hang-chow
Liu-ch'iu (Tai-wan)
Loyang
Ch'ang-an
Chü'an-chou (Zaiton)
Canton (Khanfu)
Hai-nan
South China Sea
Hanoi
ANAM CHAMPA
Sanf
CAMBODIA (CAMBOJA)
MINDANAO
SULAWESI (CELEBES)
TERNATE
Ceram
Amboina
Banda
Daru
Macassar
BORNEO
Java Sea
Demak
Tuban
Gresik
JAVA
Bali
Timor
Equator
PEGU SIAM
Malacca Straits
MALAYA
Malacca
SUMATRA
Sunda Straits
Pase
Pedir
Srivijaya (Palembang)
Satgaon
Varanashi
Patna
Tamralipti
Bay of Bengal
Kanchipura
Andaman Is.
CEYLON (Sirandib)
Delhi
Agra
Cambay
Saymur (Chaul)
Dabhol
Calicut
Quilon
Maldives
Multan
Kabul
Balkh
Daybul
Diu
Samnath
Goa
Laccadives
INDIAN OCEAN
Herat
Merv
Nishapur
Hamadan
Isfahan
Yazd
Kirman
Shiraz
Kish
Hormuz
Muscat
Suhar
Ras al-Hadd
Al-Mushaqqar
Al-Shihr
Socotra
Ras Asir
Cape Guardafui
Aleppo
Damascus
Baghdad
Caesarea
Jerusalem
Gaza
Dumat
Basra
Siraf
Wasit
Al-Ubulla
Persian Gulf
Arabian Sea
Najran
Sana
Medina
Badre
Mecca
Taif
Jedda
Mocha
Aden
Zeila
Berbera
Mogadishu
Barwa
Barbara
Seychelles
Malindi
Mombasa
Zanzibar
Kilwa
MADAGASCAR
(outer passage)
Bassa da India
(inner passage)
Sofala
Alexandria
Suez
Quzum
Al-Fustat (Cairo)
Ayadhab
Sawakin
Red Sea

according to the market opportunities. A single voyage mounted across the whole breadth of the Indian Ocean, however, incurred considerable trans-action costs, and gradually this particular pattern of trading was discontinued in favour of shorter, segmented voyages between a number of leading port-cities which were situated at the circumference of the maximum navigational circle. (The changing pattern is illustrated in the accompanying maps.)

Each year the merchants of Siraf in the Persian Gulf organised their maritime fleet for voyages to China, to Daybul and Calicut in India, and to the city–states of East Africa. Some of the goods brought back in the course of these journeys were obviously transported by the overland caravan routes to the Mediterranean ports, which in turn forwarded the cargo to the northern Frankish markets or to those of the Muslim Maghreb. But a large part of the exotic and even of the necessary imports from Africa, India, China, and the islands of the Indonesian archipelago was consumed within Islamic lands. In many ways, the articles exchanged retained their original use and symbolic meaning. The demand for Chinese porcelain in western Asia was not a trans-planted taste for chinoiserie but an evolving appreciation of fine shape, material, colour, and glazes in pottery. There was even a widespread belief in Asia that the pale sea-green celadonware of China could reveal the presence of poison in food.[4] The medieval trade of Asia was really founded on the economic and social acceptance of the four great products of eastern civilis-ation – silk, porcelain, sandalwood, and black pepper – which were exchanged for incense (Arabian gum resins), thoroughbred horses, ivory, cotton textiles, and metal goods. It should not of course be forgotten that the Indian Ocean possessed two faces, the sea itself and the arid plateau beyond the Himalayan heights. Just as the monsoon winds obeyed a global climatic law evident in the annual expansion and contraction of the pressure areas over the entire Asian landmass, so the sea-lanes of the Indian Ocean were supplemented all through history by the northern caravan routes with sturdy two-humped camels, horses, and mules as transport.

A description and analysis of the long-distance trade of Asia, following the weakening of the Mediterranean economy in the aftermath of the Roman empire, should perhaps begin with events connected with the rise of Islam. The new religion preached by Muhammad, and the astonishing military success of the Arab leaders succeeding the Prophet, have always impressed historians as being in need not only of religious and political explanations but also of a reconstruction of the economic environment. Traditional sources speak of Mecca as a commercial town, having no other resources in that desolate part of Hijaz.[5] Muhammad himself had been a factor of the richer members of the clan of Quraysh, who had grown wealthy from the management of caravan trade and from banking. The merchants of Mecca, according to tradition, had political agreements with other tribes, which secured for them the right of free passage to the lands of the Caesar, the Byzantine emperor.[6] After

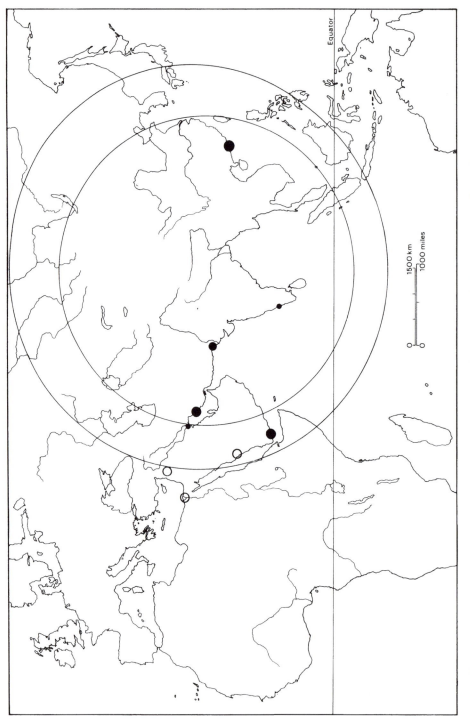

Equator

1500 km
1000 miles

Map 8. The pattern of single voyages across the Indian Ocean from the Red Sea and the Persian Gulf, *c.* 700–950.

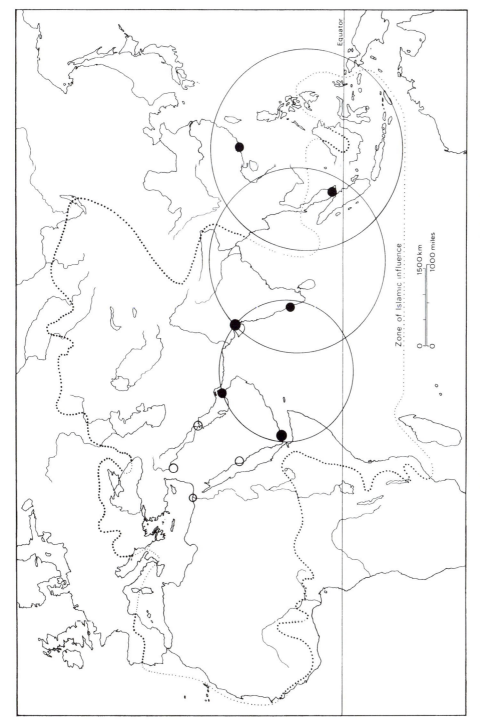

Map 9. The pattern of emporia trade in the Indian Ocean: the triple segmentation, c. 1000–1500 (each circle represents the quarterly shift of the monsoon).

Muhammad's removal to Medina and the foundation of "umma", an association of followers, much of immediate desert politics turned on the disruption of the trade and caravan traffic of Mecca. A northern town, Medina was strategically placed for raids against the Mediterranean trade of the Quraysh. After several minor forays, in January 624 a small party of Muslims surprised and captured a caravan of the Quraysh at a place called Nakhla between Mecca and the mountain town of Ta'if.[7] Two months later, Muhammad organised another raid on a Meccan caravan, this time returning from Gaza. There were 900 camels reported to be carrying goods valued at 50000 dinars. Abu Sufyan, the wealthy sheikh of the Quraysh and the leader of the caravan, managed to slip past the raiders waiting at Badr. However, the citizens of Mecca who had hurriedly come out to protect the camels refused to go back and decided to give battle. The outcome was the celebrated Muslim victory.[8] The failure of the siege of Medina (627) prepared the way for the eventual submission of the Meccans to the spiritual and temporal authority of the Prophet and the revival of the annual commercial expeditions to the Yemen, Palestine, and Syria.

These early chronological landmarks in the history of Islam were thrown up primarily by the inbred feuds of a tribal society. At the same time, they point historians in the direction of certain conclusions by revealing the presence of substantial merchants and traders engaged in long-distance exchange of some kind. That the tribe of Quraysh had inherited and fostered an active tradition of trade and money-changing we know from sources on what scholars call "Jahiliyya", the pre-Islamic period. Were they also intermediaries in an extended chain of international transactions which originated on the more fertile and productive shores of the Indian Ocean? Or were they no more than local dealers supplying the Mediterranean markets with leather, raisins of Ta'if, dates, and frankincense gathered in the mist-shrouded mountains of al-Yaman? A definitive answer would be difficult to give.[9] One way of approaching these questions is to examine the relative position and role of the Arabs as seafarers and as a sea-power. There is certainly evidence of maritime movements at this time between Arabia and Abyssinia across the Red Sea, though the Quraysh appear to have been without shipping of their own.[10] If the caravaneers of Mecca had at all carried the prestigious goods of the Indian Ocean brought from India, Ceylon, Indonesia, and China to Damascus and other western destinations, these could only have arrived at the ports of the Yemen. The Hellenistic knowledge of the monsoon winds would have made it possible for the commercial houses of Alexandria to push the trade of the Red Sea into the wider expanse of the Indian Ocean.[11] But navigation in the Red Sea was never safe and the existence of prosperous commercial cities such as Petra and Bostra may be an indication that the last section of the transcontinental trade before it reached the Mediterranean was conducted by land rather than by sea.[12]

The Arabs of Hijaz were certainly not engaged in maritime traffic. Their economic strength came from a skilful management of land caravans dependent on camels, the most frugal, patient, unruffled companions of man in arid lands. The merchants of Mecca could reach Aden, the main port of the Yemen, through the mountain road going from Ta'if to Najran and San'a. Some of the merchandise brought back from the Yemen was in turn carried to Byzantine Syria through the oasis town of Dumat al-Jandal.[13] It should, however, be noted that, in contrast to the Red Sea, the maritime trade of the Persian Gulf even in this early period retained a greater vigour. The port-city of Mushaqqar was a meeting-point for both the merchants of Hijaz and those of the Gulf.[14] With the expansion of Islam as an accelerating force of state formation within and outside the peninsula, the Arabs were forced to come to terms with the sea. First there were naval raids to western India and Iran (636–8), launched it is true from Bahrayn, which had very ancient commercial links with Mesopotamia and South Asia. Then the victors of Syria and Egypt had to face the Mediterranean style of warfare, carried on by land and sea. It took the Arabs many years before they could confront the seaborne might of Byzantium. In fact, later stories ascribe to Umar, the great conquering caliph, an actual fear of the sea and a dislike of the risks attending naval expeditions. When Mu'awiya, the governor of Syria and the future head of the Umayyad caliphate (AD 661–750), asked Umar for leave to attack Cyprus, he claimed that the Greek islands were so close that one could almost hear dogs bark and cocks crow. The caliph dissuaded his friend from the venture, saying that the Syrian sea was larger than dry land and the safety of his people greater than the treasures of Greece.[15]

Although Alexandria was occupied by the Arabs in 641, their weakness at sea was demonstrated when a Byzantine fleet came back in 645 and briefly reoccupied the city. However, the conquest of Mesopotamia, Syria, Iran, and Egypt placed at the disposal of the Muslims the nautical skills of the people of the Persian Gulf as well as of the Coptic workmen of Alexandria. A naval fleet under the command of Arab governors was put together before too long, and in 655 two hundred ships left the Nile delta to cruise off the Lycian coast. Near Phoenix the fleet fell in with the Byzantine war galleys and in the Battle of Masts the Christian Mediterranean suffered its first defeat at sea.[16] From then on Muslim naval raids against Byzantium began to multiply. Rhodes was attacked in 672, Crete two years later. From his base on the peninsula of Cyzicus, caliph Mu'awiya decided to move against Constantinople itself (674). This was the limit of early Arab success against the eastern Roman empire. The sea defences of Constantinople proved impregnable, and after three years of siege and attacks on the walls, the Muslims withdrew leaving behind, it is said, 30000 dead.[17] A second expedition against Byzantium in 717–18 was once again a costly failure. Arab advance into the Mediterranean during the second half of the seventh century followed the coastline of North

Africa. By 705 Carthage and its territory was an Islamic province with the name of Ifriqiya. In another decade the Arabs had crossed the Straits of Gibraltar and with the help of Berber converts completed the conquest of Andalusia. In the Indian Ocean itself, the Muslim occupation of Daybul, the great commercial port in western India, led up to the establishment of an Arab political kingdom in Sind (712).[18] It was admittedly a small outpost, a token presence, and yet it was an indication nevertheless that the Semitisation of the orient had not as yet reached its final boundaries.

In just over half a century from the rise of the Umayyads, much of western Asia and a great deal of the Mediterranean were transformed from a scene of decaying political institutions and divisive social practices into an area ruled by a single authority, able to marshal its immense resources. As a Nestorian Christian of the late seventh century from northern Mesopotamia, John of Phenek, commented on the rule of Mu'awiya over Persia and Byzantine Syria: "Justice flourished under his reign, and a great peace was established in the countries which were under the jurisdiction of his government . . . the earth gave us its fruits abundantly, good health prevailed, friendship shone, commerce doubled, children played with joy, there was universal plenty . . . "[19] Although Hindu India and the islands of the Indonesian archipelago were not to be brought within the orbit of Islamic world for another four centuries, the commercial expansion of Muslim merchants and traders across the Indian Ocean to South Asia and China is historically recorded from as early as the eighth century.[20] There is no evidence of any religious animosity towards Muslims in either India or China at this time. The urban settlement of migrants from the Persian Gulf and the Red Sea in eastern Africa probably did not get under way on any significant scale before the ninth century. Thereafter, it continued steadily until places such as Mogadishu, Zanzibar, and Kilwa became integral to the Indian Ocean traffic.[21] That the rise of Islam and the re-vitalising of the Mediterranean economy under Arab leadership exercised a significant impact on trans-oceanic trade seems fairly certain. The Arab military thrust was at first directed towards the north and the west, primarily because of the geographical proximity and the legendary prosperity of Iraq, Syria, and Egypt. The annual corn-fleets of the Nile were now diverted from Byzantium to supply the towns of Hijaz, Damascus, and Basra. The ancient gold of the Pharaohs, continually recovered and put into circulation, vitalised the financial capacity of the caliphate to undertake large-scale public expenditure, through a reformed currency (*c.* 690–700). These were some of the immediate gains from which any conquerors could be expected to benefit. The Islamic expansion in the Indian Ocean was less spectacular and its ethnic composition was not necessarily Arab. It was a consequence and a development of the great political and social events taking place in the Near East during the seventh and eighth centuries.

Arab achievements made it possible to unite the two arteries of long-

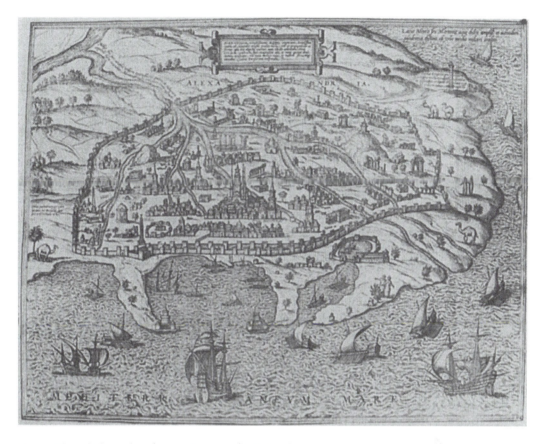

Plate 3. Plan of Alexandria, from G. Braun and F. Hohenberg, *Civitates Orbis Terrarum*, 1573.

distance trade known in antiquity between the Indian Ocean and the Mediterranean. The twin channels of the trans-continental trade of Asia – the seaborne
traffic through the Red Sea and the combined sea, river, and overland journey
across the Persian Gulf, Iraq, and the Syrian desert – were brought under the
political control of single authorities, at first that of the Umayyad caliphs and
later that of the Abbasids. Even the Mediterranean, divided as it was between
a Christian north and a Muslim south, eventually recovered much of its
economic unity through the activity of merchants and traders.[22] If this much
is evident from a mere scrutiny of the historical facts, it is also clear that the
choice of a passage either through the Red Sea or through the Persian Gulf, and
the associated volume of trade, were very much a matter of the relative importance of certain political and cultural capitals in the Islamic world. There seems
to have been a continual swing of the pendulum over the next few centuries as
to whether that centre with its strong powers of gravitation should be located
in Damascus, in Baghdad, or in Fustat, Old Cairo. When Mu'awiya, the first
Umayyad caliph, chose Damascus as the capital of the empire, he introduced
a distinct shift in demand and consumption in favour of Syria and the upper

Mediterranean connections. As a result, it was the ports and towns of Iraq that were to benefit most in commercial terms.

The old Arab caravan routes remained open, passing from Hijaz across the sandy wastes of the Great Nafud to the settlement of Dumat al-Jandal, where water was available, and then to Damascus.[23] Slowly, the functional role of the birthplace of Islam and the eastern coast of the Red Sea began to change. The demographic exodus towards the "Fertile Crescent" may have led to a drain of commercial skills and the dwindling of the special needs of the long-distance caravaneers. Mecca itself became the locus of a reverse flow of traffic. Pilgrims from all parts of Bilad al-Islam converged on the holy city, following the ancient caravan routes, as part of the annual "hajj" which all devout Muslims hoped to perform at least once in their life-time. The religious gathering in Mecca had important political and economic consequences. The cloth fair held in the vicinity of the city was one of the greatest commercial events in the economic life of the Indian Ocean, and it was to impart a strong stimulus to the textile industries of, successively, Egypt, Iraq, and western India. Above all, what made this huge periodic concourse of people possible in this part of the Red Sea was the export of grains and other foodstuffs from the Nile delta. As the Arab geographer and traveller al-Muqaddasi was to note later (*c*. 980), the sea-port of Jedda with its noble mosque and splendid palaces came to be regarded as the granary of Mecca and the emporium of al-Yaman and Egypt. He had counted and found that in a single season of the year as many as three thousand camel-loads of grains and flour were exported every week from the milling town of al-Mashtul to the port of al-Qulzum at the edge of the sea of China (the Red Sea) for supplying the pilgrim trade of Hijaz.[24]

Jedda had clearly risen to maritime fame as an economic satellite of Mecca. Many of its inhabitants were wealthy merchants, and al-Muqaddasi mentions that its ruling class was Persian.[25] This information may have some significance. For the main direction of trans-continental trade in the Indian Ocean during the eighth and ninth centuries appears to have been through neither Hijaz nor the Red Sea itself but through the Persian Gulf. People of Iranian origin were known at this time as being excellent sailors. Could it be that it was the seafaring communities of the Gulf that founded and developed Jedda as a port of Mecca? We certainly know that navigation and the movements of ships in the Persian Gulf were not impeded by strong seasonal winds and coral reefs as they were in the Red Sea. Once land was reached in the Gulf, the ocean-going ships could tranship their cargo to the river boats of the Tigris and Euphrates. For the merchants of the Near East trading beyond the bounds of the Islamic world to India, China, or Africa the Persian Gulf possessed tangible advantages.

From Babylonian times the two combined rivers, and especially the lower reaches of the Tigris known as Shatt al-Arab, with its carefully constructed system of canals and irrigation channels, had served as the waterway to the flourishing towns and cities of Mesopotamia and Syria. There were ports in the Gulf, Sasanian Ubulla and the newly founded Basra (*c.* 638), later joined by those further down the Iranian coast, Siraf, Kish, and Hormuz, which developed into true commercial emporia. Ship-owners and masters of vessels, who had to follow strict sailing dates imposed by the monsoon, could find at these ports a ready market for their imports and the goods needed for the return voyage. There was also the fact that both Iraq and Persia were centres of great civilisations with strong internal demands for the differentiated products of pre-modern exchange. Throughout the period of Islamic empires, from the eighth century to the sixteenth, these two regions were at the front of a vast market stretching out to the Central Asian steppes. To the overland traders as well as to the political rulers of the area, the control of the Gulf ports could bring rich financial rewards. The history of these commercial towns and the long-term shifts in their economic fortunes point in the direction of a rare combination of political factors and trading considerations in medieval Asia.

For many centuries the premier trading port and commercial city of Muslim Iraq was Basra, although vessels of larger tonnage often unloaded at the neighbouring port of Ubulla. The foundation of Basra, according to the Arab historian Tabari (died 923), was due to the strategic need for a strong place on the Tigris able to protect the military camps of the invaders against possible naval expeditions organised from Oman or even Hindustan in support of the Persians.[26] The rapid growth of the city and its apparent prosperity are attested by nearly all historical sources dating from the ninth and tenth centuries, and al-Muqaddasi thought that Basra exceeded even the glories of Baghdad in the extent of its resources and the number of pious inhabitants.[27] It is evident that this was a period when the seaborne trade of Iraq and adjacent places experienced conditions favourable to growth. Merchants travelling from as far away as the Frankish lands came to Baghdad and Ubulla to sail for Oman, Sind, India, and China.[28] The Abbasid revolution (749–50), based as it was on the political support of the army of Khurasan, increased the geographical importance of Iraq and Kuzistan with its valuable cultivation of commercial crops.[29] The Abbasid leaders transferred the political base of the caliphate from Damascus to Iraq, but it was not until 762 that the foundations of Baghdad were first laid under the second caliph, al-Mansur. The famous Round City, Madinat as-Salam, was a new city and it was also planned. Large urban areas outside the walled administrative centre eventually developed to accommodate a growing population of workers, artisans, traders, and the resident garrison. These new complexes had their own mosques and markets, and their own workshops for craftsmen.[30] But so striking was the original plan of Baghdad, almost unique in the history of Islamic cities, that later writers attributed a remarkable prescience to its founder in the choice of a site. "This is the Tigris", al-Mansur had said, according to Tabari; "there is no obstacle between us and China; everything on the sea can come to us on it."[31] Ya'qubi (*c.* 875) stated earlier that, as an island between the Euphrates and the Tigris, Baghdad was the harbour of the world. It received not only the river traffic from Basra, Ubulla, and Oman but also the commerce of Syria, Egypt, and North Africa in the west, and of Ajarbayjan, Armenia, Isfahan, and Khurasan in the north and the east.[32] Whatever the reason that had guided al-Mansur in the location of Baghdad, as the capital city of a vast empire it was obviously able to attract a large volume of trade in foodstuffs, raw materials, finished luxury goods, and slaves for the internal market. The productions of Iraq available for export to other countries were not negligible. "Have you not heard of the silken stuffs of al-Basra", asked al-Muqaddasi, "of its fine linen cloths, of the beautiful and rare articles produced in it, and also of its galbanum? It is a mine of pearls and precious stones, a port of the sea and an emporium of the land, and a place of manufacture ... from which dates are exported to all countries, as well as henna, floss silk, violets and rose-water."[33] When the season for shipping new dates to Wasit opened, a watch was kept on the river, and the owner of the first boat sighted had his shop decorated with curtains and carpets to celebrate the event.[34]

These contemporaneous descriptions of places and actual trading conditions in the Indian Ocean at the time of Islamic expansion reveal the presence of a social order which had probably existed for a long time, a society with a whole range of perennial preferences, from the necessities of daily life to the marginal and exotic demands of the very rich. If the legendary exploits of Sinbad the Sailor epitomised the Arab taste for travel and adventure, the stories also confirm the continuing importance of the Mesopotamian trade route. The rise of Siraf at some distance from Basra is well attested, but curiously enough never properly explained in the sources. The revolt of the Zanj (Africans) and the consequent sacking and destruction of Basra by the rebels must have severely disrupted the normal transhipment of goods through Iraq during 868 and 883.[35] But we know from an anonymous work (dating from *c.* 851) on the Indian Ocean voyages that Siraf was already a considerable port and commercial town in the Gulf. It was the terminus of a long line of oceanic traffic that stretched out in the east to the Malabar coast in India, to Ceylon, to the Malayan archipelago, and to China.[36] The location of Siraf was not happy, as the town itself was hemmed in closely between steep, barren mountains and the sea. The summer heat was extreme in Siraf. However, the main attraction of the town, which was almost as large as Shiraz, was due to the fact that large ships trading to China and other distant countries in the Indian Ocean avoided the dangers of sudden storms in the Gulf and the navigational hazards of a complex delta system near Basra.[37]

This was a feature common to both the Red Sea and the Persian Gulf, as the later pattern of trade from the tenth century to the fifteenth confirms. Ports close to the Arabian Sea gained in prominence by being closer to the monsoon winds, which changed direction with predictable accuracy. There seems to have been a division of interest and specialisation between ship-owners who served the longer routes across the Indian Ocean and those who used smaller and differently constructed vessels to tranship merchandise between Siraf and Basra, or Aden, Jedda, Aydhab, and al-Qulzum in Egypt. The commercial towns of Oman and the Yemen were particularly well placed to take on this intermediate role. Siraf was severely damaged by an earthquake in 977. By this time Suhar, the capital of Oman, and Aden were equally famous as ports of trade. A wealthy and populous city, Suhar had beautiful buildings and large markets with a Persianised ruling class. Its merchants traded with China and with Iraq, and supplied the Yemen with less exotic bulk goods.[38] Aden performed almost identical economic functions to those of Suhar, and its commercial transactions were obviously a continuing source of profit and capital gain to passing and resident merchants. Aden was also capable of withstanding siege, and as a strongly fortified town it never lost its strategic advantage in that part of the Indian Ocean.[39]

The works of Arab geographers and travellers leave no doubt at all that the inter-regional maritime and caravan trade of the Near East, important as it was, existed alongside the highly profitable trans-oceanic trade originating further east. They were aware that the subcontinent of India was ruled by a number of different Hindu princes, who were powerful but not to be compared to the imperial authority of the Chinese emperors.[40] They knew that in some parts of India trade was carried on by means of cowrie shells and that the cotton cloth exported was so fine that it could be drawn through a signet-ring.[41] The Arab political presence in Sind from 712 would have provided the basis for the growth of a Muslim community in western India, and the frontier town of Multan had a considerable number of Islamic inhabitants.[42] But the main impetus for the settlement of Muslims on the western coast of India, before the Turkish conquest of the northern provinces (1001–1192), came from the activities of the merchants of Siraf, Oman, and Hadramaut.[43] It seems that the navigation of the Indian Ocean in the direction of South East Asia and China and the transportation of the commodities produced in these areas were mainly undertaken by either Hindu ships or those from the Red Sea and the Persian Gulf. The coastal provinces of China under the T'ang dynasty gained in economic importance without as yet claiming a major stake in the seaborne trade.[44] Indeed, one of the historical puzzles in the structure of Indian Ocean commerce is the existence at this time of a direct line of voyages going all the way from the Middle East to China, in contrast to the later practice of organising trade in shorter segments based on the intermediate urban emporia of the Malabar coast and the strait of Malacca.

The anonymous work the *Relation of China and India* (851), and the *Book of Roads and Provinces* (846–85) composed by Ibn Khurdadhbih, both describe in considerable detail the sailing routes followed by Sirafian shipmasters on their way to China.[45] The first port of call for the outward-bound vessels was either Muscat or Suhar. The voyage to the western coast of India could take two directions. Merchants wishing to take on board the valuable goods supplied from the prosperous province of Sind sailed to the great city of Daybul, or the ships which already had their full complement of cargo steered for the Malabar coast where landfall was made at Kulam Mali. This was the beginning of the longest stretch of the voyage, round the southern tip of Ceylon and across the cyclone belt of the Bay of Bengal to Kalah Bar in the strait of Malacca. Once in the South China Sea, the ships worked their passage up the coast of Indo-China to Hanoi and finally to Canton, which the Arabs knew as Khanfu.[46] Most of the Gulf merchants would have made Canton the last port of call before returning home, though Ibn Khurdadhbih mentions two other ports to the north (possibly Ch'üan-chou and Hangchow) which were known to the Muslim sailors.[47] The pattern of these voyages was quite distinct and indicates that the sailors of the western half of the Indian Ocean had already mastered the problem of crossing the open sea out of sight of land. Without a knowledge of celestial navigation and the method of dead-reckoning, it would not have been possible for the ships to sail across the points indicated on the oceanic map.[48]

   When did the merchants of the Persian Gulf or the Red Sea first begin to trade to China? In a Chinese source, written about AD 500, there are references to the Roman orient and India and to the dangers encountered by the envoys of the Han dynasties in crossing the western ocean. It was mentioned that all the precious objects of land and water came from that direction, which had caused trade and navigation to be extended to those parts.[49] During the late seventh and early eighth centuries, the Persian Gulf ships were already sailing to Canton to buy, among other things, the silk textiles of China.[50] In 758 the Arabs and Persians even made a violent assault on the city of Kwang-chou (Canton) before returning by sea.[51] While the incidental references in the Chinese historical chronicles show clearly the presence of the people of the Near East in the maritime provinces of China, in the Arab accounts of the period the long voyage along the entire breadth of the Indian Ocean was always remembered as being particularly hazardous. The Persian sea-captain Buzurg ibn Shahriyar, who knew well the maritime world of Siraf, has recorded the legendary navigational skills of "al-rubban" (captain) 'Abharah, who had made the China voyage seven times. Before him no one had sailed to China in the certain knowledge of returning home without accidents, and even the famous navigator himself suffered shipwreck at the entrance to the Sea of China and was rescued as the sole survivor from his ship.[52]

   The reputation of those who succeeded in reaching Canton and who came back safely to Siraf and Oman with a cargo stood high among the seafarers of the Persian Gulf. Even so the goods of China appear to have remained a rarity in Iraq and Persia. The commercial warehouses in Canton were frequently destroyed by fire, and if the ships escaped being wrecked or plundered by pirates there were still many ports on the way where the goods could be sold.[53] Arab historical sources on early voyages in the Indian Ocean leave untouched an insistent question. Why did a direct maritime trade between China and the Near East develop in the first place, when it would have been more logical to exchange the commodities entering into the international market at some port on the Malabar coast? In suggesting a possible answer, it is important to remember that the contemporaneous sources tell us very little about the sea-borne trade carried on from the Indian subcontinent at the time when Muslim expansion began in the Indian Ocean. It may well be the case that the range of Chinese and Indonesian goods sold in Daybul, Quilon, and Calicut even in these early years was greater than it was thought necessary to record. It is very probable that the large settlement of Muslims in Canton and their navigational techniques in sailing ships out of sight of land enabled them to operate as universal carriers of cargo and passengers in all the major sea-port towns of the Indian Ocean.

This conclusion is admittedly speculative. It is strengthened by the juxtaposition of a number of ascertained facts. The heavily planked, multi-decked Chinese ships known as junks began to sail towards South East Asia only from the later T'ang period and did not reach the commercial emporia of the Malabar coast before the accession of the Sung dynasty.[54] The descriptions of the foreign trade of T'ang China, in both Arabic and Chinese languages, were of ocean-going vessels whose owners and crew came from the Near East, Japan, and Korea.[55] Muslim traders were well received at the port of Canton and they were allowed to conduct their commercial and communal affairs through the traditional Islamic institutions.[56] Just how large was the number of the Middle Eastern people settled in Canton can be seen from the account of the famous sack of the city left by the Arab historian abu-Zayd of Siraf. In 878 the rebel bandit leader Huang Ch'ao marched across Fukien in the direction of Kwang-chou, closely pursued by the imperial forces. When he failed to get an assurance that he would be given the governorship of the great port as a term of surrender, the bandit forces captured the city and slaughtered 120 000 Muslims, Christians, Jews, and Iranians of the ancient faith.[57] This was a period in the history of the T'ang dynasty when southern China witnessed intermittent rebellions, military movements, and banditry. The political uncertainties and the destructions suffered in Canton may have encouraged the Muslims to stop at Kalah Bar in the Malayan archipelago. When Mas'udi visited the Indian Ocean countries about 916, this was where the ships from the West, from Siraf and Oman, met with those that came from the Far East.[58]

It seems probable that by the tenth century Chinese merchants and junk-owners had become aware of the financial gains to be made from a direct participation in the Indian Ocean trade. Port officials in charge of collecting customs revenue were certainly engaged in buying up the high-valued imports

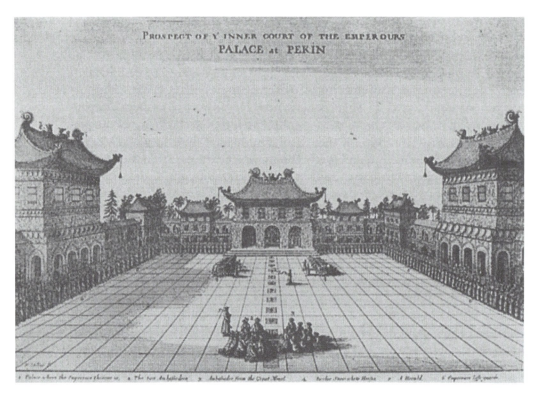

Plate 4. Imperial palace at Peking, from J. Nieuhof, *An Embassy from the East India Company of the United Provinces to the Grand Tartar Chaun Emperor of China*, translated by John Ogilby, 1669.

and reselling them at an inflated price in the open market. A common Chinese proverb stated that once the governor general of Kwang-chou passed the city-gates he was the owner of thirty million cash.[59] As the Sung dynasty (960–1126) came into power, an attempt was made to bring some administrative rationality into the organisation of the empire's maritime trade by creating a partial official monopoly:

The Imperial edict of the sixth moon of the first year of Chih-tao, A.D. 995, decreed that the inspector of shipping office, the governor, the sub-prefect and others should not hereafter make purchases of miscellaneous goods from foreign traders and the forbidden goods; if they violate this regulation, they should be liable to heavy penalties.[60]

The concern which the Sung emperors showed in encouraging and regulating the overseas trade of China points not only to the revival of Canton as a commercial city but also to the emergence of new centres such as Ch'üan-chou. Chou K'ü-fei, writing in 1178, drew attention to the fact that the coastal departments and prefectures of the empire now stretched from the north east to the south west as far as K'in-chou, the westernmost district of the province

52

of Kwangtung. The coast was visited by many trading vessels, and in its watch-ful kindness towards the foreign "barbarians" the Chinese government had established at Ch'üan-chou and Canton special inspectorates of shipping. These offices dealt with any difficulties or complaints from foreign merchants.[61]

Chou K'ü-fei knew the main geographical orientation of Indian Ocean commerce, particularly where the commodities most prized in Chinese society had their origin. The lands of the Ta-shi, the Arabs, were regarded as the greatest store of precious and varied goods. Java and Sumatra came next. The two areas formed the ancient crossroads of inter-continental trade.[62] As a source of gem stones, pearls, incense, perfumes, sandalwood, and spices, the three regions – southern Arabia, the Persian Gulf, and South East Asia – remained for more than a millennium the cornerstones of pre-modern long-distance exchange in luxury objects. It is not entirely accidental that the com-mercial goods in the stereotype lists in Indian or Chinese historical literature fall into the category of precious or high-value articles. The subcontinent of India and China had the climates and the economic resources to produce almost all the necessities of life. But not all provinces were uniformly self-sufficient. As will be shown later, the pre-modern merchant could not have operated his ships without low-value bulk cargo, which served as ballast. The range of goods brought to India or China would almost certainly have included heavy cargo such as dates, sugar, building material, and timber, just as the export of porcelain from China provided the staple ballast for ships. Among luxury goods certain items occupied a special place. Exotic aromatics always had very precise functions in the religious and social systems of ancient civilisations. The burning of incense, whether in the form of gum resins or of rare wood, was ritually as obligatory for Hindu India as it was for Confucian and Buddhist China. A Sung mandarin on retiring to the capital after having been the chief commissioner of transport in the maritime province of Kwangtung even attempted to buy a place higher up the ladder of imperial administration by bribing the court officials with incense.[63] The famous attar of roses, manufactured in Persia by distilling the petals of the flowers, was first brought to China as a tribute offering at the time of the Five Dynasties (907–60). So powerful was its perfume that even when put in glass phials sealed with wax the fragrance leaked out.[64]

The expansion in China's seaborne trade during the centuries under the Sung dynasty was part of the development that took place in the whole of the coastal provinces south of the river Yangtze. The demand for goods increased, as did the purchasing power of the urban classes.[65] Increased use of foreign imported products and greater knowledge of non-Chinese people and king-doms are reflected in the famous compilation called *Chu-fan chi* written by Chau Ju-kua in 1225. There is no indication in the work as to the exact identity of the author. A brief notice in a descriptive library catalogue from the middle of the thirteenth century refers to him as Superintendent of Maritime Trade in the province of Fukien.[66] If this is true, he would have been stationed at the great port of Ch'üan-chou, which is generally identified with the Zaiton of Marco Polo's and Ibn Battuta's travel accounts. Chau Ju-kua in the course of his official duties would have had the opportunity and the incentive to acquire a first-hand knowledge of the different branches of Indian Ocean trade and of the merchants and commodities that arrived in China from different ports. His work points out the comprehensive nature of the Far Eastern seaborne trade. It was not confined to a few items of luxury consumption but was part of a much wider system of economic exchange. The dependence of the Indo-Islamic and Chinese seafarers on the monsoon winds and the passage through the strait of Malacca is also brought out clearly in the "Description of the Barbarous Peoples". During the last half-century new historical research has succeeded in identifying the powerful political dynasty mentioned by both Arab and Chinese sources with the kingdom of Srivijaya in Sumatra with its capital at Palembang.[67] Chau Ju-kua speaks of the country of San-fo-ch'i, which is commonly identified with Palembang,[68] as one lying in the ocean and controlling the strait through which the foreigners with their ships must pass in either direction. In the old days an iron chain was used across the narrow sea passage to control merchant shipping and to deter piratical raids. After many years of peace, the chain was no longer used and lay coiled up on the beach, only to receive votive offerings from passing sailors before they faced the dreaded typhoons of the South China Sea.[69] The country of San-fo-ch'i had begun to have contacts with China from the closing years of the T'ang dynasty and had sent tribute three times during the Sung. It was, however, a powerful maritime state in its own right and had the naval capacity to intercept any merchant vessel unwilling to call at its port.[70]

After the Mongol conquest of China in 1279, the empire's maritime connections seem to have been strengthened rather than weakened. We know from Marco Polo that the capital cities of China displayed a spectacle of astonishing wealth and personal consumption on the part of their wealthy citizens. In the very noble and magnificent city of Quinsai (Hangchow), a broad canal ran parallel to the main street and market squares, and "on the near bank of this there are built great houses of stone where all the merchants who come from India and from other parts deposit their goods and merchandise that they may be near and handy to the squares".[71] The population of Hangchow was so great that a stranger, Marco Polo thought, might wonder how it was possible to feed the multitudes, and yet the daily and weekly markets were thronged by merchants and traders who brought all kinds of provisions on carts and boats for sale in the city. The port of Zaiton did not come far behind Hangchow. A centre of fine-quality porcelain and silk manufacture at this time, Zaiton was crowded with ocean-going shipping. For every ship laden with pepper which might be sent for transhipment to Alexandria

Plate 5. View of Aden from the sea, showing the Portuguese attack on the town in 1513, from Gaspar Correa, *Lendas da India*, 1858.

and the Christian lands, one hundred came to Zaiton.[72] Half a century later, when Ibn Battuta visited the city (*c.* 1343–4), it seemed to him to be the greatest port in the world, its commercial traffic exceeding that of Alexandria, Quilon, and Calicut on the Malabar coast.[73] What was the reason for the apparent wealth of Chinese merchants during the Sung and Yuan times? The Sung rulers had certainly derived a large income from sea customs and taxes paid by merchants and hence had a direct incentive to encourage overseas economic relations.[74] In addition, the government raised an impressive revenue from the sale of tribute goods sent by foreign princes. Quantities of drugs and aromatics which entered China as tribute from dependent kingdoms in South East Asia were probably as great as those imported by private merchants, although the profits of the tribute trade must be measured against the valuable presents which the imperial court returned to those rulers who had sent their envoys to China in the first place.[75]

Chau Ju-kua and Marco Polo both lived during a century which witnessed the occupation of large parts of the civilised world by the Mongols. The economic effects of these movements radiating from Central Asia are today only imperfectly understood. The waves of new conquests and the fragmentation of the old Arab empire had of course begun much earlier with the expansion of the Seljuk Turks, who conquered Baghdad in 1055. Jerusalem fell to them in 1071 and Damascus five years later. The continuing military threats alarmed China's huge northern frontiers as much as the boundaries of Islam. The disruption to the overland caravan routes caused one Sung emperor to instruct the Arab tributary envoy in 1023 to come to the Celestial empire in future by sea and not by land.[76] However, in times of peace the world of Islam actively traded with the areas around the Caspian and Aral Seas, with Central Asia, and with China. The most famous trade route was the one taken by caravans carrying silk, which passed through the Iranian cities of Hamadan and Nishapur to Bukhara and Samarkand in Transoxiana. From thence a number of routes led over vast arid deserts to the Great Walls of China, a monumental reminder to all of the gulf that separated the rich civilisation of the Chinese empire from the lands of nomadic barbarians. This was a trade in rich commodities. Gold and silver (in coins, ingots, and dust), jewellery, silk, gold-tinted paper, jade, and even costly porcelain were transported on the backs of rugged steppe horses and the formidable Bactrian camels.[77] Sizeable towns located at strategic points on the land routes fostered the caravan trade and enabled it to survive intermittently over the centuries. The urban centres in turn grew in wealth and power from the presence of transit traffic. Under the Samanid dynasty (875–999), for example, Samarkand became a city of a large population. Long walls enclosed the entire oasis under cultivation and the place was renowned for its spectacular public gardens, monuments, caravanserais, and fine buildings. Indeed, the city of the desert was the symbol *par excellence* of Muslim trade and the incessant yearnings for movement among the children of Islam. In the Iranian plateau, standing at the crossroads leading to Samarkand, Herat, or Multan in India, two large and architecturally striking towns had grown up completely surrounded by deserts. Water precariously brought in underground channels supported a limited form of agriculture in the land around these urban settlements. But the size and prosperity of Kirman and Yazd were inexplicable in the absence of income earned from industrial handicrafts or from services sold to passing merchants and their caravans.[78]

The horizontal axis of trans-continental trade in an east-to-west direction was of course supplemented by a lesser network in the direction of East Africa, orientated from north to south. The evidence for Muslim trade and demographic expansion towards the African coast comes from three separate sources. There are various oral traditions and written chronicles, dating from later periods, which ascribe a definite colonisation effort on the part of the early caliphate. The archaeological remains of towns such as Kilwa, Manda, and other places also provide a great deal of direct evidence of considerable commercial activity. Finally, the Arab geographers and travellers refer to the kingdoms of Zanj, and Ibn Battuta has left actual descriptions of Mogadishu

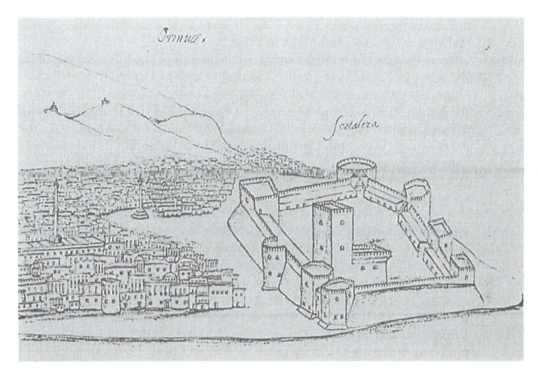

Plate 6. View of Hormuz from the sea, from Gaspar Correa, *Lendas da India*, 1858.

and Kilwa (1328).[79] The archaeological excavations carried out at Kilwa reveal the presence of large warehouses, a customs house, and a great mosque. The evidence of imported porcelain and glass found at different levels of Kilwa indicates that the settlement was important to the Indian Ocean traders from about the ninth century. Both Chinese and Islamic pottery dating from the ninth and tenth centuries has been unearthed at Manda, and the blue-glazed jars with decoration are similar to those discovered at sites in Iraq and Persia. Islamic ware of Iranian and Egyptian origin continued to be plentiful in East African settlements until the fourteenth century. As the city–state of Kilwa reached the height of its prosperity in later years, Islamic imports declined in quality and were replaced by Chinese celadon and some blue-and-white porcelain. This type of Ming pottery of course became highly popular throughout the Middle East, and in East African architecture there was a fashion for decorating the interiors of vaulted buildings and domes with inset porcelain bowls.[80] It has been claimed that Kilwa's commercial fortunes depended on its control of the gold trade of Sofala further down the coast.[81] Gold, ivory, and mangrove timber were the main exports from the region to the rest of Asia. The nationality of merchants who made the annual voyage to Mogadishu or Kilwa remains indistinct in the contemporaneous sources. But the places in the Indian Ocean with which East African towns seem most likely to have had direct commercial contacts are Daybul and Cambay in India, Aden, Suhar, and Siraf at the other end of the Arabian Sea.

From the end of the tenth century to the middle of the fifteenth, important changes took place both in the direction of Indian Ocean trade and in the larger aspects of its political, religious, and artistic traditions. The decline of the Abbasid caliphate and the rise of the Fatimids in Egypt shifted the routing of long-distance trade away from Baghdad and Damascus to Aden and Fustat. In India, the Turkish sultanate of Delhi conquered Gujarat in 1303–4, and its rich maritime towns were now within the reach of Islamic social and political influence. At about the same time the trading ports and the coastal kingdoms of the Indonesian archipelago began to accept the Muslim faith, and the process of conversion continued for the next three centuries. These new developments in the Indian Ocean ran parallel to the astonishing events taking place in the Christian half of the Mediterranean. The expulsion of the Moorish rulers from Spain and the rise of Venice and Genoa to commercial supremacy signified the symbolic beginnings of a realignment in the structure of world economy. European merchants from Constantinople, the Aegean islands, and Italy had always been active in the ports of Syria and at Alexandria. When the Fatimids shifted their seat of power from al-Mahdiyya in Tunisia to Old Cairo in Egypt, the economic importance of Alexandria as the terminus of transcontinental trade became even greater.[82] The revival of the flow of trade through the Red Sea and its economic effects on Egypt from the eleventh century onwards did not go unnoticed by contemporaneous observers. This is what al-Muqaddasi himself had to say about the capital of Misr, the ancient name by which the Nile valley was known to the Arabs:

Al-Fustat is a metropolis in every sense of the word; for in addition to having within it all the departments of the State, it is the seat of residence of the Commander of the Faithful himself. It is situated midway between the Occident and the main country of the Arabs . . . it has effaced Baghdad and is the glory of Islam and the centre of the world's commerce. The City of Peace [Baghdad] cannot compare with it in greatness. It is the treasure-house of the West and the emporium of the East.[83]

That al-Muqaddasi was not drawing on mere rhetoric to describe the preeminence of Fustat we know from the remarkable collection of business papers, belonging to Jewish merchants, discovered in a synagogue of Old Cairo.[84] The documents, letters, contracts, partnership agreements, accounts, invoices, and price lists, cover the period from *c*. 1000 to 1250. They bring to light in vivid detail the actual conditions under which a community of Mediterranean merchants organised their international business life from North Africa to India. A late eleventh-century letter describes the keen commodity markets of Alexandria and Fustat: "Please take note that no pepper, cinnamon or ginger are available in Alexandria. If you have any of these commodities, keep them, for the Rum [Byzantines] are keen solely on them. All the

Rum are about to leave for Old Cairo. They are only waiting for the arrival of two additional ships from Constantinople."[85] The most interesting revelation of the Cairo Genizah papers is the activity of Jewish traders from Tunisia, Andalusia, and even Sicily in the trans-oceanic trade. A great number of them were closely involved with western India, moving constantly between the Malabar ports, Aden, and Fustat. Joseph Lebdi of Cairo was in India in 1097–8. The family of Madmun ben Hasan was the representative of merchants in Aden at the same time. Abraham ben Yiju of al-Mahdiyya lived in India from about 1132 to 1149. He was obviously very wealthy and owned brass foundry works in India. Members of his family followed him in the Malabar trade.[86] The extent to which the Fatimid connections with North Africa had encouraged these merchants to engage in very extended commercial transactions is clear from the genizah documents. But it is also true that the shipment of goods from the Indian Ocean to the Mediterranean West – to the towns of the Maghreb such as al-Mahdiyya, Qayrawan, Palermo, or Córdoba – did not take place on the basis of direct connections. The commercial dealings of the genizah merchants between India and the Maghreb relied on intermediaries. Business was done by consigning goods to friends and relatives in Fustat or Aden, while the principal remained in India. It is significant from the point of view of commercial organisation that the leading Jewish merchants of the period with business connections in distant countries did not find it necessary to travel with their own goods.[87]

If the Cairo Genizah papers richly illuminate the multi-faceted life of one community of long-distance traders in the eleventh and twelfth centuries, they also cast some light on a baffling economic organisation known as the "karim". The Karimi merchants of the Red Sea are mentioned in Egyptian sources as being actively concerned with the spice trade of the Indian Ocean.[88] However, the word "karim" also occurs frequently in the genizah papers in the context of the India trade. For example, a fragment containing part of a letter written by Abu Zikri Kohen or Sijilmasa, who had his business in Cairo, states: "As far as the karim is concerned, I received a letter from it, from my brother-in-law Mahruz in Sawakin, saying that it contained 3000 bales and that there travelled homewards in the karim seven of our Jewish business friends."[89] Sawakin was of course a port on the Red Sea, and it seems that the karim did not touch at Aden during this season on its way home from Persia and India. From similar passages S.D. Goitein has argued most convincingly that in the twelfth century the karim was neither a guild of merchants nor a particular branch of international trade but some sort of annual convoy or a seaborne caravan. We can only speculate as to why there should have been such an organisation at this time in the history of Indian Ocean trade (Goitein has no explanations himself). There is no doubt that the total volume of Euro-Asian trade had become very considerable between AD 1000 and AD 1300. This would have made the ships and cargo of individual merchants trading by sea to India very vulnerable to pirates and political taxation. A convoy system organised by wealthy merchants may have been in a position to buy protection from the political rulers of the Middle East and to organise better protection against attacks by the pirates of the Indian Ocean.

Under the Ayyubid rulers of Egypt (1170–1260), to be followed by the Mamluks (1250–1517), the strong economic position of Cairo was maintained with intensive development of the Red Sea ports. Saladin, the Kurdish warrior who began the process of containing the military and political power of the Crusaders, also attempted to prevent the Frankish merchants from gaining direct access to the Red Sea and confined them to the Mediterranean ports.[90] The Vatican of course placed a permanent interdict on Christian trade with Muslim countries. In spite of the prohibition, Genoese and Venetian ships crowded into the harbour of Alexandria.[91] From fragmentary references to commercial negotiations and diplomatic exchanges, it seems that the Egyptian government exercised its sovereignty and control over the Red Sea and the Indian Ocean commerce, not by constructing strong naval fleets, but by instituting a system of safe-conduct passes. Merchants issued with the Egyptian passes were not only assured of the security of their persons and property, but were given good treatment by the fiscal authorities as well.[92] There is evidence that during the fourteenth century many areas of the Near East, including Egypt, experienced economic disruptions and even a sustained decline.[93] The appearance of the Black Death in Egypt in 1347 had a catastrophic effect on population and agriculture. The exact relationship between these events and the rhythm of long-distance trade through the Red Sea is not quite clear. The Cairo–Alexandria network, however, remained open.

In China the economic policy followed by the Ming dynasty (1368–1644) produced contradictory effects on maritime trade. The first emperor, Hung-wu, was an orphan of peasant origins who felt suspicious towards traders, bankers, and even the institution of money. His administrative reforms were accompanied by an official discouragement of foreign trade and of the use of silver as money. It was not until the reign of the third emperor, Yung-lo (1402–24), that a new experiment was tried in China's economic relations with the trading nations of the Indian Ocean. It took the form of a hugely ambitious series of seaborne expeditions, between 1404 and 1433. Organised by the influential Grand Eunuch Cheng Ho, the first fleet sailed from Ch'ang-lo in Fukien and went as far as Calicut in Malabar. It was composed of sixty-two ships and carried 28 000 men.[94] The fourth voyage reached Hormuz and Aden, and the later expeditions claimed to have touched even at the East African ports. What possible motive could the Grand Eunuch and even the emperor himself have had in sanctioning these costly voyages? The elaborate preparations of the fleet and the large number of men carried suggest that political and military objectives were as much in the minds of the Chinese

Plate 7. Sea-view of Canton in the seventeenth century, showing European shipping and Chinese junks in the foreground, from Nieuhof, *An Embassy from the East India Company*, 1669.

policy makers as financial and commercial ones. The inscriptions dedicated by Cheng Ho and his colleagues at the shrines of T'ien-fei, the Celestial Spouse and spiritual guardian of the sea, state that the imperial fleets in the course of their voyages subdued pirates and foreign princes who had defied the emperor's overarching authority.[95] When the expeditions were finally abandoned in 1433, this happened against a background of dissident criticism from senior mandarins that the financial gains to the treasury were meagre.[96] After the episode of Cheng Ho's voyages, future Ming emperors were determined to close China's sea-coasts to foreign visitors and placed an embargo on the trade of Chinese merchants to overseas destinations.

The long-term reasons for this change of policy are probably to be found in the problem of protecting the coastal provinces from the depredations of the ruthless sea bandits who infested the China Sea periodically. The pirates were invariably identified with Japanese raiders. Whatever their nationality, the prohibition of trade with Japan seemed one way of preventing the pirates from ravaging towns and villages close to the sea. The political ideology of excluding foreigners and especially merchants from the empire gained a practical significance as a result of insecurity at sea. Ming overseas commerce, however, continued in several forms. Traders living in coastal communities and operating private junks found ways of reaching financial agreement with the local officials to dispose of cargo brought back from smuggling voyages to the Philippines, Tongking, and Malacca. Then again, by the sixteenth century European newcomers, both Portuguese and Spaniards, made it possible for China's silver-hungry economy to acquire the metal through a quadrilateral extension of trade between India, Japan, China itself, and the New World. The silver mines of Mexico and Peru joined those in Japan to provide indispensable monetary liquidity to the whole of Asia.[97]

3

The Portuguese seaborne empire in the Indian Ocean

By all accounts the fourteenth and fifteenth centuries were unusually prosperous in the history of the Indian Ocean trade, in spite of the Mongol advance and the appearance of the plague. The vivid descriptions of commercial Asia in Ibn Battuta's travels, which extended from North Africa to China, point both to the daily rhythm of caravan journeys and to the busy existence, and the inevitable hazards, of oceanic voyages. The costly Ming expeditions organised in the early part of the fifteenth century were just one indication among many that the rich maritime towns and cities bordering the sea had a definite place in the minds and imaginations of powerful government ministers, even in imperial China. As we shall see later, these centres served as the motor mechanism through which the exchange of economic products and information of all kinds received its accelerating velocity. The evidence left by other travellers of the fifteenth century, the Persian ambassador Abdu'r Razzaq, the Venetian Nicolò Conti, or Santo Stefano of Genoa,[1] confirms the pattern of emporia trading described by Marco Polo and Ibn Battuta, a state of affairs to which Portuguese policy makers and historians were to give later a great deal of their time and attention. Indeed, the arrival of the Portuguese in the Indian Ocean abruptly ended the system of peaceful oceanic navigation that was such a marked feature of the region. The historian of "catastrophe" theories in the Asian context is fortunate in being able to assign precise dates to the watershed.[2] For the commercial communities of the Indian Ocean the challenge and competition in trans-continental trade were as wholly exogenous as the timing was sudden and unexpected.

In 1492 the Genoese sea-captain and explorer, Christopher Columbus, discovered the New World in the service of Spain, after being disappointed of Portuguese royal patronage. So far, Portugal and her seamen had no serious rival in the wider expanse of the Atlantic. Now the remarkable exploit of Columbus confronted the country with a formidable maritime challenge at its own doorstep. However, six years later Vasco da Gama won an equal if not a greater prize for the Lusitanian crown. On 18 May 1498 his small fleet, piloted across the open sea from East Africa by an Indian navigator, dropped anchor before Calicut, the Malabar emporium.[3] The way to the East round the Cape of Good Hope held out an exciting prospect, which was nothing less than the chance to liberate the vital arteries of trans-oceanic trade from Muslim politi-

cal control. All this was well known at the time, and the early Portuguese conquistadores in Asia invariably claimed that their hostility and depredations
against Muslim traders and shipping derived from the state of perpetual war
between Christendom and Islam.[4] To a large extent, the claim and the viewpoint were propagandist, a part of the make-believe world in which ideology
justified deeds. The Portuguese discovery of the route to India in fact had long
and solid historical antecedents and was based on a secure knowledge of seamanship in the dangerous and heavy seas of the Atlantic. The voyage of
Bartolomeu Dias round the Cape of Good Hope in 1487–8 was the penulti-
mate act in a chain of chronological events that had begun with Portugal's
conquest in 1415 of the Moroccan commercial city of Ceuta.[5]

Of course, the Iberian voyages of discovery across the Atlantic and the
Indian Ocean, besides inaugurating symbolically long-term movements in the
European economy, created a profound impression on the contemporaneous
world, both Asian and European. Gaspar Correa, the Portuguese historian
and official with fifty years' Indian experience since the time of Affonso de
Albuquerque (1509–15), expressed the mood and atmosphere of this period in
Malabar in his simple remark that some of the source material of his history
consisted of memoirs belonging to the Muslims and Hindus of Cannanore,
who wrote with surprise at seeing things they had never thought of before.[6]
They may well have wondered, for at the time of the Portuguese arrival in the
Indian Ocean, the great sea was still a no-man's territory, not in the power of
any particular state or prince. At sea merchants feared only the pirates and the
natural hazards of the wind and the tide. The importation by the Portuguese
of the Mediterranean style of trade and warfare, by land and sea, was a viol-
ation of the agreed conventions and certainly a new experience that had more
than one implication. It was not only the merchants of India and those of
Aden, Cairo, and Alexandria who had reason to fear the recent Portuguese
exploits; the economic interests of Venice, by now the unquestioned maritime
leader in the Mediterranean, seemed to be at stake as well. Girolamo Priuli, the
Venetian diarist, captured the feelings of gloom and uncertainty experienced
in the Signoria in the year 1501:

On the 9th of this month letters came from Lisbon of the 1st of August. And through
letters from Genoa and Lyons and other parts, it is learned that the caravels which
were expected loaded with spices are in Portugal.

 Three of the said caravels came from Calicut and one from the gold-mine which had
a large quantity of gold . . . This news . . . was considered very bad news for the city
of Venice . . . Whence it is that the King of Portugal has found this new voyage, and
that the spices which should come from Calicut, Cochin, and other places in India to
Alexandria or Beyrout, and later come to Venice, and in this place become
monopolized, whence all the world comes to buy such spicery and carry gold, silver,
and every other merchandise, with which money the war is sustained; to-day, with this
new voyage by the King of Portugal, all the spices which came by way of Cairo will be

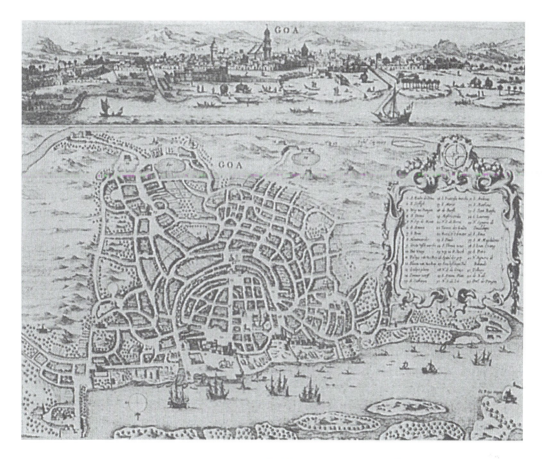

Plate 8. Sea-view and plan of Goa, from Philippus Baldaeus, *Naauwkeurige Beschryvinge van Malabar en Choromandel*, 1672.

controlled in Portugal, because of the caravels which will go to India, to Calicut, and other places to take them . . . And truly the Venetian merchants are in a bad way, believing that the voyages should make them very poor.[7]

The Arab chroniclers of Hadramaut, referring to the events of 1502–3, recorded tersely: "In this year (Radjab) the vessels of the Frank appeared at sea en route for India, Hurmuz, and those parts. They took about seven vessels, killing those on board and making some prisoner. This was their first action, may God curse them."[8]

It is now known that the attempt of the Portuguese to break into the spice market and their subsequent policy of controlling the direction and composition of Indian Ocean trade did not work out quite as was initially feared. In spite of the large volume of pepper and spices brought to Lisbon and marketed through Antwerp, from the middle of the sixteenth century eastern goods – spices, dyes, and cotton and silk textiles – were once again flowing through the

Red Sea and the Mediterranean.[9] This development was closely related to the early successes, failures, and temporising policies adopted by the Estado da India, the Portuguese empire in maritime Asia. The chronological divisions of Lusitanian presence in the Indian Ocean during the sixteenth century are fairly clear. The years from 1500 to the end of Albuquerque's governorship in 1515 were years of heroic deeds at sea, when most Asian rulers with a stake in long-distance seaborne trade were totally taken by surprise at the single-minded determination of Lisbon in seizing the most profitable ports in East Africa, the Malabar, Konkan, the Persian Gulf, and the strait of Malacca. The second period lasted from 1515 to about 1560, when the viceroyalty of Goa reached the height of its sea-power and was able to enforce a semi-monopoly in the pepper and spice trade. Through a chain of fortified settlements in the Indian Ocean, and backed up by a regular naval patrol, Goa Dorado compelled many local traders to buy safe-conduct passes from the Estado da India and to pay to it customs duties. Raiding expeditions were sent out at frequent intervals to terrorise the prosperous commercial towns of Gujarat and to inflict heavy losses on the profitable trade of the Indian merchants with the Near East.[10] During the third phase, from 1560 to 1600, there were two separate historical developments. First, the pepper trade began to revive through the Red Sea and the Mediterranean, largely as a result of the Portuguese failure to curb the formidable maritime power of the North Sumatran sultanate in Acheh, combined with the ineffectiveness of the naval blockade in Bab-al-Mandeb.[11] Secondly, the government of Goa was actively involved in creating a Far Eastern branch of commercial voyages based on the ports of Macao, Nagasaki, and the Philippines. This was perhaps far more profitable than the monopoly in the pepper trade had ever been to the Portuguese crown, and the new trading voyages to China and Japan may explain the gradual relaxation of Portuguese hold on Indian Ocean trade. The financial needs of individual officials in Goa and their natural inclination to use Asian commercial intermediaries created the basis of a partnership between the Portuguese and indigenous merchants. As the Great Mughals added Gujarat and the Deccan to their powerful military empire in South Asia, the Portuguese viceroyalty obviously felt the need to be cautious at sea without unduly weakening the principle of claiming exclusive sovereignty. This right to control the sea-lanes of Asia was never formally challenged by any local political power in the western Indian Ocean, though it was contested occasionally by Gujarati warships owned by great merchants. It was not until the appearance of the Dutch and English that the Portuguese empire was faced with new problems in terms of both international relations and the actual defence of economic interests.

Vasco da Gama's return to Lisbon in 1499 coincided with King Dom Manuel's energetic plans to modernise and develop commercial facilities in the Portuguese capital. The Tower of Belém in the suburb of Restelo, looking out to the Atlantic, is today one of the few survivals from the earthquake of 1755 to symbolise the public works undertaken by a prince who was more than just a "grocer king", as his contemporaries named him.[12] The financial prospects for Portugal in diverting the spice trade around the Cape of Good Hope were clearly apparent to the royal council, and the next few years saw plans for sending out large, annual fleets to the Indies. Apart from the possibilities of long-term gains, there was an immediate urgency brought about by a general crisis in the Mediterranean spice trade. Political troubles in the Ottoman Empire and in Egypt had led to a drastic reduction in the supply of spices available for sale in Cairo, Alexandria, and Beirut, the three traditional export markets in the Levant. The Venetian trade in the Levant during the period 1499–1502 was disrupted by a state of war with the Turks, and the price of pepper on the Rialto rose steeply as a result of scarcities in supply. The authorities in Lisbon must have been aware of the difference between the cost price of spices in Calicut and their selling price in Europe.[13] The Venetians had sent Pietro Pasqualigo to Lisbon in 1501 to seek Portuguese naval assistance against the Turks. Although Manuel did send a fleet to do battle for the Venetians, the Portuguese ships did not become seriously involved in action. Pasqualigo later reported that the king's real plans lay elsewhere, in the Indian Ocean. By 1502 the Signoria was ready to make peace with the Ottoman court and appointed a special "Giunta on the Spice Trade" to deal with the question of a commercial policy. In 1504 Francesco Teldi was despatched to Cairo with a message reminding the sultan that the Venetians had been invited to go to Lisbon to buy spices but that the Signoria preferred not to abandon its ancient marts and allies. The sultan should take appropriate action against the Portuguese spice trade so that this trade would return to its *pristino corso*. By this time, however, the situation in the Indian Ocean had slipped out of the control of the Mamluk rulers of Egypt. Within a few years the price of oriental imports was forced up to astronomical heights in Alexandria by a continued scarcity in supplies. The origin of the scarcity and the dislocation of the regular commercial voyages between Malabar and the Red Sea was of course in the policy adopted by the Portuguese.[14]

Apart from its pioneering character in the history of European seafaring, the first expedition of Vasco da Gama was significant to the Lisbon policy makers for the link it made between the ports of call in East Africa and those on the western coast of India. Was it an accident that the Portuguese first went to Calicut in Malabar rather than to Coromandel, Gujarat, or the Persian Gulf? It must have been known in every merchant house from Malacca to Venice that Calicut acted as the greatest spice market in the Indian Ocean. The Muslim traders of Grand Cairo, Gaspar Correa noted, brought to the port every year great fleets of ships, and merchants of their faith and religion were not only rich and powerful but also friends and supporters of the Hindu prince, the Samudri, who ruled over the principality of Calicut.[15] These facts are well reflected in the events that took place during the voyage of Pedro

Alvares Cabral, who left Lisbon on 9 March 1500 with thirteen ships, ten of which belonged to the crown and the rest to different syndicates of Portuguese noblemen and Italian financiers.[16] Cabral carried very detailed instructions from the king as to what he was to buy and how he was to treat with the local powers. Included in the commission was the famous clause stating that the king of Calicut, the Samudri, was to be asked to expel all Muslims from his kingdom, as they were enemies of the Holy Faith. The Portuguese would seize at least Arab ships and merchandise at sea. But as a gesture of friendship towards Calicut, Indian traders and their property were not to be touched in any way.[17]

Cabral's voyage is chiefly remembered for the large quantities of pepper and spices brought back to Lisbon and, more ominously for the Asian merchants, for the bombardment of Calicut, which lasted for two days. By firing on the leading port in Malabar, the Portuguese demonstrated to all Muslim ship-owners and no less to the local rulers that the period of unarmed trading was over in the Indian Ocean.[18] After the expedition of 1500, events began to move on rapidly both in East Africa and in India. The appointment of Francisco de Almeida in 1505 as the commander of the fleet for a period of three years marked the end of the annual voyages. From the orders given to him, it seems as if the royal council in Lisbon had spread before it a map of the whole area, with a complete key to the emporia trading network. Almeida was instructed to capture and fortify Sofala and Kilwa in East Africa. He was to build a fortress on the Angediva Islands off the Konkan coast of India, and in 1506 a letter was sent out with the suggestion that Ceylon and Malacca might be occupied.[19] Naval control of the Indian Ocean was to be strengthened by cutting off the spice trade of the Red Sea: "because it seems to us", the king wrote, "that nothing could be more important to our service than to have a fortress at the mouth of the Red Sea or nearby . . . as much as by closing it up here they are not able to carry anymore any spices to the territory of the Sultan and everyone in India would lose the illusion of being able to trade anymore except with us."[20]

Major events distinguished the period of Almeida's viceroyalty. First, Kilwa was stormed and its sultan overthrown, and then in 1508 the Portuguese faced their greatest naval challenge when a formidable Egyptian fleet under the command of Amir Hussain arrived in Gujarat and joined up with the forces of Malik Ayaz, the governor of the port of Diu. The Mamluk fleet sailed into Chaul and took the Portuguese by surprise. Almeida's son Lourenço was killed in action and the Portuguese ships were forced to withdraw. In February 1509, however, Almeida himself sailed north with a strong fleet, and in the great naval battle off Diu the combined Egyptian and Gujarati ships were defeated and scattered.[21] Although Almeida had held the line, it was not until the governorship of Afonso de Albuquerque that the original objectives of 1505 were finally realised. In 1510 the island of Goa was taken from the Adil Shahi dynasty of Bijapur, on the suggestion of the Maratha corsair Timoja.[22] The place handled the bulk of the trade passing into up-country Deccan, particularly the valuable traffic in fine horses imported from the Persian Gulf. The strategic advantages of Goa and its location as a port of call on the western coast of India provided the groundwork on which the spectacular reputation of the capital of the Estado da India was to be built. Goa's success as a commercial emporium in the Indian Ocean was to come later; but the magnitude of Albuquerque's achievement in capturing Malacca (1511) and Hormuz (1515) was immediately apparent to all spectators of the contemporaneous scene. There are three places in India, commented Albuquerque's son in his narrative of the events of these years, which serve as markets for all the trade in merchandise in that part of the world and are the principal keys of it. The first is Malacca, the second Aden, and the third Hormuz.[23] All three commanded the entrance and the exit in narrow sea passages. The failure of Albuquerque to capture Aden in 1513 was the only reverse suffered by the Portuguese in their effort to master the sea-lanes of the Indian Ocean. Albuquerque died in December 1515. His papers and letters show that he had a complete plan for the future development of Portuguese settlements in Asia, based on the permanent colonisation of the naval and trading posts by people of Portuguese descent practising Christian faith. The future history of the Estado da India between 1515 and 1600 was to prove both the strength and the weakness of Albuquerque's remarkable plan. The verdict of his fellow-countrymen is well reflected in the inscription which Count Fernão Gonçalvez ordered to be set up at the door of the monastery where he was buried: "Y quien mas hiziere passe a delante" ("he who does more, let him walk in front").[24]

During the first twenty years of the sixteenth century there were two main strands in Portuguese imperial policy in Asia. The claim to an exclusive sovereignty in the Indian Ocean was expressed through the efforts to eliminate Muslim trade to the Red Sea and East Africa and to compel Indian merchants to buy "cartazes", or naval passes, from Portuguese officials. To the Asian dimension of the Estado da India was added the European one, the diversion of the pepper and spice trade from Alexandria and Venice to Lisbon and Antwerp. These fundamental objectives were supplemented in time by a third element, the growth of Portuguese inter-port or emporia trading in Asia; this was made possible by their control over the formerly free maritime commercial cities. There seems to be a general consensus among modern historians of Portuguese oceanic expansion that King Manuel, his Conselho da Fazenda, in Lisbon, and the leading fidalgos were all motivated by an economic ideology that did not see long-distance trade as contemporary merchants would have seen it but rather as a legitimate medium for extracting political tribute through the exercise of military means.[25] It is certainly true that the aggressive attitude adopted by the Portuguese and their Islamic adversaries in the Indian

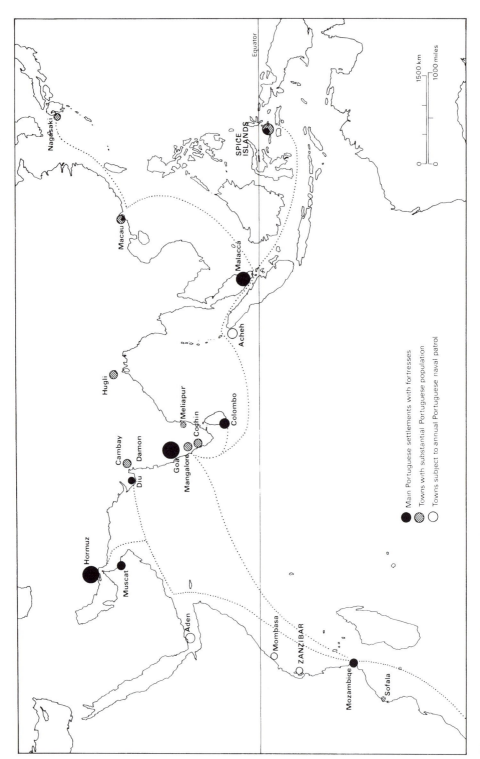

Map 10. Portuguese seaborne empire, c. 1580.

- ● Main Portuguese settlements with fortresses
- ◐ Towns with substantial Portuguese population
- ○ Towns subject to annual Portuguese naval patrol

Equator

1500 km
1000 miles

Nagasaki
Macau
SPICE ISLANDS
Malacca
Acheh
Hugli
Meliapur
Cochin
Colombo
Cambay
Damon
Goa
Diu
Mangalore
Hormuz
Muscat
Aden
Mombasa
ZANZIBAR
Mozambique
Sofala

Ocean was a fixation that did not take into account that co-existence or peaceful trading might be more profitable than waging perpetual war by land and sea. At the same time, the extent to which Portuguese officials, merchants resident in the Indies, and private individuals became involved in Indian Ocean commerce should not be underplayed. Nor can the formal policy of the Estado da India be taken as the sum total of Portugal's Asian presence. The role of accidents in history ensures alternative destinies in social progression, or why else should the conquistadores fail before the walls of Aden and succeed in Malacca and Hormuz? The Portuguese voyages to India in the early years of expansion were organised primarily by the crown and not by the indigenous merchants of Lisbon. By declaring the spice trade a royal monopoly in 1505, Dom Manual made sure that the initial official commitment to India should not pass out of government hands. It is merely a truism that all European monarchies at that time had a traditional attitude towards trade and merchants.[26] We should not attach too great a significance to the non-capitalist, non-entrepreneurial character of Portuguese trade and empire in Asia. To appreciate this, we have only to recall that when the English East India Company became a territorial power in South Asia in the second half of the eighteenth century its previous strong commercial ethos rapidly collapsed.

However, there is no doubt that in setting up an administrative structure in the capital city of Goa and in other lesser possessions and in exercising a quasi-political control over the Indian Ocean traders to the west of the Malacca strait, the Estado da India was being highly innovative. It may not have been aware of the break between the past and the present, but the policy was quite consciously adopted. As soon as Goa was secure from attack by the forces of Bijapur, it became the official seat of the Estado da India. The head of state was the viceroy, a nominee of the king in Lisbon. He was assisted by a number of informal councils composed of the head of the financial council, the Vedor da Fazenda, the Archbishop of Goa, the chief of the judiciary, the captain of the military, and the leading fidalgos living in the capital.[27] The subordinate settlements in the Indian Ocean closely followed the structure of control established in Goa, and the personality of the viceroy or the captain was the most decisive factor in the success or failure of Portuguese administration in Asia. After the death of Albuquerque, the most pressing task facing the Portuguese was to control if not altogether eliminate the commercial competition of the Gujarati merchants based on the northern ports of Diu and Cambay. The capture of Malacca had cut off the people of Gujarat from their annual voyage to the East Indies; but, as long as Diu and Cambay remained open, their Red Sea trade could not be effectively stopped. The strategy adopted was two-fold: first, to organise a naval blockade of Bab al-Mandeb every year during the trading season and, secondly, to try and capture Diu itself. The governor of the port at this time was the ambitious Malik Ayaz, who was not inclined to accept Portuguese threats against Diu without opposition. The place was strongly

DE STAD DIU

Plate 9. The island-fortress of Diu in the Gulf of Cambay, from Baldaeus, *Naauwkeurige Beschryvinge*, 1672.

fortified and beginning to take away some of the trade of Cambay itself. The Portuguese made several attempts to land at Diu, during 1520–1, when Malik Ayaz was still alive, and then during the war against Gujarat in 1530. Although the Portuguese forces looted and burned Cambay, Surat, and Rander, the fortress of Diu itself remained impregnable. The first Portuguese territorial acquisition in Gujarat did not take place before 1534, when Sultan Bahadur, the ruler of Gujarat, hard-pressed by political troubles from the north, negotiated a treaty of peace with the Portuguese governor Nuño da Cunha. He agreed to cede the small port of Bassein and its surrounding country to Goa; merchantmen bound for the Red Sea from Gujarat were to buy cartazes at Bassein and on the return voyage pay duties there. Included in the treaty was the fishing settlement of Bombay with its deep-water harbour.[28] A year later, Sultan Bahadur made even greater concessions to the Portuguese, for he was now a refugee in Diu itself, fleeing from the invading armies of the Mughal emperor Humayun. In return for the promise of military assistance, he allowed the Portuguese to build a fort in the territory of Diu. By 1538 the fortress was securely in the hands of Goa, and the town withstood two celebrated sieges from the Muslim forces in 1538 and 1546. In 1555, the Portuguese took over the government of the whole island, and the customs duties were collected by them at the port. The final naval control of the Gulf of Cambay was completed in 1559 when the small town of Daman, on the opposite side of Diu in the Gulf, was acquired.[29]

Portuguese official policy in western India between 1515 and 1560 followed a consistent logic, even though there was a great deal of individual corruption and desire for personal gain among the crown administrators.[30] On the pattern of Cochin and Goa, which effectively controlled the Malabar and Konkan trade, the Estado da India tried to create a territorial presence in the Gulf of Cambay. They also made two devastating coastal raids to the north, the first in 1529–30 and the second in 1546–8, under the command of the celebrated Viceroy João de Castro. The Portuguese admiral Manuel de Lima, under instructions from de Castro, carried out in Gujarat a repeat performance of the atrocities, in the best tradition of the early conquistadores.[31] The raids brought home a point which the merchants of Gujarat had already noted: the Portuguese determination to tax their trade and shipping through the system of cartazes. In order to set the balance right, however, it should be remembered that the viceroyalty of Goa was not generally on a perpetual footing of war with the rulers of Gujarat, as it was with the Arab or Ottoman governors in the Red Sea and the Persian Gulf. In fact, from as early as 1509, Portuguese traders had begun to settle in Cambay and to inter-marry with the local women. When the Mughal emperor Akbar conquered Gujarat in 1572, it was found that there were about sixty Portuguese in Cambay who had stayed behind to look after their affairs. At the end of the century a large number of commercial families of Portuguese origin still lived in Cambay. European travellers visiting the town at this time spoke of impressive, fine Spanish-style houses built by the prosperous Iberian settlers.[32] The active private trade carried on by these people, and their presence in numerous towns and cities of coastal India, seriously weaken the argument put forward by some historians that the Portuguese were primarily tax-gatherers in the Indian Ocean.[33] Even on the other side of the Arabian Sea, where the war squadrons of Goa were most active, the flow of trans-oceanic trade continued.[34] The sea after all is larger than the thirty-mile circle visible to the watcher in a ship's crow's-nest, and the war did not always throw its dice in favour of the Portuguese. The Arab Hadrami Chronicle describes the raid on Muscat by the Ottoman corsair Ali Bey in 1581:

On Monday, the 1st of the month of Radjab, two Turkish grabs arrived before al-Shihr port, their captain Sinan by name; on board there were 200 Turks and a like number of sailors and Indians, bound for Ras al-Hadd to the Franks. When they reached Muscat they looted it, killing some of the Franks there. Then they burned it, and with it the churches of the Frank. In the harbour they took a large galliot laden with goods bound for Hurmuz. They also took from it a galleon they found in the port. The grabs of the Frank and their own grabs – the lot they laded with the goods they had taken from the town, the Indians assisting them and looting with them.[35]

In eastward expansion in the Indian Ocean, the Portuguese policy was perhaps more influenced by direct commercial considerations than in the west, though the element of armed trading even in these areas was formally upheld. In Ceylon the Portuguese possessed Colombo and maintained a form of indirect political control over the island through nominal indigenous rulers. On the coast of Coromandel they had founded a small settlement at Meliapur, which was known as São Tomé. The supply of printed South Indian cotton textiles, which were sold in large quantities in Java and the Spice Islands, were organised from São Tomé, and in the early seventeenth century even the Dutch admitted that the Portuguese merchants of Meliapur spared themselves no trouble in fostering their business in the Indonesian archipelago.[36] The annual trade from Goa to Bengal was even more profitable to the Portuguese than the coastal trade of Coromandel. Although for a long time Bengal remained out of bounds to the citizens of Goa because of the resistance of the local Islamic rulers to the European presence, the Portuguese were eventually allowed to settle in Chittagong and Satgaon, the two deep-water ports in the province. However, in common with other Indian ports situated in the flat alluvial plains, Satgaon suffered from the continual silting up of the estuarial waters. In about 1580 the Portuguese private traders shifted their settlement to a town much further up the river, which later became known as the famous commercial city of Hugli[37] By the end of the sixteenth century or the beginning of the seventeenth the Portuguese had managed to create a highly profitable commercial network centred on the river Hugli, and as long as their control of the only large navigable port in Bengal remained strong no other European power could venture into the inland towns from the sea. The legendary wealth of India's eastern province remained out of reach to the Dutch and the English until the Mughals expelled the Portuguese from Bengal in 1632.

The principle of maritime sovereignty as expressed in the cartaze system was rigorously applied to the Asian traders of Bengal. In Malacca and the rest of the archipelago, Portuguese power was much more vulnerable to challenge. The small territory of Malacca and the township itself could be defended by land and sea, and the strait commanding the entry to the South China Sea was controlled by heavily armed Portuguese carracks. But Malacca was dependent on rice supplies from Java and it was dangerously close to the military power of the sultans of Johore and the Sumatran kingdom of Acheh. Although Portuguese armadas inflicted several defeats on the united fleets of the Javanese princes, it was difficult to patrol closely all the inland sea passages between the scattered islands, with their numerous creeks and channels. In 1513 João Lopes de Alvim, one of the Portuguese sea-captains to take part in the attack on Malacca, visited the ports of Java. Tomé Pires was on board the ship, and his unique description of the Asian trade of Java was probably based on information gathered during this voyage. From the commercial towns of eastern Java, the Portuguese pushed on to the Spice Islands. The export of rare spices from the four main producing islands – Amboina, Banda, Tidore, and Ternate – had collapsed as a result of the fall of Malacca. The Portuguese were well received at both Tidore and Ternate, which were also visited by the Spanish fleet of Magellan in 1521. It was not until the Treaty of Zaragossa (1529) that the Spanish crown formally ceded the Moluccas to the Portuguese royal house. But there was never any question as to the Portuguese monopoly in the Moluccan spice trade. It was not only that Javanese and Malays continued to ship cloves, nutmeg, and mace from the producing islands to the rest of the archipelago, but Portuguese officials and private merchants were deeply involved in transporting the spices for their own profits.[38]

The Portuguese inability to monopolise the supply of finer spices was matched by a similar development even in the trans-continental movement of black pepper. From the 1550s European dealers began to note that pepper was once again available in substantial quantities in Alexandria and Italy.[39] In the Indian Ocean the revival of trade through the Red Sea was largely the result of Asian ships successfully running the annual Portuguese blockade of Bab al-Mandeb. In the Indonesian archipelago, however, the viceroyalty of Goa for the first time encountered a naval power willing to take on its warships. The foundation of Acheh's political power in northern Sumatra was due to the conquests of Sultan Ali Mughayat Shah, who brought both Pedir and Pase under his control during the early sixteenth century.[40] At the time of his death in 1530, according to the historian Castanheda, Acheh had captured so many guns from the Portuguese that the sultan was believed to be much better equipped with artillery than was the fortress of Malacca.[41] Later, Acheh's close contacts with the Red Sea enabled its rulers to approach the Ottoman government for military equipment. Turkish arsenals were renowned at this time for the quality of their gun foundries and the skill of their artillery-men. In a tract published in 1585 Jorge de Lemos, who had been a secretary to the viceroy of Goa, pointed out that the Ottomans had supplied the Achenese with bronze guns of a calibre capable of undertaking siege warfare.[42] The fighting abilities of Acheh's men-of-war were well demonstrated in numerous sea battles with Portuguese carracks, and there were many schemes on the part of Portuguese officials to crush the naval power of Acheh by conquering its port. None of the plans came to anything, and it was Portuguese Malacca that had to withstand Achenese attacks.

The geographical limits of the Portuguese seaborne empire in Asia were reached in the Chinese port of Macau and in Japanese Nagasaki. In 1555 the Jesuit priest Mestre Belchior Nunes Barreto noted in a letter that a Portuguese "Great Ship" had arrived at the port of China from Japan. Its cargo was so valuable that all other Portuguese ships in China intended to go there.[43] In the event, the Lisbon government allowed only one "Great Ship" to make the annual voyage from Goa to Macau and Nagasaki; the captain-general of the voyage also acted as the temporary governor of Macau, which became a Portuguese enclave. In 1623 a regular captain-general was appointed to govern Macau and the commander of the "Great Ship" no longer exercised any territorial jurisdiction in Macau. The economic success of the Macau–Nagasaki trading voyages, as C.R. Boxer has pointed out, was made possible by a combination of three historical factors. It will be remembered that the Ming court had placed an embargo on China's direct trade with Japan in the aftermath of piratical raids on its coastal areas, and these fears of external dangers to China's political integrity were confirmed by a series of piratical attacks by sea in 1554–5. The official rupture of relations between China and Japan gave the Portuguese in Macau (named Cidade do Nome de Deus) the opportunity to build up what was probably the most profitable part of their Asian business. Apart from the favourable political conditions, Goa's participation in the Far Eastern trade was made possible by certain monetary features of the region. Historically, China was the meeting ground between dear silver and cheap gold. Silver mines in Japan began to produce ingot metal on a large scale from the early sixteenth century as a result of the application of the mercury amalgamation method and better mining techniques, and the whole development occurred at a time when the world supply of silver was increasing at a rapid rate owing to the working of American silver deposits. The economy of China, along with that of India, needed a constant injection of monetary liquidity to keep up its rate of economic expansion. Finally, there was the fact that the Japanese ruling classes had a clear preference for Chinese silk cloth and raw silk for the manufacture of ceremonial clothing.[44]

The Portuguese traders were able to export silver from Japan in return for supplying Chinese silk. The average return on capital was high, not only for the fortunate captain-general, who was allowed by the Portuguese crown to buy the voyage, but also for the Japanese "daimyos" and merchants engaged in the inland trade of Japan. Perhaps the only cloud to overhang official Portuguese–Japanese relations was the presence and activities of Christian missionaries in the island. In 1549 Francis Xavier, the Jesuit priest from Navarra in northern Spain, had founded the Japan mission. During the next half-century the Catholic religion found many powerful and important converts in Nagasaki itself and also in Kyoto. Although Portuguese cultural influences on certain classes of Japanese society at this time were considerable, the court of the Shoguns who ruled Japan was fearful of new Christian loyalties in the rank of Samurais as well as among ordinary people. After a period of bitter civil war, the unification of the country remained the prime ambition of the Shogunate. But neither Hideyoshi nor Ieyasu, the two great military leaders of Japan, could seriously contemplate the expulsion of the missionaries without endangering the revenue derived from the Portuguese trade. It was not until the appearance of the Dutch in Japan during the early seventeenth century that the court found a possible alternative to Macau's intermediary role. Even then the final edict banning the Portuguese from Japan was made only in 1639. The end of Lusitanian presence in Japan was as fearful as it had been promising in 1555. The citizens of Macau were unable to believe that their long commercial connections with the island were about to close, and they sent a deputation to plead with the Shogun's court. On 4 August 1640, sixty-one members of the mission were beheaded on Martyr's Mount for having disobeyed the earlier injunction not to return.[45]

The tragedy which occurred to the Portuguese in Japan was part of a larger theatre of decline. But at the end of the sixteenth century the prosperity of Goa and the prestige of its government were still undiminished. A tract written in the 1580s, bearing the title *Livro das cidades, e fortalezas*, triumphantly catalogues the Portuguese possessions in the Indian Ocean, with detailed descriptions of their trade and conditions.[46] Almost all of them had been previously important ports of trade and ports of call for Asian shipping. Sofala and Mozambique, defended by strong fortifications, commanded the East African coast for the Portuguese. Sofala had once been a major supplier of African gold. Mozambique under the Portuguese continued to have important commercial links with Cambay, particularly in the sale of Gujarat's cotton cloth.[47] Goa itself, according to the author, in the size of its population and the sumptuousness of its buildings was the most important and populous port in India, a busy centre of trade in all the commercial goods of the orient and the occident.[48] The whole of the western coast of India was marked by towns either under the direct rule of Goa or having Portuguese settlers in large numbers – Diu, Daman, Bassein, Chaul, and Mangalore; in Malabar, Cannanore, Cranganore, Cochin, and Quilon; and so the list went on all the way down to Ceylon, up the coast of Coromandel, across the Bay of Bengal to the strait of Malacca and the South China Sea. How was it possible for a small and relatively obscure nation facing the Atlantic and outside the brilliant economic mainstream of the central Mediterranean to achieve this status? Contemporary Portuguese historians and chroniclers depicted the early fidalgos in the East as belonging to a heroic band of conquistadores, comparable to the great Spanish soldiers in the New World. Military exploits and violence at sea were extolled, commerce and trade occupied a secondary place in the imagination and were regarded as unworthy of the dignity of the soldier-administrators in the empire. The key to Portuguese success in the Indian Ocean lay then in the military valour of Christian warriors sanctified by divine blessing.[49]

The Portuguese naval success was certainly impressive. In reviewing the problem, C.R. Boxer offers the following explanation. "The admitted superiority of the relatively well-armed Portuguese ships over the unarmed Muslim merchant-vessels of the Indian Ocean was reinforced by a tenacity of purpose on the part of the European intruders which was largely lacking in their Asian opponents."[50] The Portuguese were not known in Europe at the time as great warriors or soldiers, though at sea their naval skills were freely acknowledged. Cut off by their geography from taking any significant part in the military affairs of continental Europe, the Portuguese fidalgos found in Asian and African coastal kingdoms natural opportunities for acquiring a military reputation. For Asian merchants and trading cities, it was very difficult to suppress raiders from the sea who not only were equipped with ships and guns capable of destroying shore installations but came from a land-base many thousands of miles away. It is worth remembering in this context that no land-power in history has wholly succeeded in containing sea-raiders. The record of the Vikings, and later of the North African Muslim corsairs (even after the Battle of Lepanto), in ravaging coastal areas as far apart as Cornwall and Sicily, shows that the tactical problems of overcoming unexpected attacks from ships were insoluble. The Barbary raiders, like the Portuguese in the Indian Ocean, could choose their targets and the time of their attacks, and even the close patrolling of the coast by regular naval fleets could not always protect individual ports and towns. It is safe to conclude that, whether or not Asian political rulers had the necessary will to resist the Portuguese, it was impossible in practice to offer complete protection to merchant shipping crossing long sea-routes.

In such a situation, a compromise position is soon reached. The Portuguese knew from many military reverses suffered in Africa, the Red Sea, India, and Indonesia that they were too weak on land to defend a determined enemy assault. It was necessary to reach an agreement with both local rulers and merchants that would allow them to hold on to their early commercial and territorial gains. The institution adopted to legitimise the usurpation of the maritime rights of the Asian merchants was of course the cartazes system. By issuing free safe-conduct passes to the powerful political kingdoms in the Deccan and Gujarat for their trading vessels, the Portuguese tacitly acknowledged the terms of co-existence. At the same time, the Asian ship-owners found it easier to pay protection costs to the Portuguese than to suffer the devastating effects of a prolonged sea war. As individuals they went on to arm the ships with soldiers and artillery so as to offer some resistance at sea. By the first decade of the sixteenth century, the period of peaceful sailing was over in the Indian Ocean. Whoever controlled the sea was in a position of overwhelming commercial and political superiority. But such absolute power was never within the grasp of the Portuguese. Their naval victories in the Indian Ocean were due to the fact that the land-based Asian empires and strong political kingdoms were not able to put to sea effective fighting ships. Even the formidable Ottoman galleys proved inadequate later when the Turkish vessels were pitched against the Portuguese carracks in the strait of Hormuz.[51] The Portuguese territorial gains, on the other hand, were mostly made at the expense of rulers who had had no reason so far to defend their trading ports with strong military forces. The rulers of Sofala, Kilwa, and Mozambique, of Hormuz, Calicut, and Malacca, ruled over territories that were regarded throughout the commercial world of Asia as neutral ground where merchants of different nationalities could freely meet without having to pay heavy protection fees. The success of the Portuguese against places such as these must be viewed in the light of their failure or incapacity to establish a real territorial empire in Asia. No strong Asian power at the time, whether in India, the Middle East, or China, considered the Portuguese to be a serious threat to the existing balance of power. From the Red Sea to Canton and Nagasaki, no Asian ruler saw the need to construct a navy such as the Japanese built after Commodore Perry's visit to Japan in 1853. Why were they content to leave the domination of the Indian Ocean to a nation weak in economic resources and manpower? Part of the explanation may well lie in the indifference to trade reflected in Sultan Bahadur's alleged view that "wars by sea are merchants' affairs, and of no concern to the prestige of kings".[52] A more convincing answer probably lies in the fact that the regional and trans-oceanic flows of trade adjusted and redirected themselves. The supply of commodities and goods demanded by the Asian aristocracy and the ruling elites was not really interrupted by the Portuguese.

4

The Dutch and English East India Companies and the bureaucratic form of trade in Asia

By the end of the sixteenth century, the Portuguese presence in the Indian Ocean had achieved a certain degree of integration with the local political and commercial environment. The viceroy of Goa acted in much the same way as the ruler of a former free port or trading town might have done. Jan Huygen van Linschoten, the Dutch clerk in the service of Archbishop Don Frey Vincente da Fonseca, lived in Goa for five years (1583–9). His work, published under the title of *Itinerario*, is a remarkable testimony from an independent witness to the extent of Portuguese involvement in Indian Ocean trade and society.[1] Although recent arrivals from Portugal, articulate clergy and laymen, might feel that they belonged to an exclusive European culture and religion, financial and social necessity often pointed in the direction of ethnic assimilation.[2] In seaborne trade, the most visible expression of the Portuguese integration was the rise of a new and active line of trans-oceanic commerce based on a number of substantial commercial towns and cities. The maritime trade of Mocha, Aden, and Surat in the western Indian Ocean had its counterparts in other areas. There were Meliapur, Masulipatam, and Hugli in southern and eastern India; Acheh, Bantam, and Manila in the Indonesian archipelago, supplementing the trade of Malacca; Canton, Macau, and Nagasaki in the Far East. A great deal of indigenous Asian trade passed through these urban centres, and may even have been fostered by the Portuguese sale of cartazes. In the *Itinerario* Linschoten describes how the citizens of Goa earned their living by trading to Bengal, Pegu, Malacca, Cambay, and China, to every part of the Indian Ocean, both north and south. Every morning in the main street of Goa a market was held in which all kinds of imported goods were auctioned – rather like the bourse in Antwerp. The description of Goa's busy and cosmopolitan maritime traffic is followed later by the statement from Linschoten that the Portuguese allowed all inhabitants the freedom of their religion and conscience, so that Hindus, Muslims, Jews, Armenians, and Indians of all different castes could freely live together in Goa. Surprisingly, it was only the baptised members of the Portuguese empire who were subjected to the full spiritual rigour of the Inquisition.[3]

The arrival of English and Dutch ships in the Indian Ocean during the last decade of the sixteenth century of course represented to the Portuguese the greatest challenge they had yet had to face in Asia, a contest which in the long run proved fatal to their power and economic prosperity. However, the future course of events could not by any means be predicted at the time, and the formidable naval reputation of the Estado da India prevented the North European merchants from venturing out to the East Indies. From the middle of the century, English merchants made repeated attempts to gain access to the supplying markets of Asian goods, either through the eastern Mediterranean or by the overland route going across Russia and the Caspian region. The foundation of the English Levant Company in 1581, with formal trade concessions granted by the Ottoman government, was the most long-lasting result of these efforts. The commercial activity of the Company remained confined to the Greek islands and to Aleppo, the terminus of the Syrian–Iraqi caravans. Perhaps the most pressing incentive and the immediate background to the foundation of English and Dutch direct maritime expeditions to the Indian Ocean was the revolt of the Netherlands and the gradual closure of the great international spice market in Antwerp. By blockading the mouth of the River Scheldt the rebellious Dutch sea-captains could strike a fearful blow to the premier Spanish–Flemish commercial capital in northern Europe. The military struggle for the control of Antwerp, together with attacks on Spanish shipping in America by English privateers, produced an unsettling effect on the trade of all North European merchants. By 1585 Philip II had ordered an embargo against English ships and merchandise in Spain.[4] In the Low Countries, wholesale merchants engaged in the trans-regional trade of Germany and Italy continued to leave Antwerp and settle in the northern town of Amsterdam, which had hitherto been the centre of the Baltic grain trade. Within two decades from the 1580s Amsterdam developed into the leading financial and commercial city on the North Sea. The balance of economic power, which had remained firmly in Spanish–Portuguese hands for more than half a century, began to shift in favour of the Dutch Protestant community. What was happening in Europe, in a narrow stretch of land reclaimed from the sea, was to have a vital impact on the lives of people in very distant countries. During the period of Portuguese domination of the Indian Ocean, European events scarcely touched upon the Asian scene. But the Dutch and English participation in the oceanic trade around the Cape of Good Hope was very closely related to a wider international context.

It was certainly the starting-point for several new developments in the organisation of long distance trade. The first English voyage to the East Indies, commanded by Captain James Lancaster (1591–4), turned out to be a financial and maritime disaster, just as the expedition of Cornelis de Houtman to Bantam (1595–7) failed to answer high profit expectations. Conceived as speculative trading ventures, looking for new markets and sea-routes, these expeditions were only marginally different from the privateering raids that were being fitted out at the time in England and the Netherlands. The spirit of buccaneering, however, did not suit the commercial instincts of the traditional merchants in London and Amsterdam, especially when the commodities in question were articles of daily use. Their general ethics and business code incorporated the viewpoint, once actually stated, that the worst of peace was better than the best of war.[5] After a few years of experimentation, both the English and the Dutch East India Companies were incorporated into a form of commercial organisation that was quite unique, the joint-stock company with an incipient separation between the ownership of capital and its management by a professional class of merchants and salaried administrators. The emerging principle of capitalism found in the formal constitution of the chartered trading companies was not their sole contribution to innovation. After 1600 the trans-continental trade of Eurasia was no longer the exclusive preserve either of royal monopoly, such as that of the Spanish–Portuguese crown, or of numerous individual merchants and partnerships functioning as separate entities on an extended geographical distance-scale all the way from Calicut to Venice. An increasing share of it was to be taken over by bureaucratic economic organisations which possessed very different values and different concepts of economic behaviour. The resulting changes involved not only increase in the magnitude of trade between Europe and Asia but also major structural discontinuities.

The corporate structure of trade, the concentration of financial resources, and the size of the commercial purchases made by the north Atlantic merchants created a much closer link between the supplying and consuming markets than had existed before. In the seventeenth century there were at least two major suppliers of Asian goods in Europe. Later, the Dutch and English East India Companies were to be joined by the French Compagnie des Indes Orientales and a number of very small organisations operating from Ostend, Copenhagen, and Gothenburg. Although precise figures are lacking, compared to the Venetian or the Portuguese period of trade a far larger volume of eastern imports was available in the world markets in the following centuries. World demand for Indian cotton textiles, Chinese silks, indigo, raw silk, coffee, and tea proved to be highly sensitive to price changes. The joint-stock companies were significantly instrumental in changing the patterns of consumer taste in Europe. The public preference for cotton textiles as indispensable items for daily clothing needs, and the rapid extension of the market, must have suggested to enterprising Europeans that technological innovation could well begin with an import-substituting industry. The fact that the Industrial Revolution in the West originated with the mechanical spinning and weaving of cotton was surely not accidental.

The constitution and the operational arrangements of trade were worked out by the English East India Company soon after its formal incorporation by royal charter in 1600. In Holland, a number of separate companies at first attempted to conduct trade to the Indian Ocean. But competition among the agents of different Dutch concerns had the consequence of raising the price of commodities at the Indonesian ports, and the early companies earned only modest profits. In 1602, after the political intervention of the States General and Prince Maurice, a merger was agreed. Henceforth, the monogram of the Vereenigde Oost-Indische Compagnie (VOC) symbolised one of the most powerful and prestigious combinations of trade and political objectives that the commercial world of Asia had witnessed. However, the VOC retained many archaic features in its constitutional structure, reminders of its origin in the Dutch urban environment. The political and economic conventions followed in the Indian Ocean regions in the pre-Portuguese and Portuguese periods of trade did not change radically or immediately after the arrival of the North European bureaucratic companies, except perhaps in the case of the Spice Islands. Here the VOC imposed a degree of control in the key production areas which the Portuguese had never achieved and which the VOC itself was not able or willing to contemplate for other parts of Asia. The system of collective decision-making through committees and councils with delegated authority, and the operational sequences, possessed, however, a logic quite different from that usual among individual Asian merchants pursuing their separate economic interests.

The two European East India companies discovered within a decade that the whole Indian Ocean had a structural unity created by the periodic rhythm of the monsoon winds and by economic interdependence between one region and another. Cotton textiles from the coast of Coromandel in India were vital for the purchase of pepper and spices in the Indonesian archipelago. Precious metals imported from the Middle East, East Africa, and Japan supplied monetary liquidity without which rich and powerful centralised empires in Asia could not have functioned properly. This awareness of a vast integrated network of trade and finance in turn induced the bureaucratic companies to follow the natural contours of the commercial geography and design a co-ordinated system of operations stretching from the Red Sea and the Persian Gulf to the South China Sea, and controlled and directed from Amsterdam and London. That they were able to do this successfully was mainly due to the amount and the accumulation of capital, reinforced by the management's capacity for decision-making at different organisational levels. The efficient economic performance of the VOC and the East India Company, and their continued existence, depended on the ability of the directors in Europe and the officials in Asia to identify relevant problems. As national organisations with delegated sovereign powers, the Companies needed political objectives and guidelines which would define their relationships with Asian rulers and fellow-Europeans. Expansion in the volume of trade between Europe and the various Indian Ocean ports, together with the concentration of purchases, also made it essential to look for the most profitable and regular sources of supplies. The constant search for suitable trading settlements and markets in Asia was a part of both the companies' reasoning. The distribution of imported goods and the problem of long-term financial management gave rise to regular institutional practices through which buyers and sellers, investors and borrowers, could make contacts. Ships had to be built and chartered. Their outward cargo would have to be provided in time for the sailing season. The goods brought back from Asia needed buyers at the most advantageous prices. The huge amount of their permanent capital turned the Companies into bankers with a sensitive role in the money markets of Europe and Asia. The recurrent nature of the problems made it necessary to look for a systematic solution.

From the beginning, questions of political ideology exercised the minds of the Dutch and English policy makers in connection with the conduct of Indian Ocean trade. Between 1600 and 1663 the Estado da India suffered catastrophic reverses at the hands of the Dutch. No doubt Portuguese officials found it ironic that their own political thinking and methods of trading in Asia through the fort and the factory, *fortaleza e feitoria*, should have suggested to the VOC and the East India Company a workable model. The Dutch Company of course refused to recognise the legal claim of the Portuguese government to the exclusive control of the Indian Ocean. The state of war between the United Republic and Spain justified its attack on Spanish–Portuguese shipping and settlements in Asia. The weaker English Company followed a more cautious line, but it was under no illusion that the viceroy and the Inquisition of Goa would let it trade in peace in those areas of Asia where the Portuguese had substantial commercial interests. During the first decade of the seventeenth century great sea battles took place between Portuguese carracks and Dutch ships. In 1605 the VOC captured the Portuguese fort in Amboina as a first step in a general strategy for establishing naval control of the sea-routes in Indonesian waters. The defending garrisons and fleet commanders resisted the onslaught with tenacity. The Dutch assault on the fortress of Malacca (1606) was repulsed with heavy losses on the part of the attackers. Spanish forts survived in Ternate and Tidore, which grew cloves, and it was not until 1662 that the authorities in Manila withdrew the Moluccan garrisons under the threat of a Chinese attack on the Philippines. In East Africa the Dutch twice failed to take Mozambique (1607–8), the vital port of call for the Portuguese carracks bound for Goa.

The directors of the VOC had to wait more than thirty years before their naval strategy against the Portuguese maritime empire moved into its decisive phase. When Antonio van Diemen became the governor general of the VOC in the East Indies (1636–45) the war at sea reached even the bar of Goa, which was blockaded every year. On Christmas Day 1637 six Portuguese galleons left port and engaged a blockading fleet of twelve ships. After an action lasting seven hours the Portuguese galleon *S. Bartholomeus* blew up, setting on fire *'s-Gravenhage* and *Flushing*. A third Dutch ship was sunk by gunfire. The outcome of the fight between the two unequal forces demonstrated to all neutral onlookers that the Estado da India did not lack courage or seamanship but was short of men-of-war.[6] Van Diemen's greatest victory was the capture of Malacca in January 1641. From then on the screw tightened steadily by sea and on land. Johan Maetsuycker, a Catholic lawyer from Louvain and governor general (1653–78), could draw upon the harsh abilities of two great admirals, Rijklof van Goens and Cornelis Speelman, in the East Indies. In 1656 the Portuguese garrison in Colombo surrendered after a long siege. The loss of Ceylon and the cinnamon trade was followed by the fall of Cochin in 1663. It was a bitter, demoralising blow for the fidalgos of Goa and the Council of the Indies. Of all the ports of trade in the Indian Ocean, the Portuguese had the longest connection with Cochin. The success of the VOC in Malabar contained a dangerous message not only for the Portuguese but for everyone shipping black pepper from that coast. The price of pepper in the great Mughal port of Surat doubled as merchants anticipated a Dutch stranglehold on supplies modelled on the VOC's control over finer spices achieved earlier. The head of the English trading house in Surat feared an imminent Dutch attempt to ruin the East India Company's European trade in pepper.[7]

The deteriorating political relations between England and Holland in the second half of the seventeenth century produced a better diplomatic understanding between the viceroy of Goa and the East India Company. The establishment of English trade in western India was at first strongly opposed by the Portuguese. The climate of active and passive hostility provided the background to many sporadic naval engagements between the East-Indiamen and the Portuguese armadas off the coast of India. Finally, in 1622 the East India Company's officials in Surat supplied vital maritime assistance to the forces of the Shah of Persia, which captured Hormuz from the Portuguese. In a sense, the loss of the island and the port-city commanding the entry to the Persian Gulf turned out to be more than just a political incident. It marked the entry of the English and the Dutch to the Middle Eastern markets through the back door of the Indian Ocean, though the traditional access to these areas through the eastern Mediterranean still continued and trade remained prosperous. For the Portuguese the fall of Hormuz was a symbolic defeat for the Estado da India. The reconquest of the port was certainly a priority with the viceroy of Goa. But when the issue was debated soberly, as for example in the memorandum of João Corte Real in 1623, it seemed easier and more profitable to divert Portuguese trade in the Gulf to Muscat and Basra.[8] In the 1630s financial pressure on the East India Company and changed circumstances in India began to erode the ancient fear and hostility felt by the Company towards the Portuguese. The fertile agriculture of Gujarat and its industrial handicrafts were destroyed by the failures of rains and the ensuing harvest losses during the years 1630–3. The English merchants in western India needed other markets further south to sustain the Company's falling trade. The viceroy of Goa, on the other hand, could better prepare his defences against the VOC's attacks without having to fight the English shipping at the same time. In 1635, after lengthy negotiations, Conde de Linhares and President William Methwold concluded a truce and an accord.[9] However, the most lasting event in Anglo-Portuguese relations in India was the transfer of Bombay, though it could hardly have appeared significant at the time. In 1661 the small island and its magnificent deep-water harbour were ceded to Charles II by the Portuguese government in Lisbon as part of the Infanta Catherine's marriage settlement. Charles II in turn handed over Bombay to the East India Company in 1668.

The political tension which had existed between the different European traders in Asia narrowed down to a running conflict between the Dutch and the English in the second half of the seventeenth century. Eventually, after the War of the Spanish Succession, the East India Company took over from the VOC the dominating naval role in the Indian Ocean. In the 1720s a new commercial and maritime power appeared in the Indian Ocean in the shape of the second French Compagnie des Indes Orientales. The first Company, founded by Colbert (1664), had never succeeded in achieving the organisational and financial stature of the VOC or the East India Company in Asia. After its reorganisation in 1721 and 1725 the new Company was well endowed with capital and strongly supported by the French state. With the rise of France to the position of the leading European power, the way was left open for yet another cycle of war at sea on a global level among the Western maritime nations. These wars in the 1740s and 1750s gradually involved the various East India Companies in India in dynastic wars that were beginning to undermine the political cohesion of the Mughal empire. Merchants and rulers in Asia were not ignorant of the fact that the twin causes of the conflicts between Europeans were to be found in the political events originating in Europe and in the claims of one power to monopolise the seaborne trade of Eurasia to the exclusion of all others. As far as possible ruling authorities in Asia with strong military forces at their command sought to preserve the neutrality of their ports and the economic interests of the merchants trading there. But, lacking effective naval strength, they could not always prevent the Europeans fighting one another at sea.

It was this maritime dimension that created one of the crucial weaknesses in the structure of international relations in the Indian Ocean. It was a feature that steadily worsened throughout the seventeenth and eighteenth centuries. In this connection, the bureaucratic trading companies formulated a political ideology in their attitude towards the Asian merchants and princes that was as distinctive as that of the Estado da India. The principle of controlling the indigenous traders in the Indian Ocean was fully supported by the sale of safe-conduct passes and the threat of naval reprisals against shipping without such documents. The institution was useful in raising revenue, and it was a bargaining counter in negotiations with the port authorities. As early as 1618 Sir

Thomas Roe, the East India Company's envoy to the Mughal court, had claimed that both the English and the Dutch were allowed to trade in Surat because the imperial officials were afraid of their power at sea. As the maritime strength of the Portuguese was clearly ebbing, their former right to levy a tribute on the Asian merchants and shipping should devolve on the North Europeans.[10] The English Company adhered to the prescriptive policy outlined by Roe, almost to the middle of the eighteenth century. The only exception to this was the unsuccessful attempt to wage naval war on the Mughal empire during 1688–90, under the leadership of Sir Josiah Child. When the experiment failed and the financial costs were added up, it was firmly laid down by all subsequent policy-makers in London and Asia that naval power was more effective as a strategic deterrent than as a tactical weapon. The VOC had come to the same conclusion independently, on the basis of its own experience of trading in the Indian Ocean. At the beginning, however, the Dutch Directorate decided on instituting a system of exclusive treaties with the local Asian princes, binding them to sell spices and pepper exclusively to the VOC. The agreements were often obtained by threats of force. But there were many parts of Asia – the Mughal empire in India, Persia, China, and Japan – where the Dutch were not able to follow such coercive methods of trade. In these ports and markets, the VOC's officials adopted the example of the English, who relied on competitive purchasing to provide cargo for the returning ships. When relations with the representatives of the centralised empires broke down or were strained, both the Companies (English and Dutch) used their ships to impede the movement of goods belonging to the local Asian merchants. If the method invited retaliation against European property and personnel remaining at the ports and inland towns, the final settlement was always arranged through the intervention and diplomatic agency of the merchants. It was in the interest of the Companies and of the local officials alike that matters should not be pushed to the ultimate point of an open war. The financial losses to either side through lost customs and trade worked against the forced closure of a port for any prolonged period.

The attempt made by all North Europeans from the beginning of the seventeenth century to acquire a territorial settlement in the busy commercial regions of the Indian Ocean, and the associated claim to fortify the living and working quarters, were unquestionably derived from the Portuguese example. The opportunity for peaceful trading in Asia was open to the Dutch and the English. They did not take it, because they believed that neither the Portuguese nor the powerful Asian rulers in whose kingdoms they traded would allow them to do so without the sanction of arms. This argument was of course only a part of the current political ideology. The VOC, and later the East India Company, needed no explicit act of violence offered to them to justify attacks on Asian merchants and shipping. In 1622 Dutch naval squadrons destroyed eighty Chinese junks off the coast of China on the instructions of the governor general, Jan Pietersz. Coen, who believed that the policy of the Ming emperors in excluding foreign traders from China should be countered by direct violence against the Chinese at sea. Not surprisingly, such behaviour, as another Dutch official, Martinus Sonck, pointed out, united the Chinese authorities against the Dutch and gave the latter the reputation of being murderers, tyrants, and pirates.[11] If the policy of armed trading in the Indian Ocean was occasionally criticised by the Directors of the VOC and the East India Company and always held in restraint by considerations of cost, in general the use of force remained an integral part of the commercial presence in Asia. The reason for its adoption and long continuation can be traced to a combination of three factors, besides the danger from fellow-Europeans. The Companies were central distributing agencies for the commercial products of Asia and for a limited number of Western commodities and precious metals. The concentration of enormous capital resources, supported by national monopolies, gave rise to a system of trading in Asia that needed suitable geographical locations for a rational and efficient functioning of economic operations. The companies felt much safer if the enormous quantities of treasure and goods annually passing through their hands were channelled into territorial enclaves offering a certain measure of political and military security. The second factor was the element of monopoly, most strongly followed by the VOC, which attempted to exclude all rival traders by force from the highly profitable areas of the Indian Ocean's inter-regional traffic. Finally, the Companies attempted to internalise the protection costs which all overseas merchants have to incur in the form of financial payments to political authorities. They continued to pay customs duties, presents, and bribes where occasion demanded such costs, not only in Asia but also at home in Europe. The expense of constructing fortresses overseas and heavily arming the ships was recovered from monopoly profits earned in Europe by selling Asian goods, from payments received for issuing safe-conduct passes to Asian shipping, and the revenue of places such as Batavia (1619), Madras (1639), and Calcutta (1698), the three premier commercial ports belonging to the VOC and the East India Company.

It remains true, however, that the cost of building and equipping large fleets, and the running charges of fortified settlements, always imposed a heavy burden on European trade in the form of fixed overheads. The Dutch Directorate, the Hereen XVII, came to the conclusion from the beginning that these costs could be better carried if the supply of finer spices – cloves, nutmeg, and mace – was rigidly controlled and access to the producing areas in the Moluccan Islands denied to others. What began as a theoretical exercise and general instructions in distant Amsterdam became a chilling reality in the Spice Islands during Jan Pietersz. Coen's period of office as governor general. The Dutch conquered Banda, the home of the nutmeg trees, in 1620–1 and depopulated it by cutting off the supply of rice. The plantations were handed over to Dutch settlers to be worked by imported slave labour.[12] The torture

Plate 10. Sea-views of Batavia, from Baldaeus, *Naauwkeurige Beschryvinge*, 1672.

and execution of ten English servants of the East India Company in Amboina (1623), the famous "massacre", was yet another instance of how deadly serious the Dutch were in their pursuit of the spice monopoly. The conquest of Banda secured the supply of nutmegs for the VOC. But control over cloves grown in the outer islands proved more difficult to achieve. The VOC organised periodic raids against unsupervised plantations growing cloves, to cut down the trees; and the smuggling trade was not effectively stopped until the conquest of the flourishing port of Macassar in the Celebes during 1666–8. When the VOC won over the sultanate of Bantam in Java in 1682 and succeeded in closing its hitherto free markets to the East India Company and other European traders, it seemed that the Dutch were suddenly very close to gaining their long-sought mastery over the pepper trade. That danger never fully materialised, as the Dutch Company had lost its naval superiority at sea. The English removed their pepper purchases to a new settlement in Sumatra (Bencoolen) and the supply markets of Malabar remained open in India in spite of the efforts of the VOC to close them to competitive buying. At the same time, the Dutch made huge profits by selling at monopoly prices the four fine spices – cloves, nutmeg, mace, and cinnamon. In Europe, their use may have been relatively limited, but in the Indian Ocean all social communities depended on them to add distinction to gastronomic traditions.

Every trading season Dutch ships unloaded large quantities of spices, pepper, tin, copper, and sandalwood at the commercial emporia of the Indian Ocean – in Surat, Masulipatam, and Hugli, in Bandar Abbas and Mocha. The officials of the English East India Company were envious spectators of this annual traffic established by the Dutch, who financed part of their European investments from the profits of inter-regional trading. The English merchants were aware just as much as the Dutch of the high economic logic of the Indian Ocean trade and they made vigorous and successful attempts to break into it. When the East India Company allowed its servants the freedom to engage in private trade, an uncomfortable divergence appeared at once between the interest of the Company and that of its employees. The VOC kept a tighter control over its servants, though the Dutch directors could no more prevent corruption in their Asian establishments than could the English. The opportunity for making substantial private fortunes through a participation in Asia's inter-port trade arose of course from the fact that both the Companies, later joined by the French, created integrated networks of commercial houses known as factories, to which goods could be privately consigned. From the viewpoint of the Companies, the chain of factories and settlements extending over the whole of maritime Asia derived its commercial rationale from the need to diversify the commodity base. The East India Company, in common with the VOC, suffered initially from the narrow European market for pepper and spices. The Indian subcontinent, on the other hand, could supply cotton textiles for sale or barter in South East Asia, and these novel fabrics, printed or painted with striking designs and colours, awaited a rapid popularity in Europe itself and more utilitarian usage in West Africa and the New World. The search for export commodities such as indigo, saltpetre, raw silk, coffee, and tea took all the European companies from one end of the Indian Ocean to the other.

It did not take the English and the Dutch long to discover that the commercial economies of India and China held the key to the flow of goods across the Indian Ocean. From 1607 the East India Company planned to send its ships to the Red Sea and to Gujarat in western India, before the fleet went on to Bantam and the Moluccas for pepper and spices. Formal permission to trade at Surat was not forthcoming until 1612, but once established the English factory there became the most important and prosperous one in the Western zone of activity. The Dutch had attempted to reach Surat from as early as 1602, though it was only in 1617 that Pieter van den Broeke successfully opened a factory at the port-city on behalf of the VOC. The political relations between the Mughal authorities and the Portuguese were strained in these years, a fact that contributed to the Mughal willingness to grant trading rights to the North Europeans. From Surat the VOC and the East India Company quickly

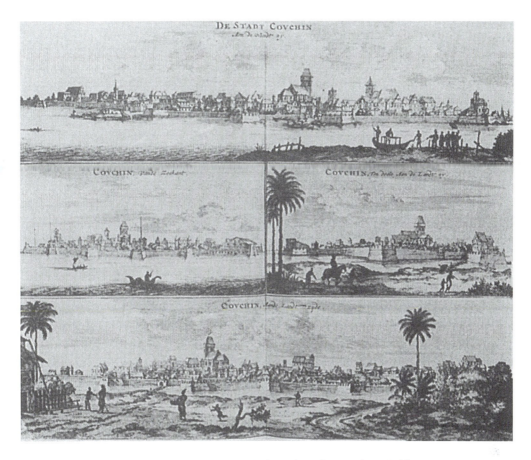

Plate 11. Sea-views of Cochin during the period of Dutch settlement, from Baldaeus, *Naauwkeurige Beschryvinge*, 1672.

extended trade to the inland commercial towns. Factories in the centres of textile weaving, such as Broach and Ahmedabad in Gujarat, were supplemented by others in more distant places situated on the caravan trunk-routes – Burhanpur, Agra, and Lahore. These three latter cities had important industries of their own, as well as being residences of the Mughal emperors. From the imperial capitals, the company servants pushed on eastward in the direction of Bihar, Bengal, and Orissa, the treasure-house of India. Not all the factories in the inland caravan towns survived the test of time or economic efficiency. Nevertheless, the effort to go beyond the wholesale markets of Surat to the producing areas was a symptom of the restless energy displayed by the English and the Dutch in creating an effective trading organisation in India linked to the larger maritime structure in Asia and Europe.

The close commercial connection between Gujarat, Malabar, and the Middle East took the Companies in the direction of the Red Sea and the

Persian Gulf in a series of exploratory voyages. That the trans-continental trade of Eurasia at this time passed through the Red Sea was already well known to the English merchants in the Levant. In 1607–8 the East India Company's commanders carried instructions to remind the Ottoman governors in the Red Sea that the English regularly traded to Cairo, Aleppo, Damascus, Constantinople, and other places within the Turkish empire. The friendship which the Grand Signor showed towards the English nation had encouraged the Company to send its ships to the area.[13] In the event, the Red Sea and its leading sea-port of Mocha remained out of bounds to the Companies until the end of the seventeenth century. This can be ascribed partly to the opposition of the Surat merchants and partly to the reluctance of the political rulers to allow non-Muslim ships to approach too close to Jedda and the Holy City of Mecca. The Companies replied to the informal embargo by periodically seizing Indian ships and their cargo.[14] It was not until the beginning of the eighteenth century, when the popularity of coffee-drinking in Europe provided the coffee-growers of the Yemen with additional demand, that the Imamate of San'a allowed the ships of the VOC and the East India Company to visit Mocha regularly. As compared to the Red Sea, the Companies had a much greater measure of success in the Persian Gulf. The lifting of Portuguese control of the strait of Hormuz in 1622 immediately stimulated the trade of Gombroon (Bandar Abbas) on the opposite mainland. The East India Company's interest in the Persian markets mainly arose from the prospect of selling substantial quantities of English woollen goods and buying the raw silk of the Caspian districts. This was a line of business in which the Levant Company had traditionally specialised, and the East India Company's grandiose plans to divert the entire Iranian export of silk along the Cape route were not received kindly in London. However, the English and the Dutch Companies continued to buy raw silk in Persia until the mulberry plantations of Bengal opened up a cheaper and more secure source of supplies in the 1650s. The factories in Gombroon remained open, selling European and Asian imports against fine wool from the province of Kirman, thoroughbred horses, and, above all, silver.

Surat, western India, Malabar, and the Persian Gulf constituted a single unit of operation in the organisation of the Companies, supplying them with many profitable items of merchandise for direct shipment to Europe. From the middle of the seventeenth century, there was a gradual geographical shift in favour of southern and eastern India. At first the Companies settled in Masulipatam, the leading port in Coromandel. The town was situated in the delta between the River Krishna and the Godavari, a region famous for its patterned cotton textiles, exported in large quantities to the Indonesian islands. Masulipatam always remained important to the Companies. But political frictions with its rulers, the court of Golconda, and awareness that the southern Carnatic districts also produced much fine cloth, caused the Dutch and the English to migrate down the coast. The VOC settled in Pulicut (1610) and later at Negapatam (1690). The East India Company obtained the right to construct a factory and a fort in the fishing village of Madras in 1639. The political fragmentation of southern India and the great wars of conquest fought between the rulers of Golconda, Hindu Vijayanagar, and later the mighty Mughal empire itself, favoured and fostered the maritime trade of the European enclaves. In the second half of the seventeenth century, the brightly coloured Coromandel chintz and other cotton piece-goods were as eagerly sought by dealers of fashion-wear in Amsterdam and London as they were by merchants trading to West Africa, Spanish America, and the West Indies. Sizeable commercial communities came to live in Madras, in Danish Tranquebar (1620) and in French Pondicherry (1674). Together with Bengal, the Coromandel factories of the Companies were destined to provide shareholders in Europe with the bulk of their profits before the rise of the China trade in the eighteenth century.

The maritime trade of Bengal did not possess the obvious fame and prestige of Surat and its frugal millionaire merchants. Suitable sea-ports capable of berthing large ocean-going ships were lacking in the area, and silting was a constant hazard. The fertile province and its legendary handicrafts were closed in by dangerous estuarial waters. Even the experienced sea-captains of the East India Company were reluctant at the beginning to navigate the river Hugli, which gave access to the inland commercial markets of Bengal. But the appearance of isolation was misleading. Exports from eastern India to all parts of the Indian Ocean were a perennial source of prosperity to merchants of every nation, and the Europeans were no exception. In fact, the English and the Dutch were long aware of its reputation as the granary of the Mughal empire, and after the expulsion of the Portuguese in 1632 they lost little time in sending commercial agents to places such as Pipli, Balasore, Hugli, and Dacca, the provincial capital. The low-lying plains and a magnificent network of inland waterways made transportation easy and inexpensive in Bengal. The trade of the Companies, based in Hugli, grew rapidly. North European buyers became a familiar sight in the wholesale markets of Kasimbazar, Patna, and Dacca, dealing in enormous quantities of raw silk, saltpetre, and every variety of luxurious muslins. After the East India Company lost its ill-conceived Mughal War (1691), the peace terms allowed the English to settle at an obscure village called Calcutta on the swampy eastern bank of the river Hugli. During the next century, a city of Georgian streets and houses, intermingled with the humble thatch-and-bamboo-mat dwellings of rural Bengal, was built on the reclaimed land. The guns of Fort William in Calcutta dominated the river, though providing little protection against a conventional military attack. The fortifications and the guns, however, were not necessary conditions of successful trading in Bengal, and the Dutch factory in Hugli throve without them. In the 1720s and 1730s, so large was the annual turnover of the two Companies that the treasures imported by them gave an ever-increasing financial liquidity to the merchants and the political elite of Bengal.[15]

The consolidation of the commercial organisation of the VOC and the East India Company in the western Indian Ocean was followed by an extension of trade to the Far East. There were several reasons. The great profits made by the Portuguese in their voyages to Malacca, Macau, and Nagasaki were well known. Japan had emerged in this period as the world's second largest producer of silver. If a part of this supply could be tapped for the Asian purchases of the Companies, it would reduce the need to export silver from Europe itself. China of course always held an overwhelming fascination for European consumers because of its unrivalled production of porcelain and silk. The VOC and the English Company found a fast-growing market in Holland, England, and France based on the consumer vogue for *chinoiserie*, which was joined later by the widespread popularity of tea-drinking. But the west European efforts to open commercial relations with China and Japan ran into major difficulties. The active junk trade from Fukien, Chekiang, and Kwangtung to Java and the strait of Malacca received rough treatment from the Dutch, and this strengthened the prejudice of the Ming imperial court against foreign "barbarians" and foreign trade. When Batavia became the centre of Dutch trade and empire in the Indian Ocean, it was hoped that in spite of the earlier acts of violence against them the Chinese junk-owners could be induced to come and live in the Dutch settlement. The great commercial families of Fukien did respond to the economic opportunity of trading with the VOC in Batavia and organised regular voyages to Java and Formosa, where the Dutch had established Fort Zeelandia as an outpost (1624). The junk trade was a source of both goods and migrant settlers.

The establishment of the Manchus on the imperial throne stabilised the chaotic situation in the coastal provinces of China created by the civil war and the downfall of the Ming dynasty in the 1640s. Some measure of international legality was restored between the VOC and the Chinese empire. But the Company remained passive, and it was only from 1727 that the Batavia government began to trade directly with Canton. This development was largely the result of the success with which the English East India Company had met in its China trade. The Company had experienced as much resistance as had the Dutch in inducing the Chinese authorities to tolerate European presence in China; in the seventeenth century, the East India Company acquired Chinese goods either from traders in Bantam or through occasional voyages sent to the mainland. But from 1710 the Company was permitted to enter Canton regularly and buy tea, raw silk, and porcelain in exchange for the much-needed silver. The mandarins, acting on imperial orders, continued to enforce the strict regulations upon which the court had always insisted in the conduct of overseas trade. Canton was the only port open to the Europeans, and they had to surrender their ships' arms and munitions before entering the river. The buying and selling of goods took place through recognised associations of Chinese merchants, the famous Hongs of Canton. The super-cargoes, or the agents of the Companies, were allowed into the city only during the trading season and had to leave with the ships. The rules were a source of friction between the Companies and the mandarins, but the relations between Europeans and Chinese were more cordial and honourable than in most parts of Asia. The atmosphere of political involution also characterised Dutch trade in Japan. The English Company abandoned Japan as a prospective commer-cial area after a few unsuccessful years (1613–23). The VOC had a far greater success in Nagasaki, both in its own right and as a counterweight to the Portuguese influence. But after the Christian disaster of 1640 the Dutch were ordered to withdraw to the small island of Deshima. There they remained for more than two centuries, closely confined and watched. They endured fre-quent personal humiliations inflicted by Japanese officials, but trade itself was very profitable. Japanese silver and copper were in brisk demand throughout Asia, and when the export of silver was banned in 1668 the VOC confined its purchases in Japan to copper, silk, porcelain, and lacquerware. These were paid for with Indian cotton textiles and Bengal raw silk.

The VOC, the East India Company, and the Compagnie des Indes Orientales shared many common institutional features. The principle of joint-stock capital, the national monopoly, and integrated organisation in Asia were innovative elements that were not widespread in European commerce at the time. Was it a historical accident that when the Industrial Revolution changed the technological frontiers of production, the new system prospered as an economic force on capitalist lines, finding new strength in the evolution of impersonal business firms? The success of Western industrialists in utilising personal or institutional savings through share capital was founded on a type of money market and financial practice that was much older than the techno-logical discoveries of the late eighteenth century. The capital market in Europe developed after 1600 almost in parallel with the growth of trade to Asia and the rising fortunes of the various East India Companies. The most powerful and revolutionary impact of the Companies lay in the public acceptance of the notion that the corporate financial liabilities were someone else's assets. Investment and capital accumulation were at once effected through this mechanism. The capital transactions of the VOC and the East India Company at the height of their commercial activity in the first half of the eighteenth cen-tury were comparable to the role played by national institutions such as the Bank of Amsterdam or the Bank of England.

The realignment in the trans-continental flow of trade between 1600 and 1750 was equally striking. Previously, Eastern goods had travelled through the Middle East and the Mediterranean in short stages, passing through many hands and frequently breaking bulk. In the later period the Companies carried these goods in single unbroken voyages to the central distribution

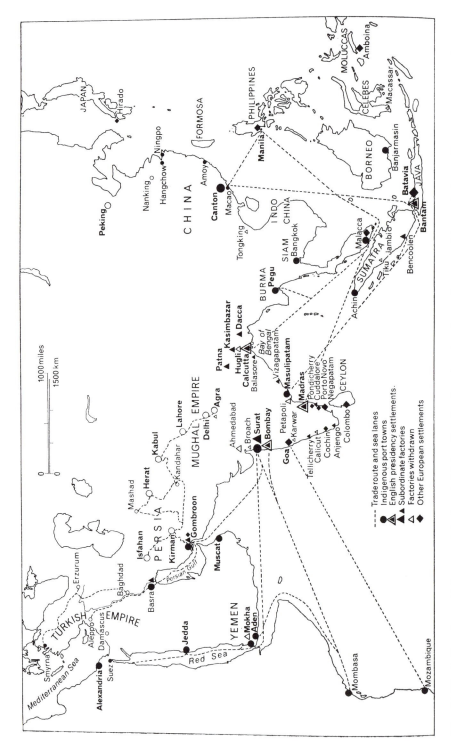

Map 11. The Indian Ocean in the seventeenth and eighteenth centuries, showing the settlements of the English East India Company and of other European nations.

Plate 12. A seventeenth-century drawing of the English factory in Surat.

points in Europe. Amsterdam and London became leading emporia in the West, and the task of re-exporting the imported goods from Asia or the New World was assumed by a secondary group of wholesale merchants drawn from all parts of Europe. The great trading regions of the Indian Ocean – India, China, and South East Asia – were drawn into a system of inter-dependent economic relations, though their internal economies continued largely to follow an autonomous rhythm of activity. The chain extended to the New World, where a new form of agricultural production and processing arose, based on African slave labour. Indian cotton textiles clothed the plan-tation populations of the West Indies and America. Silver coins bearing the arms of imperial Spain and the initials of the mint-masters in Mexico and Peru were to be found in every major trading port from Alexandria, Basra, and Mocha to Manila and Canton. The real of eight became the accepted inter-national currency of payments. Spain held the key to money supply, but the East India Companies, together with the Levant merchants, diffused the new liquidity throughout the Indian Ocean.

5

Emporia trade and the great port-towns in the Indian Ocean

From late medieval times, a number of great emporia in the Indian Ocean provided structure and vitality to its seaborne trade. The overland caravan routes linking together China, Central Asia, the Middle East, India, and North Africa also passed through urban centres performing similar functions. To see the full social and economic dimensions of emporia trading, which called for the transport of goods and the passage of men over long distances, it is necessary to form a mental image of the historical contours that divided one Asian civilisation from another in our chosen period. Arab geographers, travellers, and historians, from the tenth century to the sixteenth, were aware at all times that they lived between two if not three worlds. The land of Islam, as al-Muqaddasi observed, was touched on one side by the Sea of China and on the other by the Sea of Rome. Africa was closer to the Arabs and the Persians than were India and China, and yet the continent had recognisable frontiers beyond which Muslims found themselves in an unknown and alien environment. The configuration, then, was not merely one of physical geography but also one of cultural identity. The traditional seafaring communities of the Indian Ocean, whether or not they explicitly adopted the religious teaching and the authority of the Quran, certainly welcomed and tolerated the presence of Muslim merchants, sailors, and migrants. After a visit to the western coast of India in the year 915–16 al-Mas'udi, the author of the encyclopaedic work the *Fields of Gold*, had this to say: "at that time there were ten thousand Muslims settled there [Saymur], Bayasiras and Sirafis, Omanis, Basrans and Baghdadis and [those] from other cities, who had married and settled in those parts, including some outstanding merchants."[1] We may note the cities from which the settlers had come: Siraf, Basra, Baghdad, and perhaps Suhar in Oman. They were all commercial emporia distributing the economic products of Asia over an area much larger than the immediate hinterland. Trade, administration of political kingdoms, religious instructions, and the manufacture of industrial products – all these functions were closely woven into the fabric of Asian cities.

Although constantly intermingling with people of other faiths, Muslim traders and ship-owners in the port-towns of the Indian Ocean remained members of a distinctive civilisation. The building of the Friday mosque and its continued care always authenticated the Islamic presence. When Ibn Battuta visited Kilwa in 1328–30 he noted not only that it was a very fine and substantially built town with a predominantly African population but that its sultan Abu'l-Muzaffar Hasan was famous for his pious and charitable gifts. Later, the trading ports of the Malabar impressed the Moroccan jurist with their own vivid contrasts. It was an area dominated by fanatical Hindu warrior classes, and at the same time welcomed foreign as well as Muslim merchants. Quilon, for example, had been a port of call since the ninth century for Arab ships sailing to China. Now it traded with Chinese junk-owners also. It had fine bazaars, and the wealthy local merchants were capable of buying up single-handed an entire ship and its cargo and loading it with goods from their own warehouses. The cathedral mosque, used by the Muslim colony, was a magnificent building, constructed by the merchant Khwaja Muhazzab. During Ibn Battuta's stay in Quilon, envoys from the imperial court of China arrived in town. They had been shipwrecked, and the resident Chinese merchants provided them with clothes to continue the return journey to China. That the Muslim population in Malabar continued to prosper is also testified by Ma Huan. This Arabic-speaking interpreter accompanied some of the Ming maritime voyages organised by Cheng Ho, and he has left a remarkable account of the Calicut merchants at a time when the port was probably at the height of its commercial fortunes. When the Chinese "treasure ships" arrived at the emporium, the king sent two trade officials to negotiate with the visiting merchants and fix the price of the valuable imports. The silk piece-goods were all inspected individually, and when general agreement was reached all the parties concerned joined hands together and the Calicut broker read out the contract. The bargain was never repudiated and formed the basis for all subsequent calculation of financial transactions. Ma Huan was surprised to observe that the local merchants appeared not to use any mechanical device such as the abacus for their mathematical work, only using the fingers as indices. It was very extraordinary, the Chinese interpreter wrote, that they did not make the slightest mistake.[2] Considering that the Hindus had invented the negative number system as a way of reckoning commercial debts, the arithmetical skill of the Malabari merchants was nothing unusual.

These details from contemporaneous descriptions of the medieval period lead in the direction of a significant conclusion. The commercial towns and cities of the Indian Ocean, even in those regions which became remote and isolated in later times, lived a life of active economic exchange and social contact with people from overseas with a cultural tradition very different from their own. The transplantation of such traditions by migrating communities may or may not have been the result of trade, but once effected it strengthened the appreciation of unfamiliar values and material artifacts. However, it is worth qualifying this conclusion with an important corollary. The port-towns and caravan cities which acted as commercial emporia in the trans-continental traffic of Asia prospered and declined in a pendulum motion of long-term cycles. Their economic fortunes were not constant unchanging entities in history. In the same way, the social groups from which the merchants and traders, to take the most enterprising role in international trade, were drawn varied through time. In the eleventh and twelfth centuries, the Jewish communities of North Africa settled in Cairo and Alexandria and were as active in the India trade as the Arab merchants of the Red Sea. As the thirteenth century is approached, the Mediterranean group disappears for reasons that are still imperfectly understood. The Christian traders of Europe – Greeks, Genoese, Venetians, and Catalans – were to be found in all the leading ports of the Levant, and they played a very important part in the development of emporia trading in the Mediterranean and the Atlantic. But they did not, and were not allowed to, venture beyond Suez or Aleppo in the period before the Portuguese discovery of the Cape route. While the European urge to participate directly in trans-continental trade never slackened, the rich merchant families of southern China experienced regularly severe political obstacles in the choice of commercial destinations in the Indian Ocean. After 1433 Chinese merchants were not seen again in Calicut or in any other Indian port. But they remained as energetic as ever in the domestic economy of China, which could not function without financial intermediaries, without silver, or even without some foreign imports. Chinese junks still sailed to Malacca, to the numerous islands of the Java Sea, to Manila, but not to India, the Red Sea, or East Africa. The explanation remains elusive.

Perhaps the most enigmatic of all the social communities of the Indian Ocean was that of the Hindu merchants of India. They were not a homogenous group, The Jain traders of Gujarat, with gentle ascetical values, could neither eat, drink, nor marry with the Chettiars of the Coromandel coast, though there was no restriction on mutual business dealings between them. Both groups were renowned for commercial skills and mastery of the art of navigation and shipping. Yet all the historical information about them comes from outside, mostly from foreign sources. The obscurity was not due to a lack of literate qualities. We know that the Hindu merchants kept highly professional account books and were constantly in touch with distant markets through correspondence. When occasion demanded, as for example in the seventeenth century, a knowledge of Portuguese and English was added to the stock of local languages.[3] The historian must conclude that these men preferred to remain faceless; neither their family history, nor even the history of the community, was for sale. It is, however, certain that before the Portuguese arrival in the Indian Ocean the merchants of Gujarat, Malabar, Coromandel, and Bengal looked to the east, to the Indonesian archipelago, for direct voyages organised with their own shipping and capital. From the sixteenth century the orientation was suddenly reversed and turned westwards, towards the Red Sea and the Persian Gulf. Hindu merchants were to be found all through the Middle East in the seventeenth and eighteenth centuries. This development was undoubtedly connected with Portuguese maritime policy and was later strengthened by the naval pass-system adopted by the VOC and the East India Company. Once having found and established economic relations, the Gujarati traders and the others carried on their business in the Middle East on the basis of commercial goodwill extending over many generations. Of course, Aden and Hormuz were visited by Indian ships and Indian merchants long before the sixteenth century, and Ibn Battuta especially singled out Indian presence in Aden as a fact worth mentioning. In general, the medieval seaborne trade of India with the Red Sea and the Persian Gulf was left in the hands of Arabs, Persians, Jews, and Armenians. Portuguese atrocities against Gujarati merchants in Malacca and elsewhere in the eastern Indian Ocean, at which Pires darkly hinted, were perhaps a clear warning that they would find a commercial welcome only in the land of those who were at perpetual war with the Frankish non-believers. Islamic society did not easily tolerate the presence of people professing Jainism, but the latter were a better alternative to the Christian sword and the cannon.

The appearance of the Portuguese in Asia in 1498 not only meant a profound rearrangement of the trading relations in the area but also added a new dimension to the historiography of the subject. For one thing, they were a maritime people *par excellence*, keenly aware of the significance of international commercial routes and markets to national economies. This preoccupation with trade can be seen clearly in the opening comments of Tomé Pires, the author of *Suma Oriental*, which supplies such graphic and detailed description of the structure of emporia trading in the Indian Ocean. Pires announced in the preface to his work that he would speak not only of Asian kingdoms and regions but also of the trade they had with one another. For it was trade in general which ennobled kingdoms, made cities and citizens great, and decided peace and war.[4] There could have been few contemporary statements as explicit as this on the connection between international commerce and the economic fortunes of princes in the pre-modern period, and it may well be that Pires himself attached to trade a meaning different from our view of it as an engine of economic growth. It is one of the strange accidents of history that the work of Pires was completely lost and forgotten and never published in full under his own name. By contrast, the ambitious *Livro* of Duarte Barbosa, a contemporary of Pires, received much wider publicity. The book was translated into Italian and printed in Venice (1550) by the famous compiler of oceanic explorations, Giovanni Battista Ramusio.[5] Apart from their portrayal of the commercial world of Asia at the turn of the fifteenth century, the works of Pires and Barbosa also point out in restrained language the effects of Portuguese exploits at sea and of their attacks on the trading emporia. The depth of documentation and information continued to increase in the subsequent centuries, as Dutch and English merchants added to the Portuguese sources their own systematic reports and evaluations of commercial prospects at the various Asian ports. Many European officials of the chartered companies were deeply engaged in private trading, and they were drawn to the service in the first place by the attraction of making a fortune in the inter-regional trade of the Indian Ocean. As a result, the social base of emporia trade in the seventeenth and eighteenth centuries included, besides Asian merchants and the Portuguese, people from the Low Countries, England, France, and Scandinavia.

It is of some significance that both Pires and Barbosa arrange their accounts geographically, following the longitudinal direction of the globe. They begin either with Egypt and the Red Sea or with East Africa, and go from west to east. Pires, always the analytical narrator, took the five principal rivers of Africa and Asia – the Nile, the Tigris, the Euphrates, the Indus, and the Ganges – to mark out the shape of the *Suma*. Obviously, these writers were retracing the existing scientific conventions of geography and looking for the nearest terminus of Western trade with maritime Asia. This was a pattern copied by all subsequent European writers on the Indian Ocean. There are two distinct themes of historical causality in the *Suma Oriental* and the *Livro de Duarte Barbosa*. A concern with the mechanics of long-distance trade from China to Alexandria continually informs the narrative, intermingling with the attempt to show how the purely local economies of each Asian region or politi-cal empire connected up with the nexus of international trade. The authors saw with great precision that the seaborne commerce of the Indian Ocean functioned at this time in three natural segments. First of all, there was the stretch from the Red Sea and the Persian Gulf to Gujarat and the Malabar. The second segment included the annual voyages from the coastal provinces of India to the Indonesian archipelago. In the final segment lay the economic exchanges between South East Asia and the Far East. At each junction of the segments, great urban emporia had developed, providing cargo and shipping services to the merchants and offering on the part of the political rulers an element of neutrality. There is no difficulty in identifying these emporia. The names of the famous trading cities of Asia ring out as clear as bells in all the his-torical accounts. From the tenth century onwards, Aden, Hormuz, Cambay, and Calicut formed one quadrilateral in the Western zone. Kilwa, Mogadishu, Aden, and Jedda constituted another. In the East, Samudra-Pasè, later Malacca, Canton, and Ch'üan-chou (Zaiton) attracted the largest volume of shipping and wholesale trade. This medieval circuit of emporia was replaced after 1600 by a new one. Surat took over from Cambay in Gujarat. Bandar Abbas or Gombroon replaced Hormuz, and as civil war spread in Iran (1722) Basra once again saw some of its old prosperity restored. In the Red Sea the commercial fortunes of Mocha were built on its coffee exports, but Jedda retained its importance as an intermediate centre of redistribution. The main casualties in the later period were the city–states of East Africa and the ports of Malabar. In the Bay of Bengal and the eastern Indian Ocean, there were some new names and a few old ones: Masulipatam, Hugli, Malacca, Acheh,

Bantam, Tongking, and Canton. Some of the towns under European political jurisdiction assumed the functions of emporia trading. Goa, at first standing at the top of the list, had its importance and wealth eclipsed by Batavia, Madras, and Calcutta. The European enclaves were dependent on their Asian neighbours and counterparts for maintaining a high level of activity, but their markets were not really open to the full force of competition from Asian merchants.

The factors which lay behind the changes from the old pattern of emporia trading to the new can be found and explained. The reasons would become clearer with a closer examination of the structural features of each zone of trade. But a more general question first needs to be asked. Why was the trans-continental trade of Asia segmented in the way described by the early Portuguese writers and confirmed by medieval Arab and Chinese sources? Pires himself had no hesitation in saying that it was due to the wind-system in the Indian Ocean and the seasonal nature of sailings:

Because those from Cairo and Mecca and Aden cannot reach Malacca in a single monsoon, as well as the Parsees and those from Ormuz and Rumes, Turks and similar peoples such as Armenians, at their own time they go to the kingdom of Gujarat . . . from there they embark in March and sail direct for Malacca; and on the return journey they call at the Maldive Islands.[6]

The implied argument turns on the fact that the Western ships sailing to destinations in the South China Sea, to the east of the strait of Malacca, had to wait for several months at safe anchorages for a change of wind. At these junctions or the limits of the monsoon, intermediate centres grew up where merchants could find goods exported from other areas without having to tie up their capital in risky voyages over long periods. By minimising both time and risk, they could speed up their turnover and increase their total profits. The climatic explanation of the rise of trading cities is true in a sense. It is not, however, the only reason. Similar commercial towns and ports were to be found all over the world, in the North Sea, the Baltic, and the Mediterranean. Navigation in these seas was not influenced to the same extent as in the Indian Ocean by the seasonal direction of the wind. It is a simple historical fact that the trading emporium is a universal feature of long-distance movements of goods and men. Other explanations must be sought for the rise of places such as Aden, Cambay, and Malacca as the main centres in their time of maritime redistributive trade.

The system of emporia trading and its segmentation raise several analytically intriguing problems. Long-distance trade, whether by sea or by land, could have been conducted in a series of stages because of the nature of its organisation. Merchants and traders usually respond to business opportunities in a highly complex way, and their choice of market areas is constrained by social conventions, by the depth of local knowledge, and by the

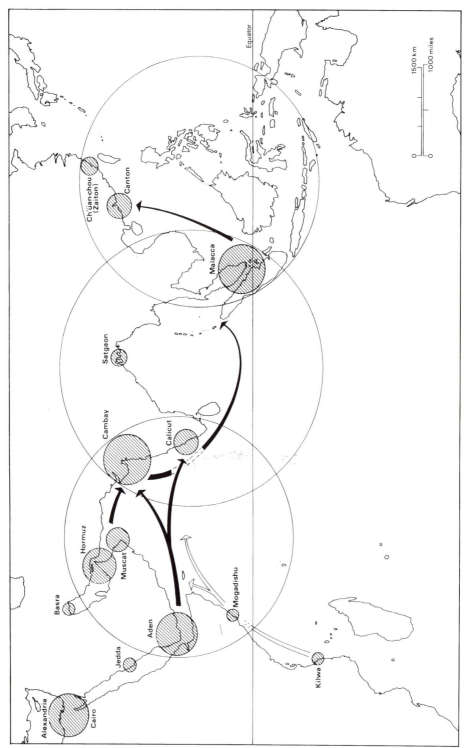

Map 12. The structure of emporia trade in the Indian Ocean before 1500.

quality of political institutions. Where these considerations played a large part in the total situation, the commercial frontiers coincided with the national and multilateral exchanges remained weak. On the other hand, there were social communities in the Indian Ocean and along the caravan routes that were truly international and always on the move. The two groups that immediately come to mind are the merchants of Gujarat and Sind and the Armenians. Both were widely scattered throughout the Indian Ocean and were considered as being exceptionally skilled in the art of merchandising. Pires thought that the people of Cambay excelled the Italians in their knowledge of commercial matters, and he counselled those Portuguese who wanted to be clerks and factors to go to Cambay for training, adding prudently that the business of trade was a science in itself which did not hinder any other noble exercise, but helped a great deal.[7] It is axiomatic that social groups, such as the Gujaratis, who possess a special ability to minimise transaction costs at the level of wholesale maritime trade cannot operate effectively except through well-established trading cities, and that their presence in turn strengthens the redistributive urban centres. The Armenians in particular never failed to locate a profitable emporium in Asia. In 1697, the directors of the East India Company declared in a rare mood of foreign appreciation that the Armenian merchants were the most ancient in the world, who had been in charge of the textile trade since the first cloth was woven. One of the Company's officials, John Fryer, had discovered in 1677 on a visit to Isfahan that the famous covered market there sold a more varied selection of English broadcloth than even Blackwell Hall in London.[8] The Armenians bought European woollens at the ports of the eastern Mediterranean, transported the bales by camel, and often undersold the exports of the chartered companies, shipped freight-free on the outward voyage. The caravan trade in European woollens was not the only area of Armenian specialisation. The members of the community were to be found in all the major textile-weaving towns of India, and they were actively involved in the production of indigo, a blue dye exported in large quantities to the Middle East. The only way that the officials of the East India Company could circumvent the Spanish ban on Protestant trading with Manila was through secret partnerships with the Armenians of Madras and São Tomé, whose ships had access to the Philippines. In 1724 an English supercargo found on his arrival in Canton for the purchase of tea that all the leading Chinese dealers had pledged their credit to Armenians.[9]

The residence of foreign merchants was an essential part of emporia trading, old and new. It did not by itself lead to the segmentation mentioned by Pires and Barbosa. The triple division arose from the need which all wholesalers have for a central location of markets and services. It would seem that under pre-modern conditions, of long-distance trade characterised by uncertainty and lack of reliable information, merchants tended to gravitate towards a central-place which had the physical resources for reducing these handicaps. If the logistics of transport – such as shipping costs, the wind-system, and the optimum period of turn-round – determined where exactly a central-place should be located in the Indian Ocean, the growth and continued use of that place were dictated by the choice offered to merchants in a whole range of competitive products and services. The presence of more than one buyer or seller of commodities for which there was fluctuating and speculative demand helped to stabilise prices, and enabled the commercial community to calculate their costs with greater confidence. The most perceptive comment on this aspect of emporia trading was made by some Armenian merchants of Julfa in 1695, in response to the East India Company's suggestion that the direction of Iranian raw silk should shift from Isfahan and Aleppo to Gombroon and Bombay. A merchant who had long been used to one sort of trade, Khwaja Calendar and his partners thought, would not give it up to take on a totally new outlet unless he was sure of making an extraordinary gain out of the move.[10] It was not merely a blind obedience to customs or traditions that claimed the loyalty of merchants to a trading emporium, but also the certainty that stocks would find a buyer at prices satisfactory to both sides of the bar-gain. Adam Smith, who gave a great deal of attention to contemporaneous international economy in constructing his theory of market behaviour, had another, more complex explanation. Smith argued that emporia trading – as for example between Lisbon, Amsterdam, and Konigsberg – was the conse-quence of risks attached to foreign investments. A merchant engaged in the carrying trade – the transhipment of goods from one external place to another – always preferred to use his home town or town of residence to warehouse the stocks, because this gave him a feeling of financial security.[11] The breaking of bulk at places other than the final consuming market was responsible for the growth of towns such as Amsterdam. The reasoning was valid in the context of a system of emporia that had already come into being; but historically multilateral commercial dealings do not antedate bilateral connections. Places such as Malacca or Aden offered to the Indian Ocean traders an unrivalled choice of commodities, a variety of currency and banking services, and ship-ping space to all destinations. In the eighteenth century, even European private traders preferred to discharge their cargo at Surat rather than at Bombay, as the market was much wider at the Mughal port-city.

It is true that political considerations, and the balance between economic gains and the cost of buying protection from an ever-hungry ruling elite, always determined in the minds of merchants the attractions of an emporium. A letter written by a Jewish correspondent in Old Cairo in about 1103 reported that the imprisonment of the Genoese by Vizier al-Malik al-Afdal had caused great concern among European merchants, as a result of which no goods could be sold. The sultan's wrath against the Italians may have been caused by the Crusaders' attacks on Palestine.[12] The bazaars of Cairo and Alexandria, however, were not forsaken by either the Mediterranean or the

Red Sea traders. Neither the government in Egypt nor the merchants could dispense with the critical intermediate role played by these two cities in the transcontinental trade of Eurasia. In 1586, another correspondent, an English agent, recorded the tyrannical behaviour of the Pasha in Cairo and the Venetian counter-threat to send away their ships empty rather than submit to the new financial demands.[13] Such incidents can be cited for all the major trading ports of the Indian Ocean throughout our period of study. But the remarkable fact remains that emporia trading continued to prosper and was an indispensable part of maritime activities in the Indian Ocean. The social resilience shown by great merchants in dealing with unstable governments, and the competition among political rulers in attracting trade to their own ports, fixed the limits of survival for a particular emporium. The neutrality of a port-city in a world dominated by land warfare and a military ethos guaranteed its continued existence.

The old network of trade, described in detail in the early sixteenth-century Portuguese sources, had certainly come into being by the tenth century. Al-Muqaddasi's description of Aden finds a strange echo half a millennium later in that of Barbosa, as if the Portuguese writer had a copy of the Arab geographical work before him. What struck both writers was the location of Aden and its natural strength as a fortress:

The town is in the form of a sheep-pen [wrote al-Muqaddasi] encircled by a mountain which surrounds it down to the sea, while an arm of the sea passes behind this mountain, so that the town is only approached by fording this arm of the sea and thus gaining access to the mountain. A through passage has wonderfully been cut in the rock and an iron gate placed at the entrance, while a wall having in it five gates has been erected on the side facing the sea from one end of the mountain to the other.[14]

It was no doubt the fortifications of Aden and the military garrison that saved the town from sharing the fate of other eminent emporia in the Indian Ocean at the hands of the Portuguese conquistadores. But the commercial importance of Aden arose from its geographical location at the entrance to the Red Sea. Ships coming from Hormuz, Cambay, or Kilwa – from the three points of the compass – were able to call at Aden and sell their cargo without having to undertake the hazardous navigation to Jedda or Suez. The range of commodities available for re-export in the markets of Aden was as comprehensive as it was representative of the pattern of economic specialisation in the Indian Ocean. There must have been a wide margin of difference between buying and selling prices, for the Arabs used to say that a merchant trading to China came as a prince to Aden, bringing with him a thousand dirhems in silver as capital and returning home with a thousand dinars in gold.[15]

It is quite evident from the works of early Arab geographers and travellers that the two areas of the peninsula known as al-Yaman and Uman – facing, as they said, the Sea of China – played an important part in the Western segment of emporia trading. Apart from Aden, the towns of Zabid and Suhar in the eleventh century also attracted a considerable number of wealthy merchants. By the fifteenth century, Muscat had taken over the former role of Suhar in Uman and had a great fishing fleet and a considerable trade in salted fish. But the branch of trans-continental trade that passed through the Persian Gulf in the direction of Central Asia and Syria appears to have broken bulk at ports mainly on the eastern flank of the coastline. When Pires and Barbosa composed their respective accounts, the island of Hormuz held the key to wholesale merchandising in the Gulf. The place possessed many advantages. It was close to the open sea, and ships from outside the Gulf could catch the first shift in the monsoon winds to make a quick passage to India or East Africa. There was no problem in finding a suitable ballast cargo. The island had ample stocks of rock salt, which was cut into huge blocks and taken for ballast by all ships which came to Hormuz, to be resold elsewhere. The most valuable export from the island, however, was fine horses, Arabs and Persians, and a large number of these highly prized mounts was sent each year to the warring kingdoms of southern India. Hormuz had become rich from the profits of maritime trade, the life-style of its noblemen and principal merchants reflecting this wealth, as did also the fine buildings and streets.

As the annual Red Sea or Gulf fleets crossed the western Indian Ocean to make landfall in Gujarat or the Malabar, they not only moved into an economically different catchment area but also entered a strongly contrasting cultural world. The coastal provinces of India shared a characteristic with China. Through their geography, climate, and industrial skills, these areas were able to export a substantial proportion of their total output, in return for precious metals and consumer goods associated with particular food habits or social customs. At the time that Pires was writing, Cambay was undoubtedly the greatest commercial city on the western coast of India. However, as a port Cambay had to reckon with two natural hazards which ultimately undermined its economic prosperity. The first was the continual silting up of the Gulf of Cambay, and the second the feared tidal bores, which were so fast and violent that they could put even a horseman in danger. The difficulty of navigation made the two neighbouring ports of Diu and Gogha berthing places for big ocean-going ships. To the south of Cambay, there was another pair of smaller port-towns, Surat and Rander, which handled a great deal of coastal and China trade but were not as yet (*c.* 1500) serious rivals of the northern city. Cambay remained in the sixteenth century the most important emporium of the kingdom of Gujarat. Why was the place so renowned in all contemporaneous accounts? The answer is always the same: because of the volume and wealth of its seaborne trade. According to Pires, the city stretched two arms: with its right arm it reached out to Aden and with the other towards Malacca. Cambay's trade with other places was held to be of less importance. It is obvious that Pires regarded Gujarat's traditional commercial links with Aden and Hormuz as something requiring little explanation or comment. But

Cambay's connection with Malacca was quite different and unique. For, he states, neither place could live without the other. "If Cambay were cut off from trading with Malacca, it could not live, for it would have no outlet for its merchandise."[16]

This is a strange and baffling statement. According to his own observation, Cambay traded actively with every part of the Indian Ocean; and he emphasised especially the eastern destinations, in Bengal, Siam, Pedir, Pase, and Kedah. As with the Genoese in Europe, there were few trading emporia in Asia where the merchants and vessels of Gujarat were not to be seen, and before the Portuguese conquests on the Malabar coast the Gujaratis had large commercial factories in Calicut as well. It appears that Pires had somehow reversed the economic position of Cambay and that of Malacca. The dependence of Malacca on Cambay was perhaps greater than that of Cambay on Malacca. The description in the *Suma Oriental* of the Red Sea and East African trade of Cambay brings out the full extent of the intermediate role of the Indian port-city. The Cairene merchants brought to Gujarat through Aden such products of Italy, Greece, and Syria as gold, silver, mercury, vermilion, copper, rosewater, woollen cloth, glass beads, and weapons. Traders from Aden itself dealt in all these commodities and in addition brought madder, raisins, opium, and horses. The return cargo of the Middle Eastern merchants included the economic products of Gujarat and those of the Indonesian archipelago: rice and foodstuffs, cloves, nutmeg, and mace, rare woods, Chinese porcelain, coarse pottery, indigo, carnelian beads, and above all cotton cloth. The textiles were traded from Aden to Zeila, Berbera, Sokotra, Kilwa, Malindi and Mogadishu, and to all places in Arabia. Pires does not refer to a direct trade between Cambay and East Africa, and it is possible that Indian ships trading with Kilwa or Malindi sailed from ports further down the coast in Konkan and Malabar.

The structure of emporia trading in the western Indian Ocean around 1500 rested on a system of commercial exchange related to the supply of distant markets, which were not necessarily close to the trans-oceanic routes. Although the sources of supply may not have been too far from the ports of shipment, the consuming markets could be situated very far inland. The overland caravan traders and the great urban centres were indispensable for the distribution of goods moving initially along sea-lanes. In the west the Red Sea, the Persian Gulf, East Africa, Gujarat, and Malabar constituted a natural unit of exchange in which the velocity of transactions was very rapid. In spite of the seasonal nature of the voyages, the duration of the trips was short and allowed the merchants the choice of a wide variety of commodities. For the merchants of Gujarat the Middle Eastern trade generated a larger volume of loanable capital than was possible elsewhere in India. In the case of the eastern Indian Ocean, the voyages became much more extended and more dependent on the precise off-take of goods. Merchants engaged in the trade of Coromandel or

Bengal, not to speak of Indonesia and China, could not really take the same type of commercial risks as the Red Sea dealers, and as a result their trade was more specialised and more dependent on a high margin of profits.

But some of the uncertainties of speculative market transactions arising from extended voyages were relieved by the role of Malacca as a central-place. The question that still remains unanswered is the historical process which made it possible for an obscure port without any natural resources to become in the fifteenth century the half-way house in the trade of China, Japan, South East Asia, and India. Pires himself provides a possible clue to the rapid rise of Malacca. While describing the seafaring qualities of the Gujarati people, he says that it was the ancient laws of the Jains that they must never kill or have armed men in their company; but now, he says, they have many men-at-arms to defend their ships. Was Pires thinking of the danger from Portuguese armadas or Indian Ocean pirates? He goes on to say that before the strait of Malacca was discovered, the Gujaratis used to trade with Java round the south of the island of Sumatra. Their sailing route was through the Sunda gap and round the point of Sumatra, ending in the port of Grise in northern Java. Here they loaded up with the spices of the Moluccas, Timor, and Banda, returning rich men. It was only a hundred years or so since the Gujaratis had given up the southern route, and the remains of their shipping, anchors and keels, were still to be seen in Grise. It would seem that the rise of Malacca was related in some way to a reorientation of trade away from Java. We know from earlier Arab and Chinese sources that the strait of Malacca was not a new discovery. The renewed use of the northern route was not due to a navigational factor. It was probably related to a change in the commercial policy followed by Javanese rulers or perhaps to an increase in piracy, which was used periodically by Malay chiefs to strengthen their political status.

Of course, the presence of Islam in Malacca, and Islamic influence over the Muslim merchants of the Indian Ocean, must not be overlooked. Pires mentioned that a large number of individual traders from Cairo, Turkey, Aden, Persia, East Africa, and Armenia accompanied the Cambay ships on their annual voyage to Malacca. Most of these would have been Muslims. Although the Gujaratis included largely Hindu sects, it is possible that Muslim converts among them may have been prominent in the trade to Malacca. In any case, the Gujaratis were perfectly familiar with Muslim jurisprudence and laws of commercial contracts, and from 1304 they had to come to terms with the Turkish conquerors from northern India. There is no doubt that the policy of Muhammad Iskander Shah in the early fifteenth century was to encourage actively the trade of Malacca by inviting the rich Muslim merchants of Pasé to settle there, and this happened before he himself accepted conversion. As Malacca prospered, the migration of traders from the neighbouring ports accelerated. But these places in turn gained from the central-place function of Malacca. The two ethnic communities of India present in Malacca, the people

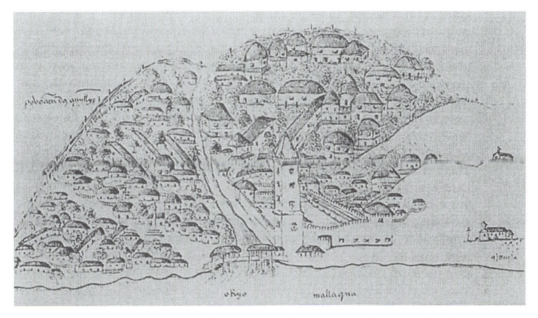

Plate 13. A view of Malacca during the Portuguese period, from Gaspar Correa, *Lendas da India*, 1858.

of Bengal and those from Kalinga (southern India), were probably mainly Hindu with some Muslims. The southern Indians occupied a position of honour in the public affairs of Malacca, and a substantial part of the port's westward trade was in their hands. It is well known that Islamic preachers had achieved a considerable following in Bengal and parts of the coast of Coromandel. There is also the intriguing evidence in the Ming imperial records on the arrival in China of some Muslim traders from the "Western Ocean" in October 1403. The second Ming emperor, Yung-lo, refused to tax their pepper sales on the grounds that the commercial tax was intended to discourage private Chinese trade overseas and was not a source of state revenue. The emperor clearly did not wish to discourage the arrival of foreign merchants with tribute goods and a week later he ordered eunuch Yin Ch'ing to go to Malacca, Cochin, and other places.[17] This is the first reference to Malacca since the accession of the Ming dynasty, and we can certainly speculate on the possible link between the Muslim visitors to the court and the mission to the emporium.

Trade between south China and Malacca appears to have continued and grown between 1405 and 1433 when the official voyages in the Indian Ocean were discontinued. In the *Suma Oriental* we still read of Chinese junks regularly sailing to Malacca – but only with a special licence from the viceroy of Kwangtung, for which the merchants were asked to pay exorbitant sums. In order to avoid these inflated charges on trade, many Chinese junk-owners sailed to Malacca or other destinations in the archipelago without a permit and sold their goods on islands near Canton, leaving the problem of tranship-ment to the mainland in the hands of professional political intermediaries. In Malacca itself the Chinese paid no taxes, rewarding the sultan's court with large presents. This was a custom they shared with other traders from the East – from Pahang, Java, Banda, the Moluccas, and Sumatra – and the presents were an important source of income to the sultan and his officials. Those who came from the Bay of Bengal and the West to trade in Malacca contributed to a duty of six per cent in addition to making personal presents of a lesser value. There is an air of enlightenment in the commercial laws of Malacca that is hardly surprising in view of its dependence on maritime traffic. Malacca possessed few domestic products of its own; dried fish, some tin, and a little gold were about all. Even the salt for preserving the fish had to be imported from other places, and the wet-rice cultivation of Java supplied its food requirements. In the absence of real productive resources, Malacca, like all true ports of trade, relied on intangible assets for its wealth: its fortunate location at the limit of the monsoons, and the mysterious affinity which mer-chants display for one another's company and the services they have to offer. Once a favourable climate of collective business confidence had been estab-lished, supported by proper administrative and legal institutions, a new emporium in the Indian Ocean could surge ahead to success. By the early six-teenth century, Malacca had come a long way from its legendary origins as a pirates' nest and become a town of considerable size. During the trading season the influx of merchants and seamen from all parts of Asia added to the weight of numbers. Pires stated that the Gujaratis alone reached the figure of a thousand traders, and they were accompanied by four to five thousand sailors. In the port of Malacca, its inhabitants affirmed, very often eighty-four languages were found to be spoken; a symbolic number no doubt, but express-ive enough nevertheless.

In any other place than a trading emporium the concourse of foreign nationals on such a scale would have presented the urban authorities with severe problems. But in the Indian Ocean, as also in the Mediterranean, there was already an ancient and honoured law of reciprocity. Rulers and princes refrained from interfering in the commercial affairs of merchants from abroad, and they in turn guaranteed good behaviour through their own law-enforcing agencies. In Malacca there were many officers, appointed by the sultan, who looked after administrative tasks such as the maintenance of law and order, the supervision of the maritime fleet, and the operation of the port and warehouses. The foreign merchant communities, however, were allowed to appoint their own officials, the "shahbandars", to safeguard the interests of each group. The shahbandar acting for the Gujaratis was considered the most important. Merchants from south China, Anam, and the islands of Riu-Kiu had in common the services of another shahbandar. The maritime laws of

Malacca and the evidence of Pires both indicate that the customs clearance of the ships and the process of buying and selling the imported goods for re-export were conducted on well-regulated principles in Malacca. The official valuation of a big, rich ship always raised the problematic possibility of arbitrary judgement and corruption. To avoid such accusations, the customs judge assembled a panel of ten merchants (five Kalinganas and five from some other nation), and together they valued the merchandise and decided on the payment of dues and presents. The sale and discharge of cargo to private merchants was institutionalised as well. On arrival at the port, the captain or the owner of the ship negotiated a single price for his goods with a group of ten or twenty local merchants, who apportioned the quantities among themselves afterwards according to the joint-contract. The system had the great merit of rapidly clearing the market without the foreign merchants having to wait for individual buyers – a point of some importance when the shipping season was governed by such precise sailing schedules. The expected range of prices in Malacca was widely known, and these must have acted as leaders in other Indian Ocean ports. Buyers and sellers were apparently satisfied with the fair method of conducting Malacca's wholesale commodity business.

The overall impression of the port left by Portuguese writers is that of a place engaged in an immensely varied and costly seaborne trade. Its commercial life functioned within a well-adjusted customary framework with clear legal conventions. Many of the customs were common to India and the archipelago. However, we know less about the business methods of the Chinese junk dealers. That all merchants, from the eastern and western Indian Ocean, made money at Malacca is not in doubt. Pires returned to this point many times. "This part of the world is richer and more prized than the world of the Indies, because the smallest merchandise here is gold, which is least prized, and in Malacca they consider it as merchandise. Whoever is lord of Malacca has his hands on the throat of Venice."[18] The design of the Portuguese on Malacca and its capture by them must have appeared catastrophic to many people. The Gujaratis, more aware and informed than anyone else of what the Atlantic sea raiders had done in Malabar and the Red Sea, informed the sultan of the true facts when Diego Lopes de Sequeira arrived in Malacca with an armada in 1509. The first ever Portuguese visit to the greatest emporium in the Indian Ocean ended in a surprise attack by the sultan's forces and the flight of the Frankish commander. When Malacca fell to Albuquerque's forces in 1511, the consequences for the Indian merchants were predictable. "It was upon the Gujaratis", Pires wrote, "that it weighed most heavily when Malacca came into Your Highness' possession, and it was they who were responsible for the betrayal of Diego Lopes de Sequeira; and today they sing in the market-place of Malacca of how the town has had to pay for what the Malayans did on the advice of the Gujaratis."[19]

Just as we are able to see a structural unity in maritime trade in the western Indian Ocean, centred on the urban quadrilateral of Aden, Hormuz, Cambay, and Calicut, so in relation to the eastern branch it can be said that a large and regular volume of trade between India, Indonesia, and China was dependent on the creation of a central-place. The Indonesian islands were too scattered and the sources of export goods were too small individually to service big ships. The Ming policy of exclusion again made it impossible for foreign merchants to call directly at Chinese ports as they had done during the Sung and Yüan periods. These two constraints, combined with other positive factors, made Malacca an ideal *entrepôt*. With the establishment of the Portuguese seaborne empire in the Indian Ocean, its network of emporia trading of course suffered a serious setback; but it was not destroyed altogether, and after a period of adjustment the maritime traffic revived. There was no point in capturing a port such as Malacca if its trade and revenue were to be lost by unsound policies. Pires himself had doubts as to how far the Portuguese were suited to commercial pursuits, and he recommended that Malacca should be provided with excellent officials, expert traders, and lovers of peace, not arrogant, quick-tempered, undisciplined, and dissolute, but sober and elderly. When Pires was secretary to the Portuguese counting-house there were few white-haired officials in Malacca, and he thought that courteous youth and business life did not go together. In the second half of the sixteenth century, as we have already seen, golden Goa became an emporium in its own right and Cambay was already a town of pronounced Portuguese presence. The main changes in the pattern of emporia trading in the seventeenth and eighteenth centuries came from two directions. The military and naval defeats suffered by the Portuguese at the hands of the Dutch and the English reduced their degree of control in the Indian Ocean and encouraged new centres of trade to return partially to the free-market transactions of the pre-Portuguese period. The second impact was made by the gradual diversion of the trans-continental trade of Eurasia from the Red Sea and the Persian Gulf to the Cape route. Ports of trade in the Indian Ocean, Surat, Masulipatam, Hugli, Mocha, Bantam, and Canton, developed a flourishing business life. Merchant communities in these cities prospered not only by serving the internal demands of Asian markets but also by supplying Amsterdam and London, the new emporia of the North Sea, with a whole selection of eastern goods: pepper and spices, cotton piece-goods, raw silk, dying material, saltpetre, sugar, tea, coffee, and porcelain. The triple segmentation of long-distance trade from Canton to Alexandria was replaced by a more random pattern based on commodity production and specialisation.

In the West, no new port reproduced the multi-directional trade of Aden, which suffered from the annual Portuguese blockade of the Red Sea. Mocha and Jedda were used by Indian and Achenese merchants to market their goods and to load up their ships with Middle Eastern and European exports. In the

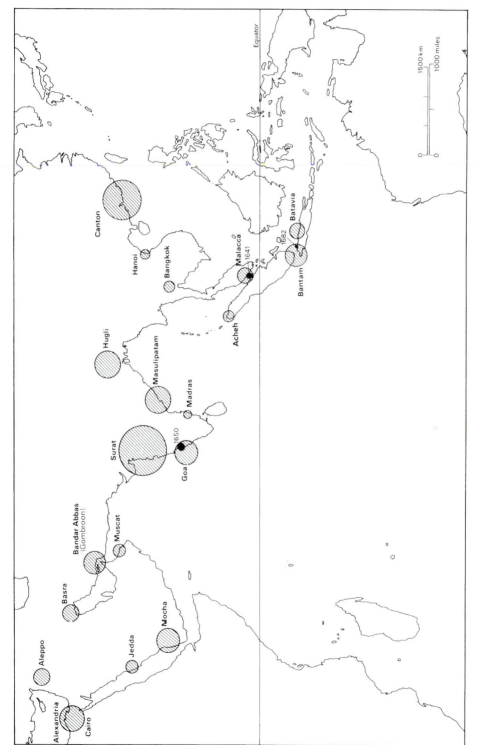

Map 13. The structure of emporia trade in the Indian Ocean after 1600.

Plate 14. A distant view of Surat and its river, from Baldaeus, *Naauwkeurige Beschryvinge*, 1672.

Persian Gulf, Gombroon and Basra played a similar role. Perhaps the port-city that had the strongest resemblance to the typology of the Malaccan emporium was Surat, exceeding even the previous reputation of Cambay as the commercial capital of Gujarat. In the eastern archipelago, Acheh, Bantam, and Macassar could fulfil only on a limited scale the function of Malacca, and one by one they were all snuffed out by the sea-power of the VOC. Canton and Surat alone survived as true independent emporia in the Indian Ocean during the later centuries. The reasons for their success can be found in a complex, three-dimensional co-ordinate of geographical location, economic and social factors, and political events. Canton had always been a leading port of China, and its viceroyalty an important prize for the higher levels of the mandarins. In the eighteenth century, it was the only Chinese port open to foreigners. Although European warships belonging to the Companies could easily have blockaded the estuary of the Pearl River and stifled Canton's seaborne trade, such acts of aggression would have remained pointless, because the imperial

116

Plate 15. A distant view of Masulipatam and its river, from Baldaeus, *Naauwkeurige Beschryvinge*, 1672.

court could still protect China's coastal cities and keep its markets closed to foreign merchants. The commercial skill of Chinese merchants in Canton made it worthwhile to cultivate the place as a free port.

Similar reasoning also applied for Surat. The town achieved its pre-eminent position in the seaborne trade of Gujarat after the province was conquered by Akbar in 1573 and brought under the Mughal imperial administration. It grew at the expense of Cambay, which experienced increasing difficulties in navigation although even in the eighteenth century it still retained its fine industries. Surat and Cambay had a common advantage: they were close to the overland caravan routes connecting Gujarat with the towns and cities of central and northern India. Under Mughal rule, some central political control was established over marauding bands of outlaws and the armies of lesser chiefs and rajas, which were always a scourge to the caravan traders. The port of Surat not only yielded a substantial revenue and personal income to the state

117

and the governor respectively, but it also commanded special respect as the place of embarkation for the annual pilgrimage to Mecca. With the revival of maritime traffic to the Red Sea and the Persian Gulf in the last quarter of the sixteenth century, the merchants of Surat were in an exceptionally favourable position to seize the initiative from Cambay, which was probably too closely involved with the Portuguese sphere of trade. When the North European trading companies came to western India, Surat was already able to supply all their immediate commercial needs. It was one of the leading centres of banking in India and a major source of capital funds. The combination of trade and finance continued for nearly two hundred years, and Surat remained the unquestioned capital of emporia trading in the western Indian Ocean.

PART II

Structure and *la longue durée*

6

The sea and its mastery

The attitudes and ideas of pre-modern people towards the sea are still relatively unexplored by historians. There are few direct sources that can be drawn upon to illustrate what people actually thought about the role that the sea played in their daily lives. This role was likely to vary according to historical divisions of labour and social stratifications among communities bordering the Indian Ocean. A group instantly recognisable in every society was the one that lived off the sea: fishermen, coral-divers, boatbuilders, rope-makers, net-menders, and so on. Their contact with the sea began in early childhood and continued through the hard toils of an entire lifetime. Such people were to be found everywhere in the Indian Ocean: in Muscat and Bahrayn, among the marshes around Basra, all along the coast of India, in Indonesia and South China. These were the original boat people, who found in the sea their daily sustenance. Often their relationship with the people of dry land was uneasy and marked by suspicion. In the Malay–Indonesian seas, for example, the Buginese community of Celebes manning fast-moving praus was feared universally as consisting of the most formidable sea-fighters in the area. There were similar seafaring communities, with a reputation of piracy, on the western coast of India. Ahmad Ibn Majid, a much-read Arab navigator of the fifteenth century, warned in his treatise that captains of vessels leaving the roadstead of Calicut should beware of a people called "al-Kabkuri", whose boats could lurk along the coconut plantations. He described them as numbering about a thousand men, ruled by their own chief, a people of both land and sea with small boats.[1] The last description suggests an inherent distinction made by even professional navigators between those who could use the sea as their natural element and those who could not.

In the social hierarchy of Asia, the position of fishermen and common seafarers always remained depressed. An English private trader, Captain Thomas Bowrey, who has left a graphic account of the countries around the Bay of Bengal (1669–79), noticed that the caste of fishermen in Coromandel called the "machuas" (or "mukkuvar", according to the pure Tamil derivative) was regarded as the lowest among the Hindu untouchables and lived apart from other inhabitants. It was in this humble community of fishermen that Francis Xavier, the great sixteenth-century Jesuit missionary, found his most ardent disciples. They had no church in which to meet and assembled in fields and on the shore, so that at times the good Father was surrounded by five or six thousand people.[2] The flimsy crafts, known variously as mussoolas or catamarans, used by the machuas were widely employed to transport passengers and bulky goods from large ships to the shore through a heavily surfing sea. Bowrey had often seen these catamarans in off-shore waters with a hard westerly wind blowing, which meant that the fishermen could not by any means get back until the wind slackened; yet their owners did not display any sign of fear, being able to swim against wind and sea. Such nautical skills were not at all rare in the Indian Ocean, though the cellular structure of an inbred society made it difficult to co-ordinate the specific skills in the form of a single national maritime tradition to be used as an arm of the state. It may well be that the lowly status of the fishermen and common sailors and their own introspectiveness made it easy for them to become pirates and sea raiders. In Ming China, according to a Fukienese official, when a terrible famine devastated the southern region in 1544 there was an increase in banditry as well as in piracy. This was a period when the imperial government was much troubled by the so-called Wo-k'ou pirates, who were thought to have come from Japan. But there was a chronic suspicion on the part of Chinese administrative officials that the raiders were rebel imperial subjects with bases within the jurisdiction of coastal China. A Ming chronicle describes the effects of the official attempt to control coastal navigation as a means of checking piracy. The traditional ferry-boats were stopped and the tithing ward system was strictly enforced. People suspected of piracy were searched and arrested. The result of this vigorous policy was to create widespread chaos in all forms of maritime activity. The report lamented that the Fukienese had long depended on the sea for their livelihood and all of a sudden were deprived of all those legitimate gains. Even the families of mandarins were not spared the inconvenience.[3]

The Ming account of the Wo-k'ou piracies brings out several overtones of ambiguity in Asian societies in so far as the sea was concerned. It was often a source of material profits but not apparently of social status or honour. The attitude of indifference among people living at some distance from the sea was, however, tempered by at once fear and fascination. Muslim pilgrims making their annual voyage to Mecca from northern India and other places after all spent many weeks at sea and they needed the services of skilled navigators to come back alive. The first personal experience by a landsman of a deep-sea vessel was not always a pleasant one. Abdu'r Razzaq, who made a voyage to India as the Iranian envoy in 1442, "fainted" when he went on board the ship at Hormuz from fear of the sea and the stench of the vessel. The ship was carrying a cargo of thoroughbred horses and must have been waterproofed, as all ships of the western Indian Ocean were, with fish glue and oil. His dismay increased when it was found that the last date for safe sailing from the Persian Gulf had passed and he was compelled to disembark at Muscat together with all other passengers.[4] The ruling elite in India and elsewhere, who were accustomed to derive their main income from an agrarian base, saw the sea as an object of diversion and a highway through which travelled the good things of life. In the memoirs of the fourth Mughal emperor, Jahangir (1605–27), a great sportsman and a keen observer, the aristocratic attitude to the sea was expressed to perfection. When the emperor was visiting Mandu in the Deccan, he was presented with fourteen of that famous Middle Eastern delicacy, pomegranates, which had been brought from the port of Mocha to Surat "in the space of fourteen days, and in eight days more to Mandu". Later, he gave the reason for his first visit to the maritime province of Gujarat: it was to hunt wild elephants and to "look on the salt sea". The visit to Cambay was enlivened not only by the sight of the rising and ebbing tides but also by the experience of sailing on board a ship. The emperor was invited to visit some Portuguese ships then in port which had been specially decorated in his honour.[5]

Jahangir discovered during his journey to Gujarat, if he did not already know it, that Cambay was a large and ancient port with many merchants, ships, and sailors. Its trade and customs brought great wealth to the province and to the political rulers. Economic activities organised on such a scale, involving long voyages by sea, needed trained personnel. Ship-owners, navigators, and builders of ocean-going vessels were likely to constitute a class of their own, separate from the traditional community of fishermen and coast-dwellers. There were of course exceptions, and in the early centuries of Arab navigation in the Indian Ocean experience of ship-handling could have been an individual chance affair. According to Buzurg, the famous Persian seaman, "al-rubban" 'Abharah had learnt the art of seamanship as a fisherman in the Gulf, having been first a shepherd in the district of Kirman. Then he became a sailor on a ship trading with India and finally commanded the "markab sini", the China ship itself.[6] When Ibn Majid came to write his treatise on navigational theory and practice (*c.* 1490), seamanship in the western Indian Ocean had become fully professional. Ibn Majid knew from experience, which he described in the book, that he himself was an exceptionally able navigator. But in due modesty he calls himself only the third in a succession of famous sea-captains; his father and grandfather had been navigators before him. The family regarded itself as being of Bedouin ancestry from the central Arabian highlands, migrating later to the coastland of Oman.[7] Ibn Majid had a poor opinion of early Muslim seamen who had left written accounts of navigational directions. Most of their descriptions were of coastal areas in the Bay of Bengal and on the Chinese mainland. The place-names they used were no longer current, and even the ports and towns had long since vanished. It is clear that this particular author considered the first Arab experience of the wider Indian Ocean as being born out of personal courage and good prep-

aration of ships. Since those early days the science of navigation had made
great progress, and sailing the sea now was a matter of abstract principles as
well as of practical experience.[8]

In the historical sources, we only rarely catch a glimpse of the social
background of the people who organised the nautical aspect of the long-
distance trade in the Indian Ocean. Portuguese historians such as Tomé Pires
were more interested in the fact that the Gujaratis refrained from violence and
the taking of lives than in the social details of the seamen. Pires confined himself merely to general statements that the Gujaratis were better navigators and
pilots than any other people in those parts of India and that they consequently
had more ships and trade. There is no reason to doubt his evidence, though
Akbar's minister Abu'l Fazl 'Allami thought that the best seamen in India
came from Malabar.[9] In fact, there were four clearly recognisable regions in
coastal India from which professional sailors were recruited. Central and
northern Gujarat in the West were supplemented by Konkan and Malabar. In
the East, the people of Coromandel had a closer knowledge of the Indian
Ocean in the direction of the Malay–Indonesian islands than anyone else in the
subcontinent. Ancient inscriptions and the evidence of cultural exchange
between Hindu India and South East Asia both confirm the ability of South
Indian and perhaps also Malay navigators to cross the open sea in the Bay of
Bengal. Finally, the low-lying districts around the Gangetic delta in eastern
India sent a steady stream of ordinary seamen to man the Indian Ocean ships.
In the eighteenth century, European East India Companies employed these
sailors even on the Atlantic voyage home. While the navigational skills of Arab
and Persian ship-masters in the period preceding the sixteenth century are well
recorded, the exact methods used by other social groups cannot yet be fully
reconstructed. Ibn Majid, writing about astronomical calculations of the
movements of the constellation of the Plough taken from various landfalls,
pointed out that it was a theory of the Chola pilots that "this measurement is
accurate on the equator and the first northern climate". Later on he gave yet
another instance of the comparisons which navigators made at that time of
each other's scientific techniques. Ibn Majid observed that few Arabs visited
the coast of Siam and its islands regularly, and that there was considerable
uncertainty about the calculations of latitudes in those areas. There were some
doubts even about the coasts of Bengal and the Carnatic regions. The South
Indians, the Cholas, sometimes disagreed with the people of Konkan, while
the Gujaratis had yet another set of values. "Each one differs with regard to
some of these measurements while with others they all agree. As for the coasts
of Hijaz and its islands and the coasts of the Arabian Peninsula and India [west
coast], all of them agree."[10]

Fragmentary as the existing evidence is, it yet throws some light on a strong
literate nautical tradition among the Middle Eastern and Indian ship-masters.
There is no reason to think that the Chinese pilots and junk-owners who

habitually found their passage through the intricate sea-lanes of the Indonesian islands, and came as far as Calicut in the fourteenth and fifteenth centuries, used any less sophisticated methods of quantitative navigation. Mathematical methods of calculating latitudes and stellar altitudes were known to the Chinese, and it is probable that from the Sung period onwards Chinese sailors made use of theoretical navigation for crossing the China Sea.[11] As well as theoretical knowledge, an Indian Ocean pilot relied upon a host of physical signs acquired through practical experience to tell him what kind of water he was in and where he might make a landfall. The nature of the sea-bed and of marine plants and fish, birds and flotsam, the shape of mountains sighted from a distance, and changes in the direction of winds – all these things carried vital messages. As the Mughal statesman Abu'l Fazl remarked, it was not easy to find men who were experienced seamen, acquainted with the tides, the depths of the ocean, the time when the several winds blew and their advantages and disadvantages. That great encyclopaedist appears to have had some knowledge of the way that an Indian deep-sea vessel was crewed, and, alone among Muslim writers of the period, he gives a description of the specific duties of the various personnel on board. In a large ship, there were twelve categories of crew. The most important was the "nakhuda", who owned the ship and decided its itinerary. He was followed in importance by the "mu'allim" or captain. According to Abu'l Fazl the function of the mu'allim was to be in charge of all navigational matters and it was his duty to see that the ship avoided danger and reached its destination. Among other members of the crew, there were chief of the sailors, "tandil", mate, "surhang", store-keeper, purser, gunners, look-outs, and common seamen.[12] Whether or not such an elaborate and differentiated staff was maintained on a typical Indian Ocean ship is not known, and it is likely that only the larger vessels carrying valuable cargo and engaged on lengthy voyages took on their full complement of officers and crew. But it is clear that the respective functions of the nakhuda and the mu'allim, which became confused in later times, were still in the sixteenth century kept separate. This impression is confirmed by a conversation recorded by a twentieth-century European sailor between himself and the captain of a Kuwaiti dhow trading with East Africa (1939). Apparently Arab ship-masters engaged in coastal trade had lost the art of theoretical navigation. When Commander Alan Villiers asked the Kuwaiti nakhuda Ali bin Basir al-Nejdi if he could make a passage from Malindi in East Africa to Calicut, he replied that he could do so only with the help of an Indian mu'allim who knew how to measure the angle of the sun with a sextant.[13]

Although direct evidence is lacking, it is not difficult to imagine that in every major sea-port and emporium in the Indian Ocean (Hormuz, Aden, Cambay, Surat, and Malacca) as the shipping season approached a great crowd of sailors, pilots, and captains gathered to offer their services to the leading merchants. Prosperous commercial firms, such as that owned by Abdul Gafur in

Surat during the late seventeenth century, employed nakhodas who continued to command the ships from year to year. Whether a voyage to India or Malacca made a profit or a loss depended to a great extent on the skills of an experienced muʻallim. He could sail out and bring home a ship confined within strict time schedules imposed by the Indian Ocean climate and discharge the cargo, where a less confident man might be tempted to remain in port through to the next trading season. A captain who left the west coast of India on the hundredth day of the year (2 March), says Ibn Majid, was a sound man, but one who attempted the passage back to Arabia after the 140th was either a merchant ignorant of the monsoon, a bankrupt, or a desperate man in dire need. Ibn Majid has given an account of a late voyage that he himself made from India to Jedda in 1471. The ship belonged to Sidqa (Sadaqa) Chelebi and was awaiting cargo for the Red Sea at Calicut. When a cargo was at last found, it was already late and the ship left port on the 135th day bound for Jedda. The passage was a rough one: Cape Hafuni, the point of Africa, was not reached until the 175th day and the entrance to the Red Sea al-Bab until the 200th. By that time the ship was beating against the north wind and only reached Jedda after another forty days. It was well past the end of the Muslim year, when customs dues were taken from ship-masters visiting the Yemen, and Ibn Majid had a great dispute with the Turkish authorities over the dates of payments.[14]

Contemporaneous accounts of voyages in the Indian Ocean and the logs of European ships in the later centuries, leave a clear impression of a fixed distance time that did not change until the advent of steam-ships. The passage time of a ship dependent on sails for speed of course varied according to weather conditions and the exact course taken. But these variations were known to contemporary sailors and could be allowed for beforehand. There were two geographical factors which exercised an overwhelming influence on sailing decisions and patterns of navigation in the whole area. The first was the fact that the Indian Ocean was made up of six separate seas, each one linked to a distinctive regional economy. The second was the seasonal pattern of the wind-system, which, besides determining the time-profile of voyages, also marked out the contours of rain precipitation and the extent of viable cereal cultivation. There was no doubt that the Red Sea and the Persian Gulf, the two long inland seas of the Indian Ocean, stood out from all the rest not only by their unusual shape but also by the problems they presented to navigation. The wider expanse of the Indian Ocean north of the Equator can be divided into two natural segments in a longitudinal direction: one to the west of Cape Comorin, the southernmost tip of the Indian subcontinent, and the other to the east. The conventional names of the Arabian Sea and the Bay of Bengal clearly recognise the nautical distinction made by pilots in this part of the Indian Ocean. Then there was the narrow sea between the islands of Sumatra, Java, Timor, Celebes, and Borneo, which would have been self-contained but for the twin passages of the Malacca and Sunda straits leading to the China

Sea. The eastern part of the Indian Ocean, as it merged into the Pacific, included most of the active commercial ports of China and took trans-continental sailors just to the edge of Japan. The Pacific itself of course remained out of bounds to Asian sailors, and it had a wind-system and currents that made it exceptionally difficult to sail in the direction of the New World. In this respect, the Asian sailors and later European navigators were fortunate in the Indian Ocean. Most of the populated areas of Asia lay to the north of the Equator, where the winds were both regular and predictable. Even in the south, landfalls on the eastern coast of Africa could be made easily, following the seasonal movements. The only area of extreme hazard to shipping in the Indian Ocean was the hurricane belt which lay between latitudes 10° and 30° south and longitudes 60° and 90° east. Mountainous waves and a swell at times travelling up to four hundred miles an hour were among the indications of the approach of a tropical storm. Even a strong ship was likely to break up if it drove against such waves, as Linschoten described in his account of the homeward voyage in 1589. The Portuguese carrack *San Tomé*, one of the strongest and most richly laden ships to sail from Goa that year, ran into a hurricane near the Cape. The pilot, trusting to the strength of her construction, let the ship drift with sails furled. When the *Santa Cruz*, the ship on which Linschoten was, reached the area, floating sea chests, pieces of masts, dead men tied to planks, and other fearful tokens showed what had happened to *San Tomé*.[15]

Any ship sailing in the southern Indian Ocean out of season faced extreme danger from storms and gales. But in the northern half the predictability of the monsoons and the known character of the various local winds made it easier for navigators to sail in the desired direction. The south west and the north east monsoons, which the Arabs called "mawsim al-kaws" and "rih al-saba" respectively, divided the calendar year into two halves. From April to September an area of low pressure prevailed in the entire region from the Equator to the Himalayan heights, and winds laden with moisture travelled in the direction of the vertical sun. The time for sailing in an eastward direction began just as the south west monsoon set in, but during the three months from June to August, when the winds were at their strongest, the ports on the western and eastern coasts of India remained closed to shipping. The changeover of the monsoons roughly coincided with equinoxes, when the sun crossed the Equator. The north east monsoon extends from October to March, with the light winds and fine weather associated with high pressure. This was the season for travelling from east to west. The climatological explanation of the Asian monsoon system is still uncertain. In 1686 Edmond Halley, the English astronomer, suggested that it was due to alternating high and low temperatures by land and sea. The reasoning was similar to that used to explain the causation of land and sea breezes at different times of the day and night, the interval in the case of the south west and north east monsoons, however, being measured in months. Halley's basic theory has not yet been fundamentally challenged, though it is realised that the real explanation of the monsoons must combine factors connected with the latitudinal displacements of zonal wind-systems and ones relating to temperature changes. It is possible that Halley, who had studied Arabic in order to translate Muslim works on astronomy, derived his theory from these sources. Ibn Majid certainly had a perfect grasp of the mechanics of the land and sea breezes. His theory of the monsoons and the intervening other winds is followed by a general explanation:

Know that the wind only blows from a cold place and we have shown this from much experience . . . In all the coasts of the world the wind only comes from the land at night, and generally only comes from the sea during the day because of the heating up of the sand by day and the coldness of the sea at night. It comes from the land, because the sea is colder than the land by day and the land is colder than the sea by night.[16]

Ibn Majid's *Fawa'id* contains a great deal more technical distinction between different kinds of winds, their deflections, and their usefulness to navigators, and it is obvious that the Indian Ocean sailor's ability to harness this particular source of energy and propulsion depended on a personal mastery of the finer meteorological details.

Each of the six seas of the Indian Ocean had its own timetable for correct departures and arrivals, which ship-masters ignored at the peril of their cargoes, ships, and crews. The science of navigation (the measurements of the latitudes, and the knowledge of shoal waters and passages through reefs and sunken obstructions) of course remained a constant. These latter hazards were particularly important for the Red Sea, the Bahr Qulzum, which shared with the Persian Gulf the terminus ports of the trans-continental trade of Asia. The Red Sea exercised a special fascination in the Indian Ocean, not only because of its ancient historic ties with the Mediterranean and the Graeco-Roman civilisations, but also because of its later connection with Islam and the annual pilgrimage to Mecca. Navigation in the Red Sea in our period fell into two separate segments, determined more perhaps by history than by the physical structure of the sea. The first section was the stretch from the Egyptian towns of Qulzum and Suez to Jedda, the port of Mecca; the second was from Jedda to the strait of Bab al-Mandeb, the "Gate of Lamentation". The entire length of the Red Sea was some 1040 nautical miles, and its breadth varied from twenty to 180 miles. It was a deep sea, with soundings exceeding more than a thousand fathoms. However, because of the presence of coral reefs which soon turned into small islands with vegetation growing on them, no one ventured to enter the natural harbours and berthing-places at the few ports that existed without an expert knowledge of local conditions. The passage from Jedda to Suez in particular was left to the specialist Red Sea ships, and few ship-masters from the Persian Gulf or India attempted to make their way to Egypt. A similar pattern of navigation applied to the Persian Gulf. The distance from the coast of Oman to the Basra river was only about 450 nautical miles, and the breadth of the Gulf varied between one hundred miles and 180, though the entrance at the Ruweia al Jebal was only twenty-nine miles in width. The southern or Arabian coast was obstructed by reefs and shoals, but the northern, Iranian side had deep water. As a result, ports such as Siraf, Kish, Hormuz, and Gombroon, all on Iranian territory, remained the main calling-points for ships that did not break bulk at Muscat or Suhar. At the end of the Gulf, the entry to Basra through the Shatt al Arab called for local pilotage, and the tranship-ment of cargo from the ports lower down the Gulf to Iraq was historically per-formed by a fleet of vessels specialising in that traffic.

If the Persian Gulf and the Red Sea were the thumb and forefinger of the Arabian Sea, the coast of India was the arm to which the hand was attached. The land of the Zanj, the eastern seaboard of Africa, was not unimportant to Indian Ocean navigators. But for Arabs at least a voyage to Kilwa, or to Sofala further south, was part of coastal navigation and did not present as much of a challenge as it did to the Indian nakhodas, or later to European captains making their way north round the Cape of Good Hope. In the Middle East, ships coming from India or the East African ports made their natural landfall at one of two places, according to the precise time of the year and to what course should consequently be taken further on. The first was Cape Guardafui in Abyssinia, and the second the rocky heights in the corner of Oman, known to the Arabs as "Ra's al-Hadd" and to the Portuguese as "Cabo de Rosalgate". Ship-masters who had set out early during the period of the north east monsoon faced no particular problem in rounding Guardafui, leaving the island of Socotra to their right, and continuing their voyage to Bab al-Mandeb. But towards April, when the light winds began to die down at the onset of the south west monsoon, calms were very frequent and a northward current set in. If this happened, ships had to stay close to the African coast before crossing over to the other side. In Oman, the point of Ra's al-Hadd was the meeting-place of two separate wind-systems, and a navigator had to take special care not to change over from one course to another, as this could easily result in his ship losing the season's passage altogether.

For a voyage to the Red Sea or the Persian Gulf from Surat or Calicut, the importance of an early start in the months from October to April was empha-sised in all sailing manuals. The log of the East India Company's ship *Society* recorded in 1685 some of the problems that could arise from a late departure. The ship was prepared for a freight voyage to Gombroon and Basra and did not get under way before 28 April. Three other ships, the *Ormuz Merchant*, the *Nizami*, and the *Mawsumi* had left the Surat river a few days earlier bound for Persia and Basra. The weather was already very stormy, and the English supercargoes had difficulty in even getting on board the *Society*. During its passage across the Arabian Sea the ship was forced to heave and drop anchor

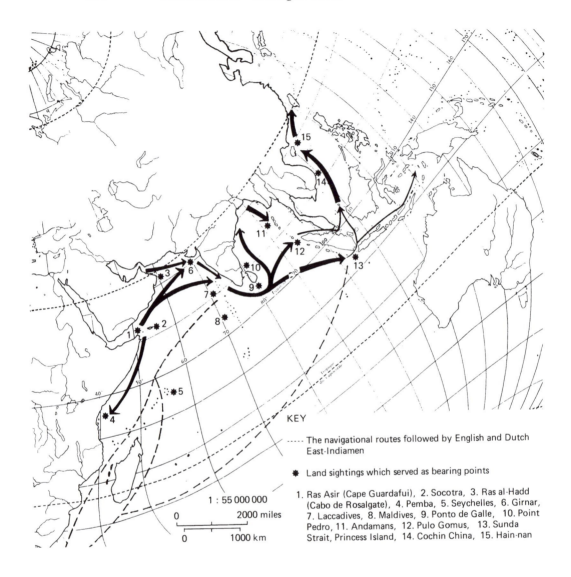

KEY

----- The navigational routes followed by English and Dutch East-Indiamen

✳ Land sightings which served as bearing points

1 : 55 000 000

0   2000 miles

0   1000 km

1. Ras Asir (Cape Guardafui), 2. Socotra, 3. Ras al-Hadd (Cabo de Rosalgate), 4. Pemba, 5. Seychelles, 6. Girnar, 7. Laccadives, 8. Maldives, 9. Ponto de Galle, 10. Point Pedro, 11. Andamans, 12. Pulo Gomus, 13. Sunda Strait, Princess Island, 14. Cochin China, 15. Hain-nan

Map 14. The main sea-lanes in the Indian Ocean.

at every tide, and the wind remained contrary. When Gombroon was reached on 2 June, there was no sign of the other ships from Surat and it was thought that they had lost their passage. However, they had already passed through the strait of Hormuz and reached Basra safely.[17] The voyage in either direction from the Red Sea or Oman was equally sensitive to correct timing. According to Ibn Majid, a ship setting out with an east wind from al-Hadd would reach the Yemen, but another from the Bay of Qalhat, a place not far from al-Hadd, would not, though both sailed within an hour of each other. Again, ships setting out for India and Hormuz from Bab al-Mandeb with a southerly wind would have no difficulty in reaching their destinations, but those fractionally inside the strait would not make it. A nakhoda coming from India and bound for East Africa at the end of the north east monsoon frequently found that the monsoon had already reversed off the Ethiopian coast, so that he was obliged to put into Aden.

For European ships there were three alternative passages from the Cape to the Arabian Sea. The first, and the one most used, was the inner passage, a route followed by the original Portuguese fleet under Vasco da Gama. After leaving the Cape, Atlantic ships followed the African coast through the Mozambique channel, passing to the westward of the notoriously dangerous Bassa da India. If the ship was bound for Surat or the Malabar coast, it crossed the Equator at about 54° E and from that point steered directly for the Indian ports. The second route was known as the outer passage and lay between the eastern side of Madagascar and the Seychelles group. Both the passages could be used during the period of the south west monsoon, the choice depending on the exact timing of the ship's arrival at the Cape. The English East India Company preferred the inner passage, though the Portuguese naval and commercial base in Mozambique remained a fixed port of call for its ships also. The Dutch ships, on the other hand, on their way to the Sunda strait, often took the direct passage of some 4416 nautical miles from the Cape across the southern Indian Ocean.

Although the passage across the Arabian Sea to western India seldom presented any problem to the Indian Ocean sailors, whether using theoretical navigation or practical experience, the exact landfall could not always be determined with certainty. An early eighteenth-century log of an English East-Indiaman records considerable perplexity about the precise location of the sand-bars and islands seen off the Malabar coast. In 1609 another ship, the *Ascension*, arrived from the Red Sea to the eastward of Diu and when it anchored in seven fathoms of water, the crew discovered that the ship had shot thirty miles inside the Bay of Cambay more than the master had thought. It was an extremely dangerous place without the assistance of a local pilot, and in fact the ship soon ran aground through the recklessness of the captain and was lost with all its cargo. For landfalls in Gujarat, Arab sailors generally used the sightings of the Girnar mountain (3662 feet) in north Saurasthra. When its twin peaks were seen as one to the north east ship-masters knew that they were approaching the Diu Head from the west, but when the mountain appeared as two separate peaks well to the east the ships were already inside the Gulf of Cambay. Although the large town at the mouth of the Gulf was one of the most prosperous emporia in western India before the rise of Surat, its location was not convenient for the ocean-going ships of larger tonnage. It was not only that the pilots needed a precise knowledge of the various channels through the sand-banks and accumulating silt, but only fourteen miles below Cambay the high spring tides rose thirty-three feet and the flood ran at a speed of six knots. These dreaded bores followed exact timing which made navigation in the Gulf only slightly less hazardous.

The approach to Chaul, Dabhol, or Calicut presented few problems, and in the pre-Portuguese period of Indian Ocean trade these famous ports, along with numerous other lesser-known towns, were visited by a steady stream of vessels from the Red Sea and the Persian Gulf. A ship-master arriving by night from Hormuz knew that he was near the vicinity of the Calicut harbour when he could see the Gujarat shipping or the Meccan vessels in the moonlight. The importance of Calicut and other Malabar ports in trans-continental trade arose of course from their role as a turntable at the limits of the two monsoon systems. Ships from the Bay of Bengal, whether coming from the eastern coast of India or the Indonesian archipelago, sailed on the north east monsoon from January onwards and arrived in the Malabar before the south west monsoon closed the ports. At Calicut and Quilon they would meet and trade with the oncoming ships from Aden, Hormuz, and Gujarat, returning to the home ports in September or October. The pattern could be reversed if the western ships wanted to go to the eastern half of the Bay of Bengal. Generally, navigation in this part of the Indian Ocean was just as predictable as in the Arabian Sea. Shipping on the coastal run to Coromandel, Orissa, or Bengal rounded Ceylon and steered north for Negapatam or one of the ports of the southern Carnatic district. The eastern coast of India lacked natural deep-water harbours, though the Asian shipping had no difficulty in anchoring in the open roadsteads. It was not until the ships reached the huge area of creeks and inlets in the Gangetic delta that navigation became difficult. The approach to the coastal waters of Bengal was characterised by the typical sights of low islands covered by mangrove trees. There were only one or two suitable passages to the main commercial towns of the region and these were all at a fair distance from the estuarial sea. The constantly changing channels through a maze of sand-banks called for the continuous sounding of depth. The composition of the sea-bed provided a clue to the depth of water. If it was soft mud, the depth increased and the ship was in a channel. If it was hard and stiff ground, there was a danger of running into shallows. The rivers themselves were so wide that an inexperienced ship-master could easily confuse his bearings in fog or mist.

In spite of its many dangers to shipping, Bengal always remained a highly profitable area of trade to Asian and European ships alike. A voyage to the north eastern Bay of Bengal, however, was a bilateral trip in great contrast to the passages through the Malacca and Sunda straits. Access to the coast of China, Siam, and Anam was possible through either of the two routes. Indian ships calling at the ports of northern Java such as Demak and Tuban or going to the Moluccas (before the sixteenth century) used the Sunda strait, and once inside the Java Sea they could have sailed to the north, to ancient Cambodia and Champa, through the passage between the tin-producing islands of Bilitun and Bangka. Arab ships on the other hand preferred to sail through the Malacca strait during the period of their China voyages, and after the emporia trade of Malacca had become established, they found that the port was a better turntable even than Calicut. The China Sea has a monsoon pattern which does not exactly correspond to the timing in the western Indian Ocean. Ships on the way to and from Amoy, Canton, or ports further north needed a lengthy stay in South East Asia before favourable winds set in. Furthermore, the much-feared typhoons often led to heavy shipping losses in the South China Sea itself. Chinese junks trading with Malacca from the beginning of the fifteenth century followed the mainland coast to Indo-China and then crossed over to the Malay peninsula. This was the western route used by sailors from Canton and Amoy. There was an eastern route as well, for shipping sailing from Ch'üan-chou, which ran through the Philippines and Borneo. These two main sea-lanes were supplemented by many subsidiary routes; a Chinese manu-script work on navigation (*c.* 1430) gives details of as many as twenty-seven different voyages between China and the Indonesian archipelago, both inside and outside the Java Sea. Chinese seafarers remained conscious even in the centuries when they sailed to the Malabar that the eastern and the western divisions of the Indian Ocean could be linked together in a single voyage only under exceptional commercial conditions. The intermediate role performed by Malacca and other South East Asian ports of course reflected the economic reality and the navigational constraints. With the rise of Portuguese trade in the Far East from the middle of the sixteenth century, it was found profitable to organise a single round voyage from Goa to Macau and Nagasaki. As usual, the ships needed more than one season to return, but the exceptional returns of Portuguese trade in China and Japan made it worthwhile to wait for a longer period of financial turnover.

A description of the six different seas of the Indian Ocean shows that navi-gationally the various areas could remain individually self-contained or be connected together in a wider framework of trade and social exchange. Ships engaged in inter-regional voyages employed masters who either possessed the necessary knowledge of distant seas or were prepared to use the science of others. "It is sensible", Ibn Majid wrote, "that every man knows his own coast best, although God is all-knowing, and it is certain that the Cholas live nearer to these coasts [in the Bay of Bengal] than anyone else, so we have used them and their *qiyas* as a guide."[18] What similarity there was between Arab and Indian methods of mathematical navigation has not been investigated in detail. In Ibn Majid's work, the science of navigation essentially depended on two separate sets of observations. The first was the measurement of the stellar altitudes from which latitudes were identified. The second was the bearings taken from the magnetic compass. By combining the two elements, a ship-master could lay down the route which the Arab navigators called "dira". There were several types of dira. The easiest course for the non-theoretical pilot was to sail along the coast, in-shore or off-shore, this requiring a considerable degree of seamanship. Coastal waters in the Indian Ocean were not any safer than the open sea. When a route called for sailing out of sight of land for many days, Arab pilots either followed a direct course between the points concerned or changed direction at some stage of the voyage. Both the methods involved the calculation of latitudes in order to fix the position of the ship and required compass steering according to strict time-keeping. The measurement of the stellar altitudes on the traditional Indian Ocean ship was performed with the aid of a board ("kamal" or "loh") held at arm's length, and there was also fixed tabulation of latitudes according to the position of the Pole Star. There is no evidence in any of the Arab works on navigation that the altitude of the sun was ever used to fix position at sea, though this fact does not prove that the Arab sailors only navigated at night. However, they did not know how to calculate longitudes and hence could not sail in a direct east to west direction unless the latitudes coincided with the points of departure and arrival. The use of the compass with magnetic needle and design circle was known in the Middle East and China from at least as early as the thirteenth century. It remains a mystery why the early European travellers in Asia stated that the Asian mariners did not know the use of a compass at sea. Chinese nagivational works describe methods of calculation, also based on stellar altitudes, taken with some sort of cross-staff, though Chinese sailors appear to have utilised compass bearings extensively and sailed close to the wind.[19]

From 1498 the Indian Ocean was no longer a legendary sea to European navigators. On his first voyage to the Malabar coast of India, Vasco da Gama had employed an Indian pilot from Gujarat to lay down the course.[20] Once the way was known, Portuguese captains found little difficulty in reaching India or the Red Sea. The Portuguese and Spanish schools of navigation founded in Lisbon and Seville trained some of the finest long-distance oceanic navigators in the sixteenth century. The Iberian pilots relied upon the use of latitudes and compass bearings, combined with an estimate of the speed of the ship, to steer a course. In addition, efforts were made in Europe to calculate longitudes as well. Without accurate sea-going chronometers longitudes could not be estimated at sea precisely, and it was not until the eighteenth century that such time-keeping instruments were perfected. However, longitude tables were theoretically prepared by mathematical computations, and the work of

Martín Cortés, among the most influential in European nautical schools, provided a serviceable table of both latitudes and longitudes.[21] The greatest achievement of Spanish and Portuguese hydrographers was to bring together the works of theoretical mathematicians and combine these with the practical experience of seamen who made voyages to the East Indies. From the second half of the sixteenth century the manuals of Cortés and Pedro of Medina were available in translation to Dutch and English navigators. Iberian charts, maps, and "roteiros", many of them found on captured Portuguese carracks, provided the foundation of North European navigational knowledge of the routes in the Indian Ocean. In the seventeenth century, Dutch and English publications on marine charts were on the same level as, or superior in quality to, the earlier ones published in Spain and Portugal. The science of quantitative navigation also developed rapidly in North Europe, and the captains of the Dutch and English East-Indiamen were carefully trained to follow generalised methods on their voyages to the Indian Ocean.

In any ocean or sea the difference between experience and non-experience in the handling of a ship was the difference between shipwreck and safe arrival. One of the most notorious examples of a captain's loss of nerve and confidence was the wreck of the East India Company's ship *Sussex* in 1738. On 9 March the ship was caught in a hurricane near the Cape and was severely battered during the night, losing its main and mizzen masts. There were ten feet of water in the hold, though in the morning, when the weather moderated, it was pumped down to a manageable level. The captain and the officers, however, decided to abandon ship and remove to the second East-Indiaman *Winchester*. Sixteen ordinary seamen led by one John Dean refused to leave and took over the stricken ship. It was a brave decision, as their subsequent tribulations showed. The ship was steered to St Augustine's Bay in Madagascar where the crew remained for three weeks to refit. But as they tried to reach Mozambique they lost the way and the *Sussex* was finally wrecked on the Bassa da India, the black spot of the Mozambique passage. Only John Dean survived to return home. He was received with acclaim from the Directors of the East India Company, which prosecuted the captains of the *Sussex* and *Winchester* for negligence and dereliction of duty.[22] The incident proved in stark terms that courage alone was not a substitute for either the nagigational knowledge of a properly trained ship-master or the full complement of crew necessary to handle the running-gear of an Atlantic ship of five hundred tons or more. The hazards faced by the Indian Ocean mariners were fewer than those confronting the Atlantic and the Pacific sailors. At the same time, losses at sea were an inevitable part of the sailor's life. A random but common cause of disaster in the Indian Ocean was the sudden appearance of a tropical storm, known variously as hurricane, cyclone, or typhoon. In 1703 the Scottish private trader, Captain Alexander Hamilton, met one of these storms off Macau on his way to Amoy from Surat. There was plenty of warning of the approaching typhoon in the form of air turbulence and distant flashing of lightning. From noon till sunset the crew waited with lowered yards and sails made fast with coils of small ropes in addition to the usual furling lines. The storm broke at nine o'clock in the evening and brought down the main and mizzen masts. Five feet of water were reported in the well and the crew worked hard to free the pumps, which had been made inoperative by the falling masts. It was not until midnight that the debris of the masts was cut away. The huge waves breaking over the deck carried away the foremast, the boltsprit, three giant guns, several anchors, the pinnace, and the yawl. However, the ship survived and with the help of spare masts managed to reach the safety of Macau.[23] Buzurg Ibn Shahriyar has left another description of a similar storm in the South China Sea many centuries before Hamilton's time. "I was sailing from Siraf to China and was between al-Sinf and China in the region of Sandal Fulat, an island at the entrance to the Sanji Sea, the sea of China, when the wind dropped to a calm and the sea became still. We let out the anchors and rested where we were a couple of days", the account reads. During the period of the calm, the crew saw in the sea a black object which turned out to be a canoe with another Sirafi ship-master, Abharah, in it. He had lost his ship earlier, and warned Shahriyar that extreme danger was imminent. For a fee of a thousand dinars' worth of goods, the captain offered his own advice and help, which were accepted by the Arab supercargoes. Abharah made the crew jettison all the heavy cargo, cut down the larger mast, and throw away all the anchors.

On the third day a cloud rose like a lighthouse, and dissolved again into the sea; then the typhoon was upon us . . . [It] lasted three days and three nights, with the ship tossing up and down without anchor or sail . . . From the morning of the fifth day the sea was good and the wind favourable . . . We arrived at China and stayed there until we had sold and bought, repaired our ship, and made a mast to replace the one we had thrown overboard.[24]

Not every ship-master was as lucky as in the case of the Sirafi ship or Hamilton's country-trader. The historical records of the European East India Companies specify in detail the losses – never very large – suffered by shipowners in each trading season in major Indian ports. Even in the relative safety of a deep-water harbour such as that of Bombay, a sudden chance squall could break a ship's cable and throw the vessel onto dangerous rocks.[25]

Stories of shipwreck and the loss of life always aroused strong emotions. In the close and small circle of sailors, ship-owners, and merchants, nothing was feared more than a ship posted overdue and never heard of again. The news of a definite shipwreck at least indicated what had happened. But a ship that disappeared without trace at sea was altogether different. The lost crew were condemned to sail on as long as the widows and orphans had memories. Indeed, John Dean, as sole survivor of the wreck of the *Sussex*, was greeted almost as if he had returned from another world, and the grant of a life pension from the East India Company was a tribute to personal courage as well as to the fact of survival itself. That the sea was a dangerous place everyone knew in the countries of the Indian Ocean. But the hazards did not deter professional seamen or long-distance merchants from sending ships to distant destinations.

7

Ships and shipbuilding in the Indian Ocean

The relative importance of seaborne and overland routes in different time periods determined the historic role of ships and caravans in the long-distance trade of Eurasia. It is axiomatic that the technology of shipping and the art of navigation must attain a certain level of development before men are able to sail safely and carry goods across the open sea. There can be little doubt that from the tenth century AD the bulk of the commodities exchanged at the trans-continental level went by sea rather than by land. This is not to say that road transport was negligible or unimportant. Few port-towns of the Indian Ocean produced export goods in any quantity. Most articles had to be brought from a distance to the places of shipment. The close relationship between ships and the organisation of road transport in pre-modern Asia arose from the geographical distribution of the main producing areas and the location of urban centres acting as commercial emporia. The movement of goods by land, whether carried by pack animals or in wheeled vehicles, was complicated. There were too many factors which decided its economic success, and not all of them were under the control of merchants and transporters. The supply and price of pack animals – camels, horses, donkeys, and oxen – they knew and accounted for in advance; but it was not possible to predict with certainty the policy of local rulers and chiefs, who were in a position to hinder the movement of the herds if it did not suit their political and financial interests. In a well-regulated market the reverse was also true. An administrator would intervene to apportion the available pack animals among the merchants, to prevent any single group from cornering the transport. In 1721, for example, the governor of Beit al-Fakih decided that the exporters of coffee must share the camels and their loads according to a fair arrangement.[1] The passage of caravans across pre-modern political frontiers was less troublesome and less regulated by government officials than it is today. At the same time, overland trade remained burdened by heavy protection charges. Organised bandits and corrupt soldiers both constantly demanded a share in the merchants' profits. Maritime trade escaped from some of these particular obstacles. The captain of an Indian Ocean ship, often carrying armed men and naval guns, was an independent and a respected figure. He was at home in an element unfamiliar and out-of-bounds to the Asian military. If he had the will to do so, he could open fire on a hostile town and inflict serious damage. Of course, no one in the

138

Indian Ocean – ship-captains, merchants, or city governors – had any real interest in resorting to such extreme measures. But the balance of power or force was more evenly distributed in the case of seaborne trade than overland.

Ship-owners in the Indian Ocean – or in any part of the world for that matter – had to overcome certain random or systematic constraints before they could make money from trade in our period. Storms and shipwrecks were the first enemy; the risk of being left without sufficient freight or cargo in a foreign port the second. It was better to load up even with unprofitable ballast goods than to add to the overhead costs of the voyage by stabilising the ship with stones. The supply of suitable timber and marine stores again raised major problems of transport and quality. The craft of shipbuilding in the Indian Ocean was not particularly localised, but difficulties in obtaining proper building materials could force it to become so.[2] Finally the technology of shipping itself imposed a restraint on merchants' freedom. As Fernand Braudel has reminded us,

Mediterranean shipping was not fundamentally different from Atlantic shipping. Techniques, insurance rates, intervals between voyages might differ, but the basic instrument, the wooden ship propelled by the wind, had the same technical limitations. It could not exceed a certain size, number of crew, surface of sail, or speed.[3]

The same observation could have been made of the Indian Ocean ships. Although the typology of Asian shipping in the design of the hull, rigging, and methods of construction remained fairly stable from the twelfth century onwards, the nautical tradition was not entirely unchanging. In the earlier centuries of Islamic expansion towards India and the Indonesian islands, the shipbuilders of the Persian Gulf and the Red Sea probably upgraded their undecked smaller crafts into bigger vessels with fuller decks offering a more watertight construction. The most innovative influence on Indian Ocean shipping, however, was the arrival of Atlantic ships from the end of the fourteenth century. Hull design was gradually modified until a stronger version of the traditional craft was produced; in many shipbuilding yards of Asia the local shipwright could turn out an identical model of the Atlantic ship. In 1652 Jean-Baptiste Tavernier, a French jeweller and an adventurous traveller, embarked on a ship at Gombroon bound for Masulipatam in southern India.[4] It belonged to the king of Golconda and sailed to Persia every year carrying large quantities of fine Indian textiles. Tavernier's description of the voyage and the ship provides intriguing information on comparative naval technology. The ship carried about one hundred Asian sailors and six Dutchmen who were pilots and gunners. The presence of Dutch personnel on board perhaps caused Tavernier to make one of those careless statements which so often destroyed the credibility of European observers in Asia. The reason why the Dutch East India Company provided the Indian princes with European pilots, Tavernier said, was that neither the Indians nor the Persians has the least knowledge of navigation. The wandering jeweller must have passd at sea many hundreds of small ships that annually crossed the Arabian Sea to trade in India but certainly did not carry any Dutch navigators. The Golconda ship sailed with a moderate, favourable wind but before long ran into heavy seas and rough weather caused by the onset of the south west monsoon. By the time the vessel reached the latitude of Goa, 16th parallel, the winds had increased to hurricane force and water was pouring into the hold. During the hot months in the Gombroon road, its timber had shrunk from the dry heat and the ship was not as watertight as it should have been. In the end, the Golconda ship was saved from foundering by an ingenious method. From its cargo of Russian leather, huge leather buckets were hurriedly stitched together by some saddlers who were on board. These were then lowered into the hold through holes cut into the decks and the buckets filled with sea water were then hauled up by means of ropes and pulleys attached to a cable strung between the main-mast and the foremast. In an hour and a half most of the water had been baled out of the ship.

The episode illuminates several aspects of Asian shipping in the mid-seventeenth century. A vessel carrying more than two hundred people as crew and passengers and fifty-five horses together with other cargo could not have been less than five to eight hundred tons in European measurements. The Golconda ship was a large one, according to Tavernier. The design of the hull incorporated multiple decking, and the method of construction was strong enough for the ship to withstand gale-force winds and finally the storm itself. Whether it could have withstood the conditions met with during bad weather in the Atlantic is another question. The point could be passed over as an academic curiosity, though it has been argued that the weak construction of Indian Ocean shipping was one of the contributing factors in the failure of the Asian merchants to develop under their own initiative European demand for eastern goods.[5] The argument is not really convincing. The technique of ship-building is seldom independent of the geographical environment in which the ships are used. It is also highly adaptive and mobile. An obvious innovation, if it does not demand too much retraining of the crew, is readily accepted. The spread of lateen rigging from the Indian Ocean to the Mediterranean is one example of this, the use in Asia of iron nails as plank fastenings from the six-teenth century another. The teak-built ships constructed in the naval yard of Goa were immensely strong and regularly sailed on the Atlantic voyage home to Portugal.[6] Later on in the eighteenth century there was a similar develop-ment in Bombay. The family of Parsi shipwrights, the Wadias, turned out numerous East-Indiamen as well as line-of-battle men-of-war for the Royal Navy.[7] The fact that ships built in the Indian Ocean were not used more exten-sively for Atlantic voyages was really due to the political opposition of ship-ping interests in Europe, which feared competition. If Asian merchants did not see any economic necessity to sell their trading products in Europe, the reason for their inaction might owe more to the contemporary structure of marketing and the social environment than to purely mechanical factors such as naval architecture.

At the same time, there is no question that the typology of Asian shipping and the methods of construction were more specialised than in the Atlantic or the Mediterranean. In Europe, two basic types of ship, the galley and the round ship, served as models for later development. From the sixteenth century to the early nineteenth the tradition of gradual and subtle improvement in hull design and rigging continued, although no fundamentally new ship appeared in the West until the discovery of the steam-engine. In the Indian Ocean, not only were there marked differences in the shape and design of hulls between one area and another, but within a single trading region there were highly specialised crafts considered suitable only for particular kinds of water and sailing conditions. Boats used to navigate the violent tidal sea in the Gulf of Cambay required handling techniques that were perfectly developed by the local sailors. These crafts could not be used for long off-shore trips. The bewildering variety of names – jalboot, ballam, boom, baghla, sambuk, shewe, kotia, ganja, gallivat, grab, and pattamar, to mention only the vessels of the western Indian Ocean – is sufficient proof of the divergent needs of the seafaring people. It is possible that some of the variations were linguistic rather than real, though professional sailors and nautical experts who have examined the modern descendants of these Asian crafts are able to appreciate the actual sailing characteristics of one type of vessel as against another. If we survey the Indian Ocean as a whole, we can reduce the multitude of ships into three regional groups. In the western half as far as Bengal, there was an Indo-Islamic tradition of shipbuilding which produced a number of common hull shapes, constructed on the same principles, the vessels being rigged with the lateen sail. In the Indonesian islands, Malaya, and Burma, two types of vessels, the prahu and the sampan, predominated. These were fast, light boats which had reached a mature and sophisticated stage of construction and handling after perhaps many centuries of evolution and continuous improvement. Although they were ocean-going boats, in the later centuries of our study neither the prahu nor the sampan appears to have been used for long-haul sea voyages. Their use was confined to inland seas. The light construction of these crafts and their limited cargo-carrying capacity obviously restricted their function and use. However, had the Javanese or the Malaccan merchants wished to become participants in trans-continental maritime trade, they would not have lacked effective models of ships to borrow from. For, besides the Indo-Islamic bulk-carriers, the deep-sea ship *par excellence* in the Indonesian archipelago and the Far East was the Chinese junk. The true sea-going junks could reach huge dimensions. All were solidly built with a unique method of construction, and their rigging of rectangular fan-shaped bamboo mats was easy to handle. The Chinese junks represented a completely separate seafaring tradition in the Indian Ocean, and a whole way of life was associated with their movements.

The geographical frontiers separating these generic ships were as marked as the ethnic and linguistic boundaries in the Indian Ocean. A large lateen-rigged vessel and a tall-masted Chinese junk moored alongside each other in the harbour of Malacca presented the two faces of maritime Asia, each striking in every way but totally different. The people who sailed the ships were divided from each other by never-to-be-crossed dietary laws and habits, just as were the caravan traders, meeting together in the tea-houses of Turfan and Urumchi. Of course it is doubtful whether the Chinese sailors crossing the typhoon belt of the South China Sea would have had much opportunity to carry on the voyage pickled pork or even live pigs, victuals utterly prohibited to Muslims. The Arabs, Persians, and Indians of the "true orthodox faith" had to deny their appetite for mutton while at sea and were forced to live on a diet of rice, ghee, and salt. The celebratory feasts on landfall, however, may have been another matter. That the social habits and traditions of the seafaring people in different parts of the Indian Ocean remained encapsulated in self-contained communities is well known historically. But it is curious that floating populations which constantly crossed cultural frontiers in the course of their routine sea voyages should have remained so distinctive in identity. The paradox can be highlighted by raising a related question: why was it that the tradition of shipbuilding and the design of ships in Asia did not become more uniform and homogenous before the age of steam-ships? After all, in the Mediterranean and the Atlantic, where the transport of goods by ship was as highly developed as in the Indian Ocean, the galleon and the East-Indiaman, Dutch or English, were instantly recognisable as sharing the same basic pedigree. It would seem that in Europe the use of technology, whether in shipbuilding or in any other area of industrial production, was more flexible and less influenced by the social environment than perhaps in Asia. Physical constraints, economic considerations, and rationality of design may consequently have been the dominating factors in the construction of long-haul ships. It is also true that, whatever the distance between Spanish civilisation and Dutch, the Arabs were even further apart from the Chinese. The sailors of Basra, Suhar, and Calicut manned their ships in the same oceanic conditions as the "boat people" of Kwangtung. Common environment and common commercial functions should logically have created, if not an identical, at least a closely related, school of naval architecture. The truth was that the shipwrights and sailors saw no reason to make their boom look more like a junk. Both kinds of craft carried commercial cargo and were handled and sailed with professional skill.[8]

In all probability, there may have been other considerations, technical and engineering, known to the local boatbuilders but now lost to historians unfamiliar with the tradition of sailing-ships. People who earn a living from the sea seldom share the landsman's image of it, as a romantic vision or its opposite, unknown terrors. They know that for man the sea is a hostile environment, but that its predictable dangers can be partially mastered with a seaworthy vessel. How could a shipwright of the Indian Ocean make sure that his owner or captain would remain alive and prosper in the boat he had built? First of all, semi-magical rituals and ceremonies provided age-old insurance against marine risks, a psychological counterweight to rational fears. A recent study of the Konjo boatbuilders of south Sulawesi (Celebes), who for many centuries specialised in building prahus, shows that the whole sequence of operations from the selection and felling of trees in the forest to the launching of the prahu is accompanied by precise ritual ceremonies. The Buginese community which sailed the prahus had of course become Muslim, and yet some of their rituals had a sinister ancestry. A live black goat sacrificed by fire just before the launching may represent a more terrible ceremony of the past. In 1668 a Spanish Jesuit priest, Father Francisco Alcina, noted that in the Bisayan Islands of the Philippines human prisoners were crushed to death by the advancing prahus at the launching.[9] The same recent study also points out that the Konjo people retained a perfect mastery of the technology that enabled them to travel to other islands and boatbuilding yards in Indonesia and to turn out copies of the prahus built in south Sulawesi. In the last analysis, the Indian Ocean shipwrights must have known the significance of proportional dimensions, the relationship between the load factor and stability, and the importance of stress distribution. Awareness of these engineering details enabled them in practice to construct ships which could withstand the combined action of waves, wind, and the weight of cargo.

Whether a vessel sailed well either before or against the wind, or wallowed deeply making life miserable for everyone on board, depended on minute details of hull construction. Experienced seamen, not only in the Indian Ocean but also in the Atlantic and the Mediterranean, knew that all ships had individual characteristics, but it was a misfortune for the owner and the crew alike to be burdened with a vessel which had acquired the reputation of being a "crank ship". In 1729 the president of Bombay, Robert Cowan, refused to load his cargo of raw cotton on a local ship then bound for Bengal because it was a crank ship. However, on closer inquiry he learned that "she is not so crank when she is light as when she is deep-loaded and therefore cotton is a proper cargo for her".[10] In the eighteenth century, a newly built East-Indiaman, designed for four effective round voyages to the Indian Ocean, underwent first a detailed survey by the East India Company's own surveyors and then a similar inspection by the commander when the ship was commissioned. The surviving papers of many East-Indiamen bring to light from a distance of two centuries all the stages in the lives of these Atlantic ships engaged in the trans-continental trade of Asia. To reconstruct the voyage of one ship, let us say that of the *Prince of Orange* (1745), would take us away from the indigenous ships of the Indian Ocean for a moment; the digression would be worthwhile.

In September 1742, Thomas Hall, the wealthy London merchant and the East India Company's shipping agent, received news that the old *Prince of Orange* had arrived back home from Bengal under the command of Captain Charles Hudson. The ship had been in service since 1730, and this was its fourth and last voyage. Four months later it was auctioned off for the sum of £1565. It was then proposed by Hall and his syndicate of owners that a new ship should be built on the old one's bottom for charter to the Company. The scheme prospered, and on 1 April 1743 contracts were signed between Hall and the Deptford shipbuilders Peter Bronsdon and Abraham Wells for the construction of a new East-Indiaman. The "Articles of Agreement" contained no fewer than eighty-nine clauses and specified the exact type and dimensions of the timberwork. The shape of the vessel and the ratios of length, beam, and height can be seen in the summary given below.[11] The timber and planks were to be of English growth, except for the sheathing below the waterline, for which Scandinavian deal was generally used. The initial contract price of the hull, fixed at £3800, was supplemented a few months later by £380 in view of the extraordinary rise in the cost of timber and labour. By the time that the ship was ready to sail the subscribers had raised a total of £10506 to fit it out properly. By January 1744, only nine months from the signing of the contract, the hull was ready for launching; and it is interesting to find that the keel fell short of the actual specifications. The builders of wooden ships, whether in Europe or in Asia, could not calculate precisely what the final measurements

The dimensions of the East-Indiaman Prince of Orange

	Contract		Survey (31 January 1744)	
	ft	in.	ft	in.
Keel	104		98	4
with scarfs of	4			
Breadth	33	2	31	10
Depth in hold	14	2	13	10
Height between decks	5	10	5	8
Rake	19	9		
Rake in the keel	7			
Rake abaft	5			
Height of the roundhouse	6			
Length of the roundhouse	22			
Measured tonnage			530 tons	

of the ship would be until the construction was completed. In the case of the new *Prince of Orange* the length of the ship was likely to have been 120–30 feet, or four times the beam. It was a long and slim ship, typical of the new generation of fast vessels.

Thomas Hall offered the ship to the East India Directorate, and in September 1744 the Shipping Committee of the Company accepted it for a voyage to the Persian Gulf and Bombay. The command was given to George Westcott junior. It was his first command, and the young captain was evidently a man of spirit. As the ship stood in at Gravesend, signing on the seamen and taking on board the cargo and provisions, it was visited by Captain Forrest, the head of the dreaded Press Gang, in search of deserters. The captain and crew of the *Prince of Orange*, however, refused to surrender the alleged fugitives and, according to the Admiralty, turned out the Press Gang with "insults and abuse". A formal apology was demanded from George Westcott.[12] The voyage of the ship, from the time that it sailed for the Indian Ocean in April 1745, can be followed in detail from the letters written by the captain. In the first letter, written from the latitude of 26.3 N and longitude 23.5 W and dated 16 May, Westcott gave a full report of the new ship's sailing qualities. The weather had been very rough in the Bay of Biscay, but when tacked in a head sea the ship had performed well. The commander thought well of the craftsmen who had fitted out the ship, and the chief shipwright, Abraham Wells, was specially praised. The ship was tight and sailed better than any merchant ship the captain knew. She went best on an even keel, and her habit of rolling deeply he ascribed to the lading of the ship. The caulking was well done and the planks in the quarter would not admit of any oakum. There were some little leaks in the bread room, which had damaged some bread. On the whole, the owners were well served by the builders. Unfortunately, the same could not be said with regard to the rope-makers. The rigging was so loaded with tar that all the ropes had stretched to half their circumference again.

Although the ambitious young commander, anxious to please his owners, had planned to go straight through the inner passage into the Indian Ocean, by August the ship's crew was so devastated by scurvy that it was no longer possible to put off a stop. On 19 August the *Prince of Orange* anchored in St Augustine's Bay in Madagascar and thirty men were sent ashore to recover. The stay lasted for a fortnight, and on 3 September they were off again. The crossing was made in good time, but as they neared the Persian Gulf the south west monsoon as usual shifted. The ship was now beating against the wind and did not arrive in Gombroon until 5 November. There were three fatal casualties so far: one soldier and one seaman died of scurvy and another seaman was drowned. Westcott did not like Gombroon and complained of the exorbitant price of provisions and fresh water. He discharged his cargo for Persia and took in twenty-three bales of Karmania wool. The passage from the Gulf to Bombay was made in the record time of twenty-one days, as the monsoon was behind the ship. In Bombay the *Prince of Orange* loaded up with coarse textiles from Gujarat, 708 bales in all. The last letter from George Westcott, dated 28 February 1746, came from the Malabar pepper port of Anjengo. The young captain's handling of the ship and his general judgement were well regarded by the Company's officials in India. In his last letter Westcott himself wrote with evident relief:

I have the satisfaction to assure you we have proceeded thus far without any accident or any other loss in my ship's company than one dead and one drowned . . . every other person that belonged to the ship is now coming home with me . . . when I see you [I shall] satisfie you that on my part nothing I could think for the owners interest hath been wanting.[13]

The *Prince of Orange* sailed from Anjengo on 1 March 1746 and was never heard of again. Somewhere between the tropical greenery of the Malabar and the cold grey Atlantic the ship vanished with all hands on board.

The financial loss suffered by the East India Company, the owners of the ship, and by the insurers could not have totalled much under £100 000. A loss of such magnitude was a relatively rare event, and the practice of risk-spreading absorbed some of the blow. Even so the social impact of a ship lost with all hands and never heard of again was very severe. The design of the *Prince of Orange* was evidently well proven, and other East-Indiamen built to the same specifications suffered no mishap. The ship may have run into a tropical storm and failed to weather it. Yet nagging doubts must remain of its habit of rolling and the weak rigging mentioned by the captain. The incidence of shipwreck in the Indian Ocean as a whole for any historical period would be difficult to quantify. Although in the pre-European age of trade Western travellers who actually saw the local ships of stitched timber commented on their weakness and high rate of loss, the regular annual commercial traffic between the great emporia in the East and the West points to a different con-clusion. Between the shipwright, the master, and the crew a degree of under-standing had been created which ensured that the ship sailed under optimum conditions. The Arab and Indian ship-masters in any case preferred to put out to sea only when the winds were known to be favourable, and from long experience acquired through generations they had learned to interpret the physical signs which foretold danger.[14] For certain seas it was important to be sailing in the right kind of ship. To try and enter the Red Sea with a large ship in the late spring was difficult, as the winds were contrary. Although the veteran Arab navigator Ibn Majid had attempted the passage in a ship of more than a thousand bahar, it was necessary for him to take shelter frequently on the way.[15]

Whether the variations in the weather-pattern were known or not, the fact remained that ships in the Indian Ocean, as anywhere else in the world, would get caught in shifting belts of winds and random storms. An Atlantic ship such as the *Prince of Orange* was designed for a double eventuality: the bad weather often met with in the Bay of Biscay, both on the way out and on the way in, and the much more dangerous gales and hurricanes in the southern Indian Ocean. To these normal requirements of naval architecture must be added the factor of armaments and defence. Edward Terry, chaplain to Sir Thomas Roe (1616–19), describes the huge ships which carried pilgrims from Surat to Mocha or Jedda as being upward of 1600 tons. Although they carried good ordnance, the ships were thought to be ill-built for defence.[16] Portuguese carracks in the sixteenth century carried so many guns on board that onlookers compared them to floating fortresses. As Western ships were kept on constant alert to go into action, their gun decks and superstructure were reinforced to take the weight of heavy artillery and to withstand the vibrations caused by the simultaneous firing of fifteen to twenty guns. These special features of European ships trading in the Indian Ocean must have presented the Asian shipwright with a novel problem of adjustment. There is evidence that, after 1500, in India and the Middle East the design of the traditional hull began to be modified to take account of the improvements offered by Iberian examples. The ships belonging to the Karimi merchants, which traded between India and the Red Sea during the pre-Portuguese period, probably carried armed men to offer better protection against pirate attacks.[17] After the Portuguese conquistadores had shown their uncompromisingly hostile intention against the Indian Ocean shipping, the wealthy merchants of maritime Asia began to equip their vessels with European-style naval guns. Whether it was the consideration of better defence or that of better cargo-carrying capacity that persuaded the indigenous shipbuilders to adopt some of the European techniques in shipbuilding, by the mid-seventeenth century the technical differences between Western and Eastern shipping had narrowed considerably. In the Far East, the Chinese junks continued with their own separate tradition; as we shall see, the original design of these vessels had been so sound that they were perfectly adapted to conditions in the North and South China Seas.

Any ship that regularly sails in oceans involving more than three weeks' voyage out of sight of land must be designed to withstand the constant pressure of waves and, in case of damage, must be capable of easy repairs. As Asian shipwrights, in common with other craftsmen, practised their art entirely in an empirical fashion, using visual methods of construction and design, systematic information on pre-modern ships and shipping is not available. But it is clear from the existing historical sources that three key considerations determined the size and shape of the Indian Ocean ships. The shape of the hull below the waterline was a function of the depth and nature of coastal waters and of the frequency of approaching harbours and roadsteads. The presence of coral reefs in particular, in the Red Sea and in Indonesia, decided whether a ship should be fitted with quarter rudders or whether the steering mechanism should have the usual stern mounting. With quarter rudders a vessel could turn around an obstacle much more quickly, whereas a conventional craft would require evasive action well before approaching a reef.[18] In general ships drawing more than four fathoms of water were classified as deep-sea vessels which needed the services of lighters and barges for loading and unloading. The transhipment of cargo was always a troublesome and costly transaction and justified only if the duration of the voyage called for economies of scale. Ships crossing the western Indian Ocean in the direction of the Malabar coast or even Gujarat considered themselves lucky if they managed to get back to the home port with a valuable cargo within the same calendar year. For voyages to China or Malacca two to three trading seasons would have been customary. On these extended journeys large ships had a distinct economic advantage over smaller ones, although it was not sensible to allow the size to increase beyond the point of acceptable loss. Finally, the coastal traders operated according to a totally different economic rationale from that of the long-distance merchants. They maximised profits on quick turn-overs. Small, fast craft, able to cross sand-bars and surfing waters, were essential for their operations, and each area of the Indian Ocean had developed specialised boats for coastal sailing.

Shipbuilding in the Red Sea was historically confined to the small craft known as "jalboot" or "sambuks". The large grain-carriers which transported Egyptian corn to Hijaz were described later as Indian ships. Whether the description signified vessels imported from the Indian subcontinent or those built after Indian designs is not known. What was certain was the fact that neither the Red Sea nor the Persian Gulf produced indigenous timber suitable for the construction of large sea-going ships. Malabar teak, supplemented by African hardwood, provided the essential raw material for Muslim shipbuilders. It is possible that the conventional cargo-ship of the western Indian Ocean, known as the Arab boom or the Indian dhangi, was originally designed and built in the shipyards of the Malabar, Konkan, and Gujarat. Throughout the Indian Ocean a thriving trade went on in the sale of newly built ships. Once the Muslim carpenters had studied the constructional features of the Indian-built crafts through repair work and the seasonal careening of the hull, it was an easy matter for them to build directly with imported timber. The traditional centres of shipbuilding in the Middle East were in Oman, Bahrain (Bahrayn) and the Gulf ports further north. The shape of an Indo-Arab boom was most distinctive. It was a double-ended ship at both the bow and the stern and the shell was built first before the insertion of the ribs or the frame timber – a method of construction common with most traditional Asian craft. There was one other feature of the boom that attracted the attention of Western observers from the earliest times. The sheathing planks were held together not by nails but by coconut-fibre ropes. The

Babarants Frigott with 2 tier of oares: Sorriotid move or life.

Plate 16. A Malabar privateering ship with two banks of oars and lateen rigging, from Peter Mundy, *Travels of Peter Mundy in Europe and Asia*, ed. R. Temple, 1914.

engineering characteristics of the Indo-Arab boom have not yet been properly studied, and as a result a great deal of confusion still remains on the question of how these vessels were constructed in our historical period. There is no doubt that the shell was built up from the horizontal keel. The planks were fixed edge-to-edge into rabbets and attached to the stem and stern-posts, raking up at a steep angle (45°). Coir ropes, passed through holes drilled at close intervals, held the timber together, being tightened against thick coconut cables inside the hull. The main problem in this method of construction was that of pre-stressing the planks once the shell was completed. For a hull a hundred feet or so in length, which was by no means unusual, and carrying heavy cargo in hold it was essential to provide internal stiffening without sacrificing cargo space. The Indian or Arab shipwright certainly solved the problem by inserting a row of carefully shaped branches of trees into the shell as ribs and fastening them to the sheathing planks. The pressure of water against the hull strengthened by these internal "spring" ribs pre-stressed the edge-jointed planks.[19]

The great merit of the stitched ship was its flexibility. The pressure of water

149

and any sudden stress worked on all the lashings. If the stitching rope broke at one point, the load immediately spread to the neighbouring cords. The popularity of the rope fastening in the western Indian Ocean probably derived from the ease with which a ship could be repaired. The legendary durability of teak gave a much longer life-span to the ships built with this timber, and with stitched vessels it was easy to replace damaged and perished planks with new pieces. Teak was also a valuable timber, and its high cost made a teak-built ship an object of considerable financial investment. However, it would be misleading to suggest that Indo-Arab shipping was entirely composed of sewn ships in the pre-1500 period. The close commercial connection between the eastern Mediterranean and the Indian Ocean from the time of the rise of the Italian city–states must have informed Muslim ship-owners and crews of the difference between a ship built with iron nails and one held together with coir ropes. In Europe the obsolescence of the Viking longship was due partly to the growth of bulk trading by sea and partly to the wider use of the saw and the drill. The method of rib or frame construction produced very strong, if stiff, vessels, and in the case of the Portuguese carracks used on the India voyage the iron treenails fastening the sheathing planks to the internal knees were as thick as a man's arm. It was suggested by R.L. Bowen in his study of the Arab dhow that ships of larger tonnage in the Indian Ocean are very likely to have been built with iron nails well before the age of European trade. There is direct historical evidence to support this conclusion. Gaspar Correa, in his account of the voyage of Vasco da Gama, written some time in the early decades of the sixteenth century, had this to say of the ships of the Malabar coast:

The ship is undecked, short, and with few ribs; the planking is joined and sewn together with coir thread, and very strongly, for it endures all the strain of sailing; and the planks are fastened in the same manner to the ribs, sewn with the same coir, and they remain as secure as if they were nailed. There are other ships which have the planks nailed with thin nails with broad heads, riveted inside with other heads fitted on, and also broad . . . Our people had seen all this in the port of Cananor . . . The ships which are thus sewn with coir have keels, and those fastened with nails have not, but are flat-bottomed.[20]

By the late seventeenth century the shipbuilders of the Coromandel coast around Masulipatam had thoroughly mastered the technique of European naval construction, and according to Thomas Bowrey many English private traders had their ships built in these yards. Although Bowrey does not mention explicitly that iron nails were used in these ships, he does refer to the excellence of the iron foundries which operated in the area and produced spikes, bolts, and anchors. But the iron industries of southern India were not new. For many centuries local smelters and ironsmiths had been engaged in making fine sword blades and even guns among luxury objects, and it was not beyond their capacity to produce iron bolts for shipbuilding. When William Methwold lived in Masulipatam (1618–22), he noted that the large ships of six hundred tons or more built on the coast were fastened with iron, whereas the small coastal traders of twenty tons which came from Bengal each year in a fleet had their planks "only sowne together with cairo (a kinde of cord made of the rinds of coconuts), and no iron in or about them".[21]

References made by Marco Polo and other early Western travellers to the sewn ships of the Indian Ocean may have been a case of noting only what was unfamiliar and newsworthy. As long as the Asian shipwright had the use of a wood-drill or a gouging chisel, he could make holes in a hard timber such as teak and utilise iron treenails for fastening the sheathing timber to the internal frames. The larger the ship and the higher the total cost of construction, the easier it was for the owners to absorb the extra cost of iron. The relative superiority of early Portuguese shipping was due, as many naval actions in the Indian Ocean proved in the first decade of the sixteenth century, to better sea-manship and the use of artillery. The Asian tendency to copy the hull shapes of the Iberian carracks and galleons probably began as a step towards building better fighting ships with rows of heavy guns on either side. For vessels armed in this way, it was of course necessary to mount the artillery lower down in the hull in order to provide better load distribution. The intermediate gun deck in its turn called for the use of gunports pierced in the sides of the hull. The use of strong internal ribs, knees, and floor timber and iron nail fastenings made it possible to preserve the strength of the hull even when there were openings in it. With the method of shell construction the hull naturally becomes the load-bearing structure in the ship, and it is doubtful if the Indo-Arab stitched vessel could have accommodated gunports in the style of European armed ships. Whatever the reason, after 1500 a new class of ships appeared in the Indian Ocean which had many of the characteristics of Iberian galleons. When built in the Persian Gulf the new ships were called "baghlas". In northern Gujarat and the Malabar, they were known as "kotias", but, to add to the wealth of nautical terminology, an Arab- or Muslim-owned kotia trading across the Arabian Sea could only be referred to as a "ganja". There were subtle differ-ences between them which made them instantly recognisable to the local sea-faring communities. But the main feature that distinguished these ships from the traditional boom was the arched and square transom stern, highly carved and ornamented. It is probable that the large size of a stately baghla and its increased cargo-carrying capacity were associated with the European method of frame-building.

The element of conjecture in a historical reconstruction of Indian Ocean shipping can be reduced through indirect reasoning. Perhaps one indication of whether a ship was shell-built or frame-built was in the presence or absence of caulking. A caulked ship bore the unmistakable mark of frame-construction, as the gaps in the edge-jointed planks were tightly filled in with oakum, a mix-ture of fibres and melted pitch. This method of water-proofing the hull was unnecessary with shell-construction. Asian shipwrights normally carved each piece of timber according to the shape of the hull suggested to them by the length of the keel, the stem, and the stern-posts. Whether or not they rabbeted the edges, each plank was fitted to its neighbour several times (to take account of the seasoning process) until a perfect join was obtained. The mixture of lime, fish oil, and resin applied to the hull below the waterline was to keep it relatively free from boring worms and other marine encrustations. An interesting example of the preference for the traditional method of shipbuilding, at least on the part of the Mughal rulers, comes from the records of the English East India Company in 1647. The shahbandar of Tatta had bought a Portuguese ship from the captain-general of Daman and a second one of about 250 tons from that of Portuguese Chaul. The vessels were intended for the commercial services of the crown prince Dara Shukoh. The Mughal harbour-master requested the services of an English captain to bring the last ship up to Surat. But the vessel was rejected by the agent of the prince because it was caulked in the European manner and did not have the rabbeted edge-joints which, it was claimed, were "only known to these people". The ship had two flush decks and could easily accommodate twenty to twenty-four pieces of ordnance. It was bought by the East India Company for 13 500 rupees and was employed in the trade of the Persian Gulf.[22]

Indo-Arab ships from all the famous emporia of the Indian Ocean regularly sailed to the straits of Malacca and Sunda. But the South East Asian shipbuilding industry had developed a type of vessel that had its origin in the outrigger canoes of early Indonesia. The cargo-carrying prahus which were engaged in the inter-island trade of the area in the early sixteenth century were keeled and fully planked vessels bearing little resemblance to the ship depicted in the sculpture of the Borobodur temple in central Java (eighth century AD). This famous carving shows a ship under full sail with two tripod masts and outriggers on one side. The later prahus had cross-beams projecting through the hulls on which a superstructure of platforms could be built to seat rowers if necessary. But the normal cargo-carrying prahu was a shell-built craft in the tradition of the Indo-Arab boom, though it had a curved bow and stern. The planks were fastened either by ropes passing through projecting lugs or by dowels. Above the stern there was a square rudder housing to take the two quarter-rudders. An Indonesian ship used a different type of rigging from the usual lateen sails of the western Indian Ocean. The masts were generally in the form of a tripod, and the square sail was attached to a yard and a boom which could be tilted at an angle to the masts. The "sombala tanja" rig, as it was known in the local Makassarese language, could sail very close to the wind and take advantage of the light winds which often prevailed in the Java Sea.[23]

The Indonesian prahus had obviously evolved from earlier crafts utilising both sail and oars, and with the growth of maritime trade between the different islands their cargo-carrying ability was given more emphasis than the

Plate 17. An Indonesian prahu under full sail: stone-carving from the Borobodur temple in Java.

need to carry passengers or armed men for warfare. From contemporaneous Portuguese descriptions of the Indian Ocean, it is clear also that at the turn of the sixteenth century the merchants and seafarers of South East Asia (with the exception of the Achenese, perhaps) were not competing with Chinese, Indian, or Arab ships for the transport of commodities over long distances. The reason for this development is almost certainly to be found in the structure of political power among the maritime kingdoms of the archipelago. Each successful port and its ruler created clear stratifications of military and naval power. The commercial and economic ties with other areas continued only as long as the small principality was able to maintain its warrior image by land and sea. Under such conditions local traders may have been reluctant to stay away from their home ports for too long or to commit a large proportion of their capital to distant voyages. Pires raises a curious paradox in his account of the seaborne trade of the north Javanese ports. There was evidently an active commercial exchange between the various kingdoms of Java and Malacca, and yet most of the shipping, according to Pires, was bought in Malacca and built in Pegu. After the capture of Malacca, the Portuguese armadas destroyed so many local ships that the Javanese merchants were left with no more than ten junks and a similar number of cargo "pangajavas", which were proper ships. The Javanese were incapable, Pires claimed, of building ten junks in ten years.[24]

It is possible that inter-island cargo in the Indonesian archipelago before the Portuguese arrival was carried in a class of vessels different from the war prahus built in the south Celebes. The reputation of the Malayan sea raiders certainly remained as fearsome as that of any group of naval fighters in the Indian Ocean. Even the Chinese visitors to Malacca, who arrived in strongly built junks carrying a large crew, were afraid of the Malayan privateers.[25] In fact, the official indifference towards foreign trade and shipping under the Ming dynasty had created a false impression of Chinese weakness in protecting the empire's coastline, as the Portuguese discovered to their cost. Because maritime trade was denied official protection, private merchants and their

153

Plate 18. A Chinese junk with bamboo-mat sail, from Nieuhof, *An Embassy from the East India Company*, 1669.

ships were vulnerable to attack by foreign men-of-war. However, in the seventeenth and eighteenth centuries, no less than in the earlier history of China, the war-junks in the service of the government were perfectly capable of serious naval action. The ships built by Cheng-ho for the early Ming expeditions to the western Indian Ocean were capable of carrying a very large number of armed men, though later accounts greatly exaggerated their size.[26] Muslim observers who saw some of these ships in the harbour of Calicut were greatly impressed. Ibn Battuta was completely carried away by his own rhetoric when describing the ships of China in the Malabar ports. The largest vessel among the fleet that visited the coast was called a junk and it carried a complement of a thousand men, six hundred of whom were sailors and the rest soldiers, including archers and fire-throwers.[27] The actual figures are obviously stylised, as there would have been no room even on the largest junk to carry cargo, if it had to victual such a number of crew. The junks were built in Zaiton and Canton, carried four decks, and had rooms, cabins, and saloons for merchants. The larger class of ships was accompanied by three smaller types, called the half, the third, and the quarter. Such was the reputation of these floating warehouses that anyone who wished to go to China sailed only in the junks.[28] That the merchants of south China were regular visitors to the Malabar coast was confirmed by a persistent local tradition that many local seafaring people were descended from Chinese settlers. Abdu'r Razzaq, writing a century later, noted that the

154

men of Calicut were brave navigators who went by the name of "sons of China".[29]

From the middle Sung period to the time of the early Ming emperors, Chinese ship-owners were undoubtedly active in the intermediate stage of emporia trading that included western India. From the middle of the sixteenth century, after the official ban on maritime ventures, private ships belonging to the merchant houses of Canton, Amoy, Ningpo, Hangchow, and Nanking went no further than the Philippines, Java, and Sumatra. If the ship-owners preferred to localise their commercial activities within a smaller area of trading ports in South East Asia in the later period, it was for reasons other than the technology of shipping. Contemporary European ships may have appeared more seaworthy and capable of sailing under adverse weather conditions than Chinese junks. In reality, the junk was an immensely strong construction and had a rigging that could withstand gale-force winds with less strain than the Western square-rigged ship.[30] The large ocean-going junk had developed from the river craft which dominated the economic life of internal China. There was a variety of river boats suitable for different navigational needs. But the essential feature of Chinese boatbuilding was present in all the different types of vessels. It was part of a tradition totally different from the techniques followed in the western Indian Ocean and in Europe, though many river boats of eastern Bengal in India had features in common with the Chinese junks. The shipwrights of China did not make use of the keel, the stem- and stern-posts as the starting points of their construction. A sea-going junk was built up from a flat or slightly rounded floor nailed to a series of solid bulkheads which took the place of ribs and internal support. The stern of the ship ended in a square open space which was closed by a transom. The bow was finished in a similar way, though it was more tapered than the stern. The sheathing planks were laid edge to edge with scarfed joints and were nailed to the bulkheads. There was often double planking at the critical points of the hull. The whole structure was finished off with deck beams and deck planking. The technique of building ships with solid bulkheads naturally provided a number of watertight compartments, adding to the safety in case the hull was breached at one point. As the foremost scholar of Chinese science and technology, Joseph Needham has lent his authority to the conclusion that a longitudinal section of the bamboo with its septa intact may have suggested to the early Chinese shipwrights how to build their boats.[31]

The flat bottom and the shallow draught of the typical junk made it an ideal craft for sailing in shoal or estuarial waters. In the open sea, however, the junk was in danger of becoming a leeward sailer with its lugsails. The problem was overcome by using leeboards and centre-boards as well as the axial rudder. In an Indo-Arab ship the keeled hull and the great lateen sail gave the helmsman a degree of control over the vessel which was lacking in the Chinese junk. The steering gear of the Chinese ships was consequently more scientifically developed than in the west. The merit of the large, vertical, transom-mounted rudder of the junk, no matter how critical it was to the vessel's control, might have escaped the attention of casual onlookers. But there was no doubt about the unusual and striking character of the junk's rigging. Even a dedicated caravan traveller such as Ibn Battuta noticed that the sails of the Chinese ships in Calicut, numbering three to twelve, were made from split bamboo and woven like mats. These sails, he said, were never lowered but were allowed to float freely in the wind while ships remained at anchor.[32] Multiple sheeting attached to the battens of the sail controlled its position in relation to the direction of the wind, and its aerodynamic balance enabled the junks to sail to windward. A sea-going junk sailing over long distances had several masts, as did also the ships of the western Indian Ocean. The latter never adopted the Chinese rigging, in spite of its ease of handling, remaining strongly attached to the quadrilateral lateen sail. As a means of propulsion, the lateen sail was highly efficient, and ships rigged with it were capable of achieving high speeds. The main drawback of the lateen rig was the size of the sail area and the difficulty of tacking the ship in a head wind. Even a small ship of 250 tons or so had a mainyard nearly as long as the mast itself. The mainsail attached to the yard was enormously heavy and cumbersome for the crew to handle when the wind was fresh. To move from the starboard tack to the port tack, the sailors had to release the mainsheet and the tack purchase and move the entire sail to the opposite side. It was a difficult and dangerous operation and not often undertaken. The lateen-rigged ship sailed best downwind, though it was also capable of sailing as close to the wind as four points.[33]

The limitations of the lateen sail in executing complicated movements at sea are among the possible reasons why the Indo-Arab boom or baghla performed less well in battle than a Portuguese square-rigged ship. The Italian visitor to the Mughal court, Niccolao Manucci, narrates the story of an experimental, model ship being constructed by European craftsmen on Aurangzeb's orders, as the emperor was anxious to commission a number of government warships. The European artillery men in the emperor's service gave a highly effective demonstration of the model ship's capacity to fire guns in all directions.[34] However, in the early eighteenth century the fighting ships used by the Maratha privateer Kanhoji Angria were all of traditional design and were equipped with long-range guns. With these he could batter his opponent's ships while remaining beyond the range of their guns.[35] The men-of-war belonging to the sultan of Muscat had a formidable reputation in the Arabian Sea. In 1695 an Omani fleet of sixteen sail was sighted in Indian waters. The Muscat Arabs had begun to fit out large warships during these years, no doubt to provide an effective force against the European privateers who descended on the Arabian Sea from the West Indies in the 1690s. The French ship *Legier*, of forty guns, ran into two Muscateers, of sixty and eighty guns respectively, off Goa and was promptly engaged. The action and cannonade continued until nightfall, and under cover of darkness the *Legier* managed to get away. She arrived in Goa in a shattered condition; her captain had been killed.[36] We have no information as to how the Omani ships were rigged. There is no reason to think that they had other than the familiar lateen sails. It would appear from the numerous contemporary accounts of sea fights between organised Indian naval units and Western ships that the latter indeed possessed an edge over the Asian ships in discharging their broadsides accurately. At the same time the fighting ships manned by the Sanganians of northern Gujarat and the various Malabar chiefs were universally feared by all merchant ships, whether these were Asian or European. For the Portuguese, to fall into the hands of Malabar privateers was to invite certain death; the Sanganian sailors, according to Alexander Hamilton, never surrendered and fought to the death.[37] From the available evidence one must conclude that if the balance of sea-power was unevenly distributed between the Asian merchants and the Europeans, it was perhaps more the result of different economic, social, and political considerations than of the technology of shipping. For when Asian seamen turned predators and had a tangible motive for gaining the day, even a heavily gunned East-Indiaman such as the *Derby* (1735) proved a victim.[38] As we shall see in another chapter, European maritime trade in the Indian Ocean vitalised itself with a very precise political and economic ideology. The heavy armament of its ships and the will to fight followed on from that ideology.

The ship-owners of India and the Middle East of course did not lack either suitable timber, carpenters, artillery men, or arms dealers (mostly European after 1500) to bring their vessels up to the same defence standards as Western shipping. Whether or not they used merchant vessels in the same way as Europeans is another question. As many Portuguese writers recorded in the sixteenth century, the ship-owners of Gujarat began to arm their shipping and carry armed men in order to resist attacks at sea. The fierce naval battles between Portuguese ships and those belonging to the sultans of Acheh also prove that this particular Sumatran kingdom had not lost the traditional Indonesian will to engage in sea fights. Accurate information about the ordnance carried on board Indian ships can be found in later Dutch records. From the end of the seventeenth century, the officials of the VOC kept very extensive registers of local shipping and their cargo at all the major trading ports of India. Some idea of the size of the ships and of their armaments, commercial destinations, owners, and captains can be gathered from these records. As an example, let us take the list of naval passes issued at Surat in the year 1718–19.[39] Out of the thirty-two ships which asked for Dutch passes, twenty-three belonged to the port of Surat; five were from Gogha, two from Broach, one from Cambay, and one from Sind. The largest ship in the list, the *Sulaymani*, was owned by the famous and long-established commercial house of Shaikh Muhammad Fazil. Her burthen was given as 1200 candies or about four hundred tons. She carried twenty-seven guns and was destined for Jedda, Mocha, and Aden under the command of nakhoda Muhammad Umar. Abdul Gafur, the most important ship-owner and merchant of Surat, fitted out six ships in this season. Their tonnage varied from 150 to four hundred and their armament from eighteen to thirty-five guns. The destinations of four ships were in the Red Sea; one was sent to Bengal and one to Malacca and China. Even the smallest ship, the *Isfahan Merchant* of forty candy-burthen, carried eight guns. She was bound for the Malabar coast and Persia. Most of the ship-masters can be identified as Muslims from their names, and the majority of the ships appear to have sailed in the direction of the Bay of Bengal and further east than the Red Sea and the Persian Gulf.

The Dutch pass-lists, like all pre-modern shipping and customs records, have limitations as historical records.[40] The movements of ships at sea were uncertain and governed by volatile commercial conditions. The ports mentioned in the Dutch pass-lists were only the approximate destinations of the ships, which would almost certainly have called at other intermediate ports in the course of their voyages. Many ship-owners, particularly of the small coastal vessels, never troubled to take out European passes. However, sometimes even an imperfect and tantalising glimpse of the past is better than a complete blank. The overall impression conveyed by this particular type of Dutch source and other European records, Portuguese, English, French, and Danish, is that of a flourishing shipbuilding industry and merchant fleet in all parts of the Indian Ocean. In the early eighteenth century, the number of junks calling at Canton was no less than 5000, if we are to believe Alexander Hamilton. The figure may not have been entirely exaggerated.[41] We know that there was a constant interchange of ideas between European ship-owners and shipwrights and local shipbuilders. Thomas Bowrey thought that the master carpenters of the Krishna–Godavari delta on the Coromandel coast could construct and launch ships as well as any shipwright. They knew and discussed the technical reasons behind the nautical designs, and many of them had learned the technique of European construction from English craftsmen.[42] Hamilton relates how, in 1703, the ruler of Badagara, the small northern Malabar kingdom, came aboard his large and well-armed ship and spent three hours inspecting it minutely. The "valunnavar", as the raja was called in the local language, found Hamilton's company congenial, and he informed the Scottish captain that he would build a ship of the same dimension, though his rivers lacked sufficient depth of water to launch a vessel of that size. Hamilton came back to the area in 1707 and learned that the ship had just been finished. When he offered to buy it, the ruler replied that he would be glad to sell it to Hamilton. But first he must make at least one commercial voyage in the ship, as religious tradition forbade the sale of a new ship until the new owner had done this.[43] In the later period of our study, European country-traders made little technical distinction between ships built in the West and those built in the countries of the Indian Ocean. If anything, they seem to have preferred the local ships, as the standard of finish and the general workmanship remained high.[44]

8

The land and its relationship with long-distance trade

The relationship between land and sea in human civilisation all through history has been determined at several levels. First of all, there is the geographical factor, largely though not entirely beyond the control of man. Technological knowledge and constraints, closely interwoven with social and cultural habits, constitute the second dimension. Lastly, the random elements of time, wars, famines, and the rise and fall of political empires, added their own imprints on the varying fortunes of ports, cities, merchant communities, and all those who stood to gain from long-distance maritime trade. How far the Indian Ocean made its influence felt in the vast sweep of land in the north and the south west, in the direction of Asia and Africa, is a fascinating question. The sea, of course, as Fernand Braudel has pointed out in another context, is not responsible for the sky that looks down on it.[1] The global climate controlling the rhythm of seasons and the boundaries between aridity and dense vegetation was an autonomous phenomenon that played a vital part in forging the links between the Indian Ocean and the lands around it. Even in areas far beyond the immediate reach of the sea, as in the great chain of towns and cities that held together the Central Asian caravan trade, the pull of the maritime civilisations remained strong. The repeated migrations of nomads from the steppe towards China, the Middle East, and India are difficult to explain in terms of single or direct causation. The religious and cultural influence exercised by Buddhism and Islam in Central Asia and the periodic political expansion of imperial China in that direction obviously alerted the steppe people to the possibilities that lay beyond their pastures.

A map of the Indian Ocean shows that, while the two monsoon systems imposed a uniform sequence of maritime and even economic activity throughout Asia, the geographical contours were highly diverse. Very far back in time continental drift (plate tectonics) probably determined the strange coastal shape of the Arabian peninsula, southern India, and South East Asia. Volcanic activities on the other hand were responsible for the only large group of islands in the Indian Ocean, the Indonesian archipelago. China and the eastern seaboard of Africa had relatively unbroken lines of coast-land, which certainly contributed to easier navigation and the growth of port-towns. It may be interesting to speculate to what extent this fact explains the absence of indigenous African population in the trans-regional trade of the Indian Ocean

and the reluctance of Chinese navigators to sail beyond the straits of Sunda
and Malacca. Their own coastal waters and places of trade may have provided
the African and Chinese ship-masters with as much economic incentive as they
needed. What is certain is that the navigational knowledge and the skills of the
Arab and Indian sailors were born out of the conditions inherent in the
environment they were accustomed to sailing nearer home. For the Arab or
Iranian navigators, to sail out of the narrow confines of the two inland seas
into the wider Indian Ocean probably called for the same level of seamanship
and commercial motivation as a direct voyage to India or East Africa. Equally,
the captain of a Gujarati or Malabar ship who wished to go round Cape
Comorin and sail to the ports of Coromandel and Bengal needed a training in
practical or theoretical navigation that would have been sufficient for trans-
regional trips. It is apparent from the historical records going back to the times
of the Cairo Genizah records (tenth- to eleventh-century) that a strictly coastal
trader in the Indian Ocean was in a different category of specialisation from
one who engaged in trans-oceanic trade. But the ships on which the latter
sailed from, let us say, the ports of Malabar to Aden or Suez would have
carried cargo to any destination considered profitable, whether this involved a
short or a long voyage.

The location of sea-ports in the Indian Ocean, as in any other part of the
world, was the result of an interaction between geographical features, historical developments, and economic considerations. The relative weight of
each element varied, of course, through time, and a port that had established
itself as a busy and profitable centre of trade remained in use longer than was
justified by geographical advantages. The two well-known examples in our
period are the Indian ports of Cambay and Surat. Long after continual silting
of the navigational channels had closed direct access to the waterfronts of the
two cities, they continued to be the chief emporia for a most varied group of
merchants. The deep-sea vessels were berthed ten to twenty miles away, and
the cargo was brought to the city warehouses in shallow-draught lighters. The
risk and inconvenience involved in the transhipment of goods were considerable but were discounted in view of the commercial advantages of Cambay
and Surat. The example of these two cities and their historical experience illus-
trates another striking point about pre-modern sea-ports. Most of these were
located at or near the mouths of rivers, often at some distance from the open
sea. The reason for this preference on the part of ship-masters and merchants
is not difficult to explain. Ports with natural deep-water harbours were not
often found in the coast-land of Asia, and in the Red Sea the approach to those
that existed was obstructed by coral reefs. The estuarial waters of a large river
provided some shelter from the force of the elements, wind and waves. The
inland ports could also be better defended against pirates and hostile warships,
either with chains stretched across the river or, after the invention of gun-
powder, with guns mounted on shore-batteries. In some cases, the rivers also

acted as highways for the transport of heavy goods produced in areas far from the port of shipment. But these towns and cities always paid a price. Navigation in the estuaries of silt-carrying rivers was most hazardous, and eventually the sea became so far away in such places that a port-city which once had a relatively unobstructed passage was no longer safe or economically viable.

There were nevertheless ports in the Indian Ocean which possessed open sea-fronts. The marvellous situation of Aden of course invited comments from all contemporary geographers. Muscat was another port with direct access to the sea, and its navy could command both trade and passage through the Gulf of Oman into the strait of Hormuz. We can do no better than to turn to Alexander Hamilton's description to see what the place looked like at the turn of the seventeenth century:

> The City of *Muskat* is very strong, both by Nature and Art; but the Buildings very mean, as most Fabricks are under the Oeconomy of a People who abominate Luxury and Pride, as the *Muskat Arabs* do. The Cathedral built by the *Portugueze*, still retains some Marks of its ancient Grandeur, and is now converted into a Palace for the King, when he resides there, which is generally a Month or two yearly. The Wall of the Town that faces the Harbour, has a Battery of large Cannon, about 60 in Number, and there are 8 or 10 small Forts built on the adjacent Rocks or Mountains, which guard all the Avenues to the Town, both by Sea and Land; and there are none permitted to come in or go out of the Harbour between Sun-set and Rising.[2]

The geographical location of Muscat was not its only point of merit. Hamilton, inveterate gossip that he was, comments on the fair administration of the city's Arab governors. On one occasion when the commander of a country-ship from India failed to get paid for his freight by a local Arab merchant, he went to the governor in an angry mood to complain. He was asked to come back later, when justice was promptly done to him, and the governor explained that the delay was deliberate in order to give the captain time to get rid of his anger. If this was just one instance of the complex interplay between social factors and physical determining a merchant's decision to call at a particular port of the Indian Ocean, it is not hard to imagine that a similar logic would have been applied to all the others. The changing fortunes of Calicut from the fourteenth century to the eighteenth are another example. Calicut had a palm-fringed sea-front, typical of so many ports of the Malabar coast. Its harbour was deep enough to cause no trouble either to the traditional Asian shipping or to the deeper-draughted Portuguese carreiras in the sixteenth century. But in 1772 the English traveller James Forbes claimed to have seen, during low tides, waves breaking over the tops of sunken temples and mosques, thus echoing the local legend that the ancient city where Vasco da Gama had made his first landfall in India had been swallowed up by the sea.[3] The Calicut road, apparently, was no longer entirely safe. The town experienced over this period political and commercial changes that were no less dramatic. The small kingdom and its capital had grown to prosperity and fame with the revival of trans-continental trade through the Red Sea after the decline of the Abbasid empire, and was well administered by the dynasty of Samudri Rajas, the Sea Kings, whose title reflected Calicut's dependence on the sea. The arrival of the Portuguese and their anti-Islamic policy, as we have already seen, destroyed the city's free trade and made the position of the Muslim merchants difficult. Its own Malabari population continued to be bred up as merchants, and those ships which were prepared to run the gauntlet of Portuguese armadas could still trade at Calicut. Economic prosperity, however, decidedly moved away to Goa and the neighbouring Cochin.[4]

The problem encountered by Calicut when faced with the weight of Portuguese sea-power was a common one in the Indian Ocean. Very few ports were prepared to lay out money to construct sea defences against hostile forces. The strict vigilance exercised by the rulers of Muscat and by the officers of imperial China over foreign shipping was an exception. The relative scarcity of natural harbours in any case made it difficult to build proper sea defences, and Asian shipping, so often forced to use open roadsteads, remained vulnerable to bad weather and enemy attacks. The estuarial ports were not in danger to the same extent, but their access to the sea could easily be cut off by a naval blockade. To historians the question why the political elites of the Indian Ocean refused to become serious naval powers must remain a perennial mystery. However, in the last analysis no one – not even the Portuguese – was prepared to strangle the uninterrupted flow of maritime trade which was such an obvious source of civic wealth. The exact location and the history of port-towns in Asia continued to be a function of mainly economic considerations. Here again there are puzzling questions to which no definite answer can be given. While the general pattern of emporia trading in the Indian Ocean may explain why Canton, Malacca, Calicut, Cambay, Aden, and Hormuz enjoyed positions as central-places, it is not quite clear why two neighbouring towns sharing the same geographical location and advantages should have a dissimilar history of success. Surat and Rander, for example, were well placed in the sixteenth century to profit from Cambay's commercial decline. The first became the treasure-house of the Mughal empire and the latter did not. Amoy's commercial services in the seventeenth century were considered superior to those of Canton, and yet the Manchus, once their political power had become secure, returned to the old imperial policy of encouraging the foreign trade of Canton and of the province of Kwangtung. In the council chambers of Peking and Delhi, commercial matters may not have figured as largely as political and military ones. But the imperial officials in the coastal provinces of China and India must have known the iron-clad logic that determines the decision of merchants and ship-owners to use a particular port-city. What advice they sent to the court escapes our knowledge.

That transport costs in the case of articles whose value was low in relation

to their bulk were an important consideration in the choice of a port of shipment we know for certain. In 1732 two English supercargoes in charge of the
East India Company's coffee purchases in the Yemen wrote a remarkable
memorandum on the economics of transporting the beans and on the location
of the plantations in relation to the three main ports of the area. The Court of
Directors in London had been urging the agents to try and persuade the
wealthy coffee dealers of the great inland market of Beit al-Fakih to send their
stocks to Mocha. This would have saved the Company the expense of keeping
an office in Beit al-Fakih, which was at a considerable distance from Mocha.
The argument of the supercargoes against the suggestion turned on the fact
that the plantations which brought their products to the markets of Mocha
and Beit al-Fakih were entirely separate and that, as long as the ports of
Hodeida and Lohaya were available to the merchants of the inland town, they
would not incur the extra cost of transporting coffee to the more distant
Mocha.[5] In a competitive market marginal differences in the cost of camel hire
would affect prices and therefore demand. Financial calculations in their turn
fixed the boundaries of supply areas and the centres of marketing.

Perhaps there were also other, non-quantifiable, reasons why a port-city
should become a commercial metropolis. An urban location is more than a
point on a geographical surface. It always mirrors the presence of active,
vigorous, and far-sighted businessmen. Just as the success of a merchant
prince shows his ability to grasp economic opportunities not visible to others,
so the presence of such a man in a town puts it in a position of competitive
advantage in relation to other urban areas. The argument can be elaborated
with actual historical examples taken from our period of study. It certainly
coincides with the view of John Henry Grose, who visited Surat in the middle
of the eighteenth century. Commenting on the rapid rise of Surat during the
quarter of a century following Akbar's conquest of Gujarat (1572), Grose
wrote: "The City on the bank [of the river] is perhaps one of the greatest
instances in the known world, of the power of trade to bring in so little a time
wealth, arts, and population to any spot where it can be brought to settle."[6]
Why, then, do merchants settle in one town or port and not in others? Here we
turn to the random elements of time which interact with the systematic factors.
Accidents of birth, political upheavals, insecurity of food supplies – all these
could have contributed to the population density of a town. When Canton was
made the only port open to foreign merchants in imperial China in the early
eighteenth century, the artisans and traders who had supplied the markets of
Amoy moved away from the place. In the seventeenth century, following the
relative decline of Malacca, the port of Bantam in north west Java witnessed
a substantial influx of Indian and Chinese traders, and the European trading
companies in search of pepper invariably turned in the early years to the markets of Bantam for their purchases. The periodic blockading of the port by the
Dutch affected not only its maritime trade but also the prosperity of the pepper

plantations. After the VOC finally completed the conquest of Bantam in 1682, no foreign merchants were left there to compete with Batavia. The junk-owners of coastal China had long been accustomed to trade at the Dutch colonial metropolis, in spite of the VOC's earlier depredations against Chinese shipping. The Ch'ing conquest of Taiwan in 1683 greatly stimulated the activities of junk traders, and Batavia's markets began to be well stocked with all the prized exports of China.

The settlement of Chinese merchants, carpenters, building workers, and labouring families was an infallible sign that a maritime town in South East Asia was climbing up the ladder of urban wealth. The process was not without its dangers to the newcomers, as the brutal massacres of the Chinese population in Manila (1603 and 1639–40) and in Batavia (1740) demonstrated. Panic reactions such as these, however, were an exception in the great trading emporia of the Indian Ocean frequented by foreign merchants, and when institutionalised violence became endemic the city in question suffered immediate and catastrophic demographic decline. In Gujarat, Ahmedabad was renowned for its architectural splendours and fine industries. In the 1720s military campaigns in the area, conducted by the Marathas and disaffected Mughal officers, led to repeated assaults against the city. Many cotton and silk weavers and rich traders left the place in search of better conditions elsewhere, and Surat, which had previously had little weaving industry of its own, benefitted at the expense of Ahmedabad. In 1725, when its leading merchant, the "Father of the City" Nagarseth Khulsalchandji, made an agreement with the besieging Maratha army and thereby saved the town from plunder, the grateful citizens settled a perpetual income on the Nagarseth's family in recognition of his political skill.[7] That the policy of the ruling elites was a vital element in the economic development of a port-town needs little emphasis. But it is also true that the violence and insecurity engendered by a predominantly warrior society in all parts of the Indian Ocean were contained and localised, so that the function of a town ruined by warfare could be taken over by another. There were of course exceptions. The decline of Kilwa's trade after the Portuguese arrival is a case in point. Commercial activity all along the East African coast appears to have suffered diminution as a result of Portuguese naval policy.

The coastal areas and the port-towns were naturally the meeting-ground between the Indian Ocean and those who directly or indirectly lived off the sea. But the bond between land and sea did not end there. It is certain that the maritime trade of Asia could not have been sustained for any length of time without the presence of inland urban centres and a productive agriculture capable of producing a food surplus and industrial raw materials. The caravan trade was the most spectacular symbol of this indivisible bond, though the humbler river boats and crafts played a role no less important. Both the Euphrates and the Tigris in Mesopotamia were used to transport trade goods,

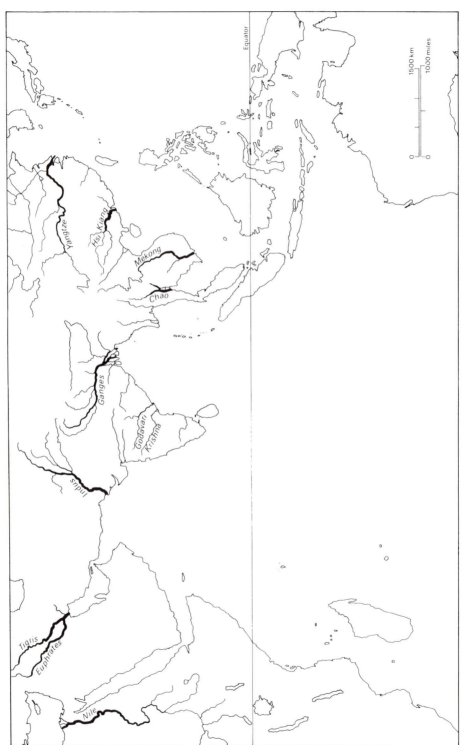

Map 15. Main river systems used by long-distance traders.

though the first was more navigable than the second. The freight traffic mainly consisted of dates, silver coins imported from the Mediterranean, and the luxury goods of Europe. The Indian ships waiting at Basra for their return cargo could not leave the Shatt al-Arab until the boats came down from Baghdad. The Indus and the Ganges were the two main rivers of India to carry a substantial volume of goods destined for the Indian Ocean. Navigation of the Indian rivers presented no particular hazards to the boats, but it was highly seasonal. During the dry months of the year, coinciding with the onset of cold weather and frosts in the Himalayan glaciers which fed the perennial rivers, the water level fell so low that neither the Indus nor the Ganges was accessible, throughout its full length. As the rains came with the south west monsoon, from June onwards, the rivers rose and became much more navigable. Huge, flat-bottomed boats were used to carry all sorts of heavy goods, and in Bengal the inland waterways provided the main means of commercial transportation. There were other great rivers in India, South East Asia, and China which had a comparable role: the Godavari and Krishna, the Mekong in Indo-China, the Yangtze in China. Indeed, the premier commercial city of ancient China, Hangchow, may have owed its economic pre-eminence to the Yangtze, one of the longest rivers in Asia. The wealth of the rice-growing areas in the Yangtze delta is well recorded in Chinese histories. The river made it possible to transport economic products and stimulated trade.

The management of river boats was always a very specialised affair, and travelling on the rivers, though entirely natural to the delta people, was not popular with those who were not born to it. The caravan trade was another matter. The arterial roads of Asia, traversing the frontiers of powerful empires and awesome landscapes, conveyed both men and goods. It is difficult to say what proportion of goods entering the flow of inter-regional exchange was carried by road in relation to those travelling by inland waterways. That the latter mode of transport was more economic, efficient, and trouble-free is certain. But not all populated areas of Asia were fortunate enough to have a network of water transport, and for these regions roads and beasts of burden remained the only way of reaching out to the outer world. Over centuries and even millennia the caravan trade had become highly organised. Many port-towns of the Indian Ocean lived a life of organic dependence on the uninterrupted traffic of the caravan routes. For ports close to the Gulf of Suez, it was a necessity without which the commercial links between the Indian Ocean and the Mediterranean would have collapsed. The caravan routes through upper Mesopotamia and Syria provided a passage no less vital to the trade of the northern Levant and the Persian Gulf. Perhaps the most spectacular examples of the symbiosis between sea-ports and road travel were the Iranian commercial emporia which successively supplanted one another: Siraf, Kish, Hormuz, and Gombroon (Bandar Abbas). These were the terminal points of a caravan journey that often began on the edge of the Gobi desert and continued through

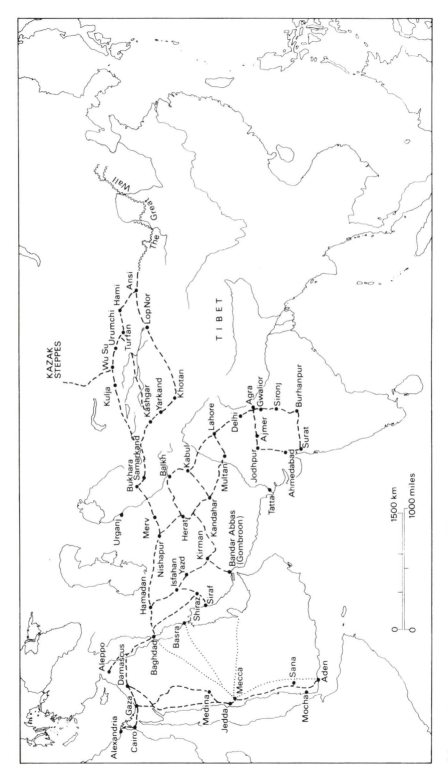

Map 16. Main caravan routes in Asia, 618–1750.

the famous oasis towns of Central Asia and the Iranian highland. Many medieval travellers, apart from Marco Polo and Ibn Battuta, have left detailed descriptions of such journeys. From the pen of an English merchant (1753) we have direct evidence of Gombroon's commercial connection with Central Asia. Dealers who bought English broadcloth from the East India Company's factory in Gombroon came not only from the desert towns of Kirman and Yazd but also from as far away as Mashhad and Urganj near the Aral Sea.[8] In India, Cambay and Surat both depended on the caravan trade to keep their markets supplied with the commodities of upper India. When Maharaja Jaswant Singh of Jodhpur died in 1678 commercial confidence suddenly collapsed in Surat, because it was feared that political disturbances in the kingdom which lay across the caravan route might interrupt the arrival of Agra convoys.[9]

We have seen that the main sea-lanes of the Indian Ocean served as conduits of trans-continental, as well as inter-regional, trade. A similar distinction can be made for the great highway systems of Asia. There were roads along which caravans travelled from one end of Asia to the other, while ports serving shorter, more localised voyages were connected to the hinterland by lesser roads which remained outside the influence of trans-continental caravans. Three celebrated land-routes in our period bridged the three continents of Asia, Africa, and Europe. In the West, several routes connected together the cities of the Muslim Maghreb and established a regular traffic between Egypt, Tunisia, and Morocco. Towns such as al-Mahdiya, Qayrawan, Fez, Marrakesh, and Sijilmasa were as much a part of trans-continental exchange as those of Iraq, Syria, and Egypt, even when the volume of traffic fluctuated according to a given political situation. Alexandria and Fustat were the two main turntables of the North African caravans, which met there the last stage of the Indian Ocean trade. Goods brought to Suez or Qulzum by sea were unloaded and forwarded to Cairo and Alexandria by camel caravans; the markets of these two cities in turn supplied the qafilas setting out for North African destinations. The last stage of the trade between the eastern Mediterranean and the Indian Ocean, whether it flowed through the Persian Gulf or the Red Sea, was conducted by land. And the starting-points of the longest stretches of land-route in Asia originated in Palestine and Syria, at port-towns which had been active since antiquity. The routes all converged on Baghdad, the meeting-place of caravans coming from Iran, India, Central Asia, and China. From Baghdad the caravan traders had a choice of two routes: one short, leading to the sea, and the other long. The first went through the fertile province of Khuzistan to Shiraz, Siraf, Kish, or Hormuz. The second was the main highway which continued in numerous stages to the capital cities of northern India and the Great Wall of China. This was the silk road of ancient times, though it might equally well be called the cotton road, as the fine textiles of the Indian subcontinent were transported to the Middle East in small bales packed on the backs of camels and horses travelling along it.

After leaving Baghdad, caravans going to India or Central Asia first reached Hamadan, an old Iranian town. The second stage was the journey to Nishapur or Mashhad. The road passed to the south of the high Elburz mountains which separated the arid Iranian plateau from the humid cereal-growing lands of the Caspian Sea. At the end of the second stage, the route divided into three branches. One went to Balkh and Kabul and thence to Multan, Lahore, and Delhi in India. The second formed a loop connecting Herat, Kandahar, Ghazni, and Kabul. The third was the trans-Asian route to China. While individual travellers and merchants wishing to go to China overland from the Middle East or Europe had no option but to follow the entire length of the journey, it was more common for trade caravans to terminate their operations at some well-recognised intermediate point of exchange. Bukhara and Samarkand remained all through our period the two main destinations of the caravans coming from Aleppo and Baghdad. Here these would join up with traders who had travelled from Turfan, which lay at the heart of the Central Asian crossroads, and also with those who came from Kashgar, Yarkand, and Khotan.

It is not possible to state with certainty which of the three possible routes were used by caravan traders beyond Samarkand and Kashgar. The most ancient route appears to have passed through the southern edge of the Takla Makan desert, which contained a number of oases, as far as Lop-nor. This was the staging-post for the next stretch of the journey, to the oasis region of Turfan. Marco Polo recorded how caravans rested at the great city of Lop-nor before beginning their desert crossing with camels and donkeys. Crossing the Takla Makan in a south to north direction from Lop-nor meant a journey of more than thirty days. Although water was to be found in small quantities, it was essential to carry all one's food-stocks. If the parties ran out of supplies before the desert ended, there was no alternative but to slaughter the baggage animals, though people preferred to save their valuable camels.[10] The old southern road fell into disuse for reasons that are not properly understood. It may have been due to climatic changes which desiccated the area or to factors associated with political developments. Whatever the real reason, the main passage of caravans in our period probably lay across the southern slopes of the snow-capped T'ien Shan range, which the Chinese called the Heavenly Mountains. While the description "silk road" is a recent European invention, the Chinese themselves described the middle passage as "T'ien Shan Nan Lu", the Road South of the T'ien Shan. From Turfan the road led either to Urumchi over mountain passes or to Hami, and thence across the great Gobi to the frontier towns of the Kansu and Shensi provinces of China. The Gobi traverse was as fearsome as the Takla Makan. Chinese caravan-masters who organised the annual journeys spoke of the loss of their transport animals as having to

Plate 19. A league-tower or kos-minar, marking the old highway from Delhi to Agra in northern India.

throw away so many camels on the "business of the Gobi".[11] It was recognised that a highly valuable trade such as the carriage of heavy jade stones might lead to the sacrifice of many camels in the desert. No caravan-master and his crew of camel-pullers looked upon the prospect of losing their camels with equanimity. For without the endurance and strength of the two-humped camels the Central Asian caravan trade would have come to a complete stop.

The presence of desert and high mountains made the two routes through the Takla Makan and the southern T'ien Shan hazardous and called for careful planning. At the same time the natural obstacles partially protected the caravans from attacks by the nomadic steppe people. There was yet a third road, which was particularly susceptible to political disturbances. It ran to the north of the Heavenly Mountains from Urumchi to Wusu, where one branch led through gaps in the Jungaria trough to the Kazak steppes and the other went on to Kulja and the Ili valley. When the steppes were quiet or under the authority of strong rulers, it was possible for the trade caravans to leave Samarkand and the valley of Zarafshan to follow the northern road to China. At Turfan, Urumchi, and other oasis-towns of Central Asia, the world of China met the world of Islam, the people of "Great Religion" having little real objection to making profits in trade with those of "Little Religion", as the Chinese liked to call the Muslims. From the tenth century onwards Islam had been gradually moving eastwards across the steppes and the valleys of the T'ien Shan, to become a dominant political as well as social force by the time the Ming rulers came to power in China (1368). There were indeed many Chinese commercial houses in the northern provinces which were engaged in the caravan trade of the Gobi and which belonged to families converted to Islam. Their social status was lower than that of the Confucian Chinese, but no political obstacles were put in the way of their business dealings by the imperial bureaucracy.

It may well be asked what relevance there was for the Indian Ocean in the caravan trade of Transoxiana and the Gobi. We have already looked at the link between the ports of shipment and the great trunk-roads of the Middle East and India. The trade of Central Asia had no such direct connections with the sea, and yet the whole region itself exercised a vital influence on the lives of people closer to the monsoon belts of the Indian Ocean. In terms of direct relationships, the Central Asian caravan trade was complementary to the trans-continental maritime commerce of Eurasia. The price of Chinese silk, porcelain, and other exotic articles brought by sea to the markets of Baghdad, Cairo, and Constantinople would fluctuate according to the quantities expected by the overland caravans. The rhythm of trade and its volume were themselves functions of the two separate conduits. When the overland route was obstructed or made politically unsafe, the seaborne trade gained at its expense. The real key to the economic success of the Central Asian caravan trade lay in diplomatic and military relations between the Chinese empire and the leaders of the Mongol and Turkish nomads who controlled the critical points of the vast route. It should not be forgotten either that the history of the Middle East, northern India, and China is punctuated by repeated incursions of steppe people, who settled down permanently among the indigenous urban and agricultural population of those areas. The infusion of Turko-Mongol influence into ancient Chinese and Irano-Semitic civilisations renewed period- ically distant ties with Central Asia. If the first Mughal emperor, Babur, remained homesick to the end of his life for the gardens and orchards of his native Ferghana, his descendants in India continued to live in marble palaces that resembled tents rather than houses. The recently arrived Turani soldier- courtier fought for political influence in Delhi with the similarly placed Iranian

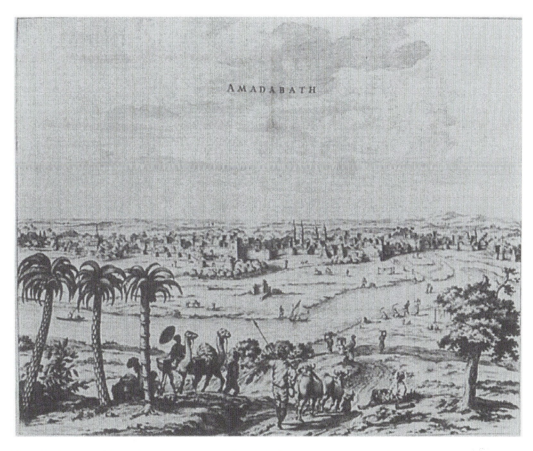

Plate 20. A view of the Indo-Islamic city of Ahmedabad in Gujarat, from Baldaeus, *Naauwkeurige Beschryvinge*, 1672.

nobleman. Mounts for both came largely from the northern pastures. Strong, rugged, dependable horses, whether bred in the Ili valley or in Ferghana, populated the stables of Indian rulers always anxious to keep up the fighting quality of their cavalry. The horse trade alone justified the continued connections with Central Asian caravan routes.

The overland trade followed geographical lines which had been worked out over many centuries, and the relative merits of alternative road-systems were well understood. The trade was also highly organised. A caravan composed of a thousand camels in the Gobi or the T'ien Shan posed many problems, of discipline, work-sequence, forage, and protection. A Chinese caravan-master occupied a position not unlike that of a captain in charge of an Atlantic ship. His experience of the actual routes and of the management of baggage animals and men earned him the appointment, and the authority of the caravan-master made him superior in status to the merchants, often the sons of the commercial house employing him. As long as the caravan was on the march, its master had

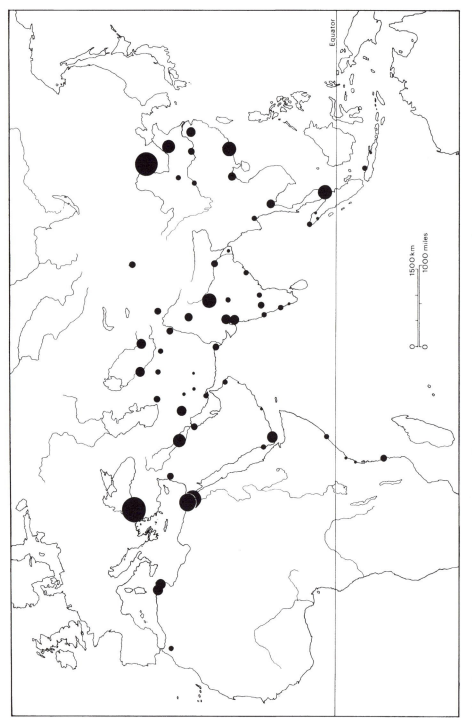

Map 17. The pattern of urbanisation in the Indian Ocean: the primate and secondary cities, 650–1500.

the last word on how the camels were to be loaded and where they were to make camp. Below him there was another hierarchy. The head camel-puller also served as the cook, and after a meal break, when he uttered the words "let us drink tea", all the other camel men took up the cry, this being the agreed signal that it was time for the caravan to be on the move again. This description of the Gobi travel routine comes from the account of the epic journey made by Owen Lattimore in 1926. Without a similar type of discipline the caravans of the earlier centuries could not have traversed such hazardous routes and returned to China with viable profits. The question of protection and war damage remained endemic. When Ibn Battuta arrived in Bukhara (1333), he noticed that all but a few of its mosques, madarasas, and bazaars were lying in ruins. The destruction of Bukhara he ascribed to Tinkiz (Chingiz Khan) the Tartar. The signs of Tartar military advance were visible everywhere, but the area itself had been pacified. This was not the case in North Africa. The pilgrim caravan of which Ibn Battuta was the qadi had set out from Tunis bound for Hijaz with an escort of several hundred horsemen and a detachment of archers; the show of force kept marauders at a distance from the caravan. The journey across the Syrian desert from Damascus to Medina and Mecca was regulated by strict stages and social conventions. The fear of the desert caused the caravans to travel through in forced marches. He who entered the desert, a local proverb said, was a lost man and he who left it was reborn. At the well of al-Hijr, four days' march from Medina, water was available in abundance, but no one drank from it, as the Prophet had forbidden his followers to draw water there. The Christian merchants of Syria were allowed to come as far as the neighbouring oasis of al-'Ulá with its palm trees and water-springs. The passage beyond was open only to true believers.[12]

The social conventions prevalent among the members of a large caravan reflected partly their functional needs and partly the force of historical tradition. Merchants belonging to different religions, as in the case of Syrian Christians, could trade with Muslims and supply the pilgrims with provisions and other goods, provided they did not violate the exclusive enclaves of Islam. India was another country where such accommodating principles saved merchants from continual political harassment, though the cost of protection remained high. The presence of an international community of traders, merchants, and bankers at an Asian city was an indication not only of its advantageous location but also of the quality of its political administration. The caravan trade in particular was wholly dependent on the existence of urban centres, providing a mirror image of the co-ordinates that bound together port-towns and sea-lanes. The exact nature and character of commercial cities on the coasts of the Indian Ocean and the caravan routes in the premodern age still await detailed historical study. However, some general features can be outlined without too many qualifications. In examining the typology and the internal morphology of the Asian town, it is useful to recall the triple distinction drawn by Fernand Braudel in his history of the Mediterranean. The historical evolution of early Western towns, Braudel argues, contains three stages. First of all, there are towns that are scarcely distinguishable from the surrounding countryside except for their population density. Then there are places walled in and living a separate life of their own, owing little to their immediate hinterland. Finally, the primate cities occupy a unique position of national influence, just as they are in turn completely subject to the political will of the prince or the senators.[13] In this analysis Braudel is looking out on the world through the eyes of the townsmen. When the viewpoint is changed, he is able to point out, all economic systems operating on the principle of the division of labour recognise a centre, some focal point that acts as a leading mechanism to other places. In the Mediterranean of the fifteenth and sixteenth centuries that centre was a narrow urban quadrilateral comprising Venice, Milan, Genoa, and Florence.[14]

Was there such a "world economy" in the areas we are concerned with? It is certainly plausible to say that the whole of the Indian Ocean and the eastern Mediterranean was held together by the urban gravitation of Malacca, Calicut, Cambay, Aden, Cairo, Alexandria, and Venice. The arterial flow of goods and men on the east–west axis is inconceivable without the history of these trading cities. The functional role of caravan cities – Aleppo, Baghdad, Samarkand, Turfan – was not very dissimilar. Examples of Braudel's other two types of town are easily found. Anyone who has seen Yazd, standing at the crossroads of Afghanistan and Central Asia, is aware of the sudden transition from the sands of a true desert to a thriving, prosperous, and industrious urban centre. It is true that Yazd drew some of its food supplies from nearby plantations irrigated by water brought from the mountains in underground channels (qanats) which also supplied the town. But Yazd was a solitary urban location in a landscape empty of human population, though sheep incredibly still found grazing in the desert. A journey through the countryside of Gujarat would bring the traveller to towns that were fully walled and with sumptuous houses built by wealthy citizens, merchants, land-owners, and officials. There were also numerous semi-urban places with perhaps no more than a dozen brick-built houses surrounded by mud-and-straw huts, and intersected by a single street which also served as a market.

Throughout our period the geographical outlines of the urbanising process stand out with great force. Towns and cities have existed in Asia longer than recorded history. They dominated the economic, social, and political life of the area extending westwards from the plains of India to the Mediterranean shores of Africa and Muslim Spain. The numerical strength of urban centres was matched by advanced development in architecture and social amenities. Two possible explanations can be put forward for the urban vitality of Islamic civilisations. Arab, Turkish, and Mongol conquerors successively settled in lands which had enjoyed a high degree of urbanisation from antiquity. The military and political organisation of Islamic empires also called for a rapid transition from the nomadic camp to the garrison town. The peasants carried on their backs the financial burden of the empire and its culture, while townsmen dominated both. In time Islam came to look on towns as the true repositories of the faith. The whole historical development bred the twin religious and political paradoxes of Muslim urbanisation. The tradition of jurisprudence made no distinction between one member of the faith and another, between different classes or communities. Therefore the citizens of towns enjoyed no special political privileges. Unlike the medieval experience of Christian Europe, there was no historical necessity in Islam to treat the towns as politically autonomous and separate from the countryside. At the same time, the presence of religious leaders and the ruling elite in towns ensured that these acted as nodal points through which a conquering religion and people could assert their power. The enormous influence exercised on the Muslim sense of self-identification by cities such as Baghdad, Damascus, Cairo, Qayrawan, Seville and Córdoba had its origin in a living and continuous tradition of treating urbanisation as a unique symbol of imperial aspirations and artistic expression. Whether it was al-Muqaddasi in the tenth century or Ibn Battuta in the fourteenth, as he travelled from one city to another throughout the Bilad al-Islam the qualities that recommended a place were first the purity of its religion, followed by the visual attractions of monuments, buildings, squares, and public gardens. Ibn Battuta tells us the remarkable story of the ruin and depopulation of Delhi, which the schizophrenic sultan, Muhammad Tughluq, caused by ordering all the inhabitants to remove to his own new capital of Daulatabad in the far-distant Deccan. The city was built as much to glorify the imperial status of the sultan of Delhi as to strengthen his military plans in the south. Daulatabad was a fine town with spacious bazaars and wealthy merchants. But the transplantation of population was effected by means of exemplary acts of cruelty.[15]

As we turn in the direction of China, a different world of urban construction opens up, a world that owed few ideas to either the Islamic, the Hindu, or the European city. In China, walled settlements containing the ruling lineage families had appeared during the Shang period, most of these being in the north–central areas. With the imperial unification of China under the Han dynasty, Chang-an in the Shensi province became the first of several capital cities of the ancient empire to record a long history of successful commercial and administrative occupation. By the time the Sung dynasty came to power, the urbanisation of China had gathered full momentum in both the north and the south. The four primate cities, Chang-an, Lo-yang, K'ai-feng, and Hangchow, were supplemented by at least 170 other smaller urban centres throughout the empire. The Ming emperor, Yung-lo, moved the capital from Nanking to Peking in 1421, and the urban splendours of the new imperial capital fully reflected the power and refinement of Chinese civilisation under

Plate 21. An encampment scene from Babar-Nama, 1598, showing the feeding and tending of horses, camels, and mules around the tents.

Plate 22. A Chinese walled-town.

the Ming and Ch'ing rulers. A comparison between the Chinese towns and Islamic or Indian ones presents several significant functional similarities, as well as contrasts in morphology. The twin urban function of administration and commercial service was basic to all towns and cities in Asia, as it was also in Europe. In China, however, there was a much greater awareness of the urban–rural contrast and the distinct role played by cities in the political administration of a country. The Chinese word for the city (Ch'eng) was the same as that for walls, and the walled city satisfied the imperial bureaucracy's passion for order and regularity. Town-planning based on the grid pattern and the square shape was much more common in China than it was in the Middle East or India. Cosmological ideas and the four cardinal points of the compass obviously influenced the design of Chinese planned towns and of the residences of emperors. But there was also another type, the unplanned city which had grown in size and status from a small market town drawing its economic sustenance from trade and industrial handicrafts. When these unplanned but economically important towns came under the control of strong rulers, they attempted to impose a planned structure upon them; a mixed typology was a common feature of the Chinese urban environment.

The morphology of the planned city in China presented a complete contrast to that of the congested, circular Indo-Islamic towns with their multi-storied buildings. In southern Arabia and the land adjacent to the Red Sea, urban buildings almost resembled sky-scrapers and towers. In a Chinese town, the

179

buildings were mostly single-storey, and the prosperous houses were surrounded by landscaped gardens. The principle of constructing houses on an extensive scale was facilitated by the choice of a site close to water transport, which eased the problem of movement within the towns. Canals running at right-angles to one another supplemented a similar network of streets and public squares. The city-gates were complemented by water-gates. Their opening and closing at prescribed times in the morning and evening regulated the flow of daily activity and also served a political purpose. Potential troublemakers whether they were within the walls or in the rural areas outside could be kept isolated and under control. For a detailed description of Hangchow in its great days under the Yüan dynasty, we cannot do better than turn to Marco Polo who saw it through the eyes of a Venetian:

the city of Quinsai is so large that in circuit it is in the common belief a hundred miles round or thereabout . . . there are squares where they hold market, which on account of the vast multitudes which meet in them are necessarily very large and spacious . . . And the streets and canals are wide and great so that boats are able to travel there conveniently and carts to carry the things necessary for the inhabitants . . . And let no one be surprised if there are so many bridges, because I tell you that this town is all situated in water of lagoons as Venese is, and is also all surrounded by water, and so it is needful that there may be [*sic*] so many bridges for this, that people may be able to go through all the town both inside and out by land.[16]

Marco Polo's account of Hangchow runs to many more pages, and it is clear that, even to a Venetian, the city appeared well planned and richly built.

The Indo-Islamic towns and those of China represented two separate civilisations. In between there was yet another form found in South East Asia that bridged the different urban traditions of the western and eastern Indian Ocean. An Islamic town was typically identified in our period by the presence of the Friday mosque and the square surrounding it. Covered bazaars and shops, formal public gardens, and an inner citadel–palace invariably accompanied the place of worship. The buildings were mainly rectangular with flat roofs and constructed in stone or brick, though the poorer housing was made of clay mixed with straw. In South East Asia stone was used only in areas where it was easily available, and the remains of vast palaces in Java and Cambodia reflecting Hindu architectural and artistic traditions demonstrate that the technique of construction in stone was neither new nor a challenge to the people of the area. But the most common form of house building was in wood or bamboo. Solid teak, supplied from the magnificent forests of upper Burma and Siam, provided a splendid and durable building material. When polished or gilded the timber presented a most agreeable visual appearance. Buildings standing on wooden pillars, with steeply arched roofs made of bamboo mats or more permanently of baked tiles, indicated to the sailors of the Indian Ocean as they approached the towns upstream on a river that they had arrived in an environment where the distinction between land and water was imperfectly drawn. Houses built on stilts or wooden platforms provided a measure of security against flooding and wild animals. But few towns in South East Asia composed of such houses could rival the aspects of an Indo-Islamic city. In parts of Java, Sumatra, and Malaya, where the population had accepted Islam, the mosque made its appearance. There were many mosques in Acheh, whose citizens were devout Muslims and regularly sailed to the Red Sea. In size and in the scale of commercial activity the place came to occupy in the seventeenth century the leading position among ports not under the control of Western trading companies. "This City is the fairest and most populous of any that ever I saw or heard of that is inhabited by Malayars or Javas", wrote Captain Bowrey (*c.* 1669), with the qualification, "but indeed it cometh far short for decency and buildings and uniformitie of the meanest City in Arabia, Persia, or the maine land of India; but the good soile, wholesome air, and plenty of gold doth add very much to the goodness of the place."[17]

The port or caravan town in Asia was the valve that regulated the flow of trans-regional trade in Eurasia. It supplied commercial services in all forms: brokers able to enter into contracts guaranteeing deliveries of trade goods at a future date, markets supplying them on the spot, and bankers who smoothed out payments through the mechanism of credit and bills of exchange. Local mints, dockyards, and shipping – and, in the case of caravan towns, transport animals and their forage and stabling – all these essential components of the overall machinery were brought together in the urban centres. The last and final condition of economic success, however, remained the quality of political life, at once the most difficult to achieve within a consensus and liable to deteriorate with time.

9

Commodities and markets

Pre-modern trade had many distinctive characteristics. The commodities exchanged between one region and another cannot be classified neatly into categories familiar to historians of the international economy in the age of the Industrial Revolution. The mixture of goods was much more random than was the case later. The result of the application of machinery to the production system was to create among other things an unceasing demand for raw materials and an equally compelling search for overseas markets able to absorb industrial manufactures. Large areas of the world, whole continents even, went over in the nineteenth century to the production of cereal grains, commercial crops, and minerals which were exported to the industrialised countries of the West and paid for by the import of finished consumer goods. The long-distance trade of the Indian Ocean before 1850 or 1800 obeyed a different logic. The demand for raw materials, or the transport of grains and foodstuffs, was common enough. Some of the coastal and inland areas of the Middle East, India, and China also specialised in the manufacture of industrial products. But the composition of trade between, let us say, India and China was not mainly determined by the nature of that specialisation. The factors which dominated the movement of goods in Asia's seaborne and caravan trade are not difficult to identify. The most important consideration was the ability of a local economy to create a surplus over and above the subsistence demand and to maintain this level of productivity over a sufficiently long period of time. Throughout the length and breadth of Asia there were surplus and deficit areas. The density of population, the incidence of rainfall, the fertility of land, and the level of technology continuously interacted among themselves as forces marking out rich communities from the less fortunate. The passage of time was punctuated by a large variance as well. The devastations caused by wars and droughts dried up supplies of commercial goods and destroyed the livelihoods of both artisans and farmers. Prosperous urban centres and rural industries, which existed in mutual economic interdependence through the intermediary of merchants and traders, suffered in equal measure from such calamities.

The contrast between good times and bad and its inevitable effect on trade can be seen from the following two eye-witness accounts, separated by nearly four centuries. The caravan cities of Central Asia were especially vulnerable to military encounters between their political rulers and the nomads of the steppe. When Ibn Battuta visited the capital city of Khwarizm (Kunya Urgench) on the upper reaches of the river Oxus, it was still densely populated and frequented by merchants from China and India. Other more famous towns of Transoxiana were not so fortunate. "The city of Bukhara . . . ", Ibn Battuta wrote, "was formerly the capital of the lands beyond the Oxus. It was destroyed by the accursed Tinkiz [Chingiz] the Tartar, the ancestor of the kings of Iraq, and all but a few of its mosques, academies, and bazaars are now lying in ruins."[1] Balkh was an utterly ruined town and uninhabited, as was also Merv. Once an urban centre decayed beyond a certain point it was impossible to revive its fortunes, as merchants and artisans tended to move away permanently to other places. The effects of famines and harvest failures on urban and rural industries were less long-lasting, though the short-term consequences were very serious. In the 1730s all the textile-weaving districts of southern India actively engaged in the export trade to South East Asia, Europe, and the Middle East suffered a series of catastrophic famines. The English East India Company's chief merchant, Tomby Chitty, prepared a detailed report on the supply situation in 1731:

From Tinvanem Vieravande. We sent four People here to purchase Cloth, they wrote us that by the Famine and Great Price of Cotton thread great part of the Inhabitants were dead and many left the place, that those that remain were very poor and not to be trusted with money, they sent our money back . . . [From] Acheravacum and Mudarandarum. There was formerly six hundred weavers here now but two hundred . . . [From] Trecaleecoonam and Cale Collum. We sent our people here with money and orders to advance on every piece of Long cloth . . . they found the Country in a very miserable Condition by the late Famine and not above twenty weavers where formerly was hundred, those that Remain said they could not get thread for Long cloth but they would weave Sallampores . . .[2]

The report listed many other places, all with the same story of disruption to the textile production.

The two accounts describe not isolated events but regular occurrences. Scarcity of thread could be traced back to the failure of the cotton crop, and shortage of grains and food drove away large numbers of spinners and weavers from the famine-stricken areas to those which were relatively better off. Merchants, however, were not able immediately to adjust the existing network of trade. The consequences of over-supply were just as serious for exporters as those of under-supply. The chance arrival of an additional ship at a port with the same type of cargo ruined the market for the vessels which had arrived earlier, and the local merchants continually strove to keep themselves informed of shipping movements. In 1724, after a period of harvest failures in the neighbouring Yemen, fourteen ships arrived at Jedda from Egypt, deeply laden with grain. It was reported in the town that five more were expected and that five vessels had been lost at sea. The exporters of Malabar rice to Mocha were disappointed in their expectations of profit that year, as all kinds of provisions were selling at low prices. The English correspondent at Jedda thought that the arrival of the rains and the successful harvest would "have a good effect on the cloth market" though as yet he had not "found the benefit of it".[3] Pre-modern trade was not altogether a matter of chance; but it was characterised by a high degree of fluctuation from year to year.

A perennial anxiety haunting the merchants at every major port of trade was that a sufficient quantity of bulk goods might not be available to counter-balance a cargo of rich and fine articles. That a sailing-ship would need ballast to stabilise it was known to everyone concerned with seaborne trade. Roughly hewn stones, ingots of iron and other heavy metals, and even water jars and tanks were considered suitable ballast in the Indian Ocean. However, the most efficient use of shipping was to maximise the cargo space and freight revenue by loading bulk goods which had a saleable value. It was also mandatory for all ships sailing to distant ports to reduce insurance risks, and the danger of shipwreck called for an upper ceiling for cargo value. Prudent ship-owners and merchants consigning their goods to overseas agents made sure that the vessels of their choice carried mixed cargoes. Apart from the problems of prices, costs, and the tastes of the consuming markets, the commodity composition of Asian seaborne trade remained subject to considerations arising from shipping and insurance finance. To organise the supply of a suitable bulk cargo was not an easy matter. The traditional ballast commodity in the Middle East for ship-ment to india, Africa, and South East Asia was dates. Baskets of dates provided the standard measurement of shipping space and of the size of the vessel. A perishable agricultural product, dates needed proper harvesting, packing, and transport to the ports of embarkation, and the timing of their arrival had to be carefully co-ordinated with the sensitive sailing dates of ships setting out for specific Indian Ocean destinations. For example, it was not unusual for Indian ships to be kept waiting at Shatt al-Arab already loaded up with silver and gold coins because the river boats from Baghdad had not come down with their cus-tomary loads of dates. There was a limit beyond which it was dangerous to detain the ships because of the onset of the monsoon winds outside the Persian Gulf. In such cases, the Basra ships sailed with non-commercial ballast and whatever bulk goods could be hastily put together. The financial loss to mer-chants caused by an unsuitable cargo was not negligible, and it reflected badly on the reputation of the ship-master and of the agent in charge.

A geographical map showing the pattern of commodity production and exchange in the Indian Ocean would also reveal certain regional imbalances. The Middle East was a large area of consumption which imported from other parts of Asia food products, aromatics, medicinal plants, and manufactured goods. Whether or not the Islamic world suffered a perpetual deficit on its balance of trade is debatable. There is little doubt that its trade with India, the

Indonesian archipelago, and China was balanced by the export of precious metals, gold and silver. The Middle East appears to have enjoyed a financial surplus with the Christian West, Central Asia, and the city–states of eastern Africa. The favourable balances materialised in the form of treasure, and what was not retained at home as a store of wealth flowed out again in eastward directions. It is important to note that the ability of the Arab empire in the early days of the caliphate to absorb imported goods and services (a trend that continued later) rested as much on the exchange of commodities as on the profits of passing trans-continental trade or on the government tax-gathering machinery. Imperial expenditure and the life-style of private Muslim merchant families both found an outlet in the Indian Ocean trade.[4] The position of the Indian subcontinent was very different. Its diversified economy and climatic variations generated a wide spectrum of commercial goods, and the subcontinent remained all through our period the leading exporting nation of Asia. Taken as a whole, the caravan and seaborne trade of India was orientated more towards exports than imports, and the favourable balance was settled in precious metals. Beyond this broad generalisation, it is possible to differentiate between the finer details and the basic characteristics of India's commodity trade. The demand for imported goods from both inland and coastal provinces was for a large number of miscellaneous articles: exotic food products, such as the fresh and dried fruits of the Middle East, spices from Indonesia, aromatics, silk, glass, porcelain, finely wrought metalware, precious stones, and horses. The exports were cotton textiles, foodstuffs, and industrial raw materials (dyes, cotton and silk thread, timber, and raw metals).

The balance between exports and imports must, in the nature of things, have varied from region to region and year to year. Concepts of national income accounts, balance of trade and payments, capital movements, and invisible earnings from shipping and banking services can be applied to the analysis of pre-modern trade, though it is important to remember that in the absence of instant central banking transactions at an international level the mechanism of trade functioned in a way different from that in modern practice. This aspect of pre-industrial exchange will be discussed in the next chapter. For the time being it is sufficient to note that India's trade to the Middle East was dominated by the import of treasure, just as exports to South East Asia were balanced by imports of spices, aromatics, and Chinese goods. In the seventeenth and eighteenth centuries there was even a considerable re-export of silver from the subcontinent in the direction of Java, Sumatra, Malaya, and China. Indian trade to the Philippines during these latter centuries formed part of a larger structure. Large quantities of cotton textiles were exported to Manila and were then sent to Spanish America by way of the galleon trade to Acapulco. The returns to India were made largely in silver. The existence of these bullion flows in separate and often self-contained channels through the main geographical network of maritime trade indicates that there were several

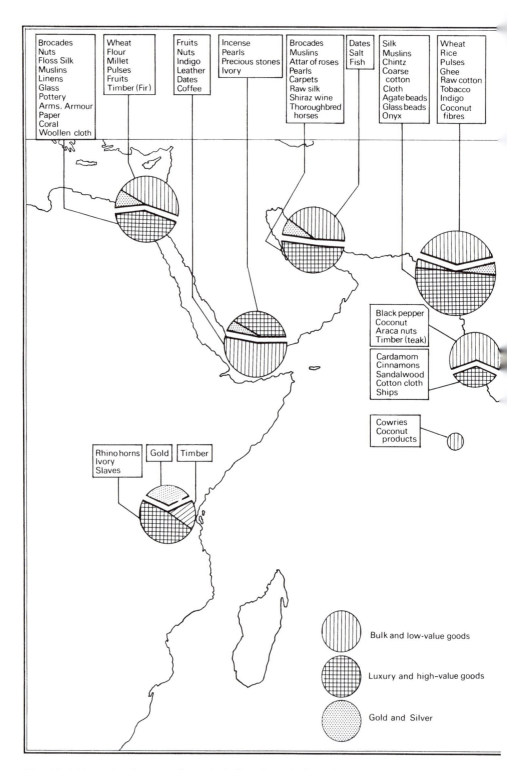

Map 18. Main regional exports from the Indian Ocean before 1750.

186

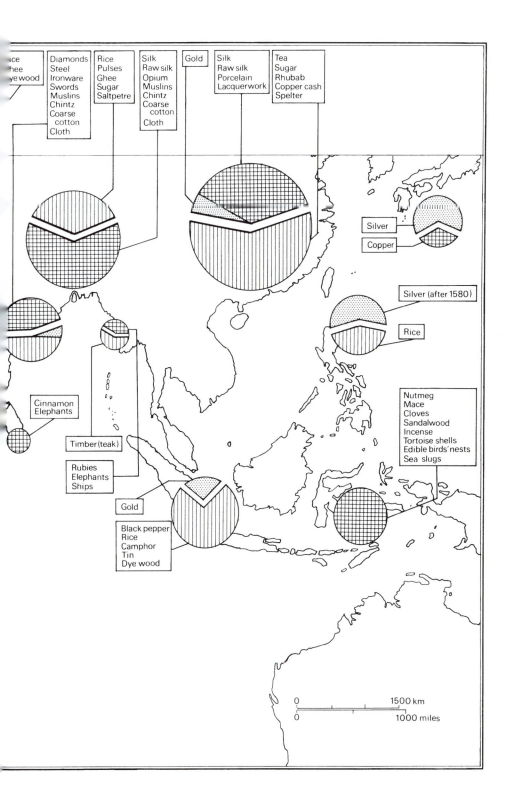

ce
hee
ye wood

Diamonds
Steel
Ironware
Swords
Muslins
Chintz
Coarse
 cotton
Cloth

Rice
Pulses
Ghee
Sugar
Saltpetre

Silk
Raw silk
Opium
Muslins
Chintz
Coarse
 cotton
Cloth

Gold

Silk
Raw silk
Porcelain
Lacquerwork

Tea
Sugar
Rhubab
Copper cash
Spelter

Silver

Copper

Silver (after 1580)

Rice

Nutmeg
Mace
Cloves
Sandalwood
Incense
Tortoise shells
Edible birds' nests
Sea slugs

Cinnamon
Elephants

Timber (teak)

Rubies
Elephants
Ships

Gold

Black pepper
Rice
Camphor
Tin
Dye wood

0   1500 km
0   1000 miles

levels of commercial and financial operations which did not necessarily inter-link. A Spanish embargo against Protestant and Muslim merchants kept the Philippines isolated from the rest of the Asian emporia trade and gave Armenians, Catholics, and even Hindu traders an advantage over other groups. There were also other areas of maritime venture in Asia (Indo-China and Japan) which were handled only by specialist business houses.

While Japan was undoubtedly a Pacific island–empire at the fringe of trans-continental trade, the prosperous Tongking delta was on the regular path of Arab and Indian ships on their way to China. In the earlier centuries (the ninth to the fourteenth) the area was an important source of many commodities which were in demand in more than one Asian country: red lead, silk cloth, gold, and lacquer work. Yet Indo-China never formed an integral part of active emporia trade, an attribute it shared also with trade to Siam. No such qualifications attach to the Indonesian archipelago and China. The monopoly position occupied by the Moluccas in the production of the finer spices, and the quality of the local black pepper, ensured that South East Asian islands would remain high on the list of Asian merchants' ports of call. The spice and pepper trade, in combination with the wet-rice cultivation of the Javanese, created a level of purchasing power throughout the main commercial centres which could be used on the imports of Indian and Chinese consumer goods.

Seaborne trade was an economic necessity for the survival of many island communities and a strong force in the consolidation of political power. In this respect, Chinese experience and policy could not have been in greater contrast. China did not need foreign trade to maintain its standard of living or the pace of its economic life. The massive strength of China's internal economy guaranteed a level of taxes and of income to the imperial exchequer which was an object of wonder to foreign travellers and a source of envy to the warlike people around China's land frontiers. The attitude of successive governments in China towards seaborne trade was conditioned by this sense of financial independence and the huge military resources of the empire. The policy in general was to retain some official initiative in external trade and relations, either by controlling commercial affairs within China or by restricting the freedom of private merchants to organise overseas voyages. Yet, in spite of China's economic self-sufficiency, maritime and overland trade both proved irresistible to the ruling elites and wealthy individuals. The desire for rare articles not obtainable in China was one reason why overseas trade remained open. The use of silver as a measure of value and exchange was another. The precious metal entered China through a well-known network of long-distance trade. The reverse of this was of course the foreign demand for China's luxury products. The presence of non-Chinese merchants in the empire's frontier towns and sea-ports served to remind the mandarins constantly of China's rank among the league of Indian Ocean civilisations. The commodity composition of Chinese foreign trade reflected the reality and the contradictions of the situation. China's exports were historically dominated by two highly valued articles: silk textiles and fine porcelain. To these were added later tea, sugar, copper alloy, zinc, nickel, and occasionally gold. As well as silver, China imported in return gum resins, sandalwood, perfumes from India and the Middle East, tortoise shells, black pepper, and war horses from Central Asia. The actual list of imports was much longer, and the items were carefully recorded by the imperial officials.[5]

For purposes of analysis, it is worth distinguishing between three categories of commodities, each group being identified by the distance over which the goods were transported. In all but the most sparsely populated areas of Asia there was an active local trade between villages and district towns or between one cluster of villages and another, linked perhaps by a weekly market or by travelling pedlars. Agricultural produce, industrial raw materials, textiles, and pottery – all these items of daily consumption formed part of the local exchange economy. A day's journey on foot or by slow-moving carts was the measure of its extent: fifteen to twenty miles in all. Above this level, and a long way removed from it, was the inter-regional trade supplying mostly wholesale merchants and markets. Commodities entering this circuit also satisfied a whole range of demands: the needs of areas deficient in food, particular kinds of industrial goods, luxury items, and specialised products limited by the local climate and geography. The distances between regional markets varied widely, and trade moved by land, rivers, and the sea. The camel caravans which set out from the northern towns of China for the Gobi traverse discharged their cargo at Turfan, Urumchi, or Kulja, and these urban bazaars in turn supplied other northern and western areas of Central Asia. The Gobi traders covered many thousands of miles in the course of their annual return journeys, but it was inter-regional trade all the same. In contrast, the sea voyage between Muscat and the ports of Gujarat was no more than twelve hundred miles and much easier in terms of risks and turn-round time. At the third level was what many historians regard as the true long-distance pre-modern trade, a trade that was trans-continental in its dimensions and very distinctly marked by the nature of the commodities exchanged. The articles carried by this trade found markets and buyers by virtue either of transplanted social demand or of a totally independent psychology of value. Their names at once spring to mind. They were the great products of civilisation: silks, brocades, the fabulous superfine cotton fabrics, porcelain, jewellery, spices, and thoroughbred horses. Trans-continental trade had two further characteristics. We have already seen that the shipment of luxury goods called for counter-weights in the form of bulk goods, to spread the risk of shipwreck and to provide ballast. As the buying and the consuming markets were far apart, commodities which travelled from China, South East Asia, or India to the eastern and western Mediterranean were marketed through a series of commercial emporia. Goods could break bulk at any of these intermediate points of their entire journey or be consigned from agent to agent to reach the principal in one intact package. With the development, in the bureaucratic chartered companies, of North European methods of trade in the Indian Ocean, trans-continental trade took on recognisably modern forms: central distribution agencies operating at an international level on highly capitalistic lines, grafted onto a pre-modern system of production. The Asian merchants who partici-pated in the trans-continental trade were inter-regional traders as well because of the presence of bulk goods in their ships. The European East India Companies, on the other hand, combined a multitude of functions. The luxury and bulk goods transported by them were marketed at the inter-regional level in the Indian Ocean and at the same time carried all the way to Europe. This development was to lay the foundation of the nineteenth-century trade in raw material and foodstuffs.

The theoretical premises and the generalisations put forward so far about the commodity flow of Asian trade should be capable of being tested against the actual historical evidence. What do contemporary writers and surviving records tell us about the objects of trade and the places from which they were exported? As first-hand impressions, we might look at the writings of al-Muqaddasi and Chau Ju-kua, both of whom describe the geography and the trade of the Indian Ocean in days long before the rise of the great circuit of emporia commerce controlled by Malacca and Cambay. The early evidence can be followed up by an examination of the surviving shipping invoices dating from the eighteenth century. The work of al-Muqaddasi shows all the signs of an accurate and scientific mind, and he was careful enough to qualify his statements, which the demands of rhetoric required him to make in stereo-type form.[6] By the tenth century the Arabian coastlines commanding the entrance to the Red Sea and to the Persian Gulf were already closely integrated into the wider circle of Indian Ocean trade. For al-Muqaddasi says of al-Yaman:

The commerce of this province is important, for here are the two chief ports of the world, as well as the fair of Mina, and here is the sea which stretches as far as China. There are also Juddah and al-Jar, the two granaries of Egypt, and Wadi-Qura, the mart of both Syria and al-Iraq, and al-Yaman, the country of kerchiefs, cornelian, leather and slaves. To Uman the following articles are exported: apothecaries' drugs, all kinds of perfumery, musk even included, saffron, sappan wood, teak wood, the wood of the sasam tree, ivory, pearls, brocade, onyx, rubies, ebony, coconut, sugar, sandarach, aloes, iron, lead, canes, earthenware, sandalwood, glass, pepper and other articles. Aden receives in addition, ambergris, [fine linen cloths called] shurub, leather bucklers, Abyssinian slaves, eunuchs, tiger skins and other articles, which, were we to mention them in detail, would unduly prolong the book. Chinese wares are proverbi-ally famous.[7]

Compare this list of commodities with that compiled by Chau Ju-kua in the early thirteenth century. Merchants who came from the lands of the Ta-shi or the Arabs to trade in the strait of Malacca brought pearls, ivory, rhinoceros horns, frankincense, ambergris, putchuk, cloves, nutmegs, benzoin, aloes, myrrh, dragon's blood, asafoetida, borax, opaque and transparent glass, coral, rosewater, brocades, satins, woollen cloth, and other miscellaneous products.[8] The Chinese writer's knowledge of the Indian Ocean goods acquired in distant Fukien was less sure than that of the Arab geographer, though it is striking that both should emphasise so many articles which fall into the category of high-value cargo.

In fact, they knew perfectly well that the staple products of the trading regions entered the flow of long-distance exchange as much as did the luxury goods. These commodities did not share the prestige in possession conferred by the latter, but each writer took pains to describe the main agricultural crops and their role in trade. For example, Chau Ju-kua had this to say of Java:

there is a vast store of pepper in this foreign country and the merchant ships, in view of the profit they derive from that trade, are in the habit of smuggling [out of China] copper cash for bartering purposes. Our Court has repeatedly forbidden all trade [with this country], but the foreign traders, for the purpose of deceiving [the government], changed its name and referred to it as Su-ku-tan.[9]

Everyone connected with the maritime trade of Asia was aware of the fact that the black pepper of Indonesia or Malabar was a heavy-weight ballast article, which could be purchased very cheaply in its areas of native growth. The widespread mass demand for it, however, yielded a large revenue on the merchants' turn-over. The drain on copper currency, used in everyday transactions in China, obviously caused anxiety to the imperial government, and the prohibition of its export for the purchase of pepper was a part of the official apparatus of pre-modern government control of the destabilising side of international trade. Chau Ju-kua's comment on the prevalence of smuggling and the re-routing of trade reveals that medieval economic regulations were no more successful than some of their modern counterparts, official interference sometimes enhancing the value of an article which would otherwise have been regarded as one of ordinary daily use.

It is not known whether the ships that left the eastern and western ends of the Indian Ocean to trade at intermediate ports in the early centuries carried manifests and comprehensive documentation of their often miscellaneous cargo packed in bales, bundles, baskets, and jars. Actual owners of the goods, if they were travelling with them, would certainly have kept a detailed record of what was shipped for purposes of internal accounting, as well as establishing the liability of the ship-masters and insurers. During the eighteenth century Asian owners of ships captured by European privateers and men-of-war were able to provide accurate manifests of the cargo if the matter went to court or arbitration. Whether the institution of marine documents was a practice surviving from the pre-European period of trade or a more recent borrowed innovation is uncertain; but there is no doubt that itemised invoices were later kept by Asian and European traders throughout the Indian Ocean. From the lists found among private commercial papers and official records, the composition of Asian maritime trade can be reconstructed in considerable depth. Illuminating evidence of imports into China from the Philippines is provided by a Chinese shipwreck inquiry carried out by district officials in Amoy in 1749. The ship had sailed from the Ilocos area in Luzon, with a mixed cargo, to trade for Chinese Yung-ch'un linen. She ran into a typhoon near the Fukien coast and was lost with all her cargo, though none of the crew lost his life. The subsequent official inquiry established the following list of goods carried on the vessel:[10]

Rice	1300 tan
Canvas	207 pieces
Ox hides	41 pieces
Lard	8 jars
Tobacco	8 chests
Betel nuts	60 packages
Sesame seeds	19 packages
Dried meat	44 piculs
Sappanwood	38 piculs
Coconut meat	8 jars
Copper fragments	2 piculs
Silver dollars	3900

It is evident that the ship carried two main forms of purchasing power: rice and silver. As Manila was a large receptor of Spanish American treasure, there is no difficulty in accounting for the presence of silver reals of eight on the invoice. These would have been used to buy Chinese industrial goods and would have circulated in China in the form of bullion. The shipment of a considerable quantity of rice on the Ilocos vessel is, however, surprising. It shows that South East Asia was acting as a food-surplus area to the coastal province of Fukien, and perhaps also to Kwangtung. There is independent evidence of this from the imperial records, which prove that population pressure in these areas of China had become intense in relation to available food resources and that the deteriorating situation was used as an argument in favour of relaxing the prohibition on foreign trade. While authentic examples of policy considerations in economic affairs are rare in our period of Asian history, the Chinese document of 1727 on the above point is highly revealing and worth quoting at some length:

Governor-General Kao Ch'i-cho [1676–1738] of Fukien, in his confidential memorial on the lifting of the sea ban, pointed out that "the population is dense while the land is limited in the five prefectures of Foochow, Hsing-hua, Ch'üan-chou, Chang-chou, and Ting-chou, so that the rice produced there is insufficient to meet the demand. Most of the sea-going vessels bring back rice on their return. The lifting of the ban on overseas trade would therefore greatly benefit the people of the coastal areas." Permission was granted to act as proposed. Owing to the food deficit in Fukien and the tendency of the unemployed there to become bandits, the ban was lifted in this province ... However, the sea off Kiangsu and Chekiang is adjacent to that off Fukien ... Now that the ban has been lifted in Fukien, but not in Kiangsu and Chekiang ... inconsistencies will certainly arise with respect to the patrolling of the coast ... The proposal of the merchants of Kiangsu and Chekiang that they be permitted to trade in the South Seas, like the Fukien merchants, should be accepted.[11]

The rice trade between Luzon and Amoy was one of the results of the lifting of the ban on sea voyages.

Apart from rice and silver, local products were not carried in significant quantities on the Luzon ship. The heterogeneous nature of pre-modern trade and the mixture of goods involved would appear unbelievable unless attested by the actual evidence of surviving invoices. The diminutive scale of transactions shows that the difference between the large wholesale dealer and the small speculative trader was not sharply drawn. If a commodity could be sold no matter how minute its relative quantity, it was shipped. The cumulative revenue from these sales at least helped to pay for the costs of the voyage. If we turn from the inter-regional trade of the South China Sea to the Indian subcontinent, these characteristics can be seen in numerous examples. In 1729 the country-ship *Carolina* left Calcutta carrying the following goods destined for Surat:[12]

Baftas, brown	1477 pieces	Rs 2363
Gurrahs, brown	1352 pieces	Rs 2771
Gurrahs, white	1432 pieces	Rs 3007
Soosies	600 pieces	Rs 3556
Mulmuls, brown	1951 pieces	Rs 4389
Taffetys, fine	400 pieces	Rs 2350
Muga, saries	374 pieces	Rs 693
Muga, dhuties	242 pieces	Rs 441
Cuttanees	121 pieces	Rs 726
Raw silk	61 maunds	Rs 10 012
Iron balasore	1490 maunds	Rs 6384
Sugar	2000 bags	Rs 16 000
Ginger	440 maunds	Rs 1210
Rattens		Rs 45
Salt petre		Rs 224
Rice	6310 maunds	Rs 5084
Benjamin	1027 maunds	Rs 3065
Gunnies		Rs 484

The first nine items on the invoice are various kinds of textiles: pure cotton as well as cotton-and-silk mixtures, for which the Bengal handloom weavers were famous. Raw silk, sugar, and rice were of course traditional exports from the province. But the large amount of raw iron, which came from the foundries in Orissa, is a little unusual, and its export to Gujarat indicates the concentration of the industry in eastern and southern India and the latter's dependence on trading networks for distribution. The cargo of the *Carolina* would, when sold in Surat, have yielded a substantial profit to the shareholders in the voyage. When measured by the standards of an English East-Indiaman, which carried home upwards of one million rupees' worth of goods, the ship was not a rich one. On the other hand, it was possible to organise a greater number of voyages, and in smaller ships, in the coastal run from Surat to Bengal than between London and the Indian ports. The *Carolina*'s consignment reflects the breadth of the Surat market even in its days of relative decline. By contrast, the *Rose Galley* sent from Calcutta to Malacca and Kedah in 1731 had on board only two thousand maunds of rice valued at Rs 1600, one hundred chests of Bihar opium (Rs 29 000) and a few pieces of textiles for presents. Opium had a huge mark-up on cost prices in South East Asia and China. The profits of the *Rose Galley* could not have disappointed the owners.[13] The range of cargo, however, was very limited.

The commercial voyages just discussed were all organised by Robert Cowan, the English governor of Bombay, and by his compatriots and partners in various Indian Ocean ports. The account books, ships' papers, and letters found among his private papers throw considerable light on the regional balance of trade, the choice of different commodities, and the expected level of profit. The element of speculation and the uncertainty of adequate returns were constantly discussed by all correspondents. A trading emporium such as Surat offered special attractions to all types of traders because of the range of its service facilities. In 1728 Richard Upton wrote to Cowan, "Surat generally engrosses all those whose schemes are not deep enough to take in a large compass, and even for those who are no great schemers, Surat is a very convenient port." The trade to South East Asia, on the other hand, was carried on in small vessels and was hardly worthy of notice.[14]

Bengal's seaborne trade and the flow of its export goods had apparently turned in the eighteenth century in a different direction, towards the western Indian Ocean and Europe. Two centuries earlier Pires had noted the high price that Bengal cotton textiles fetched in Malacca and their wide currency throughout the eastern islands.[15] The reputation of Bengal's textile industry for the production of fine luxury fabrics had not diminished, and the agricultural prosperity of the province gave to the area a unique cost advantage, which merchants did not fail to notice; though excessive rains or flooding could, of course, destroy the local cotton crop and raise the price of coarse cloth, which was often in short supply. Richard Bourchier, a correspondent of Cowan, regretted in 1728 that he could not provide the exact types of cloth asked for because of temporary scarcities. On the other hand, he wrote, "I believe you will find the cargoes now sent you as reasonable as any goes hence this season, and should cotton grow cheap as rice has done in all probability all goods will be reasonable the next year."[16] The type of cotton cloth sold in the Red Sea markets was mainly the cheaper and coarser sort, and such was the prevailing shortage of these goods (which required a proportionately higher amount of raw cotton) that Bourchier found it difficult to load up even a ship of sixty tons.

There are other examples in the correspondence of Robert Cowan and his associates that illustrate the fine balance between prospective profit or loss. In 1729 Cowan informed his friend Philip Martin in Basra that he fully shared the latter's dismay at the unexpected arrival of the ship *Fame* at that port with a consignment of goods which were not at all meant for the area. The super-cargo had in fact been actually forbidden to go to Basra. Furthermore, the arrival of these goods, he realised, could harm the sale of the cargo of the *William*, which had been expressly sent to Basra. The voyage of the *William* made a loss of twenty per cent in the event, and Cowan wrote that for such disappointments there was no remedy but patience. From the late 1720s, for a decade or so, the inter-regional trade of the Indian Ocean seems to have gone into a considerable recession. The civil war in Iran following the downfall of the Safavid dynasty (1722), famine in southern India, wars and troop movements in Gujarat – all these extraneous events added to the effects of any cyclical patterns there may have been in the time-path of international trade even in this early pre-industrial and pre-capitalistic period. Evidence of competition and over-trading by the servants of the European East India Companies certainly heightens the impression that these were difficult times. From Bengal, Henry Frankland in 1727 complained that the maritime trade of the province had seen its best days and was in great decay if not altogether lost. The voyages barely made such returns as could have been earned from "the common interest of our money by our Inland Trade".[17] Frankland was not alone in taking a gloomy view of the commercial scene. The English governor of Madras, James Macrae, also reported that the port's trade had dwindled to nothing because of the great losses recently suffered. It was becoming difficult to find enough subscribers for new and fresh voyages. There is some exaggeration in these complaints of hard days: both Cowan and Macrae made fortunes in the country trade during these years which were large by contemporary standards.[18] Cowan thought that a profit of eighty per cent was a poor return, and he was constantly trying to anticipate the market in order to avoid a possible over-supply. In 1729 he sent five hundred bags of Bengal sugar hurriedly to Cambay with instructions to sell it quickly. He thought that sugar would be cheaper in Surat that year than it had been during the past twenty years, because of the expected number of ships reported to be on their way from Bengal and Malacca laden with the commodity. Two great ships belonging to Mahmud Ali, the leading merchant of Surat, had already reached the Malabar carrying cargoes of sugar.[19]

A detailed examination of the evidence found in the Cowan papers and other similar collections dating from the first half of the eighteenth century raises two separate questions. The first is as to the general conclusions which can be drawn from the records of English inter-port trade; the second as to the extent to which the methods depicted in eighteenth-century documents of buying and selling different commercial goods had earlier origins. Did the Asian merchants of Surat, Bandar Abbas, Mocha, Masulipatam, and Canton feel the same chill winds of economic depression and over-trading as did the Europeans? And did they in the days of Malacca's supremacy as a trading emporium have the same speculative outlook in committing their capital to a particular article as did the English country-traders of Bombay, Madras, and Calcutta in the 1720s? To raise questions is not, however, the same as to find reliable answers to them in history. In the absence of comparable private commercial documents from Asian business firms, we are forced back to the European sources for information. The general reports compiled by the officials of the trading companies all refer to the decay of trade and its effects on Asian and European merchants alike in the 1730s. There is no doubt that the seaborne trade of Surat, busy and valuable as it was, was subject to periodic depressions and boom conditions. Scarcity of money, famines, and warfare took their toll of merchants as well as of the common people. In 1622, the ancient trading emporium of Hormuz, held by the Portuguese for more than a century, was retaken by the Shah of Persia with the help of the English East India Company's warships. The immediate effects of the conquest were not favourable to the merchants of Surat, who had apparently built up good business relations with the Portuguese. The hostile policy adopted by the Dutch and English towards the port of Surat caused great anger among the indigenous population against the North Europeans. As the Dutch merchant Francisco Pelsaert noted in his description of the Mughal trading city,

because of this decay, we are cursed not only by the Portuguese, but by the Hindu and Muslims, who put the whole blame on us, saying that we are the scourge of their prosperity; for, even though the Dutch and English traders were worth a million rupees annually, this cannot be compared to the former trade, which was many times greater, not merely in India, but with Arabia and Persia also.[20]

When Bandar Abbas was established as an alternative to Hormuz, the Gulf trade once again returned to its former prosperity in the 1650s.

By the seventeenth or eighteenth century, according to the evidence in European sources, the fundamental structure of buying and selling markets for the bulk of the goods commonly exchanged in the Indian Ocean was already well developed. If the commercial practices these sources reveal are compared to those described in Pires' more fragmentary account of Malacca's maritime laws and economic institutions, it would seem that the basic techniques of merchandising changed little during the intervening century. Malacca itself imported the traditions of emporium trading from other longer-established ports in the Indian Ocean. The works of Muslim geographers and the commentaries of legal experts on Islamic laws also confirm the impression that, from the tenth or eleventh century, the growth in the volume and value of Asian trade led to an extension of the legal and economic practices which had evolved in the context of particular national or imperial needs. Foreign merchants who came to trade at any one of the great Asian emporia, whether it was Aden, Calicut, Malacca, or Canton, had to make sure that the port was able to provide four essential commercial and legal services without which a wholesale dealer could not function. First of all, the provision of ships' cargo required the existence of "spot" or forward markets with clear price indicators and continuity of supply. Almost as important were local monetary institutions and the operations of bankers, who were expected to provide credit in case of need or exchange the proceeds of local sales for foreign bills. The settlement of accounts between dealers, and the process of recovering debts, also called for either a binding consensus among merchants themselves or recourse to courts of law. Finally, there was the matter of a market for shipping space or, as the contemporary ship-owners called it, the freight business. Many merchants with consignments of high-value goods preferred to spread the risk and ship them in many different bottoms rather than in their own vessels in single lots. If the article was a contraband, the freight business provided a measure of safety to merchants and considerable profits to the ship-owners.

Deductive reasoning enables us to suggest the above schema of emporia trading, which is corroborated by the later, post-seventeenth-century evidence. Just how far back in time the common features can be found is uncertain. Many of the commodities transported in the later period over long distances were also part of inter-regional and trans-continental trade during the earlier (eighth to fifteenth) centuries; it is perhaps safe to assume that the economic mechanism of exchange was not too dissimilar either. Some of the early sources are not entirely lacking in elements indicative of wholesale trading and speculation in maritime ventures. The Moroccan traveller al-Idrisi, for example, who used the experience of his twelfth-century contemporaries as the basis of a comprehensive geographical work on Islamic lands gives an informative account of the Indian port of Daybul in Sind:

This is a populous place, but its soil is not fertile, and it produces scarcely any trees except the date-palm. The highlands are arid and the plains sterile. Houses are built of clay and wood, but the place is inhabited only because it is a station for the vessels of Sind and other countries. Trade is carried on in a great variety of articles, and is conducted with much intelligence. Ships laden with the productions of Uman, and the vessels of China and India come to Debal. They bring stuffs and other goods from China, and the perfumes and aromatics of India. The inhabitants of Debal, who are generally rich, buy these goods in the bulk, and store them until the vessels are gone and they become scarce. Then they begin to sell, and go trading into the country, putting their money out at interest, or employing it as may seem best.[21]

Al-Idrisi obviously took an interest in the trading towns of India. In describing the citizens of Broach in Gujarat, he once again returns to the theme of maritime speculation and voyages to distant lands. The reference to bulk trading and the practice of storage in expectation of better prices underlines the basic logic of any foreign trade which claimed to be more than a peddling activity. For both luxury precious articles and ballast goods large-scale operations allowed merchants to reduce costs, and the policy of keeping an inventory of goods was grounded as much in the expectation of better profits as in the predictability of prices.

Violent price fluctuations, and even a wide range between the lowest and the highest points, were generally disliked. For those who lived permanently close to the producing markets and had long experience of the nature of price volatility, the unstable behaviour of a commodity did not matter much. But a travelling merchant or the agent of a principal resident abroad could not take the same risks and anticipate the direction of changes to his advantage. To a buyer in this category, the Indian Ocean emporium offered two possibilities. He could approach the dealers who specialised in spot transactions and kept stocks, and a mutually satisfactory bargain could be negotiated on the basis of competitive prices. The other alternative was to operate through a broker and leave a list of goods to be purchased and shipped for the coming trading season. This was essentially a form of forward commodity dealing which avoided the speculative effects of rapid market changes. Not all the goods carried across the Indian Ocean were bought or sold through the exercise of a choice between the two methods. Some were available only in the spot market, while others could not be procured at all unless one contracted for them in advance. The sale of coffee in the Yemeni port of Mocha and in the great inland town of Beit al-Fakih was wholly conducted in the warehouses of individual dealers who had bought stocks of coffee during the months before the arrival of the foreign ships. Fine Indian cotton textiles and Chinese silk cloth, on the other hand, needed much greater planning in terms not only of the commercial contract of supply but also of the organisation of production. The overseas markets in the Spice Islands and the Persian Gulf for certain types of textile were completely specific as to the design, colour, and texture of the products. The degree of specialisation in weaving these fabrics was often so great that, if the contracting merchants failed to take delivery, they could not be sold in the local market.

Black pepper, cloves, nutmeg, and other finer spices, coffee, tea, and food grains appear to have changed hands mostly in the spot markets in either the port towns or the caravan cities. In the records of the Dutch and English East

India Companies, dating from the late seventeenth and early eighteenth centuries, very detailed reports are available on the wholesale coffee markets of the Yemen. These reveal that the economic considerations involved in merchants' decisions and the daily movements of the market had all the features of sophisticated international commodity trading. The main factors which established an equilibrium in prices (constantly changing for individuals of course) were the size of the annual crop and the number of ships actually visiting the ports of shipment. The situation was, however, complicated by anticipation, and English merchants trading in Mocha sometimes thought that the fluctuations in coffee prices in the Yemen were very similar to the behaviour of the bourses and exchanges in Europe.[22] The news of favourable or unfavourable prices in the intermediate markets of Jedda and Cairo immediately caused movements in Mocha and Beit al-Fakih. This is not surprising, as the bulk of Yemeni coffee was exported to the West, to Egypt, to Syria, and to other parts of the Ottoman empire. Iraq and India came next, and after 1700 exports to Western Europe steadily increased. The presence of so many buyers in the market during a narrow trading season provided the coffee dealers with the opportunity to mark up their prices continuously from the day that the market opened to the time when the news of any fresh arrival of ships was no longer credible. From that point prices gradually fell to the level at which the local dealers conducted business among themselves. By varying the time of their arrival, foreign merchants could take advantage of the different gradations of prices, and the same result could be obtained by spreading total purchases over a period of time. The dealers profited equally well from not selling their entire stock to a single buyer at a particular level of prices. One English buyer noted in the 1720s that the traditional discount given to buyers of large quantities did not apply in Mocha and Beit al-Fakih. But there was no difficulty in the way of buying in smaller lots. The coffee market of the Yemen was characterised by two types of seller. At one end of the scale there were very large dealers able to influence prices by releasing or withholding stocks. At the other end there were numerous small men whose cumulative sales jointly affected prices. Even peasants brought their crops of coffee to the market of Beit al-Fakih, as the coffee-growing hills were not too far off. They responded to price fluctuations by not coming to the market if they thought that the trip was not worthwhile.[23]

The chance preservation and discovery of historical material on the Yemeni coffee trade reveals a picture that is familiar to all commodity dealers today. The question that naturally arises is as to the prevalence of similar conditions in other commodities and other ports of trade in the Indian Ocean. It is apparent that the commercial practices adopted in Mocha and Beit al-Fakih were imported from Middle Eastern business centres elsewhere, because the coffee trade did not start to grow significantly before the late fifteenth century. It is inconceivable that the wholesale markets of Alexandria, Cairo, Aden, and

Baghdad should have been any less advanced. It is certainly evident that the Indonesian ports were able to supply as much pepper as foreign ships wanted from spot markets, though of course the prices behaved in accordance with the forces of supply and demand. There was, however, an important exception in the case of the pepper market in both Malabar and South East Asia. From time to time the local rulers, if they were strong enough to stand up to the economic power of the merchants, cornered the supplies and sold them at semi-monopoly prices. Similar situations arose at times in the sale of tea in Canton, where the Chinese merchants were organised into Hongs on the orders of the imperial government after the accession of the Manchu dynasty.

If an export commodity was sold in the spot market for immediate or short-term delivery, it made little difference whether the buyer was a foreign visitor or an indigenous merchant exporting abroad. But in the case of items which required advance orders and forward transactions local dealers possessed an undoubted advantage over any other group. The two classic examples of commodities sold in forward markets are indigo, a blue dye used in the textile industry, and cotton piece-goods. Once again the mechanism of marketing is reconstructed from historical descriptions and records left by the officials of the European trading companies. Indigo was manufactured from a green annual plant, and its cultivation constantly migrated from region to region according to the local structure of costs. During the sixteenth and seventeenth centuries large quantities of the dye were exported from Gujarat and northern India. The finest and best variety of Indian indigo was sold in the wholesale market of Biana, a small town near the Mughal imperial capital of Agra. Francisco Pelsaert has left a most illuminating account of forward transactions in the sale of the commodity. Wealthy Indian dealers and Armenian merchants heavily involved in the Middle Eastern cloth trade advanced money to the indigo farmers long before the time of the harvest and the processing of the dye. This group secured the best quality and the largest stocks, and the leading member was by tradition allowed to fix the price when the market opened for general dealing. Small traders or foreign buyers who came all the way to Biana to buy indigo either bought in the open market for spot cash or negotiated advance orders for the coming season. Prices were highly sensitive to the force of demand from this type of trader.

The qualities and varieties of indigo sold for export were limited enough to make it possible for the buyers to compare prices over a whole spectrum, and they could easily decide whether it was profitable to buy in the open market or to contract in advance. The cotton textile trade in India and the silk industry of China were different. The range of products was enormous, and the variety differentiated by type of yarn, number of threads per square inch, design, and colour was so great that only an expert familiar with the trade could make a safe and intelligent comparison of the prices asked by weavers or intermediate dealers. Furthermore, the high cost of the fine luxury products, especially in the case of silk piece-goods, made it a highly speculative venture on the part of producers to undertake the weaving of those types at their own risk. A commercial agreement between wholesale merchants in touch with the consuming markets and weavers reduced the element of risk on both sides. The merchant was assured of receiving supplies on time, before the seasonal sailing dates of his ships, and the producers knew in advance that they would not be left with costly unsold stocks on their hands. The whole system of marketing cotton or silk textiles in pre-modern exchange economies incorporated a most important element of capitalism, that of advance finance. Of course the textile industries of India and China (or other parts of Asia) included weavers who were independent producers and sold their output directly in the open market. This type of cloth was often traded locally, and the sellers could establish from their own experience the relationship between quantities to be produced and possible demand. The export market, however, was seldom accessible to industrial producers, and the need for pre-planning and a considerable amount of organisation allowed merchants to assume the role of entrepreneurs. The advance contract system which developed as a result has been described by some historians as a "putting-out" method of industrial production in which the buyers gave to the weavers all the necessary raw materials and received the finished goods for a fixed price. This was the system prevalent in Europe before the Industrial Revolution, and historians have taken the textile production and trade of Asia as merely its variant.

The extension of the "putting-out" model to Asia is neither valid nor analytically complete. A merchant who is in a position to advance raw materials to weavers is also able to assume almost all the functions of an industrialist, with the exception of labour supply. In the case of the cotton and silk industries, with their huge product variations, he must know exactly what type of yarn to buy and where to get it processed. The successful weaving of very fine cotton cloth is due as much to the elaborate and multiple processing of the thread as to the final weaving on the loom itself. The merchant and his agent must constantly keep in touch with the weavers through all the stages of production from the time that the contract is given out to the time of the final delivery. There is no historical evidence to show that this was the normal practice in the Indian or Chinese textile industries. The merchant remained overwhelmingly concerned with trade and assumed the role of a financier as a secondary consideration. The process of weaving was supervised, mainly to make sure that the producers did not sell off the textiles to other buyers offering better prices and thus breach their legal contracts. If the weavers were unable to obtain the right kind of threads the system of supervision also provided a warning that some adjustment might be necessary in the final choice of the shipments overseas. While the detailed history of the Chinese silk industry has yet to be written in English (and may modify the above conclusion), the Indian method of buying and selling cotton piece-goods for export to the

Asian or European markets, from the seventeenth century onwards, is fully known. The great merchants at the ports of shipment employed either their own agents or independent brokers working for commission to advance money to weavers specialising in the particular kind of fabrics wanted. The acceptance of the part payment of the final price bound the weavers legally to deliver the cloth to the contractor at the specified time. Sometimes the price was fixed in advance; on other occasions it was negotiated at the time of completion, in accordance with current market conditions. The Islamic law of contract (salam sales) regarded the advance payment system as a sale of entities and not merely as a promise of future delivery.[24] The commercial conventions in the Indian textile trade were well established. From October to December, in the dusty plains of Gujarat, in Coromandel, and in Bengal, brokers and textile agents travelled from town to town, from village to village, in search of skilled and credit-worthy weavers who would accept an advance of money and agree to supply cloth at a future date, to be used in the wealthy households of Iran, Java, and even Japan.

The commodities of the Indian Ocean were sold in three types of market and were handled by several different classes of trader. The great commercial emporia of Asia had their counterparts in the immensely rich resident merchant families, comparable to territorial nobility. These merchants, towns, and cities were multi-functional, dealing in a wide range of goods and spreading the financial risks in a dozen different directions. Below this typology there were markets and traders who were still large but specialised in particular goods or commercial services. At the bottom of the scale the urban bazaars and weekly country fairs supplied goods to the consumers at the retail level; these markets were supplemented by the business carried on by pedlars. Long-distance maritime trade included small traders whose individual transactions were no greater than those of local pedlars. The role of this group is difficult to measure in terms of market shares. The small traders accompanied the annual fleet of ships which set out from the ports of India or China, carrying their wares in numerous packs and baskets. These goods were sold from their shoulders in Malacca, Bantam, or Batavia, causing profound irritation to the larger shippers. The pedlars obviously undercut the great merchants on many items of export. However, it is doubtful if their activities were ever more than marginal to the main volume and direction of seaborne trade.

10

Capital and trade in the Indian Ocean: the problem of scale, merchants, money, and production

The historical overview of long-distance trade takes little account of features that define and describe an economic region. The subject, by its very nature, lends itself to a high degree of theorisation and abstraction. Whether trade is carried on by sea or land, the emphasis is generally on the scale of distance over which merchants travel and transport their goods. It is, of course, recognised that the character of the local economy and the changes taking place in it deeply influence long-distance trade, as do the political institutions of nation–states. Nevertheless, for most historians this assumption is the point of departure and not part of the analysis. The logic of international trade is mainly determined by the discrete existence of markets. Producers are separated from consumers by a double filter, that of geographical space and time. It is this particular feature of commercial transactions that turns trade into an activity involving the use of capital and its accumulation. A local region, even in the remote historical past, could have an exchange economy based on division of labour and the implied condition of capital accumulation. However, for a closed economic system with a limited spatial dimension it is not necessary to develop a more advanced circuit of capital which translates values into relative prices and economic surplus into money or productive capital. But inter-regional or long-distance trade cannot by definition function without capital, money, and prices. The time-interval between the initial investment made by merchants in purchasing export goods, their despatch and sale in distant markets, and the final returns gives rise to actual operations as well as conceptual measurements that are entirely capitalistic. How far a local economy is integrated into the wider system of economic exchange depends both on its internal development and on the scale of commercial influence.

In the history of Asia, seaborne and caravan trade played a major cultural role throughout our period of study, from the rise of Islam to the mid-eighteenth century. It has been pointed out how certain items of trade – gold and silver, silk, fine muslins, spices, incense, and horses – were looked upon as great products of civilisation, indispensable accompaniments to a refined and luxurious way of life. But we also know that the trans-oceanic trade of Eurasia was not supported by high-value precious goods alone. The technology of sailing-ships demanded the transport of bulk goods in combination with precious articles. Moreover, many regions around the Indian Ocean supplemented their food production with imports from areas of high agricultural surplus. An active trade in food grains and many different kinds of foodstuffs enabled the chronically deficient regions to specialise in the production of commodities for which there was a steady demand. The level of production in these areas was conditioned not only by the local geography and economy but also by the volume of long-distance trade. The strength of urban centres in different parts of Asia – the Middle East, Central Asia, and China – was derived precisely from the strong flow of maritime and caravan trade. In the Red Sea and the Persian Gulf, entire communities depended on food imports from Egypt and India for their daily survival. Even in the rice-growing provinces of coastal China, density of population had by the sixteenth century created sufficient pressure on food resources to warrant rice imports from the sparsely inhabited agricultural lands of South East Asia. The available historical evidence leaves little doubt about the close relationship between economic prosperity and long-distance trade – between social institutions and the consumption of goods obtained by trade – and the overall role played by merchants in quickening the pace of exchange. The question that is much more difficult to answer is the exact scale and the quantitative dimension of Indian Ocean commerce in our millennium.

Merchants and business organisations rarely preserve their records for the benefit of posterity. Once the practical reason for record-keeping is removed, commercial documents are either destroyed or deposited with law courts or religious foundations, according to the social usage of the time. To family inheritors, even when they were engaged in trade, the business papers of another generation made little sense. The surviving documents remain difficult to interpret to this day. Calculations of profits, before the age of double-entry book-keeping, could be carried out with ease only by contemporary participants perfectly familiar with running accounts. The obscurity and the special nomenclature may have been deliberately adopted in order to discourage outside investigations. The result of the secretive attitude of merchants in the context of the Indian Ocean trade is a severe lack of documentation on the content of commercial dealings. It is not until the appearance of the great European bureaucratic trading companies in the seventeenth century that some idea of relative quantities can be established. An examination of commercial accounts, invoices, and letters from the time of the Cairo Genizah records to the first half of the eighteenth century, however, proves beyond any question that the actual quantities handled by individual merchants and partnerships were small in relation to the total theoretical capacity of the local economy that generated the surplus economic products. Pre-modern merchants, in Asia as well as in Europe, recorded their transactions in minute units of monetary or volume measurement. The convention cannot be explained merely in terms of an exactitude created by the accounting mind. The scale of operations was really small. When all the individual dealings, the numerous shipments and bargains, were added together, the total quantities and values may not have been inconsequential for the regional economy. There were good reasons, as we shall see, why the pre-modern merchant did not adopt centralisation as the only method of trade.

The commercial invoices and correspondence which have survived through chance reveal a strange world of financial transactions. The business methods of medieval merchants are seen graphically illustrated in the following letter written by Abu Imran Musa in Alexandria to a correspondent in Old Cairo (*c.* 1058–9):

Ibn Yahya to please do this [for me]. I have requested the indigo [?] . . . and the garments and the woollen cloaks and the handal [? leather or fur garments]. Let him leave this until, God willing, I arrive. Musa of Sfaqs is also carrying for me a sealed bag of coins which arrived from the West containing dinars . . . If God decrees his safe arrival I would like my master please to take delivery of it from him. With him, I have also sent [a quantity] of olive oil. Please take delivery of everything. Similarly, I have sent with Abu Ali Hassun b. Yahya two bags of coins: a bag of Rumi dinars and a bag of dinars from Tripoli, Syria, and Egypt. If God decrees the safe arrival of these bags and if you consider it desirable to sell, then please try to sell them. Write [and tell] me the weight of each bag and the separate amount that each one fetched. By this you will be doing me a favour.[1]

Similar letters would have been written from the Malabar coast, Aden, and the trading towns of North Africa by the compatriots of this Jewish merchant of Egypt. In the Indian Ocean itself, merchants shipped their goods in numerous bundles, packs, and jars. The correct delivery of the items to the rightful owner at a port of call presented the ship-master with no small problem. In 1717 the Surat ship *Nizami* arrived in Bengal at the port of Hugli with a typical cargo shipped from the West: pepper, raw cotton, tobacco, rosewater, dried fruits, aloes, spelter, coral beads, and asafoetida. The first three items alone were carried in substantial quantities.[2] Expressions which were perfectly idiomatic in Arabic and Hebrew eight centuries ago may appear strange in a modern translation. The striking point of Abu Imran Musa's letter is the fragmentation of transactions. Professional merchants, experts in the business of moving goods over very long distances, divided their risks and operations. A quantity of olive oil and three sealed bags of gold coins, that was the measure of this particular consignment. The gold coins may have been valuable; olive oil was an article of daily life.

Although the sizes of individual transactions in the Indian Ocean trade may appear small in comparison with those in the later or modern period, it is important to relate the scale to other quantitative dimensions of the economy and to take into account its qualitative character. A true demographic perspective can be gained if we remove four out of every five persons now in the densely populated areas of Asia. Many parts of India, the Middle East, and Central Asia in our period were completely uninhabited or very thinly populated. Demographic expansion following a favourable run of years was abruptly brought to an end by natural calamities – famines, floods, or epidemics – and by the outbreak of large-scale warfare. Urban centres and whole economic regions with a large demand for goods imported from external sources could suddenly disappear from the merchants' list of profitable markets because of unpredictable social disasters. The fluctuations in the flow of economic activities, and especially in the volume of long-distance trade, aroused the interest of contemporary observers. The variations and the general movements are well recorded in historical sources. On the other hand, the proportion and the exact weight of trade in the total economic activity of a region will never be known for any pre-modern period. All that can be said with certainty is that certain areas of the Indian Ocean were heavily dependent on external trade, both as suppliers and as consumers of commodities. Changes in the level of trade for these regions were invariably expressed in terms of prosperity and depression. Two examples can be taken from the sources to highlight this point. In 1679 Streynsham Master, the English governor of Madras, went on a tour of inspection in southern India. It was an area of concentrated weaving and exported its products to other parts of India, to South East Asia, and to the Middle East. For some unknown reason, perhaps connected with the policy of the local political authorities and the sultans of Golconda, the overseas demand seems to have shifted for a period from Masulipatam, the main port-town, to producing areas further south. The neighbouring small towns and the rural weavers supplying the export trade through Masulipatam suffered great hardship, and Master noticed during his travels signs of economic decay. He was continually pressed by the local merchants to accept their services and re-establish the Company's own textile purchases in the region. When the offers were rejected, as Master recorded in his diary, the merchants "being wholly disappointed of the imployment they aimed at . . . departed with sorrowfull countenances".[3] The economic and political links between trade, industry, and government revenue in Mughal India were explicitly mentioned in a letter written by the East India Company's Court of Directors a decade later. Although the Mughal emperor was believed to attach little importance to foreign commerce, the Company thought that "he draws more annual profit from Trade especially from his Manufacturers within the Land than all the princes upon the face of the earth and it is no great pleasure to a great prince to see such multitudes of subjects starve for want of employment".[4] Was the Company guilty of an exaggeration, repeating a popular belief rather than the reality? Considering how the markets of Europe were flooded with Indian cotton textiles within a space of three decades during the second half of the seventeenth century, the statement does carry a certain conviction.

That the coastal areas of India, Indonesia, and parts of China had become highly commercialised by the beginning of the seventeenth century is evident from contemporary European descriptions. The records of the Dutch and English East India Companies demonstrate after 1600, in a wealth of details, the exact nature of the commercial economy, its inner workings, strengths and weaknesses, and the regional variations. How far back in time did the process of change begin? The question subsumes another, broader, one: whether the historian is in any way right to adopt an evolutionary approach in the discussion of economic and social structures. A moment's reflection is enough to convince one that division of labour, industrial production, and long-distance trade were part of the social community from pre-historic times. It will be difficult to find a society in any age or place which did not have some of the features of an exchange economy based on the concept of relative values, money use, and the market. Communities practising subsistence agriculture and industrial production almost certainly co-existed with those which were subject to the influence of the market mechanism and the control of capital. Seen in this light, the question of the origin of commercialisation in the various areas of the Indian Ocean takes on a different character. The problem is to identify the substantive changes in the systems framework and the functions and operations of that framework. In a study concerned with long-distance trade the obvious starting-point of such an analysis is an examination of the role of merchants, commercial and legal institutions, monetary arrangements, and the method of production itself. However, it will be useful first to recapitulate the chronology of the main events and its significance to the economic developments.

In an earlier chapter, it was pointed out how our period of Asian history was shaped by an interaction, a struggle, between five separate forces of civilisation. The spread of Islam in both the West and the East created a zone of unification. At the same time the process of conversion ran into conflict with the Hindu social system in the Indian subcontinent and with the equally strong sense of identity possessed by the Chinese empire. The Turco-Mongol conquests and migration into the civilised lands of Asia were politically catalytic. The administrative norms of the various military–bureaucratic empires found in Asia from the eleventh century onwards represented a refashioning of the ancient imperial traditions (as, for example, those of Iran or even of Babylon) in the mould of the steppe people. The European arrival in the Indian Ocean, and the growth of western seaborne trade, finally introduced both new economic institutions and the novel concept that sea-power was an instrument of state policy. There is no question that the ancient lands overrun by Islamic armies and settlers had already evolved a sophisticated economic system which could support long-distance trade and the apparatus of the state. Although the caravan traders of Mecca and Hijaz may appear in the existing sources as mere tribal carriers, the fact remains that they were intermediaries between two segments of the trans-continental trade of Eurasia. By the tenth century, according to the descriptions of al-Muqaddasi, many regions of the world of Islam were fully integrated into a structure of distant economic exchange, both as producers and as consumers. The systematic examination, carried out by many Arab geographers, of production, commodities, and trade, and of the roles of towns, shows that Egypt, the Yemen, Iraq, Oman, and parts of Iran already possessed local economies dependent on the market mechanism.

Lack of evidence makes it difficult to reconstruct the exact nature of the commercial economy of the Indian subcontinent for the period corresponding to that covered by the Arab writers (i.e. the eighth to the eleventh century). Yet there can be little doubt that the Middle Eastern port-towns received a substantial volume of their imports from the coastal regions of India, and that the caravan trade to Central Asia and the Iranian highlands remained active, subject only to temporary political barriers. The commercial advance of Sung China into the circuit of Indian Ocean trade is, of course, well recorded. Neither India nor China could have supported its political superstructure and habits of civilisation without an instrument of economic extraction. However, there was a qualitative difference between Indian and Chinese participation in long-distance trade, maritime or landborne. Chinese merchants and traders were as skilled, commercially motivated, and innovative as Indian. Both groups built ships and sailed to distant seas when the opportunity arose. But all through history the merchants of China were subjected to a degree of central government control that was absent in India. The attitude and the policy of the successive imperial dynasties in China created a strange paradox. One of the most advanced entrepreneurial groups in Asia was forced to operate outside the reach of the state system and to create its own system of self-protection. Indian merchants were not altogether free from state control; but in general they could trade wherever they pleased.

The thirteenth and fourteenth centuries were spectacular periods of expansion for Islam. The Turkish conquest of Gujarat (1303–4), the most active maritime province of India, coincided with renewed migration of Islamic communities to East Africa and with a vigorous age of town construction on different parts of that coast. The gradual acceptance of Islam by the rulers and people of the Indonesian islands was yet another sign of the Muslim advance in an easterly direction. It was during these two centuries also that the pattern of emporia trading seems to have grown to maturity, culminating in the twin commercial scales of Malacca and Cambay in the fifteenth century. If the historian is to be able at all to identify and speak of an Asian system of economic exchange, or even of a "mode of production", in which commercial capitalism was the dominant feature, he will have to look seriously at the rise of emporia trade in the Indian Ocean in this period. The developments that followed the foundation of the Portuguese seaborne empire in the early sixteenth century can be viewed in two separate perspectives. European maritime expansion, particularly the integration of America into the western commercial system, acted as a powerful force drawing together the countries of the Indian Ocean and parts of the African continent. The emerging pattern of long-distance trade and of economic exchange and specialisation represented the beginning of a "world economy". It has certainly been interpreted as the first stage in the history of capitalism, leading eventually to the dominant role of industrial capital and the social transformations of the early nineteenth century.[5] In the Indian Ocean, the diversion of a large proportion of trans-continental trade to the Cape route, the forcible restructuring of the emporia trade, the injection of a huge volume of monetary liquidity in the form of American silver, and the rapidly growing demand for Asian commodities (after 1600), were all part of the larger global movement. At the same time, it is possible to argue that purely internal forces in the Mughal and Ming empires, and in other parts of Asia, were working towards intensification of the market, development of commercial capital, a greater degree of industrial control exercised by merchants over artisans, and monetisation of state fiscal arrangements.[6] In functional terms, what happened in Western Europe during the sixteenth and seventeenth centuries may not have been quite so unique after all. One can find strong parallel developments in many areas of the Indian Ocean – areas long associated with emporia and trans-continental trade.

There were, of course, major differences between the paths taken by respectively European and Asian economic developments, just as different Asian countries had distinctive structural features. It is not our purpose here to examine these points of similarity or contrast. We shall return to the analytical points raised earlier: to the role played by merchants, money, and production in the Indian Ocean. The close relationship between capital, as a prerequisite of long-distance trade, and merchants is taken for granted by historians; but it is not at all evident why one particular social group – the merchants – should also have become axiomatically the legal owners, managers, and beneficiaries of capital. The logical answer to this historical puzzle must surely depend on tracing the stages through which capitalism evolved in the past or quite simply on recognising its functional categories. Just as there is division of labour in economic production as a whole and in its component parts, so the utilisation of capital involves to a lesser or a greater extent specialisation. It is possible theoretically to conceive of a perfect world of capitalism in which the supply of capital, claims to its ownership, its utilisation, and the distribution of the economic surplus created by it are completely separate processes controlled by their own separate sets of assumptions and incentives. Such a world exists today in many industrial societies. In the past, the merchant community had little alternative to taking on most of these functions itself, and the whole weight of social, legal, and political traditions in Asia remained tilted, whether by accident or by deliberate preference, towards keeping the merchants as capitalists separate from other groups in society. It is not that there was no pre-industrial capitalism in the Middle East, India, or

China; but the merchants or bankers in these trading nations of Asia could not turn their investments into spheres of public interest protected by law and encouraged by the state. Members of the public who invested their money in the bonds of the republics of Venice or Genoa or the Bank of Amsterdam were not free from financial risks. But the bonds had the qualities of legal recognition and of mortgage value. The Indian or Chinese merchants lending money to the ruling elites or helping with the realisation of taxes were unable to institutionalise their public credits into marketable assets.

One of the most difficult questions in the history of Indian Ocean trade is to determine how merchants and small traders raised their initial commercial capital. We know that laws of contract and partnership existed and that legal conventions made it possible for a junior merchant to borrow capital from a senior member. Examples of these commenda contracts in medieval Islamic trade are numerous and their provisions are not too difficult to interpret. Bonds raised on the value of a ship or its cargo constituted another instrument of credit. The borrower accepted a fixed rate of interest and repaid the principal, together with the interest, either at the overseas port of shipment or at the conclusion of the voyage. The risk of shipwreck was borne by the lender. The most flexible form of capital transactions, however, was provided by bills of exchange. All the leading emporia of the Indian Ocean had active markets in precious metals in addition to normal commodity markets. Bills of exchange drawn on one port-town by another provided temporary finance for merchants who wished to make speculative investments and reduced the risk involved in moving liquid capital in the form of gold and silver for those with surplus funds on their hands. These practices were essentially the technical devices of an ongoing capital market without which the maritime trade of Asia could not have existed to any significant extent. The problem of capital accumulation is a different one. If a merchant had sufficient credit, it was not difficult for him to raise capital through one form of monetary instrument or another. There is little historical information as to how that credit was established in the first place or as to its subsequent value with bankers.

Although direct evidence is lacking, it is possible to gather some idea of this process from scattered references in contemporary sources. However, it is important to remember that capital accumulation among merchants must have taken different paths in the various countries of Asia. The experience of Islamic societies in particular is likely to have been in marked contrast to that of, let us say, India. This was not only because Islamic laws against the practices of usury and money-lending created a social barrier against the profession of bankers; but the Muslim encouragement of merchants and trade derived its authority from the Prophet himself and created a paradox. How could merchants trade without capital, and what was to regulate the supply of capital without its price (interest payments)? It was difficult or unusual for Muslims to become bankers, though money-changers or "sarrafs" were common enough. The question of interest charges was settled by Islamic merchants indirectly, either by dealing through bankers of another faith or through disguised payments of premiums. But, whereas the occupation of merchant in Islam was open to all members of the faith, in India it was kept confined to closed groups identified by their caste at birth. Evidence from sixteenth-century China refers to land hunger and rural hardship as constituting the motive force behind the merchants' adoption of the profession.[7] Lack of economic opportunities in the countryside can certainly push the children of the impoverished landed classes in the direction of large-scale commerce. It must be asked how these people raised their working capital and, if they had no capital of their own at the beginning, why the established commercial firms opened their doors to young, aspiring members?[8] In India, the most successful mercantile groups in the long-distance maritime trade of Asia came not from harsh barren lands, but from regions of high agricultural production: Gujarat, southern India, and Bengal. The inland trade, on the other hand, was dominated by merchants from the arid regions of northern India, Rajasthan, the Punjab, and the province of Agra.

There were clearly many contradictory movements in the formation of mercantile classes in the trading nations of Asia in our period. But capital could accumulate in the hands of merchants in three ways. The main source was family wealth, supported by the wealth of the trading community to which the family belonged. There is no doubt that a Chinese merchant of Fukien or Kwangtung did not operate alone any more than the Gujarati bania families were independent of their common Jain community in Cambay or Surat. Similar groups were to be found in Cairo, Alexandria, Aden, Mocha, Hormuz, and Isfahan. The wealthy Armenian families of Julfa were engaged in the caravan and seaborne trade of Asia from Anatolia to Tibet and from Gombroon to Canton in the seventeenth century. The family firm trained the younger members in calligraphy, accountancy, and the use of foreign languages. When they were old enough to accept financial responsibility, a trial sum would be assigned to them to manage on their own and they would graduate to positions as the firm's factors in provincial branches. From that point onward inborn talent alone determined how high the youthful merchant would climb. John Fryer gives an amusing description of the Armenian merchants of Isfahan (1677):

the Armenians being skilled in all the intricacies of trade at home, and travelling with these into the remotest kingdoms, become by their own industry, and by being factors of their own kindred's honesty, the wealthiest men . . . they are a kind of privateers in trade, *No Purchase, no Pay*; they enter the theatre of commerce by means of some benefactor, whose money they adventure upon, and on return, a quarter part of the gain is their own: from such beginnings do they raise sometimes great fortunes for themselves and Masters.[9]

If the immediate family, kinsmen, and benevolent friends diverted some of their surplus wealth in the direction of new entrants, to a limited extent an experienced Asian merchant also invested and managed funds belonging to the rich landed classes and the ruling elites. The actual arrangements were never institutionalised and remained a matter of private treaty; but there are many examples from seventeenth-century India which reveal that a leading merchant actively trading by land and sea had access to capital owned by the Mughal princes or aristocracy. During the first half of the eighteenth century, two brothers in the North Indian family of the Fatechands became bankers to the nawabs of Bengal, the managers of the provincial mint and friends of the Mughal emperor himself in Delhi.[10] Similar connections between the mandarins of Canton and the junk merchants of Batavia and the islands of Indonesia were common. The third way of capital accumulation for a merchant was the game of chance. An individual, through his entrepreneurial ability, was able to identify profit-making opportunities in the market, and his high-risk ventures succeeded through either planning or luck. For such men, once the business grows beyond a certain size it becomes an immense machine of capital generation. The problem for them is no longer how to raise capital but how to reinvest it profitably. For the traditional line of specialisation is quite often unable to absorb the commercial surplus. This was the reason why all great Asian merchants were forced to diversify their business activities into numerous different spheres of economic interest.

In general, the supply and ownership of capital employed in the long-distance trade of the Indian Ocean remained in the hands of professional merchants. This would have been the case in Europe also, though the development of public banks as deposit-accepting institutions may have opened the door to capital transfers between public and merchants. It was really the rise of the Dutch and English East India Companies with joint-stock capital that lent financial respectability to the method of capitalisation through shares and fixed-interest bonds. The practice separated the owners and the managers of capital and thereby redistributed the profits and further accumulation of capital. The commercial economy of Asia, however, remained in our period less differentiated in terms of function and legal practice. It was taken for granted that merchants worked for profits. They provided the capital and kept the gains as a reward for the taking of risks. While there was a natural connection in the popular mind between tangible wealth and the occupation of merchant, the reality was somewhat different. The great majority of the merchants engaged in the emporia trade of the Indian Ocean probably earned no more than a modest living. A few families rose to positions of real wealth comparable to those of the great landed classes. But, unlike the Asian bureaucratic officials or the hereditary landowners, merchants suffered from a perennial erosion of their material status. They had no direct access to political or military power, and the Asian state systems (except, perhaps, in China) did not completely concede to the merchants the principle of financial independence under the law.

The dividing line between private property and concentrated mercantile wealth was a fine one. It was recognised everywhere that merchants and traders had as much right to spend their money on the good things of life as did other members of society. Chinese sources frequently spoke of the legendary fortunes of the salt merchants of Shansi, and their Arab or Indian counterparts are equally well recorded in history. What these had in common was the ability to support a life-style generally found only among the ruling elites. The descendants of a successful commercial house might indeed invest their money in urban property, garden houses, fine stables, and personal possessions; but there was always a limit beyond which it was not possible to increase the private consumption of merchants, even if no political danger had been incurred in attracting the attention of the tax-gatherers to the firm's economic success. In most cases, the outlook and attitude of Asian merchants were no different from those of entrepreneurs elsewhere. They remained frugal and reluctant to adopt an ostentatious way of life. The separation of personal expenditure from the assets of the firm left the merchants with an awkward problem. What were they to do with the profits of a trade which went on reproducing itself endlessly for as long as the business remained successful? If the question had been put to any pre-modern Asian merchant, the answer would probably have been the same as any modern business firm would give: reinvest the profits in further growth. The logic of growth was a relentless one. This was the starting-point historically of a conflict between the principle of private property and financial gains made in trade. How far the state would allow a business organisation to grow with unfettered control over its resources was never settled in the past. If a rich merchant used his money well, it was possible to make powerful friends in government. The grant of official monopolies or exclusive rights to farm fiscal revenues, or the management of national currencies, might be given to particular merchants as a result of political intervention. But the spectre of arbitrary expropriation was never far off from the scene of pre-modern commerce. The vulnerability of merchants to unpredictable shifts in official policy furnished the greatest threat to the continuity of Asian business houses and their uncontrolled growth.

The limits to legal recognition of mercantile wealth as the abstract assets of a business concern demand an explanation. This was not a phenomenon confined to Asia alone. In 1692 the English East India Company published a pamphlet in which it was pointed out that no man was obliged to give financial security for his property. The Company did not see any reason why Parliament should impose such restrictions on its trading capital and force the Company to wind up its balance-sheet every twenty-one years, as was being proposed.[11] Although the Directors of the East India Company refused to mention it, the reason for the public criticism of the Company was quite clear. It was suspected of being an association of monopolists which shut the corporate door against the admission of new members and investors. It had become uncomfortably powerful in political terms and had even dared to wage war against the Great Mughal (1688–90), which it had lost. In all the commercial emporia of the Indian Ocean, merchants were allowed to buy and sell freely, with minimum state intervention. The regulations and maritime laws in these towns actively encouraged market operations which inevitably gave rise to large-scale capital transactions. But there was a remarkable difference between the ownership of land and that of commercial capital. The concept of private property in land was not limited in Asia either by size or by the type of owner. Religious foundations, charitable institutions, sovereign princes, widows, and orphans, were all entitled to own land and enjoy its income. This was never the case with trading capital. The merchant and his working stock remained indivisible. Capitalism as a commercial activity was universal in the Indian Ocean. There was little social or legal admission of capital's productive role as distinct from its owners.

That social conventions and the financial needs of the state defined the relationship between Asian political rulers and merchants is readily seen. Trade remained a specialised occupation below the professions of arms, of administration, and even, in the case of China, of farming. The attitude of official contempt towards traders in general is one of the best-recorded themes of Asian history. A Mughal official who visited Bombay at the end of the seventeenth century was greatly impressed by the sight of its European military garrison. But of the English as traders in India, he had this to say: "The profits of the commerce of these misbelievers, according to report, does not exceed twenty lacs of [200 000] rupees. The balance of the money required for the maintenance of the English settlement is obtained by plundering the ships voyaging to the House of God [Mecca]."[12] It was common knowledge throughout the Indian Ocean that the Asian ships which every year crossed the Arabian Sea from Mocha or the Persian Gulf carried large sums of money in Spanish silver or Italian coins. The treasure ships proved an irresistible prize to European privateers, to pirates, and even to the East India Companies when their political relations with the Mughal empire were not cordial. In normal times, the annual Middle Eastern fleet supplied India and China with the means to sustain their monetary institutions. Precious metals obtained through trade were as great an inducement to Asian princes to encourage merchants as were the direct customs duties paid by them. If the political or social attitude towards the trading community was generally hostile in Asia, its origin lay in the supposition that the accumulation of capital, and even commercial profits, were made at the expense of the public. But merchants and traders survived, flourished, and proliferated over centuries because of the vital economic role performed by them in pre-modern societies.

Perhaps the most immediate and powerful means of self-protection available to merchants was in their command over money. Commercial understanding of international currencies complemented the ability to move precious metals over long distances and make payments separated by time and space. The link between the flow of trade in the Indian Ocean and movements of gold and silver essentially resolved itself into two areas of interaction. First of all, there was the need to establish a common measure of value and an index of prices which could be understood and utilised without the need to master complicated linguistic conventions. Secondly, these values or prices had to be expressed in terms of physical objects or of an analogous system which created purchasing power. In China a roll of silk or a basket of rice was treated as money of account for a long time, just as in the desert areas of North Africa a standard unit of moulded salt helped to fix the exchange ratios of traded goods. Commodity money was rarely used in the Middle East and India. These regions inherited a strong imperial tradition in which the issue of dynastic coins – of gold and silver supplemented by copper – was regarded as a mark of national sovereignty and as a monetary necessity. The inconvenience and disadvantages of using commodities to express values in international transfers were only too apparent. Neither silk nor rice could circulate in the form of physical payments; their role as money was limited to accountancy. The supply of gold and silver, on the other hand, remained strictly limited and the relative scarcity preserved the value of these metals. Simple metallurgical tests and weighing easily determined the intrinsic worth of coins fashioned out of the scarce metals. Once a particular coin had assumed a leading role in international banking – as, for example, the Arab gold dinar, the Venetian ducat, or the Spanish real of eight – the merchants did not need to carry out detailed assay of the coins before accepting them in payment. The stamp of the mint dies was sufficient proof of their authenticity and intrinsic value.

The use of precious metals as money and currency varied in different parts of the Indian Ocean. Throughout the Middle East and the Indian subcontinent money was identical with national or regional currency. A gold or silver coin of fixed weight and alloy conferred on its owner the legal claim to buy certain units of goods and services. Prices could be expressed as so many coins per fixed unit of goods or, more commonly, as the reverse, so many units of commodities for a single nominated coin. The prevailing shortage of coins and precious metals in pre-modern societies kept the nominal prices of many articles low. Items of daily use in particular had their prices quoted in varying standards of quantity rather than in a varying number of coins. The issue of regnal coins was an obligatory act of royal accession for both Hindu and Muslim rulers. For the latter, the unauthorised minting of coins constituted an act of rebellion; the concept of a legal tender was very strong in Islamic states. By contrast, the failure of South East Asian countries to develop strong national currencies based on gold and silver appears inexplicable. The ports of trade and the commercialised areas of production must have used some system of currency and money. Pires hints that in Malacca gold and silver were regarded and traded as bullion.[13] From the second half of the sixteenth century, once Spanish American silver coins had established their authority in the Indonesian islands and in Malacca, the export of pepper and spices was financed by reals of eight. Chinese copper coins were also popular as a means of international exchange in South East Asia, and indigenous coins made from tin or a low-value alloy served as internal monetary units.

Historically, the area which attracted the largest volume of precious metals in the course of international trade was China, which remained ahead even of the Indian subcontinent. But Chinese monetary practices were both unique and more inclined to experimentation than those of other regions of Asia. The only official currency issued in China was confined to copper pieces, which achieved astronomical quantities during periods of economic prosperity and high government expenditure. While strings of copper cash provided a general form of purchasing power, silver in bullion was considered as a more valuable form of money. Instead of coining bullion, Chinese merchants, traders, and bankers used precision scales and metal cutters to derive a standard unit of gold or silver. The system had the great merit of keeping the government and its agents out of the commercial usage of money, and its origin probably lay in the periodic attempts of the imperial court to discourage the monetary function of imported silver. However, China was also the first country in the world to issue paper currency. Paper notes were printed as early as the seventh century, though it was not before the ninth century that these were considered reliable. The first Ming emperor, T'ai-tsu (1368–98), attempted to replace gold and silver as money by issuing official paper currency. The financial experiment was not successful. The value of the paper notes soon collapsed, and by the middle of the fifteenth century China had once again returned to the conventional usage of silver.[14] The method of making monetary payments in uncoined bullion remained. Foreign merchants and Chinese junk traders who imported silver into China had their treasure assayed by recognised bullion dealers, and the die stamp of these dealers turned the imported coins or bars into circulating medium. For domestic use silver was generally melted down after a time and recast in the form of the famous shoe-shaped ingots.

In India and the Middle East, the government maintained the value of currency by insisting on frequent recoinage. As Islamic coins were hammered pieces without a protective stamped edge, clipping was easy. The low amount of base metal added to the alloy (which remained more than ninety-five per cent fine) also led to a certain amount of natural wastage through wear. Both gold and silver are soft metals. The convention adopted for preserving the intrinsic mint value of currency was an ingenious one. It was clearly recognised that, given the rigidity in the supply of money caused by using metallic currency, merchants and professional bankers would be forced to accept and handle a large number of coins of different mints and different values. The system of exchange was determined by a sliding scale of discounts and premiums. For example, freshly minted coins bore a theoretical value of one hundred. All issues later than the current year from the identical mint and identical dies were discounted at a variable rate and the same principle was applied to the issues of non-local and foreign mints. For national currency, when, after a time-lag of perhaps no more than three or four years, the discount equalled the mint charges for coining, there was no longer any incentive to keep the coins. They were returned to the foundry for recoinage. The monetary arrangements placed enormous monopoly powers in the hands of currency dealers and government mint officers.

There are many complaints in seventeenth-century European sources that the system was open to abuse by money-changers, bankers, and mint officials.[15] Market factors, of course, decided in the final instance how far the would-be monopolists could go in pressing their financial advantage. It was not too difficult for merchants to manipulate the general public in collusion with the mint. But it was much more difficult for one group of professional money-dealers to keep the balance of financial power in their hands exclusively if merchants engaged in long-distance trade opposed them. For gold and silver constantly crossed national and regional frontiers in response to changing economic conditions. Periodic gluts and famines in bullion supply were an endemic feature of pre-modern societies, and the movements at times completely destabilised national currencies. The most frequent and obvious source of disruption came from changes in the value of a well-known currency. Debasement or enhancement in the mint value of a coin, whether undertaken in response to financial exigencies or as a matter of considered policy, immediately set off a chain reaction. It could easily lead to an inflow or outflow of precious metals if the policy of neighbouring countries or trading partners remained unchanged. Alterations in the ratio of gold to silver in any case constantly threatened monetary stability, and the relative demand for the two precious metals, arising from speculative and storing motives, tended to fix market prices which differed from those of the official mints.

While gold and silver were indispensable as universal measures of value in the Indian Ocean, copper coins supplied the needs of poorer people. The role of copper in the emporia or trans-continental trade was less complicated than that of the precious metals; it was traded mainly as a commodity. Cowries fulfilled a function similar to that of copper coins as token currency, though their monetary value was more widespread. Trade to coastal and inner Africa demanded a huge quantity of cowrie shells, together with Indian beads made from semi-precious stones. Token currency satisfied the transaction demand for money at one end of the market. At the other end, there were exclusively banking instruments, bills of exchange, personal bonds, and discounted bills. These were all known to Asian merchants and used to create credit. It is not possible to ascertain the importance of banking instruments, as against precious metals, in financing Indian Ocean trade. Gold and silver supported the superstructure of banking transactions, and the ability to settle final payments in one of the two metals was essential in upholding one's financial credit. It was this linkage between long-distance trade and treasure that accounted for the constant movement of precious metals between one emporium and another.[16]

The most important temporal watershed in the international migration of treasure in our period took place in the sixteenth century, with the European discovery of the Cape route to India. In the earlier centuries gold and silver had moved along the existing network of trade, and the characteristic feature of the monetary system underpinning the international payments had been the exchange of a large number of national currencies against each other. The transactions arose out of the need to pay for goods, as well as the more specialised trade in precious metals. The money of certain dominant states – Egypt, Venice, and Genoa, for example – was treated as leading reserve currencies. Altogether, the annual production of precious metals remained small, and there was considerable delay before large quantities of coins or bullion responded to the forces of demand. Within half a century of the discovery of America and the Cape route to Asia, the *ancien régime* began to give way. As gold and silver brought back from America entered European monetary circulation, there was a rising level of government expenditure on the part of countries able to claim a share of this newly created purchasing power. Some of the European demand moved in the direction of Asia, and the continuing export of Asian goods paid for with Spanish American gold and silver reflected as much the expansion in money supply as Asia's comparative advantage in industrial production. The pattern of trade in precious metals also began to change across Europe and Asia. In the place of small individual transactions in numerous coins of different denominations, silver was traded on a large scale, either in the form of stamped ingots or coined into reals of eight. The shortening of the journey time taken for the Spanish American silver to reach the trading emporia of the Indian Ocean increased the velocity of exchange. The economic effects of the easing of the money supply must have been considerable in the commercial regions of the Middle East, India, Indonesia, and China. From the middle of the sixteenth century, Japanese silver mines added their output to that of the central and South American production centres in Mexico and Peru.

The connection between commercial capitalism in Europe and the inflow of American treasure received much attention in Europe. The question was discussed and debated from the sixteenth century to the eighteenth. As early as 1571 the Spanish writer Thomas de Mercado pointed out the way in which Spain's trade to the New World had the effect of raising the prices of cloth at home, together with the prices of imports from Holland.[17] From the latter half of the seventeenth century both merchants and theorists became aware that the outflow of silver from Europe to Asia was caused by changes in the international economy. Did the rising volume of financial liquidity stimulate economic production in Europe and Asia? If the answer is a positive one, it can be argued that the increase in the flow of commercial transactions created surplus value and established a firm link between mercantile capital and production. If, on the other hand, the answer is negative, it will be right to assume that the commercial capitalism of the sixteenth and seventeenth centuries was no more than a more intensive exploitation of the previous system. Historians familiar with the description of events in the original sources will be aware that these questions and assumptions are not likely to go beyond plausible suggestions. The response of different countries in different periods to economic opportunities varied widely, and the gains and losses may well have cancelled one another out and produced a static aggregate situation. It is much more interesting to recast the problem and ask what was the nature of the relationship between long-distance trade and economic production in pre-modern Asia.

We have seen in an earlier chapter that the range of commodities exchanged included agricultural products, industrial raw materials, and finished manufactured goods. The level of international demand for these goods fluctuated from year to year and from season to season. But from the tenth century, if not earlier, the pattern of specialisation and the basic structure of selling markets had become established. Merchants knew what items were demanded and how much they could sell in a particular trading area. Speculative dealing and a temporary imbalance between supply and demand could create uncertainties in the market. Merchants and dealers lived and continued to live with that knowledge. Many new commodities entered the flow of exchange during our period of study, and likewise the prosperity of one particular group of economic regions declined in time so that they were replaced by others. The production system in general – and especially those people engaged in export industries, whether these were agricultural or manufacturing – felt the impact of long-distance trade through two separate mechanisms. First of all, the familiar multiplier effect of an increase in demand expressed in the form of a higher volume of exports was as evident in the pre-modern economy of Asia as it was in the nineteenth and twentieth centuries. Exports of coffee, raw silk, cotton and silk fabrics, pepper and spices, brought considerable rural and urban income to the producing areas. The second mechanism was the control exercised by merchants in organising the system of production itself. The point of contact between producers and merchants was not just at the level of the market-place where commodities were exchanged for money: long-distance trade imposed a whole range of economic considerations on merchants, varying from consumer taste, transport costs, and control of quality to the time and reliability of delivery. The constant effort of wholesale dealers to resolve these problems gave rise to an industrial relationship that was highly distinctive and identifiable by both producers and merchants. The organisation adopted was a two-way process. Merchants advanced money to agriculturists or artisans in return for an obligation to deliver the contracted goods on time and in accordance with the stipulated quality. The producers secured in this relationship contracted customers who had close knowledge of distant markets.[18] The maritime and caravan trade of Asia was not a matter of chance or pure speculation. The same could also be said of the system of production. The capitalism of trade, in spite of the absence of fixed capital, was a fact of daily life for the Asian artisan and the farmer alike.

11

Conclusion

It is not easy for historians of the present age to take a backward glance at the period before 1800 and recreate its images. For European historians especially organic links with that distant past are so far lost that the social landmarks of even the late eighteenth century are scarcely recognisable in terms of living experience. To suggest that the year 1750 might constitute a symbolical meridian in time is to invite an insistent question. What kind of life-cycle for human civilisation in general came to an end around that period? Was it perhaps feudalism; or is the statement just another instance of empty rhetoric imitative of the Gallic tradition and able to offer nothing more than a vague generalisation? As the question echoes back, the reasoning behind the original comment in the opening page of chapter 1 gradually re-emerges. The great sailing vessels which in our period of study were to be found in every port of the western Indian Ocean, from Basra to Cambay and from Calicut to Mombassa, can still be seen in Bombay harbour alongside the modern freighter and tanker. No European East-Indiaman, however, sails today through the Bay of Biscay to the island of Madeira to take on board fifty-odd casks of malmsey and then cross the line, as contemporary logs describe the Equator, to make landfall at the palm-fringed sea-front of Cochin or Calicut. If the Kwaiti booms and their Indian fellow-vessels continue to cross the Arabian Sea, they do so, it could be said, either as part of a backward economy or because their owners are not rational beings. Modern technology is intolerant of the living past going beyond, shall we say, the 1850s, let alone the 1750s. The sailing-ship, whether it was European or Asian, lived on for a century or more beyond the mid-eighteenth century. Its eventual disappearance can be traced back to the invention of the steam-engine. There is no particular difficulty in citing other examples which support the theory of a fundamental structural break between our period of study and the one that followed it. Fernand Braudel expressed the idea well when he commented:

Even at the end of the eighteenth century, vast areas of the earth were still a garden of Eden for animal life. Man's intrusion upon these paradises was a tragic innovation ... What was shattered in both China and Europe with the eighteenth century, was a biological *ancien régime*, a set of restrictions, obstacles, structures, proportions and numerical relationships that had hitherto been the norm.[1]

221

It would be futile to enter into a debate here as to whether the golden age of mankind should be located in the present or in the past. However, it is certain that the merchants and sailors of the Indian Ocean or the Atlantic did not know in the mid-eighteenth century that they were "irrational", "backward", and "deprived" people. On the contrary, they had every reason to believe that the pattern of long-distance trade based on the transport of goods in sailing-ships, in wagons, and on the backs of camels had proved its rationale through several millennia and needed no further theoretical justification. If the present study of Indian Ocean trade points in the direction of any systematic conclusion at all, this is that the process of economic exchange was shaped by the social and political systems of different civilisations and their attitudes towards one another. In the economic equations of merchants and others involved in the business of distant trade, the influence of demand factors was overwhelmingly important. This is very far removed from the present-day situation in which international trade is primarily a function of the variables on both the supply and the production sides. The close relationship between rapid technological development and the total stock of material goods and services is a fundamental determinant of modern social values. In our period, the technology of production had stabilised itself over many centuries and was treated as if it was a constant. The force of change and the opportunity for accumulating wealth came mainly from shifts in demand and from improvements in the institutional arrangements of economic exchange which lowered costs.

At the same time, a historical study of the period in question makes it quite clear that the long-distance trade of Eurasia was not conducted on the basis of a socially determined exchange of goods and services between different communities or state systems.[2] The *use* and *function* of the commodities traded originated in a spectrum of values, and in turn influenced the nature of demand. But the process of exchange itself was an economic transaction or a market-orientated activity. Few historians would disagree with the view that pre-modern markets were highly imperfect as mechanisms allocating economic resources.[3] The notion that there is an abstract force called the market which maximises output through competition for scarce resources is the legacy of a doctrinaire theory. Its universal acceptance has unquestionably impeded an understanding of the way in which economic resources are utilised and allocated in a given historical situation. Attention has already been drawn to the fact that the supply or production functions in pre-industrial economies were relatively rigid and derived from a complex involving many different levels of human society. The system of distribution on the demand side of the economy, however, was strongly dependent on the allocative role of relative prices. The type of trading relations examined in the present study was primarily an activity carried on by professional merchants acting as profit-seeking individuals. Of course they represented at times the interests of political rulers and even of the governments of powerful centralised empires; but they cannot be equated by any stretch of the imagination with state officials or administrators.

Relative prices measured in units of gold and silver provided the merchants with the key to economic success. A roll of silk, a basket of rice, a standard mould of salt were all useful as measures of value in conveying exchange ratios to the local population of a trading region unaccustomed to the use of money. For the final calculation of profits, merchants who transported a variety of goods over long distances needed to convert these commodity currencies into acceptable money of account. Our historical sources leave no room for doubt that the "universal almanac" of exchange tables and currencies, together with the system of weighing precious metals and heavy goods, was as essential to pre-modern merchants as financial newspapers are to today's businessmen. From the sixteenth century, European treatises on Asian currencies and weights reveal in minute detail the full operation of the price mechanism in the Indian Ocean. That the Asian merchants themselves kept complete notes of these relative values is attested, to take only one example, in Ma Huan's work (1413–51). The incense produced in Champa (central Vietnam), he wrote, was expensive; its weight in silver was the price charged. The king of Cochin minted a gold coin called the fanam, each one weighing one fen and one li on the Chinese steelyard (0.013191 oz troy). It was ninety per cent fine and exchangeable for fifteen silver coins of four-li weight (0.00479 oz troy each coin). The currency and weights of Calicut were recorded with equal exactitude. Only a compelling motivation and commercial need can explain Ma Huan's attention to metrology.[4]

It may be asked, what then is a market and its connection with trade? Economists use the term "market" in a much more restrictive sense than do historians, geographers, or anthropologists. To avoid confusion, a general definition is needed. Theories on markets, it was suggested in another historical study of early trade, can be grouped into three conceptual categories, all of them characterised by the necessary assumption that the term involves an exchange of some kind:

A market may be defined first of all as a form of economic behaviour. It is also a locus in space where the physical process of exchange takes place. A corollary of the spatial definition of the market is its dynamic features; time is an important second dimension in its measurement. Finally, a market can be taken as a sociological phenomenon, in which various social groups perform differentiated functions, between merchants and brokers, or the pedlar and householders, and the political relationships which characterise the contact between rulers and merchants in particular also involve wider questions of power and social stratifications.[5]

Karl Polyani made a theoretical distinction between trade and market and raised the question, when and how does trade get linked with markets?[6] If the above definition is accepted, the relevance of Polyani's question can be properly appreciated. Trade or economic exchange did not, historically, necessarily occur in the market-place. It could have taken place in the counting-house of a great merchant or on board a ship. Nevertheless, the economic relationships were "market" transactions.

In the area of the Indian Ocean, the strongest influence of the market was to be seen in the great trading emporia. The concept of a "port of trade", as elaborated by Polyani, is too restrictive for a general study of central-places or "world economies". An emporium offered political security to visiting merchants, and provided facilities for anchorage, loading and unloading of ships, warehousing, banking, and the enforcement of contracts. But it was more than an institution for administered or treaty trading in which government agencies played a leading part.[7] The Indian Ocean emporia in our period were markets in every sense and fulfilled multifarious functions. Merchants found in these places a choice of goods and of buyers and sellers, as well as the opportunity to compare prices. Above all, the political neutrality of the leading emporia before the age of Portuguese sea-power was an essential element of their economic success. Rulers whose income came mainly from commercial dues paid by merchants were more aware of their true interests and welfare than were the officials of great centralised empires with strong agricultural revenue. Even so, as many examples from the eighteenth century prove, Mughal ruling elites strove hard to preserve the neutrality of ports under their administrative care.

The temporary residence of foreign merchants at a commercial emporium highlighted only one aspect of the social dimension of long-distance trade. It was taken for granted by everyone concerned that merchants or their agents must travel if they were to make money by trade. The appearance of funduqs in Arab towns, in which ethnic visitors found shelter and protection, was followed by the assignation of entire "mahallas" or quarters to them. The Gujarati bania merchants in Mocha, Gombroon, Constantinople, and even Moscow, shared the foreign quarters of the city with Jews, Armenians, and Syrians from Aleppo. There seems to have been a great "diaspora" of merchants, in which certain ethnic groups displayed special skills both of survival and of profit-making. However, some caution is needed in using the term "trading diasporas" as an analytical tool. The argument that merchants who live and operate through dispersed communities constitute a special social category because they need to work through family or common friends is not really valid as a theoretical proposition. Merchants and traders in our period conducted business through close-knit groups, irrespective of their location; whether they lived at home or in foreign lands, that is how they worked. Furthermore, Jewish and Armenian merchants alone had no proper homeland to which they eventually hoped to return. The behaviour and outlook of these particular members of a nation in diaspora were likely to be very different

Plate 23. The Armenian church in Julfa, Isfahan.

from those of travelling merchants with solid connections at home. Even the Armenians living in Kashgar, Khotan, Delhi, and Hugli in the seventeenth century could point to their own suburb in Isfahan, the little town of Julfa on the far side of the Zayandah-Rud, as a national home. Their fine brick-built church, with its elegant, classic lines, opened its doors to the members of the

English East India Company who could find no consecrated ground to bury their dying colleagues. The concept of "trading diaspora" is invalidated by epistemological reason alone. For example, if it is postulated that such a community is spatially dispersed (a necessary assumption in argument), that they strive to monopolise the trade in certain commodities, that they possess a social and political organisation of an informal nature, and that they exchange commercial information through friends belonging to the same group, it can be easily shown that it is not the fact of spatial dispersion which determines the rest of the proposition but the general characteristics of human behaviour. Historians would be unable to find a single instance in which such a hypothesis can be applied without qualifications destroying the theory.[8]

Of course, a community of merchants living beyond their immediate cultural and political environment can be the object of a historical or anthropological study. The examination of the behaviour patterns of such communities in West Africa provides illumination of many different aspects of long-distance trade. The connection between the organisational requirements of trade and the migration of bania merchants to different parts of India was observed by an official of the English East India Company as early as 1696, as we can see in the following passage from a letter written by Samuel Annesley:

It has been the policy of the Brokers by degrees to settle in all places of the Investment their relations and creatures to carry it on . . . whereby they have done in a manner what they pleased, and it is your Honour's true interest (as I presume) to take the quite contrary measures, and little by little to dysplace them . . . It has been the ancient custome of the Indians to make all bargains by the mediation of Brokers, all Forreigners as well as the natives are compelled to submit to it: the Armenians, Turks, Persians, Jews, Europeans and Banyans.[9]

The significant point about this information is that the migrating communities operated through kinship connections and that they took their commercial organisation with them.[10]

In functional terms, however, there is no difference between modern commercial firms with branches across the world and the seventeenth-century agents of the house of Abdul Gafur, living in Mocha, Gombroon, and Canton and receiving their instructions and trade consignments from the head office in Surat. Even in the much-debated area of protection costs, there is a similarity between present-day multi-national corporations and pre-modern merchants buying political favours and economic concessions from rulers who welcomed an extra source of revenue. But the exact nature of the problem facing the merchants of our period in protection costs remains very indistinct. The historical sources frequently refer to unjust taxes or imposts levied on domestic and foreign merchants by governments in urgent need of money. And information about regular rates of commercial duty charged on long-distance trade is particularly well recorded. On the other hand, there are few references to any internal calculations by merchants as to the costs of buying protection. As the long-distance trade of the Indian Ocean was unarmed before the Portuguese period, the solution to the problem is likely to have been non-systematic. Merchants gave presents to powerful sovereigns according to their special relationships, and they organised protection for their ships and caravans against pirates and bandits. With the appearance of the Portuguese in Asia, and later of the Dutch and English bureaucratic companies, the consideration became more insistent. Asian traders and ship-owners were forced to buy safe-conduct passes from the Europeans, who in turn incurred considerable costs in enforcing their demands and protecting their settlements on land.[11]

The cost of obtaining political protection for merchants in our period of study cannot be quantified, just as transport costs also remain indistinct. It can be surmised that, if the two items together exceeded the expected rate of commercial profit, long-distance trade could hardly have flourished and continued. The seventeenth- and eighteenth-century evidence shows that all types of merchants and traders, great and small, bargained hard with ship-owners over the cost of freighting their goods to overseas ports.[12] There was ample competition in the provision of shipping space for them not to have to encounter monopoly prices. At the same time, the master or owner of a ship regarded it as an item of capital expenditure which was subject to normal calculations of financial yield and depreciation. If there was no point of equilibrium between these two separate sets of costs and profits (those of ship-owners and merchants freighting goods respectively), the maritime trade of the great Asian emporia would have come to an abrupt end. In the absence of detailed account books, these historical calculations cannot be precisely made. It is, however, worth bearing in mind two other points concerning pre-modern transport. The ship-owners of the Indian Ocean often included captains and crews for whom voyages to overseas destinations were a way of life. Whether these people always charged rationally calculated freight rates is doubtful. Likewise, the owners of camels, oxen, horses, and other beasts of burden were hereditary nomadic communities, selling or hiring out their animals to caravan traders. The professional caravan-masters and their animal-handlers themselves looked on trans-continental trips as another way of life. What they regarded as an adequate or satisfactory standard of living and remuneration we shall never know; but we can be certain that, as long as the camels were crossing the Gobi, the Thar desert or the great Nafud, their masters ate just enough food so that both could live and come home. It was imperative that caravan-leaders and ship-captains should have a close understanding with the military authorities in whose areas of action they had to trade. The cost of such protection would have been passed on to the merchants.

The opportunity for political authorities to make financial gains at the expense of merchants would not have arisen without a concentration of wealth. The pre-industrial capitalism of Asia possessed a remarkable feature. Other factors of production, land and labour, were considered socially divisible; anyone who possessed sufficient purchasing power could buy land and employ labour. But capital utilised in trade and industry remained firmly in the hands of mercantile groups. The notion that the possession of title to commercial investments yielding permanent income might be better than the direct taxation of merchants does not seem to have suggested itself to Asian rulers. Had it done so, the other necessary condition would have followed: the need to define such titles and rights under the law. This historical study has demonstrated, it is hoped, the strength of commercial capitalism in Asia. Because it remained legally undefined and socially misunderstood (being associated with usury, engrossing, and monopolies), the area of the social ownership of capital, and of its specific utilisation, management, and accumulation, also remained confined. Of course, the long-distance trade of the Indian Ocean was a capitalistic activity, however that may be defined. No one in our period of study quantified the amount of capital invested in agriculture, in clearing the fields, digging irrigational channels and wells, planting orchards, or building roads. The amount of money invested in Chinese silks, Indian muslins, spices, incense, and fine horses was visible to all. Weavers, spinners, silkworm-rearers, metal-smiths, and the owners of spice plantations, all received their economic rewards through the price mechanism. The link between long-distance trade, commercial capitalism, and production for the export market remained strong. Its exact nature and relationship with the rest of the Asian economies should appropriately be the object of another, separate historical study.

Notes

INTRODUCTION

1 Braudel, *Civilization and Capitalism*, I (1981), 26.
2 Braudel, *The Mediterranean*, I (1972), 14.
3 *Ibid.*, I, 276.
4 See J.T. Fraser and N. Lawrence, eds., *The Study of Time II* (1975).
5 T.W. Rhys Davies, ed., *The Questions of King Milinda* (1890), I, 64; Watanabe, "Causality and Time", in Fraser and Lawrence, eds., *The Study of Time II* (1975).
6 Al-Muqaddasi, *Ahsan al-Taqasim* (1901), 103–4.
7 IOR, Abstract of letters received from Bombay, 20 December 1718, vol. 449, para. 30, p. 322; Despatch Book, 21 July 1738, vol. 107, para. 11, p. 441.
8 Al-Muqaddasi, *Ahsan al-Taqasim* (1901), 23.
9 *Ibid.*, 29.
10 Braudel, *The Mediterranean*, I (1972), 20.
11 Braudel, "Histoire et sciences sociales: la longue durée" (1958).

CHAPTER 1

1 The letter is translated and analysed in Udovitch, "Formalism and Informalism in the Social and Economic Institutions of the Medieval Islamic World", in Banani and Vryonis, eds., *Individualism and Conformity in Classical Islam* (1977), 61–81. The commercial life of the Cairo Genizah merchants has been described in detail in Goitein, *A Mediterranean Society*, I (1967).
2 The quotation is given in Holt, Lambton, and Lewis, eds., *The Cambridge History of Islam* (1970), IA, 224; the original reference is to Ibn al-Furat, *Ta'rikh*, ed. Zurayk and Izzedin, VIII (Beirut, 1939), 65ff.; see also G. Wiet, "Les Marchands d'épices sous les sultans mamlouks", in *Cahiers d'Histoire Égyptienne* (1955).
3 IOR, Factory Records Surat, Diary, 1 October 1744, vol. 29, p. 15; *ibid.*, 11 January 1747, vol. 31, p. 50.
4 For some tentative discussion of the problem, see Steensgaard, *Carracks, Caravans, and Companies* (1972); Chaudhuri, *The Trading World of Asia and the English East India Company 1660–1760* (1978).
5 For the degeneration of navigational knowledge among Arab ship-masters, see Villiers, *Sons of Sinbad* (1969), 186.
6 See Schrieke, "Some Remarks on Borrowing in the Development of Culture", in his *Indonesian Sociological Studies* (1955), I, 225–37; Renfrew, "Trade as Action

at a Distance: Questions of integration and communication", in Sabloff and Lamberg-Karlovsky, eds., *Ancient Civilization and Trade* (1975), 3–59.

7   Renfrew, 22–3.

8   Hiskett, "Materials Relating to the Cowry Currency of the Western Sudan" (1966).

9   IOR, Despatch Book, 6 September 1682, vol. 90, para. 7, p. 38; Original Correspondence, 23 February 1684, vol. 43, no. 5103, p. 2.

10 IOR, Despatch Book, 18 January 1717, vol. 99, para. 26, pp. 74–5.

11 Ibn Majid, *Kitab al Fawa'id*, 252.

12 This was because it was eaten hot, straight from the fire.

13 Bernier, *Travels in the Mogul Empire* (1891), 250.

14 *Ibid.*, 251, 438.

15 The quotation is in Étienne Balazs, *Chinese Civilization* (1974), 91.

16 Adam Smith, *The Wealth of Nations* (6th edition), vol. II, bk iv, ch. 9.

17 See Fairbank and Teng, "On the Ch'ing Tributary System" (1941), 167.

18 Arendonk, "Kahwa", article in the *Encyclopaedia of Islam*, new edition.

19 See Chaudhuri, *The Trading World of Asia and the English East India Company* (1978), ch. 12.

20 Hassanein Rabie, "Some Technical Aspects of Agriculture in Medieval Egypt", in Udovitch, ed., *The Islamic Middle East, 700–1900* (1981), 60.

21 al-Muqaddasi, *Ahsan al-Taqasim* (1901), 327.

22 E-Tu Zen Sun and Francis, eds., *Chinese Social History* (1956), 214; on migrations, see also Will, *Bureaucratie et famine en Chine* (1980).

23 For references to all these events, see *The English Factories in India 1630–1633*.

24 IOR, Original Correspondence, 9 January 1675, vol. 35, no. 4062, p. 6; Chaudhuri, *The Trading World of Asia and the English East India Company* (1978), 179.

25 E-Tu Zen Sun and Francis, eds., *Chinese Social History* (1956), 225; Will, *Bureaucratie et famine en chine* (1980), 184, for the effects of civil wars at the end of the Ming dynasty in the seventeenth century.

CHAPTER 2

1   The term "world economy" is used here in the sense adopted by Fernand Braudel: of a well-defined economic area under the influence of a central-place or central region. As long as there is a functional and possibly hierarchical relationship between the centre and the peripheral areas, the *level* of the relationship can be left to vary. For example, in a pre-modern economy the element of integration is seen in the commercial relationship between different port-cities. This is entirely different from the large-scale economic integration brought about by the Industrial Revolution and European imperialism in the nineteenth century. In a sense the term "world economy" is semantically misleading, and the geographical "central-place theorem" is a better approximation of the theory. For a discussion of these problems, see Braudel, *Civilisation matérielle, tome 3: Le Temps du monde* (1979); Wallerstein, *Modern World-System* (1974).

2   Islamic historians, brought up on the strict tradition of documentation, would no doubt want to know the nature of the urban growth and of its relationship with

Islam. All that is being assumed here is that a great many new towns and cities were founded with the expansion of Islam, which is taken to be essentially an urban-based religious and political system. Our assertion makes no assumption whatsoever about the degree of urbanisation in, for instance, Sasanian Iraq. For a discussion of Islamic urbanisation, see Grunebaum, "Islam: Essays in the Nature and Growth of a Cultural Tradition" (1955), and "Three Comments on Orthogenetic and Heterogenetic Urban Environment: Hellenistic and Muslim Views on Cities" (1954); Fischel, "The City in Islam" (1956). For a recent discussion of the connection between demand for food production and Islamic urbanisation, see Watson, *Agricultural Innovation in the Early Islamic World* (1983), 132–6.

3 The inscription is dated AD 1030–1: Hultzsch, *South Indian Inscriptions* (1891), II, 105; Coedès, *The Indianized States of Southeast Asia* (1968).

4 Gompertz, *Chinese Celadon Ware* (1958).

5 Wolf, "The Social Organization of Mecca and the Origins of Islam" (1951). An Arab poet spoke of the region: "There winter and summer are equally desolate. No bird flies over Mecca, no grass grows. There are no wild beasts to be hunted. Only the most miserable of all occupations flourishes there, trade." Quoted by Wolf.

6 Kister, *Studies in Jahiliyya and Early Islam* (1980). The authenticity of these traditions cannot be verified in a rigorous manner. It is interesting that the problem of protection on the desert caravan routes is mentioned by Strabo in the classical age. For a discussion of this point, see Bulliet, *The Camel and the Wheel* (1975), 94.

7 Guillaume, *The Life of Muhammad: A Translation of Ishaq's Sirat Rasul Allah* (1955), 287.

8 *Ibid.*, 289–304. Details of the caravan, the number of camels, the value of goods, and the individual share of the Meccan families in the expedition are given by Muhammad ibn 'Umar al-Waqidi, *Kitab al-maghazi*, ed. Jones (1966), summarised in Wolf, "The Social Organization of Mecca and the Origins of Islam" (1951), 333.

9 The attempt by many modern historians of early Islam to present the Arabs of Hijaz as great traders seems implausible on the basis of the evidence available. They were certainly involved in exchanging local goods for the products of the Mediterranean; but the distribution of Indian Ocean imports is more problematic. The people of Southern Arabia were clearly engaged in this branch of transcontinental trade. Whether the Meccans were also connected with it is not documented. For a review of the historical evidence on Roman commerce with the Indian Ocean, see Rostovtzeff, *The Social and Economic History of the Roman Empire* (1979), I, 94–7; II, 576 n. 17, n. 18.

10 Hourani, *Arab Seafaring in the Indian Ocean* (1951), 45.

11 The anonymous author of the commercial tract *Periplus Maris Erythraei* (first century AD) ascribed the Greek discovery of the regular monsoon winds in the Indian Ocean to a pilot named Hippalos, before whom navigators had followed the coasts. See *Periplus Maris Erythraei*, ed. McCrindle (1879), 110, 138; new trans. by Huntingford (1980), 52.

12 On the dangers to navigation in the Red Sea, see *ibid.*, 77–8. On the ancient

trading cities, see Rostovzeff, *Caravan Cities: Petra and Jerash, Palmyra and Dura* (1932).

13   The trade route and the stages of the caravans passing from South Arabia to the Mediterranean are discussed in Groom, *Frankincense and Myrrh* (1981); see also Grant, *The Syrian Desert* (1937).

14   Kister, *Studies in Jahiliyya* (1980), 130.

15   The story is given in three versions by al-Tabari in *Ta'rikh al Tabari*, I, 2820–2. The source is Sayf ibn 'Umar (died *c.* AH 180/AD 796). Cyprus is not mentioned by name but is assumed to be the object of the raid. I should like to thank M.A. Cook for this bibliographical note on sources.

16   Hourani, *Arab Seafaring* (1951), 58–9.

17   Canard, "Les Expéditions des Arabes contre Constantinople dans l'histoire et dans la légende", in his *Byzance et les Musulmans du Proche Orient* (1973).

18   For a discussion of the role of Arab cultural influence, see Lombard, *The Golden Age of Islam* (1975), 7.

19   Mingana, *Sources Syriaques* (1970–8), I, 175, 181; Brock, "Syriac Sources for Seventh-Century History" (1976). This evidence was brought to my attention by M.A. Cook.

20   Drewes, "New Light on the Coming of Islam to Indonesia" (1968); Schrieke, "Javanese Trade and the Rise of Islam in the Archipelago", in his *Indonesian Sociological Studies* (1955); Tibbetts, "Early Muslim Traders in South-East Asia" (1957).

21   The first dated evidence of the Muslim presence in East Africa is the Kufic inscription of AH 500/AD 1107 in the mosque of Kizimkazi in Zanzibar. See Chittick, *Kilwa: An Islamic Trading City* (1974); Garlake, *The Early Islamic Architecture of the East African Coast* (1966).

22   For a discussion of all these points, see Lombard, *The Golden Age of Islam* (1975).

23   For the importance of Dumat al-Jandal, see the article by Vaglieri in the *Encyclopaedia of Islam*, new edition.

24   al-Muqaddasi, *Ahsan al-Taqasim* (1901), 320–1.

25   *Ibid.*, 127.

26   al-Tabari, *Ta'rikh*; the reference is taken from Muhammad Bal'ami's Persian version, French trans. Zotenberg, *Chronique* (1867–74), III, 401. On the foundation of Basra, see also al-Muqaddasi, *Ahsan al-Taqasim* (1901), 181; on the topography of Mesopotamia, see Le Strange, *The Lands of the Eastern Caliphate* (1905).

27   al-Muqaddasi, *Ahsan al-Taqasim* (1901), 184.

28   Ibn Khurdadhbih, *Kitab al-Masalik w'al-Mamalik*, in Goeje, V.

29   For a discussion of the economic geography of the area, see Lombard, *The Golden Age of Islam* (1975).

30   Lassner, *The Topography of Baghdad* (1970).

31   al-Tabari, *Ta'rikh*, I, 272, quoted in Hourani, *Arab Seafaring* (1951), 64.

32   al-Ya'qubi, *Kitab al-Buldan*, in Goeje, VII, 237–8; Hourani, *Arab Seafaring*, 64.

33   al-Muqaddasi, *Ahsan al-Taqasim* (1901), 206–7.

34   *Ibid.*

35 M.A. Shaban has argued that the revolts of the Zanj and of the African population in lower Mesopotamia had the support of the Gulf merchants and that the disturbances were in some way connected with the control of the African seaborne trade. No argument is given for this interpretation, however; see Shaban, *Islamic History* (1976).
36 '*Aḫbar as-Sin wa'l-Hind* (1948).
37 *Ibid.*, 7, para. 13, 41 n. 13.2.
38 al-Muqaddasi, *Ahsan al-Taqasim* (1901), 142.
39 *Ibid.*, 135–6.
40 *Aḫbar as-Sin wa'l-Hind* (1948), 11–12, paras. 24–5. See also Ibn Khurdahbih's references to India cited in Elliot and Dowson, *History of India* (1867–77), I, 13–17.
41 *Aḫbar as-Sin wa'l-Hind* (1948), 13, para. 38.
42 On Multan, see al-Istakhri, *Kitab al-Akalim*, in Elliot and Dowson, *History of India*, I, 27; *Hudud al-'Alam* (1937), 89:32.
43 al-Mas'udi, *Muruj al-Dhahab* (1861–77), II, 85–6.
44 Wang Gungwu, "Nanhai Trade" (1958).
45 *Aḫbar as-Sin wa'l-Hind* (1948), n. 38; Hourani, *Arab Seafaring* (1951), 70–4.
46 Chau Ju-kua, *Chu-fan chi* (1911), 15.
47 Hourani, *Arab Seafaring* (1951), 72.
48 Tibbets, *Arab Navigation in the Indian Ocean* (1971).
49 Chau Ju-kua, *Chu-fan chi* (1911), 7.
50 Hourani, *Arab Seafaring* (1951), 62.
51 Wang Gungwu, "Nanhai Trade" (1958), 79.
52 Buzurg ibn Shahriyar, *Kitab 'Aja'ib al-Hind* (1981).
53 *Aḫbar as-Sin wa'l-Hind* (1948), 6, para. 11.
54 Jung-pang Lo, "Maritime Commerce and the Sung Navy" (1969).
55 Kuwabara, "P'u shou-keng" (1935); Reischauer, "Notes on T'ang Dynasty Sea Routes" (1940–1).
56 Chau Ju-kua, *Chu-fan chi* (1911), 16.
57 Hourani, *Arab Seafaring* (1951), 76–7.
58 al-Mas'udi, *Muruj al-Dhahab* (1861–77), I, 308.
59 The source of the saying is Nan Ch'i Shu (*c.* AD 457) in the biography of Wang K'un, an honest governor of Kwangchou, quoted by Kuwabara, "P'u shou-keng" (1935), 53; see also Wang Gungwu, "Nanhai Trade" (1958).
60 The source is Sung-hui-yao, quoted by Kuwabara.
61 Chau Ju-kua, *Chu-fan chi* (1911), 22–3.
62 *Ibid.*
63 The source is Chang-shih-k'o-shu, quoted by Kuwabara, "P'u shou-keng" (1935), 54.
64 *Ibid.*, 19–20.
65 Wang Gungwu, "Nanhai Trade" (1958).
66 Chau Ju-kua, *Chu-fan chi* (1911), 35; Wheatley, "Geographical Notes on Some Commodities Involved in Sung Maritime Trade" (1959).
67 Coedès, *Indianized States of Southeast Asia* (1968); Meilink-Roelofsz, *Asian Trade and European Influence* (1962), 13.

68 For a review of the historical material on South East Asia, see Wolters, *Early Indonesian Commerce* (1967). For the identification of the capital of Srivijaya with Jambi, see Wheatley, "Sung Maritime Trade"(1959), 11.

69 Chau Ju-kua, *Chu-fan chi* (1911), 61–2.

70 Ibid.; Wang Gungwu, "Nanhai Trade" (1958).

71 Marco Polo, *The Description of the World* (1938), I, 326–8.

72 *Ibid.*, I, 351.

73 Ibn Battuta, *Travels* (1929), 46, 287.

74 The available figures are summarised in Wheatley, "Sung Maritime Trade" (1959), 24.

75 Fairbank and Teng, "On the Ch'ing Tributary System" (1941–2).

76 Kuwabara, "P'u shou-keng" (1935), 14, n. 10.

77 Bulliet, *The Camel and the Wheel* (1975); Pope, *Chinese Porcelain from the Ardebil Shrine* (1956).

78 Le Strange, *Lands of the Eastern Caliphate* (1905), 285, 300–2, 463–5; Gaube, *Iranian Cities* (1978).

79 Ibn Battuta, *Travels* (1929), 110–13.

80 Chittick, "East African Trade with the Orient", in Richards, ed., *Islam and the Trade of Asia* (1970), 97–104; Chittick, "The 'Shirazi' Colonization of East Africa" (1965).

81 Chittick, "Observations on Pre-Portuguese Accounts of the East African Coast", in Mollat, ed., *Sociétés et compagnies de commerce en Orient* (1970).

82 Goitein, *Mediterranean Society* (1967), I, 29–42.

83 al-Muqaddasi, *Ahsan al-Taqasim* (1901), 323. Muqaddasi had a critical approach in his descriptions of the Islamic towns, shown by the following comment on Baghdad: "Baghdad was once a magnificent city, but is now fast falling to ruin and decay, and has lost all its splendour. I did not find it a pleasant place, nor an attractive city; and any eulogy of mine regarding it is merely conventional. The Fustat of Misr in the present day is like the Baghdad of old; I know of no city in Islam superior to it": *ibid.*, 51.

84 Goitein, *Mediterranean Society* (1967), I, 1–28.

85 *Ibid.*, I, 44.

86 Goitein, "Letters and Documents on the Indian Trade in Medieval Times", in his *Studies in Islamic History and Institutions* (1966), 337.

87 For a discussion of this point, see Chapter 1; Udovitch, "Formalism and Informalism in the Social and Economic Institutions of the Medieval Islamic World" (1977).

88 Fischel, "The Spice Trade in Mamluk Egypt" (1958); Ashtor, "The Karimi Merchants", in his *Studies on the Levantine Trade* (1978).

89 Goitein, "The Beginnings of the Karim Merchants", in his *Studies in Islamic History and Institutions* (1966).

90 Labib, "Egyptian Commercial Policy in the Middle Ages", in Cook, ed., *Studies in the Economic History of the Middle East* (1970), 63–77.

91 Ashtor, "The Venetian Supremacy in Levantine Trade", in his *Studies on the Levantine Trade* (1978).

92 Wiet, "Les Marchands d'épices" (1955).

93 Lopez, Miskimin, and Udovitch, "England to Egypt, 1350–1500", in Cook, ed., *Studies in the Economic History of the Middle East* (1970).
94 Duyvendak, "The True Dates of the Chinese Maritime Expeditions in the Early Fifteenth Century" (1938); Ma Huan, *Ying-yai Sheng-lan* (1970).
95 Duyvendak, "The True Dates".
96 *Ibid.*, 388, 395–6.
97 Boxer, *The Great Ship from Amacon* (1963); Atwell, "International Bullion Flows and the Chinese Economy" (1982).

CHAPTER 3

1 *India in the Fifteenth Century*, ed. Major (1857).
2 The "catastrophe theory" deals with such situations as two converging systems cannot reconcile without a conflict; in its mathematical form the theory studies the limits beyond which a catastrophe becomes unavoidable.
3 See Gaspar Correa, *Lendas da India*, ed. de Lima Felner (1858), I; an English translation of selections from the *Lendas* is published in *The Three Voyages of Vasco da Gama*, ed. Stanley (1869) and in *The Journal of the First Voyage of Vasco da Gama 1479–1499*, ed. Ravenstein (1898).
4 See Vasco da Gama's alleged speech to his ship's officers before burning an Arab ship: Correa, *The Three Voyages of Vasco Da Gama* (1869), 313–14.
5 Magalhães-Godinho, *L'Économie de l'empire portugais aux XVe et XVIe siècles* (1969), 41; Boxer, *The Portuguese Seaborne Empire 1415–1825* (1969), 18.
6 Correa, *Lendas da India* (1858), I, 2.
7 Extracts from Girolamo Priuli's diary are printed in English translation in *The Voyage of Pedro Alvares Cabral to Brazil and India*, ed. Greenlee (1938); the original version is in Girolamo Priuli, *I Diarii* (1933–8).
8 Serjeant, *The Portuguese off the South Arabian Coast* (1963), 43.
9 Braudel, *The Mediterranean* (1972), I, 543–70.
10 See Pearson, *Merchants and Rulers in Gujarat* (1976).
11 Boxer, "A Note on Portuguese Reactions to the Revival of the Red Sea Spice Trade and the Rise of Atcheh, 1540–1600" (1969).
12 The "Manueline" style of Portuguese architecture of course derived its name from that of the king, and the monastery of the Jerónimos begun in 1499 represented its finest expression. For a discussion of this point, see Lach, *Asia in the Making of Europe* (1965), vol. I, bk i, 98–100.
13 *Ibid.*
14 For the Venetian reaction to the disruption in spice supplies, see Weinstein, *Ambassador from Venice: Pietro Pasqualigo in Lisbon, 1501* (1960), 70–84.
15 Correa, *Lendas da India* (1858), I, 75.
16 *The Voyage of Pedro Alvares Cabral*, ed. Greenlee (1938), xviii.
17 *Ibid.*, 180.
18 *Ibid.*, 84–5.
19 "Regimento que levou D. Francisco de Almeida quando foi por capitão-mor para a India", *Cartas de Affonso de Albuquerque seguidas de documentos que as elucidam*, ed. de Bulhão Pato, II (1898), 272–334 (5 March 1505); III (1903), 268–76 (1506).

20 *Cartas de Affonso de Albuquerque*, II, 311 (5 March 1505).
21 The Egyptian armada and the events leading up to the battle of Diu in February 1509 are described by all contemporary historians of early Portuguese expansion in Asia: see João de Barros, *Ásia* (1945), déc. II, liv. iii, cap. 4, 117ff.; Correa, *Lendas da India*, I, 923ff.; Fernão Lopes Castanheda, *História do descobrimento & conquista da Índia pelos Portugueses* (1924–33), liv. ii. caps. 96–7, 426ff. A useful description with full editorial references to the above works will be found in *Crónica do descobrimento e conquistà da Índia pelos Portugueses (códice anónimo, Museu Britânico, Egerton 20,901)*, ed. de Albuquerque (1974), 180–7.
22 *Crónica do descobrimento*, 203.
23 *The Commentaries of the Great Afonso D'Alboquerque*, ed. Gray Birch (1884), IV, 185.
24 *Ibid.*, 209.
25 For a discussion of this point, see Niels Steensgaard, *Carracks, Caravans, and Companies* (1972), 81–103; Pearson, *Merchants and Rulers in Gujarat* (1976), 52–6.
26 An example of this attitude is the demand for £10 000 made by James I of England after the English East India Company's capture of Hormuz from the Portuguese in 1622. The king claimed the present from the Company with the remark "Did I deliver you from the complaint of the Spaniard and do you return me nothing?". See Chaudhuri, *The English East India Company* (1965), 64.
27 *Livro das cidades, e fortalezas, que a Coroa de Portugal tem nas partes da India, e das capitanias, e mais cargos que nelas há, e da importancia delles, [1582]*, Centro de Estudos Históricos Ultramarinos, Portugal: Studia, No. 6 (1960), 5–10.
28 Pearson, *Merchants and Rulers in Gujarat* (1976), 76.
29 For a description of Portuguese towns on the western coast of India north of Goa, see *Livro das cidades, e fortalezas*, 18–32.
30 Gaspar Correa was particularly concerned about the growing corruption among Portuguese officials and gave many examples of it in his *Lendas da India* (1858), which of course remained unpublished during his life-time.
31 See D. João de Castro's letter to King D. João III, 15 December 1546, printed in *Cartas de D. João de Castro*, ed. Sanceau (1955), 263–4.
32 Commissariat, *A History of Gujarat* (1938), I, 509; Jean-Baptiste Tavernier, *Travels in India*, ed. Crooke (1925), I, 56–7.
33 Steensgaard, *Carracks, Caravans, and Companies* (1972), 83.
34 Salïh Özbaran, "The Ottoman Turks and the Portuguese in the Persian Gulf, 1534–1581" (1972), 70.
35 Serjeant, *The Portuguese off the South Arabian Coast* (1963), 111.
36 Meilink-Roelofsz, *Asian Trade and European Influence* (1962), 189.
37 S. Chaudhury, "The Rise and Decline of Hugli, a Port in Medieval Bengal" (1967), 33–67.
38 Meilink-Roelofsz, *Asian Trade and European Influence* (1962), 157–64.
39 Braudel, *The Mediterranean* (1972), I, 550–1.
40 Boxer, "A Note on Portuguese Reactions to the Revival of the Red Sea Spice Trade and the Rise of Atcheh 1540–1600" (1969), 415.

41 Castanheda, *História*, livro vii, cap. 100, 179, quoted by Boxer, "A Note", 416.
42 Jorge de Lemos, *Hystoria dos cercos* (1585); cited in Boxer, "A Note", 423.
43 Boxer, *The Great Ship from Amacon* (1959), 22.
44 *Ibid.*, 1–8.
45 Boxer, *The Christian Century in Japan 1549–1650* (1951), 385.
46 *Livro das cidades, e fortalezas, que a Coroa de Portugal tem nas partes da India [1582]*, Centro de Estudos Históricos Ultramarinos, Portugal: Studia, No. 6 (1960).
47 *Ibid.*, 40.
48 *Ibid.*, 5–10.
49 For a discussion of the attitudes of the early Portuguese historians, see Harrison, "Five Portuguese Historians", printed in Philips, ed., *Historians of India, Pakistan and Ceylon* (1961), 155–69.
50 Boxer, *The Portuguese Seaborne Empire* (1969), 49–50.
51 Özbaran, "The Ottoman Turks and the Portuguese in the Persian Gulf", 64.
52 Quoted in Boxer, *The Portuguese Seaborne Empire* (1969), 50.

CHAPTER 4

1 Linschoten, *Itinerario 1579–1592* (1955–7).
2 Boxer, *The Portuguese Seaborne Empire* (1969), ch. 11.
3 Linschoten, *Itinerario 1579–1592* (1955), 136.
4 *Calendar of State Papers Foreign 1584–1585*, 15/25 July 1585, vol. XIX, p. 602.
5 *The Court Minutes of the East India Company 1664–1667*, 40 (25 May 1664).
6 *The English Factories in India 1637–1641*, 35 (2 January 1638).
7 *The English Factories in India 1661–1664*, p. 218; IOR, Factory Records Java, 28 March 1660, vol. 3, para. 3, p. 308.
8 "Discursos sobre los medios que se deven tomar para la redificación del comercio de Ormuz . . . ", *Documentação Ultramarina Portuguesa*, II, 450–7, quoted by Steengaard, *Carracks, Caravans, and Companies* (1972), 354.
9 "The Accord between the Viceroy of Goa and the English President and Council", 10–20 January 1635, *The English Factories in India 1634–1636*, 88.
10 Foster, ed., *The Embassy of Sir Thomas Roe* (1926), 344–5.
11 Meilink-Roelofsz, *Asian Trade and European Influence* (1962), 267.
12 See *ibid.*, ch. 9.
13 *The First Letter Book of the East India Company 1600–1619*, 129, 249.
14 On the embargo, see Niebuhr, *Travels through Arabia* (1792), I, 235; on the policy of seizing Indian ships trading to the Red Sea, see *The English Factories in India 1618–1621*, 237–40 (9 March 1621).
15 Chaudhuri, *The Trading World of Asia and the English East India Company* (1978), 188.

CHAPTER 5

1 Al-Mas'udi, *Muruj al-Dhahab* (1861–77), II, 85–6.
2 Ibn Battuta, *Travels in Asia and Africa 1325–1354* (1929), 238–9; Ma Huan, *Yang-yai Sheng-lan* (1970), 140–1.

3 *The English Factories in India 1661–64*, 23; Private Papers of Sir Robert Cowan, Inward Letter Book, 15 March 1727 (letter from Laldas Vitaldas, merchant of Surat, to Cowan, written in Portuguese), no. 1A,D654/B1/4D.

4 Pires, *The Suma Oriental 1512–1515* (1944), 4.

5 *Ibid.*, lxv.

6 *Ibid.*, 269.

7 *Ibid.*, 41.

8 Fryer, *A New Account of East India and Persia* (1909–15), II, 249.

9 IOR, Factory Records China, Canton Diary, 30 June 1724, vol. 25, p. 5.

10 IOR, Original Correspondence, 11 March 1695, vol. 50, no. 5984.

11 Adam Smith, *The Wealth of Nations* (6th edition), vol. II, bk iv, ch. 2, p. 454.

12 Goitein, *Mediterranean Society* (1967), I, 45.

13 Foster, ed., *The Travels of John Sanderson 1584–1602* (1931), 135.

14 Al-Muqaddasi, *Ahsan al-Taqasim* (1901), 135.

15 *Ibid.*, 148.

16 Pires, *The Suma Oriental* (1944), 45.

17 Wang Gungwu, "The Opening of Relations between China and Malacca, 1403–5", in Bastin and Roolvink, eds., *Malayan and Indonesian Studies* (1964), 87–104.

18 Pires, *The Suma Oriental* (1944), 286–7.

19 *Ibid.*, 47.

CHAPTER 6

1 Ahmad Ibn Majid, *Kitab al-Fawa'id fi usul al-bahr wa'l-qawa'id* (1971), 202.

2 Bowrey, *A Geographical Account of Countries Round the Bay of Bengal* (1905); 41–4; Lucena, *Vida do Padre Francisco de Xavier* (1600), 117; Schurhammer, *Francis Xavier*, II (1977). 471.

3 So Kwan-wai, *Japanese Piracy in Ming China* (1975), 52, quoting from *Ming Shih*.

4 Abdu'r Razzaq, *Matla' al-Sa'dain*, in Major, ed., *India in the Fifteenth Century* (1857), 7–8.

5 Rogers and Beveridge, eds., *Tuzuk-i-Jahangiri* (1909), I, 391, 416–17.

6 Buzurg Ibn Shahriyar, *Kitab 'Aja'ib al-Hind*, trans. extract in Hourani (1951), 114–15.

7 Tibbetts, *Arab Navigation in the Indian Ocean* (1971); "Introduction" to Ibn Majid, *al-Fawa'id*, 7.

8 *Ibid.*, 71–2.

9 Abu'l Fazl, *'Ain-i-Akbari*, I (1867), 280.

10 Ibn Majid, *al-Fawa'id*, 182.

11 Needham, *Clerks and Craftsmen in China* (1970), 40–70.

12 Abu'l Fazl, *'Ain-i-Akbari*, I (1867), 280–1.

13 Villiers, *Sons of Sinbad* (1969), 186.

14 Ibn Majid, *al-Fawa'id*, 232–3.

15 Linschoten, *The Voyage* (1885), II, 236.

16 Ibn Majid, *al-Fawa'id*, 143–4.

17 "Journal of Voyage to Persia 1685", British Library, Additional MS 19282.
18 Ibn Majid, *al-Fawa'id*, 182.
19 Miquel, "Origine et carte des mers dans la géographie arabe" (1980); Ferrand, *Introduction à l'astronomie nautique arabe* (1928); Needham, *Clerks and Craftsmen in China* (1970).
20 On this point, see Tibbetts, "Introduction" to Ibn Majid, *al-Fawa'id*, 9–10.
21 Cortés, *Breve compendio de la sphere y de la arte de navegur* (1551).
22 Foster, *John Company* (1926), 197–209.
23 Hamilton, *A New Account of the East Indies* (1930), II, 117.
24 Hourani, *Arab Seafaring* (1951), 115.
25 On the difficulties of navigating in the Bombay harbour, see Findlay, *A Directory for the Navigation of the Indian Ocean* (1897), 928–32.

CHAPTER 7

1 IOR, Factory Records Egypt and Red Sea, 20 July 1721, vol. 1, no. 29, pp. 54–5.
2 For example, Pires says that the merchants of Pase in Sumatra bought their sea-going ships in Malacca because of the scarcity (or non-availability) of teak wood in the local country. On the other hand, Madapolam on the Coromandel coast of India was especially mentioned in 1675 as being suitable for shipbuilding; it was on a large river and timber logs could be floated down from the forests further up stream. See Pires, *The Suma Oriental 1512–1515* (1944), 145; *The English Factories in India 1670–1677*, 277.
3 Braudel, *The Mediterranean* (1972), I, 296.
4 Tavernier, *Travels in India* (1925), I, 203–7.
5 Moreland, "The Ships of the Arabian Sea about A.D. 1500" (1939), parts 1 and 2.
6 On Portuguese shipbuilding in India, see Boxer, *Portuguese India in the Mid-Seventeenth Century* (1980), 27–8.
7 Wadia, *The Bombay Dockyard and the Wadia Master Builders* (1955).
8 We do not know what influence the actual techniques of construction in each region exercised on those of the other, although the design may have remained distinctive. Gaspar Correa's description of the flat-bottomed but nailed vessels of the Malabar could easily have been adapted from the Chinese junk. See n. 19.
9 Horridge, *The Konjo Boatbuilders and the Bugis Prahus of South Sulawesi* (1979), 23; Horridge refers to the work of Francisco Alcina, S.J., *Historia de las Islas e Indios de Bisayas* (1668), in the Biblioteca Real, Madrid.
10 PRO, Northern Ireland, Belfast, Private Papers of Sir Robert Cowan, Outward Letter Book, 24 March 1728/9, no. 34, D654/B1/1A; IOR microfilm reel 2015.
11 PRO, Chancery Masters' Exhibits, Private Papers of Thomas Hall, C103/131.
12 IOR, Admiralty Office to the East India Company, 19 February 1744/5, Miscellaneous Letters Received, E/1/33, No. 8.
13 PRO, Chancery Masters' Exhibits, Private Papers of Thomas Hall, Westcott to Hall, 28 February 1746, C103/131; the other letters from Westcott are in the same bundle. See also Richard Bourchier to Hall, Anjengo, 16 February 1746, *ibid.*, C103/132, no. 3; IOR, Despatch Book, Court of Directors to Bombay Council, 18 February 1747/8, E/3/110, para. 24, p. 47.

14 See Buzurg ibn Shahriyar, *Kitab 'Aja'ib al-Hind*, English extract in Hourani, *Arab Seafaring* (1951), 116–17.

15 Ibn Majid, *al-Fawa'id*, 231–2.

16 Foster, ed., *Early Travels in India 1583–1619* (1921), 301.

17 See ch. 2, p. 38. Marco Polo has a long description of the organised pirates of Malabar and Gujarat who cruised on the coast with upwards of a hundred ships. The merchants who traded by sea knew this danger from the pirates so well that, according to Marco Polo, "they go many together and so well armed and so well prepared that they have no fear of them when they find them, for they defend themselves bravely and very often do them great harm": Marco Polo, *The Description of the World* (1938), 418.

18 Horridge, *The Design of the Planked Boats of the Moluccas* (1978), 6.

19 For a discussion of the engineering considerations, see Horridge, 39–41. From Gaspar Correa's description of the vessels of Malabar at the time of the early Portuguese voyages, it is quite clear that these had ribs, though the number was not great. Correa, *Lendas da India* (1858), I, 122; English trans. Stanley, ed., *The Three Voyages of Vasco Da Gama* (1869), 239–40. Moreland was wrong in saying that the Indo-Arab ships were built without ribs or frames: see Moreland, "The Ships of the Arabian Sea about A.D. 1500" (1939).

20 Correa, *Lendas da India*; see also Bowen, *Arab Dhows of Eastern Arabia* (1940), 21. The reference to the thickness of the treenails in Portuguese ships is in the *Narrative of the Voyage and Vicissitudes which Befell the Great Ships Aguia and Garça 1559*, in Boxer, ed., *The Tragic History of the Sea, 1559–1565* (1968), 29. Moreland, of course, denied the authenticity of Correa's evidence on the ground that he was writing several decades after the time of Vasco da Gama's first voyage to Malabar. By then the Malabar shipwrights, Moreland argued, had already learned to copy the Portuguese methods of ship construction. It never occurred to Moreland that the idea of iron fastenings in Malabar ships may have come from the Chinese junks which regularly visited the area long before the Portuguese arrival. For a discussion of European and Asian shipbuilding traditions, see also Greenhill, *Archaeology of the Boat* (1976).

21 Moreland, ed., *Relations of Golconda* (1931), 36, 40; Bowrey, *Countries Round the Bay of Bengal 1669 to 1679* (1905), 102.

22 *The English Factories in India 1646–1650*, 90–1; see also Qaisar, *The Indian Response to European Technology* (1982), 21.

23 Horridge, *The Konjo Boatbuilders* (1979), 6.

24 Pires, *The Suma Oriental* (1944), 195. The term "pangajava" used by Pires is puzzling. He distinguishes between the war prahus of the Buginese, which were engaged in privateering throughout the archipelago, and merchant prahus (pangajavas): *ibid.*, 227.

25 Pires, 122–3.

26 Jung-pang Lo, "Chinese Shipping and East–West Trade from the Tenth to the Fourteenth Century" (1970), 173.

27 Ibn Battuta, *Travels* (1929), 235.

28 The junks were not necessarily owned by the Chinese, because when Ibn Battuta prepared to sail for China in a fleet of thirteen junks, his ship was prepared by Sultan Samari and its factor was Sulayman of Safad: *ibid.*, 236.

29 Abdu'r Razzaq, *Matla'al Sa'dain* in Elliot and Dowson, eds., *The History of India*, IV, 103. Correa repeats the memory and the legend of Chinese arrival in India (the Ming expeditions) during the early fifteenth century, in the following passage: "in one year more than eight hundred sail of large and small ships had come to India from the parts of Malacca and China and the Lequeos, with people of many nations, and all laden with merchandise of great value which they brought for sale ... they were so numerous that they had filled the country and had settled as dwellers in all the towns of the sea-coast". Correa, *Lendas da India* (1858), I, 69–70; Stanley, ed., *The Three Voyages of Vasco Da Gama* (1869), 146–7.

30 Needham, *Clerks and Craftsmen in China and the West* (1970), 68–9.

31 *Ibid.*, 66.

32 Ibn Battuta, *Travels* (1929), 235.

33 Bowen, *Arab Dhows of Eastern Arabia* (1949), 10.

34 Manucci, *Storia do Mogor 1653–1708* (1907–8), II, 47.

35 IOR, Despatch Book, 19 November 1719, E/3/100, para. 19, p. 6.

36 IOR, Original Correspondence, 29 April 1695, E/3/51, nos. 6021, 6023.

37 Hamilton, *A New Account of the East Indies* (1930), I, 80.

38 IOR, Factory Records Surat, Diary, 18 January 1735/6, vol. 20, p. 42.

39 Algemeen Rijksarchief, The Hague, Koloniale Archieven Oost-Indie, vol. 1805, p. 81.

40 See Das Gupta, *Indian Merchants and the Decline of Surat* (1979), 282.

41 Hamilton, *A New Account of the East Indies* (1930), II, 128; for contemporary estimates of shipping in China, see Jung-pang Lo, "Chinese Shipping" (1970).

42 Bowrey, *Countries Round the Bay of Bengal 1669 to 1679* (1905), 102.

43 Hamilton, *A New Account of the East Indies* (1930), I, 168–9.

44 On the quality of the Bombay-built ships, see Karaka, *History of the Parsis* (1884), II, 66–7.

CHAPTER 8

1 Braudel, *The Mediterranean* (1972), I, 232.

2 Hamilton, *A New Account of the East Indies* (1930), I, 44–5.

3 Forbes, *Oriental Memoirs* (1813), I, 322–3; see also Hamilton, *A New Account of the East Indies* (1930), I, 177, 251; Das Gupta, *Malabar in Asian Trade* (1967), 137 n. 1.

4 This statement was actually made by John Fryer, *A New Account of East India and Persia* (1909), I, 140–1.

5 IOR, Factory Records Egypt and Red Sea, 30 May 1732, vol. 2, no. 268, p. 93.

6 Grose, *A Voyage to the East Indies* (1772), I. 98.

7 Commissariat, *History of Gujarat* (1957), 420, 423; a copy of the Deed Settlement is printed in full.

8 IOR, Factory Records Persia, 26 March 1753, vol. 16, para. 5, p. 3.

9 IOR, Original Correspondence, 17 February 1679, vol. 39, no. 4577, para. 20, p. 4.

10 Marco Polo, *The Description of the World*, ed. Moule and Pelliot (1938), I, 56–7.

11 Lattimore, *The Desert Road to Turkestan* (1928); and, on the caravan roads, *Inner Asian Frontiers of China* (1940), 172–3.

12 Ibn Battuta, *Travels in Asia and Africa* (1929), 73–4, 171–2.
13 Braudel, *Capitalism and Material Life* (1973), 401.
14 Braudel, *The Mediterranean* (1972), I, 387.
15 Ibn Battuta, *Travels in Asia and Africa* (1929), 204.
16 Marco Polo, *The Description of the World*, ed. Moule and Pelliot (1938), I, 152.
17 Bowrey, *A Geographical Account of Countries Round the Bay of Bengal* (1905), 293–4.

CHAPTER 9

 1 Ibn Battuta, *Travels* (1929), 167–75.
 2 *Records of Fort St George: Diary and Consultation Book 1731*, 96–7.
 3 PRO, Northern Ireland, Belfast, Private Papers of Sir Robert Cowan, letter dated 22 October 1724, D654/B1/544; IOR microfilm reel 2036.
 4 Purchasing power was created by three elements in the national economy: exports, invisible earnings, and government expenditures. The fact that the economy of the Middle East or any other region of Asia during the period was non-mechanised and imperfectly integrated does not affect the argument. The existence of long-distance trade was itself an indication of the operation of the general economic forces.
 5 See Chau Ju-kua, *Chu-fan-chi* (1911).
 6 Al-Muqaddasi, *Ahsan al-Taqasim* (1901), 51.
 7 *Ibid.*, 147–8.
 8 Chau Ju-kua, *Chu-fan-chi* (1911), 116.
 9 *Ibid.*, 78.
10 Chao Ch'uan-ch'eng, "A Ship's Voyage from Luzon to China in the Eighteenth Century', in E-Tu Zen Sun and John de Francis, *Chinese Social History: Translations of Selected Studies* (1956), 353–9.
11 *Ibid.*, 358–9.
12 PRO, Northern Ireland, Belfast, Private Papers of Sir Robert Cowan, Carolinas Invoice dated 17 October 1729, no. 16, D654/B1/544; IOR microfilm reel 2031.
13 *Ibid.* See Captain Thomas Garland's letter to Robert Cowan dated 15 November 1730 from Achin Road, no. 62A; IOR microfilm reel 2020.
14 *Ibid.*, no. 13A; IOR microfilm reel 2022.
15 Pires, *Suma Oriental* (1944), 92.
16 PRO, Northern Ireland, Belfast, Private Papers of Sir Robert Cowan, no. 14, D654/B1/544; IOR microfilm reel 2022.
17 *Ibid.*, letter dated 2 April 1729; IOR microfilm reel 2013. *Ibid.*, letter dated 6 December 1727, no. 11; IOR microfilm reel 2019.
18 Cowan's fortune, for example, was valued at about £40000. See *ibid.*, Outward Letter Book; IOR microfilm reel 2017.
19 *Ibid.*, letter dated February 1729; IOR microfilm reel 2015.
20 Pelsaert, *The Remonstrantie* (1925), 39.
21 Al-Idrisi, *Nuzhat al-Mushtaq*, in Elliot and Dowson, *History of India*, I, 77.
22 For a description of the Yemeni coffee trade and reference to sources, see Chaudhuri, *The Trading World of Asia* (1978).

23 La Roque, *A Voyage to Arabia* (1742), 106.
24 Hamilton, *The Hedaya* (1870).

CHAPTER 10

 1 Udovitch, "Formalism and Informalism in the Social and Economic Institutions of the Medieval Islamic World", in Banani and Vryonis, eds., *Individualism and Conformity in Classical Islam* (1977), 69.
 2 Algemeen Rijksarchief, The Hague. Records of the VOC, KA 1783, 92.
 3 Streynsham Master, *The Diaries* (1911), II, 146 (consultation, 31 March 1679)
 4 IOR, Despatch Book, 30 May 1690, vol. 92, p. 103.
 5 For a variety of historical and present-day discussions of the problem, see Adam Smith, *Wealth of Nations*, (6th edition), vol. II, bk iv, chs. 7–8; Karl Marx, *Capital*, III, ch. 20; Dobb, "Capital, Accumulation, and Mercantilism", in his *Studies in the Development of Capitalism* (1963); Kriedte, *Peasants, Landlords, and Merchant Capitalists* (1980). See also ch. 2, n. 1 for a discussion of the term "world economy".
 6 On this point, see Braudel, *Civilization and Capitalism: The Wheels of Commerce* (1982), II, 581–99; Balazs, "The Birth of Capitalism in China", in his *Chinese Civilization and Bureaucracy* (1974); Chaudhuri, *The Trading World of Asia and the English East India Company* (1978).
 7 On China, see Brook, "The Merchant Network in 16th-Century China: A Discussion and Translation of Zhang Han's 'On Merchants' " (1981), 165–214.
 8 The most immediate motive for a merchant house to give employment to a member of the landed classes is of course either family ties or the hope of obtaining political patronage.
 9 Fryer, *A New Account of East India and Persia* (1912), 249. On Indian merchants, see also the "Memorie of Alexander Hume" (1730), Stadsarchief Antwerpen, Antwerp, General Indische Compagnie, vol. 5769. See also IOR, Original Correspondence, 16 January 1695, vol. 50, no. 5960.
10 Little, "The House of Jagatseth" (1920).
11 "The Humble Answer . . . of the East India Company", in IOR, India Office Tracts, vol. 268.
12 Khafi Khan, *Muntakhab al-Lubab*, in Elliot and Dowson, eds., *History of India*, VII, 354.
13 Pires, *The Suma Oriental* (1944), 286–7.
14 Atwell, "International Bullion Flows and the Chinese Economy *circa* 1530–1650" (1982).
15 IOR, Factory Records Miscellaneous, 7 January 1667, vol. 3, p. 5. Many other references can be cited also.
16 For examples of bank transactions and precious metals in the western Indian Ocean in the seventeenth and eighteenth centuries, see IOR, Original Correspondence, vol. 27, no. 2905; Factory Record Surat, Diary, 26 May 1670, vol. 3, p. 65; Original Correspondence, 21 December 1672, vol. 33, no. 3722, pp. 13–14; Bombay Public Proceedings, 30 November 1722, vol. 5; Factory Record Surat, Diary, 1 September 1740, vol. 25, p. 15.

17 Thomas de Mercado, *Summa de tratos y contratos* (1571), fol. 95.
18 On the organisation of the Indian textile industries, see Chaudhuri, *The Trading World of Asia and the English East India Company* (1978), pp. 253–75.

CHAPTER 11

1 Braudel, *Civilization and Capitalism* (1981), 69–70.
2 On the anthropological interpretation of trade as a form of economic exchange, see Sahlins, *Stone-Age Economics* (1972); Polyani, "Traders and Trade" (posthumous paper), in Sabloff and Lamberg-Karlovsky, eds., *Ancient Civilization and Trade* (1975); Dalton, "Karl Polyani's Analysis of Long-Distance Trade and his Wider Paradigm" in *ibid.*
3 See North, "Markets and Other Allocation Systems in History: The Challenge of Polyani" (1977).
4 Ma Huan, *Ying-yai Sheng-lan* (1970), 136.
5 Chaudhuri, *The Trading World of Asia and the English East India Company* (1978), 132.
6 Polyani, "Traders and Trade" (1975).
7 *Ibid.*; see also Polyani, "Ports of Trade in Early Societies" (1963); Polyani, Arensberg, and Pearson, eds., *Trade and Markets in the Early Empires* (1957).
8 The concept of a "trade diaspora" was formulated by an anthropologist, Abner Cohen: see his essay "Cultural Strategies in the Organisation of Trading Diasporas", in Meillassoux, ed., *The Development of Indigenous Trade and Markets in West Africa* (1971).
9 IOR, Original Correspondence, 16 January 1695/6, vol. 50, no. 5960, pp. 3–4.
10 This point has been emphasised by Philip D. Curtin in his discussion of the "trade diasporas": see his *Economic Change in Precolonial Africa* (1975), I, 59–68. The criticism of the concept of "trade diaspora" made here does not, of course, in any way detract from the highly original contribution made by Curtin's historical research on pre-colonial trading communities in West Africa.
11 For a discussion of protection costs in long-distance trade, see Steensgaard, *Carracks, Caravans, and Companies* (1972); Chaudhuri, *The Trading World of Asia and the English East India Company* (1978).
12 For European sources on freight rates, see *ibid.*, 211, 590.

Glossary

Ashrafi	Arabic word meaning "more noble", generally used as a royal title; hence gold coins bearing that title came to be known as ashrafis. The full title was "al-Malik al-Ashraf".
Baghla	A large deep-sea vessel used by Arab, Persian, and Indian sailors; the hull shape was strongly influenced by that of Portuguese ships.
Bahar	An Indo-Islamic weight measure used in wholesale trade and for calculating the tonnage of a ship, the weight varied from 200 kg to 370 kg.
Bahr	Arabic word for sea.
Bayasirah	A social community among the tribes of Oman who were considered as being of depressed status.
Bilad al-Islam	The world or lands of Islam.
Boom	The name given to an Islamic double-ended ship, generally found in the Red Sea and the Persian Gulf.
Candy	A European corruption of the Indian word "khand", meaning a lump. Also a weight measure of *c.* 305 kg used for measuring the tonnage of a ship.
Catamaran	Name given to a South Indian fishing boat.
Ch'eng	Chinese word for wall; hence a walled town.
Chola	The name of South Indian people and of a dynasty.
Dhira	Arabic linear measure equivalent to 66.5 cm.
Dirhem	An Islamic silver coin, 4 grams in weight.
Dinar	An Islamic gold coin, 4.25 grams in weight.
Dira	Arabic term for a ship's course or route; technical navigational term; could also refer to a compass.
Fanam	A South Indian or Malabar coin, generally of silver.
Fen	Chinese weight equivalent to 0.37 grams.
Ganja	An Indo-Islamic ship.
Genizah	A Hebrew word for a depository, attached to a Jewish synagogue, for "burying" documents bearing the name of God. In the text refers to a particular collection of medieval merchants' documents.
Ghee	Clarified butter.
Kamal	A board used for calculating stellar altitudes; see also "loh".
Karim	A term which often occurs in Islamic historical sources and refers to a particular class of merchants engaged in seaborne trade. Its meaning is uncertain.

Kotia	An Indian double-ended ship; see also "boom".
Lac	A corruption of the Indian word lakh meaning one hundred thousand.
Li	A Chinese weight, used in the bullion trade, equivalent to 0.037 grams.
Loh	An instrument used for calculating stellar altitudes, used by navigators at sea; see also "kamal".
Machua (Mukkuvar)	An Indian name given to the caste of fishermen in South India.
Maghreb	The Arabic term for West or North Africa.
Mahalla	A neighbourhood or quarter in an Indo-Islamic city.
Markab Sini	The Arabic term for a China ship.
Mawsim al-kaws	Arabic navigational term for the south west monsoon; see also "rih al-saba".
Mu'allim	Arabic navigational term for a pilot, navigator, and ship's captain.
Mussoola	A European corruption of an Indian word denoting a fishing boat found in South India; see also "catamaran".
Nagarseth	An honorific title given to a prominent Indian merchant, meaning "the (chief) city merchant".
Nakhoda (Nakhuda)	An Indo-Islamic term used for a ship's captain or owner.
Pangajava	A word used by the Portuguese writer Tomé Pires to describe a type of Indonesian ship.
Prahu	An Indonesian ship.
Qadi	An Islamic judge.
Qafila	Arabic word for caravans.
Qanat	Islamic subterranean aqueducts.
Qiyas	Arabic term for deduction by analogy; also used by navigators to describe the technique of stellar measurement.
Radjab	Arabic term for the seventh month of the Muslim calendar.
Rih al-Saba	Arabic navigational term for the north east Monsoon; see also "mawsim al-kaws".
Rubban	Islamic term for a ship's captain or master.
Sarraf Sombala	An Islamic money-changer who also acted as a banker.
Tanja	An Indonesian term for the rigging of a prahu.
Surhang	Indo-Islamic term for a ship's mate.
Tandil	Indo-Islamic term for the chief of sailors on a ship.
Umma	Quranic term for people and religious communities.
Wo K'ou	Chinese word for Japanese pirates.
Zanj	Arabic name for African tribes from the east coast.

Guide to sources and further reading

Sources

The sources on which this study is based can be classified into three clearly recognisable types. Documents originating with individual merchants, commercial partnerships, and trading companies constitute the first category, one that is obviously of great importance and at the same time of uneven depth and coverage. Contemporary treatises on trade and merchants, travel accounts, and historical works on the geography, people, and political kingdoms of Asia form the second category. Government regulations, edicts, and maritime laws constitute yet another type. A strong chronological division runs through all these different kinds of source, marked by the European arrival in the Indian Ocean around the turn of the fifteenth century. Without the fortunate preservation and the survival of historical documents in Western languages relating to European trade and empire in Asia, our knowledge of commercial activity in the Indian Ocean would have remained seriously deficient. It is evident that the relative paucity of source material from the Asian side is attributable to poor preservation rather than to a lack of systematic record-keeping. The personal papers of European private merchants trading in Asia occasionally contain letters, invoices, and even commercial accounts which were written and prepared by their Asian business partners. These differ very little in their conventions from Western documents.

The commercial history of Asia before the tenth century is documented in a very fragmented way. Most of the available information comes from Islamic sources rather than from Indian, Chinese, or Indonesian ones. The most significant pre-Islamic and Hellenistic source on the Indian Ocean is the Alexandrine work *Periplus Maris Erythraei* (first century AD), which is fairly accurate on coastal geography and the wind-system. The commercial activities of the Meccans during the life-time of Muhammad are mentioned by Ibn Ishaq (died in AH 150/AD 767), in his *Sirat* as transmitted by Ibn Hisham, and similar details are to be found in the historical works of al-Waqidi (died AH 207/AD 823) and of al-Tabari (died AH 310/AD 923). The goods carried by the Meccan trading caravans and their size, destinations and places of origin given in these sources reflect the participation of the Arabs of Hijaz in the long-distance trade of the peninsula, though the exact details cannot be properly verified or assessed in terms of quantitative importance. The interpretation of the Quranic references to the tradition of "ilaf" and "rihla" (in summer and winter) likewise remains difficult. The first term is generally taken to refer to the safe-conduct agreements organised by the caravaneers in order to pass through the territory of other tribes, while the second simply means a journey, which for the Meccans may have been commercial and pastoral. Tabari's work is useful for a description of the Islamic expansion into Syria, Iraq, and other places, and its Persian version prepared by Muhammad Bal'ami contains several additional details on the trade of Mesopotamia. Two Islamic works that specifically describe seafarers, ships, and voyages in the Indian Ocean are *'Ahbar as-Sin wa'l-Hind* (in two parts, the first anonymous and dated 851, and the second by Abu Zayd al-Sirafi in about 916) and Buzurg ibn Shahriyar's *Kitab 'Aja'ib al-Hind* (c. 900–53). These were compiled from accounts by actual sailors and merchants engaged in the trade of India and China and appear to be authentic in spite of the inclusion of many fantastic sea stories.

From the tenth century, Islamic evidence on trade rapidly improves in volume and quality. This was the period of famous geographers and travellers writing about the world of Islam and also about non-Islamic people. The most important and illuminating work for our study is al-Muqaddasi's *Ahsan al-Taqasim* (c. 908), which was composed on the basis of the author's personal travels in the Islamic countries and also of the works of other geographers and scholars. Muqaddasi possessed a critical mind and was highly aware of his own contribution to scholarship. The long account of his contrasting experiences in different walks of life and different situations, though it disturbs some modern historians, was probably no more boastful than many present-day authors' prefaces drawing attention to the wide range of historical libraries and archives visited. Muqaddasi's observations on the economic life of the Arabian peninsula, Iraq, Iran, Syria, and Egypt are full of interest and reveal a thorough knowledge of the role played by long-distance trade and sea-ports in bringing economic prosperity to an area. The studies made by al-Istakhri preceded the work of Muqaddasi, and these were edited and utilised by Ibn Hawqal in his *Kitab al-Masalik wa'l-Mamalik*. This reflects an extensive knowledge of the geography and people of Asia. Finally, there is the encyclopaedic work of al-Mas'udi, dating from the first half of the tenth century. Mas'udi appears to have visited India, China, and the eastern islands some time around the turn of the century and mentions the presence of Muslim trading communities in western India. Ibn Khurdadhbih was a contemporary of Mas'udi, but his *Book of Roads and Provinces* was different from the standard geographical treatises of the time. Khurdadhbih was the Director of Postal Services in Jibal and an important court official in the Abbasid caliphate. His work on roads and towns was probably intended as a practical guide for subordinate officials. The anonymous Persian work *Hudud al-'Alam* (982) contains very detailed information on the geography of Asia, though it is less useful for the commercial history of the Indian Ocean countries. Description of India and the neighbouring regions can also be found in al-Idrisi's *Nuzhat al-Mushtaq* (1154) which was written in the Norman Christian court of Sicily as a guide to a silver planisphere constructed by the author.

In marked contrast to the Islamic sources, Chinese works dealing with maritime trade and voyages are very scarce for the period before AD 1000; the only major treatise describing the Indian Ocean countries and their trading products is *Chu-fan-chi*, composed by Chau Ju-kua (c. 1225). It is, however, unusually detailed and provides accurate information on South East Asia. The author's knowledge of India and the western Indian Ocean was more vague. The scattered Chinese sources on T'ang and Sung maritime trade are extensively discussed and summarised by Kuwabara (1935) and in the introduction to *Chau Ju-kua* (1911), edited by F. Hirth and W.W.

Rockhill. For the Central Asian caravan trade and a description of the trading cities of China during the period of the Mongol conquest, Marco Polo's classic account remains indispensable. Doubts whether Marco Polo actually saw as much of China as claimed in the book are expressed by a minority of modern historians. However, it is a criticism more applicable perhaps to the work of another famous medieval trans-continental traveller than to Marco Polo. The Moroccan jurist and scholar Ibn Battuta claimed to have travelled by land and sea all the way from North Africa to the heart-land of Islam, to East Africa, Central Asia, India, South East Asia, and China. His description of caravan routes, sea voyages, and important towns appears both auth-entic and accurate as far as India and thereafter becomes a little stereotyped. It is not known how extensively Ibn Battuta travelled in China, though probably he managed to reach the busy Chinese port of Zaiton (Ch'üan-chou). Ibn Battuta's *Rihla* remains, in spite of some later reconstruction from memory, the best Islamic travel account of trans-continental routes. Ma Huan's *Ying-yai Sheng-lan* (first published in 1451 and now available only in Ming editions dating from the seventeenth century) is in a dif-ferent category altogether as a contemporary treatise on maritime trade. Ma Huan acted as an interpreter and translator to the naval fleets sent by Cheng Ho between 1404 and 1433, and his book was written from personal notes and papers kept during the voyages. As a source of commercial information on Indian Ocean ports, trading products, currency and the system of weights and measures, Ma Huan's work is unsurpassed. For economic historians of Asia, the only comparable material to that provided by Ma Huan is the collection of personal papers belonging to the medieval Jewish merchants of Egypt and North Africa, found in a genizah or depository attached to a synagogue in Old Cairo. The collection was discovered by European orientalists in the second half of the nineteenth century, and the three most important collections are now in the university libraries of Oxford and Cambridge and in the British Library, London. A detailed description and summary of the documents can be found in the four-volume study made by S.D. Goitein and in Udovitch (1967). The Cairo Genizah collections are the only direct source material to come from the actual commercial transactions of merchants engaged in the Indian Ocean trade during the period from the tenth century to the eleventh.

For the fifteenth century, the account of Abdu'r Razzaq, the Persian envoy to India, adds some interesting details of the sea voyage from the Gulf ports. Navigation and shipping routes in the Indian Ocean are also thoroughly covered by his near-contemporary Ibn Majid. The latter's *Kitab al-Fawa'id* (c. 1490) is a technical treatise on navigation by a professional Arab pilot, and shows the exact methods used by Asian ship-masters in crossing the sea out of sight of land. The problems in quantitat-ive navigation as seen by contemporary Islamic, Gujarati, and Chola navigators are discussed in detail in the work, as are timings of voyages to different seas of the Indian Ocean and wind-systems. Although, from the frequent references made by Ibn Majid to the navigational techniques of the Gujarati and Chola pilots of India, it can be inferred that the Indian ship-owners and captains were as active in the Indian Ocean as were the Arabs and Persians, no concrete historical source material is forthcoming on the subject from the subcontinent. Indeed, the silence of Indian personnel on com-mercial affairs, whether deliberate or accidental, is a feature that goes back to the pre-Islamic period of Indian history. From scattered inscriptions found in western and southern India, we know that merchants of South Asia traded extensively both by land and sea. A Tamil inscription on stone, found in Sumatra and dated 1088, refers to a corporation of "one thousand and five hundred", echoing similar references to actual associations of merchants (Settis) made in South Indian inscriptions from the tenth century. Translations of these texts are given in Nilakanta Sastri (1978). Indian commercial source material from the Islamic period is as sporadic as for the earlier years. Only indirect references are to be found in historical works such as those of Akbar's minister Abu'l Fazl and Muhammad Hashim, Khafi Khan. It is possible that at some future date the business papers of Indian trading houses, so often mentioned in European sources, will be discovered. But for the time being there is no indication as to exactly where these might be located.

With the addition of Portuguese sources from the end of the fifteenth century, documentation of Indian Ocean navigation and trade becomes much fuller, a trend that accelerates with the foundation of the Dutch and English East India Companies in about 1600. The bulk of the Portuguese documents is to be found in the national archives of Lisbon and Goa, but a great many of the state papers were destroyed during the earthquake of 1755 in Lisbon. References to Portuguese sources are given in Boxer's works, cited in the Bibliography, and in Pearson (1976). Apart from the Portuguese documents, the enormous business archives of the bureaucratic companies founded in Amsterdam and London illuminate in a wealth of statistical detail both their own trading operations and those of the indigenous merchants of the Indian Ocean. These sources are fully discussed in Chaudhuri (1978), Das Gupta (1979), and Glamann (1958). Contemporary European works on geography, trade, and Asian societies also provide comprehensive information, though a certain caution is necessary in their use as historical sources. European observers of early Asia often misunderstood the nature of the social institutions they were commenting on, and even plain statements of fact were sometimes wrong. The inaccuracies can, however, be identified in most cases. The full list of European printed works mentioned in the Bibliography is too long to be discussed here. But in this study the following authors have been extensively utilised: Barbosa, Pires, Bernier, Tavernier, Hamilton, and Grose (the names are arranged in chronological order). Attention should be specially drawn to the collections of private papers belonging to Sir Robert Cowan and to Thomas Hall. These cover the years from about 1720 to 1740 and touch on many different aspects of Indian Ocean trade.

Further reading

The reference notes to each chapter in this study indicate the most important secondary works on the subject. However, as a guide to further general reading, it is useful to reclassify the main works according to a number of analytical themes. For the economic and social role of long-distance trade, for merchants, markets, the institutions of capitalism and food habits, Braudel's monumental three-volume study *Civilisation matérielle* (1979) is indispensable. Although Braudel is not an expert on Asian history, and his detailed statements of fact or even his interpretations may strike an Asian regional expert as slightly odd or out of place, there is no question that his intuitive understanding of historically important social relationships is a constant stimulus to further thinking. When this study is read alongside his *The Mediterranean* (1972–3), the two works provide a marvellous insight into the technique of historical analysis and writing. Similar in approach to Braudel, but with a greater relevance to our subject, is Lombard's *The Golden Age of Islam* (1975). It is an excellent introduction to the economic history of the Middle East during the early period of Arab expansion. Indian Ocean trade and shipping up to about AD 1000 are discussed in Hourani, *Arab Seafaring* (1951), and up to the fourteenth century in *Islam and the Trade of Asia*, edited by Richards (1970), which contains a number of essays from specialists on different areas.

The most original and powerful analysis of the cultural significance of long distance trade and its social origins is to be found in the works of Polyani cited in the Bibliography. The anthropological interpretation of trade as an economic exchange is discussed in Sahlins (1972). Critiques of Polyani's ideas are made by Dalton, "Karl Polyani's Analysis of Long-Distance Trade and his Wider Paradigm", in *Ancient Civilisation and Trade*, edited by Sabloff and Lamberg-Karlovsky (1975), and by North (1977). The diffusion of cultural traditions and the exchange of ideas through trade have been analysed by Schrieke, "Some Remarks on Borrowing in the Development of Culture", in his *Indonesian Sociological Studies* (1955), I, and by Renfrew, "Trade as Action at a Distance: Questions of Integration and Communication", in *Ancient Civilization and Trade*, edited by Sabloff and Lamberg-Karlovsky (1975). The typology of Asian merchants and the organisation of maritime trade were first theoretically raised by van Leur (1955). For a recent restatement of his ideas and a critique, see Steensgaard (1972). For a criticism of van Leur, see Meilink-Roelofsz (1962) and Chaudhuri (1978). For the problem of political protection and its financial costs, see Lane (1966), Steensgaard (1972), and Chaudhuri (1978). For the migration of merchants and its social interpretation, see Cohen, "Cultural Strategies in the Organization of Trading Diasporas", in *The Development of Indigenous Trade and Markets in West Africa*, edited by Meillassoux (1971), and Curtin (1975). A detailed and carefully researched case-study of Indian merchants in Surat during the eighteenth century is made by Das Gupta (1979), and of English merchants in Bengal during the same period by Marshall (1976). The theoretical analysis of Asian merchants should be tested against the evidence presented in such studies as the above two. For the role of money, precious metals, and capitalist development in long-distance trade, see Atwell (1982), Chaudhuri (1978, 1984), Glamann (1958), Kriedte (1980, 1981), Perlin (1983), and Wallerstein (1974).

Bibliography

PRINTED SOURCES

ORIENTAL

Abdu'r Razzaq (1470), *Matla' al-Sa'dain*, ed. M. Shafi, Lahore, 1941–9; selected trans. in English from E. Quatremère's French version in R.H. Major, ed., *India in the Fifteenth Century*, London, 1857, and in Elliot and Dowson, IV, 95–126.

Abu'l Fazl, *'Ain-i-Akbari* (1595), ed. H. Blochmann, 2 vols., Calcutta, 1867–77; trans. in 3 vols.: vol. I by H. Blochman, rev. D.C. Phillott, vols. 2 and 3 by H.S. Jarrett, rev. J. Sarkar, Calcutta, 1927–39, 1948–9.

'Ahbar as-Sin wa'l-Hind, Relation de la Chine et de l'Inde redigée en 851 (anonymous), texte établi, traduit et commenté par Jean Sauvaget, Paris, 1948.

Ibn Battuta (died 1377), *Rihla*, ed., with French trans., C. Defremery and B.R. Sanguinetti, 4 vols., Paris, 1853–1914; ed. English trans. H.A.R. Gibb, *The Travels of Ibn Battuta A.D. 1325–1354*, London, 1929; full edn, 3 vols., Cambridge, 1958–71.

Brook, T., "The Merchant Network in 16th-Century China: A Discussion and Translation of Zhang Han's 'On Merchants' ", *Journal of the Economic and Social History of the Orient*, vol. 24, 1981, 165–214.

Buzurg Ibn Shahriyar (c. 900–53), *Kitab 'Aja'ib al-Hind*; French trans. L.M. Devic, *Les Merveilles de l'Inde*, Paris, 1878, from a copy of MS 3306, Aya Sofia Mosque, Istanbul; Arabic text and rev. French trans. L.M. Devic in P.A. van der Lith, *Le Livre des merveilles de l'Inde*, Leiden, 1883–6; English trans. P. Quennell, London, 1928, and G.S.P. Freeman-Grenville, *The Book of the Wonders of India, Mainland, Sea, and Islands*, London and The Hague, 1981; English extracts in G.F. Hourani, *Arab Seafaring*, Princeton, NJ, 1951.

Chau Ju-kua, *Chu-fan-chi* (c. 1225, 1242–58), English trans. F. Hirth and W.W. Rockhill, *Chau Ju-kua: His Work on the Chinese and Arab Trade in the 12th and 13th Centuries*, St Petersburg, 1911.

Elliot, Sir H.M., and J. Dowson, eds., *The History of India as Told by its Own Historians*, 8 vols., London, 1867–77; repr. Allahabad, 1972.

Fairbank, J.K., and S.Y. Teng, "On the Ch'ing Tributary System", *Harvard Journal of Asiatic Studies*, vol. 6, 1941–2, 135–346.

Goeje, M.J. de, ed., *Bibliotheca Geographorum Arabicorum*, Leiden, 1870–1906.

Ibn Hawqal, *Kitab Surat al 'Ard*, or *Kitab al-Masalik wa'l-Mamalik* (988); Arabic text in Goeje, vol. II; selected English trans. in Elliot and Dowson, I, 31–40.

Hudud al-'Alam (anonymous), English trans. V. Minorsky, *Hudud al-'Alam, the Regions of the World: A Persian Geography 372 A.H.–982 A.D.*, London, 1937; 2nd edn ed. C.E. Bosworth, London, 1970.

Hultzsch, E., ed., *South Indian Inscriptions*, Madras, 1891.

Al-Idrisi, *Nuzhat al-Mushtaq* (1154), selected Arabic text and English trans. in S. Maqbul Ahmad, *India and the Neighbouring Territories as Described by the Sharif al-Idrisi*, part 1, Aligarh, 1954; part 2, Leiden, 1960; selected English trans. in Elliot and Dowson, I, 75–93.

Abu Ishaq Al-Istakhri, *Kitab al-Aqalim* (*c.* 951), Arabic text in Goeje, vol. I; selected English trans. in Elliot and Dowson, I, 26–30.

Ibn Ishaq (died 767), in English trans. A. Guillaume, *The Life of Muhammad: A Translation of Ishaq's Sirat Rasul Allah*, London, 1955.

Jahangir (1624), *Tuzuk-i Jahangiri*, ed. Syud Ahmud, Ghazipur and Aligarh, 1863–4; English trans. A. Rogers and H. Beveridge, 2 vols., London, 1909–14.

Khafi Khan (*c.* 1664–1732), *Muntakhab al-Lubab*, English trans. in Elliot and Dowson, VII.

Ibn Khurdadhbih (*c.* 850–911), *Kitab al-Masalik w'al-Mamalik* ("Book of Roads and Provinces"), Arabic text in Goeje, V; selected English trans. in Elliot and Dowson, I, 13–17.

Ma Huan (1433), *Ying-yai Sheng-lan* ("The Overall Survey of the Ocean's Shores"), English trans. J.V.G. Mills, Cambridge, 1970.

Ibn Majid Ahmad, *Kitab al-Fawa'id fi usul al-bahr wa'l-qawa'id* (*c.* 1490), Arabic text from MS 2292. Bibliothèque Nationale, Paris, in G. Ferrand, *Pilote des mers de l'Inde et de la Chine et de l'Indonésie*, 2 vols., Paris, 1921–3; English trans. G.T. Tibbets, *Arab Navigation in the Indian Ocean before the Coming of the Portuguese*, London, 1971.

Al-Mas'udi (died 956), *Muruj al-Dhahab wa-Ma'adin al-Jauhar*, Arabic text and French trans. in C. Barbier de Meynard and Pavet de Courteille, *Les Prairies d'or*, 9 vols., Paris, 1861–77; English extracts in Elliot and Dowson, 1, 18–25.

Al-Muqaddasi (died 1000), *Ahsan al-Taqasim fi ma'rifat al-aqalim*, Arabic text in Goeje, III; English trans. G.S.A. Ranking and R.F. Azoo, Calcutta, 1901; French trans. A. Miquel, Damascus, 1963.

Periplus Maris Erythraei, ed. and trans. J.W. McCrindle, Calcutta, 1879; original text in Hjalmar Frisk, *Le Périple de la mer érythrée*, Goteborg, 1927; new English trans. from this version by G.W.B. Huntingford, *The Periplus of the Erythraean Sea*, London, 1980.

Serjeant, R.B., ed., *The Portuguese off the South Arabian Coast, Hadrami Chronicles, with Yemeni and European Accounts of Dutch Piracies off Mocha in the Seventeenth Century*, Oxford, 1963.

Al-Tabari (died 923), *Ta'rikh al-Tabari*, Arabic text ed. Th. von Noldeke, Leiden, 1879, and Muhammad Abu al-Fadl Ibrahim, 10 vols., Cairo, 1960–77; French trans. from Muhammad Bal'ami's Persian version in M. Hermann Zotenberg, *Chronique de . . . Tabari*, 4 vols., Paris, 1867–74.

Al-Waqidi (died 823), *Kitab al-maghazi*, Arabic text ed. M. Jones, 3 vols., London, 1966.

EUROPEAN

Albuquerque, Affonso de, *Cartas de Affonso de Albuquerque seguidas de documentos que as elucidam*, ed. Raymundo Antonio de Bulhão Pato, vols. II–III, Lisbon, 1898, 1903.

  The Commentaries of the Great Afonso D'Albuquerque, ed. W. de Gray Birch, vol. IV, London, 1884.

Baldaeus, Philippus, *Naauwkeurige Beschryvinge van Malabar en Choromandel*, Amsterdam, 1672.

Barbosa, Duarte, *The Book of Duarte Barbosa: An Account of the Countries Bordering on the Indian Ocean and Their Inhabitants, 1518*, ed. and trans. M.L. Dames, 2 vols., London, 1918–21.

Bernier, François, *Travels in the Mogul Empire, A.D. 1656–1668*, trans. from French by Irvine Brock, rev. and annotated by A. Constable, London, 1891; repr. Delhi, 1968.

Bowrey, Thomas, *A Geographical Account of Countries Round the Bay of Bengal 1669 to 1679*, ed. Sir Richard Temple, Cambridge, 1905.

Cabral, Pedro Alvares, *The Voyage of Pedro Alvares Cabral to Brazil and India*, ed. and trans. W.B. Greenlee, London, 1938.

Calendar of State Papers, Foreign Series, of the Reign of Elizabeth, vol. 19 (August 1584–August 1585), ed. Sophie Crawford Lomas, London, 1916.

A Calendar of the Court Minutes of the East India Company 1635–1679, ed. E.B. Sainsbury, 11 vols., Oxford, 1907–38.

Castro, João de, *Cartas de D. João de Castro*, ed. and annotated by Elaine Sanceau, Lisbon, 1955.

Correa, Gaspar, *Lendas da India*, ed. Rodrigo José de Lima Felner, 4 vols., Lisbon, 1858, repr. Liechtenstein, 1976.

  The Three Voyages of Vasco Da Gama and his Viceroyalty from the Lendas Da India of Gaspar Correa, trans. H.E.J. Stanley, London, 1869.

Cortés, Martin, *Breve compendio de la sphere ye de la arte de navegur*, Seville, 1551.

Cronica do descobrimento e conquesta da India pelos Portugueses (codice anómino, Museu Britânico, Egerton 20,901), ed. Luis M. de Albuquerque, Coimbra, 1974.

English Factories in India 1618–1669, ed. W. Foster, 13 vols., Oxford, 1906–27.

English Factories in India (New Series) 1670–1684, ed. Sir C. Fawcett, 4 vols., Oxford, 1936–55.

The First Letter Book of the East India Company 1600–1619, ed. G. Birdwood and W. Foster, London, 1892.

Forbes, James, *Oriental Memoirs*, 4 vols., London, 1813.

Foster, W., ed., *Early Travels in India 1583–1619*, London, 1921. (Accounts of Ralph Fitch, John Mildenhall, William Hawkins, William Finch, Nicholas Withington, Thomas Coryat, and Edward Terry.)

Fryer, John, *A New Account of East India and Persia, being Nine Years' Travels 1672–81*, ed. W. Crooke, 3 vols., London, 1909, 1912, 1915.

Gama, Vasco da, *The Journal of the First Voyage of Vasco da Gama 1497–1499*, ed. and trans. E.G. Ravenstein, London, 1898.

Grose, John Henry, *A Voyage to the East Indies*, 1st edn London, 1757; 2nd edn, 2 vols., London, 1772.

Hamilton, Alexander, *A New Account of the East Indies*, first published Edinburgh, 1727; modern version ed. W. Foster, 2 vols., London, 1930.

Linschoten, Jan Huygen van, *The Voyage of John Huygen van Linschoten to the East Indies, from the Old English Translation of 1598*, ed. A.C. Burnell and P.A. Tiele, 2 vols., London, 1885; *Itinerario, Voyage ofte schipvaert van (Jan Huygen van Linschoten) naer Oost ofte Portugaels Indien 1597–1592*, ed. H. Kern and H. Terpstra, 3 vols., The Hague, 1955, 1956, 1957.

Livro das cidades, e fortalezas, que a Coroa de Portugal tem nas partes da India [1582], Centro de Estudos Históricos Ultramarinos, Portugal: Studia, No. 6, Lisbon, 1960.

Lopez, R.S., ed., *Medieval Trade in the Mediterranean World: Illustrative Documents Translated with Introductions and Notes*, London, 1955.

Lucena, Joam de, *Historia da Vida do Padre Francisco de Xavier*, Lisbon, 1600.

Major, R.H., ed., *India in the Fifteenth Century, Being a Collection of Narratives of Voyages to India*, London, 1857.

Manucci, Niccolao (1699–1709), *Storia do Mogor*, trans. W. Irvine, 4 vols., London, 1907–8.

Master, Streynsham, *The Diaries of Streynsham Master 1675–1680*, ed. Sir Richard Temple, 2 vols., London, 1911.

Niebuhr, Carsten, *Travels through Arabia and Other Countries in the East*, trans. R. Heron, 2 vols., Edinburgh, 1792.

Pelsaert, Francisco, *Jahangir's India: The Remonstrantie of Francisco Pelsaert*, ed. W.H. Moreland and P. Geyl, Cambridge, 1925.

Pires, Tomé, *The Suma Oriental of Tomé Pires: An Account of the East, from the Red Sea to Japan, Written in Malacca and India in 1512–1515*, ed. and trans. Armando Cortesão, London, 1944; repr. Wiesbaden, 1967.

Polo, Marco, *The Description of the World*, ed. and trans. A.C. Moule and P. Pelliot, London, 1938.

Priuli, Girolamo, *I Diarii*, 2 vols., Citta di Castello, 1933–8; selected English trans. in W.B. Greenlee, ed., *The Voyage of Pedro Alvares Cabral: see under* Cabral.

Records of Fort St George: The Diary and Consultation Book 1731, Madras, 1930.

Roe, Sir Thomas, *The Embassy of Sir Thomas Roe to India 1615–1619*, ed. W. Foster, London, 1926.

Roque, Jean de la, *A Voyage to Arabia Felix* (1716), English trans., London, 1742.

Sanderson, John, *The Travels of John Sanderson 1584–1602*, ed. W. Foster, London, 1931.

Smith, Adam, *An Enquiry into the Nature and Causes of the Wealth of Nations* (1776), repr. from the 6th edn, London, 1905.

Solis, Duarte Gomes, *Discursos sobre los comercios de las dos Indias*, ed. M.B. Amzalak, Lisbon, 1943.

Tavernier, Jean-Baptiste, *Travels in India* (1640–67), trans. John Phillips, London, 1677; new edn trans. V. Ball, 2 vols., London, 1889; Ball's trans. rev. and ed. W. Crooke, London, 1925.

ARCHIVAL SOURCES

India Office Records, London
East India Company: records listed under General Correspondence, Factory Records, Proceedings, and Marine Records.

Public Record Office, London
Private Papers of Thomas Hall; Chancery Masters' Exhibits, C103, nos. 130–3, C111, no. 95.

Public Record Office, Northern Ireland, Belfast
Private Papers of Sir Robert Cowan, The Londonderry Estate; microfilm copy in India Office Library, London.

British Library
Additional Manuscripts 19282, 38871–3.

Algemeen Rijksarchief, The Hague
Vereenigde Oostindische Compagnie, VOC (United East India Company): records listed under Uit Indie Overgekomen Brieven en Papieren and Bataviaas Inkomend Briefboek.

Stadsarchief Antwerpen, Antwerp
General Indische Compagnie (The Ostend Company): "The Memorie of Alexander Hume", 1730, in vol. 5769.

Archivo General de Indias, Seville
Records on bullion mining and movements listed under Contaduría, Contratación, Indiferente General, and Audiencia de México.

MODERN WORKS

Arendonk, C. van, "Kahwa", article in the *Encyclopaedia of Islam*, new edn, Leiden, 1960– .
Ashtor, E., *Studies on the Levantine Trade in the Middle Ages*, London, 1978.
Atwell, W.S., "International Bullion Flows and the Chinese Economy *circa* 1530–1650", *Past and Present*, no. 95, 1982, 68–90.
Balazs, E., *Chinese Civilization and Bureaucracy: Variations on a Theme*, trans. H.M. Wright, New Haven, Conn., and London, 1974.
Banani, A., and S. Vryonis, eds., *Individualism and Conformity in Classical Islam*, Wiesbaden, 1977.
Bertin, J., ed., *Atlas of Food Crops*, Geographical and Chronological Survey for an Atlas of World History, École Pratique des Hautes Études, VIᵉ section: Sciences Économiques et Sociales, Paris and The Hague, 1968.
Bowen, R.L., *Arab Dhows of Eastern Arabia*, Rehoboth, Mass., 1949.
Boxer, C.R., *The Christian Century in Japan 1549–1650*, Berkeley and Los Angeles, 1951.

The Great Ship from Amacon: Annals of Macao and the Old Japan Trade 1555–1640, Lisbon, 1959.

"A Note on Portuguese Reactions to the Revival of the Red Sea Spice Trade and the Rise of Atcheh, 1540–1600", *Journal of South-East Asian History*, vol. 10, 1969, 415–28.

Portuguese India in the Mid-Seventeenth Century, Delhi, 1980.

The Portuguese Seaborne Empire 1415–1825, London, 1969.

The Tragic History of the Sea, 1559–1565, Cambridge, 1968.

Braudel, F., *Afterthoughts on Material Civilization and Capitalism*, trans, P.M. Ranum, Baltimore, Md, 1977.

Civilisation matérielle: économie et capitalisme, XVe–XVIIIe siècle, 3 vols., Paris, 1979; English trans. S. Reynolds, vols. I–II, London, 1981–2. Vol. III, London, 1984.

"Histoire et sciences sociales: la longue durée", *Annales, économies, sociétés, civilisations*, vol. 13, 1958, 725–53; English trans. in P. Burke, ed., *Economy and Society in Early Modern Europe: Essays from Annales*, London, 1972.

The Mediterranean and the Mediterranean World in the Age of Philip II, trans. S. Reynolds, 2 vols., London, 1972–3.

Brice, W.C., ed., *An Historical Atlas of Islam*, Leiden, 1981.

Brock, S.P., "Syriac Sources for Seventh-Century History", *Byzantine and Modern Greek Studies*, vol. 2, 1976, 17–36.

Brook, T., "The Merchant Network in 16th-Century China: A Discussion and Translation of Zhang Han's 'On Merchants' ", *Journal of the Economic and Social History of the Orient*, vol. 24, 1981, 165–214.

Bulliet, R.W., *The Camel and the Wheel*, Cambridge, Mass., 1975.

Cahen, C., "L'Histoire économique et sociale de l'orient musulman médiéval", *Studia Islamica*, vol. 1, 1955, 93–115.

Canard, M., *Byzance et les Musulmans du Proche Orient*, London, 1973.

Chao Ch'uan-ch'eng, "A Ship's Voyage from Luzon to China in the Eighteenth Century", in E-Tu Zen Sun and J. de Francis, eds., *Chinese Social History: Translations of Selected Studies*, Washington, DC, 1956.

Chaudhuri, K.N., "Circuits monétaires internationaux, prix comparés et spécialisation économique, 1500–1750", in J. Day, ed., *Études d'histoire monétaire*, Paris, 1984.

The English East India Company: The Study of an early Joint-Stock Company 1600–1640, London, 1965.

The Trading World of Asia and the English East India Company 1660–1760, Cambridge, 1978.

Chaudhury, S., "The Rise and Decline of Hugli, a Port in Medieval Bengal", *Bengal Past and Present*, vol. 86, 1967, 33–67.

Chittick, N., *Kilwa: An Islamic Trading City on the East African Coast*, 2 vols., Nairobi, 1974.

"The 'Shirazi' Colonization of East Africa", *Journal of African History*, vol. 6, 1965, 275–94.

Coedès, G., *The Indianized States of Southeast Asia*, ed. and trans. W.F. Vella and S.B. Cowing, Honolulu, 1968.

Les Peuples de la péninsule indochinoise, Paris, 1962.

Commissariat, M.S., *A History of Gujarat*, 2 vols., Bombay, 1938–57.

Cook, M.A., ed., *Studies in the Economic History of the Middle East*, London, 1970.

Curtin, Philip D., *Economic Change in Precolonial Africa: Senegambia in the Era of Slave Trade*, Madison, Wisc., 1975.

Das Gupta, A., *Indian Merchants and the Decline of Surat*, Wiesbaden, 1979.
  Malabar in Asian Trade 1740–1800, Cambridge, 1967.

Digby, S., "The Maritime Trade of India" (1982): *see under* Raychaudhuri and Habib, eds., *The Cambridge Economic History of India*.

Dobb, M., *Studies in the Development of Capitalism*, London, 1963.

Drewes, G.W.J., "New Light on the Coming of Islam to Indonesia", *Bijdragen Tot de Taal-, Land-en Volkenkunde*, Deel 124, 1968, 433–59.

Duyvendak, J.J.L., "The True Dates of the Chinese Maritime Expeditions in the Early Fifteenth Century", *T'oung Pao*, vol. 37, 1938, 340–412.

Fairbank, J.K., "Tributary Trade and China's Relations with the West", *The Far Eastern Quarterly*, vol. 5, 1941, 129–49.
  and S.Y. Teng, "On the Ch'ing Tributary System", *Harvard Journal of Asiatic Studies*, vol. 6, 1941–2, 135–246.

Ferrand, G., *Introduction à l'astronomie nautique arabe*, Paris, 1928.

Findlay, A.G., *A Directory for the Navigation of the Indian Ocean*, 4th edn, London, 1897.

Fischel, W., "The City in Islam", *Middle Eastern Affairs*, vol. 7, 1956, 227–32.
  "The Spice Trade in Mamluk Egypt", *Journal of the Economic and Social History of the Orient*, vol. 1, 1958, 157–74.

Foster, W., *John Company*, London, 1926.

Fraser, J.T., and N. Lawrence, eds., *The Study of Time II*, New York, 1975.

Furber, H., *Rival Empires of Trade 1620–1750*, Minneapolis, Minn., 1976.

Garlake, P.S., *The Early Islamic Architecture of the East African Coast*, London, 1966.

Gaube, H., *Iranian Cities*, New York, 1978.
  and E. Wirth, *Der Bazar von Isfahan*, Wiesbaden, 1978.

Gerber, H., "The Muslim Law of Partnerships in Ottoman Court Records", *Studia Islamica*, no. 53, 1981, 109–19.

Glamann, K., *Dutch Asiatic Trade 1620–1750*, Copenhagen and The Hague, 1958.

Goitein, S.D., *A Mediterranean Society: The Jewish Communities of the Arab World as Portrayed in the Documents of the Cairo Geniza*, vol. I, Berkeley, Los Angeles, and London, 1967.
  Studies in Islamic History and Institutions, Leiden, 1966.
  "Two Eye-Witness Reports on an Expedition of the King of Kish (Qais) against Aden", *Bulletin of the School of Oriental and African Studies*, vol. 16, 1954, 247–547.

Gompertz, G.St G.M., *Chinese Celadon Ware*, London, 1958.

Grant, C.P., *The Syrian Desert*, London, 1937.

Gray, B., "The Export of Chinese Porcelain to India", *Transactions of the Oriental Ceramic Society*, 1964–6, 21–37.

Greenhill, B., *Archaeology of the Boat: A New Introductory Study*, London, 1976.

Groom, N., *Frankincense and Myrrh: A Study of the Arab Incense Trade*, London, 1981.

Grunebaum, G.E. von, "Islam: Essays in the Nature and Growth of a Cultural

Tradition", *American Anthropology*, vol. 57, 1955, 141–58.

"Three Comments on Orthogenetic and Heterogenetic Urban Environment: Hellenistic and Muslim Views on Cities", *Economic Development and Cultural Change*, vol. 3, 1954, 75–6.

Guillaume, A., *The Life of Muhammad: A Translation of Ishaq's Sirat Rasul Allah*, London, 1955.

Gungwu, Wang, "The Nanhai Trade: A Study of the Early History of Chinese Trade in the South China Sea", *Journal of the Malayan Branch of the Royal Asiatic Society*, vol. 31, 1958, 1–133.

"The Opening of Relations between China and Malacca, 1403–5", in J.S. Bastin and R. Roolvink, eds., *Malayan and Indonesian Studies: Essays Presented to Sir Richard Winstedt*, London, 1964.

Harrison, J.B., "Five Portuguese Historians", in C.H. Philips, ed., *Historians of India, Pakistan, and Ceylon*, London, 1961.

Hiskett, M., "Materials Relating to the Cowry Currency of the Western Sudan", *Bulletin of the School of Oriental and African Studies*, vol. 29, 1966, 122–42, 339–66.

Holt, P.M., Ann K.S. Lambton, and B. Lewis, eds., *The Cambridge History of Islam*, 4 vols., Cambridge, 1970.

Hornell, J., *The Origins and Ethnological Significance of Indian Boat Designs*, Calcutta, 1920.

Horridge, G.A., *The Design of the Planked Boats of the Moluccas*, London, 1978.

The Konjo Boatbuilders and the Bugis Prahus of South Sulawesi, London, 1979.

Hourani, A.H., and S.M. Stern, eds., *The Islamic City*, Oxford, 1970.

Hourani, G.F., *Arab Seafaring in the Indian Ocean in Ancient and Early Medieval Times*, Princeton, NJ, 1951.

Huart, C., "Yazd", article in the *Encyclopaedia of Islam*.

Johnson, M., "Cowrie Currencies in West Africa", *Journal of African History*, vol. 11, 1970, 17–49, 331–53.

Jung-pang Lo, "Chinese Shipping and East–West Trade from the Tenth to the Fourteenth Century", in M. Mollat, ed., *Sociétés et compagnies de commerce en orient et dans l'océan indien*, Paris, 1970.

"Maritime Commerce and its Relation to the Sung Navy", *Journal of the Economic and Social History of the Orient*, vol. 12, 1969, 57–101.

Karaka, D.F., *History of the Parsis*, London, 1884.

Kirkman, J.S., *Men and Monuments on the East African Coast*, London, 1964.

Kister, M.J., *Studies in Jahiliyya and Early Islam*, London, 1980.

Kriedte, P., *Peasants, Landlords, and Merchant Capitalists, Europe and the World Economy 1500–1800*, Göttingen, 1980.

H. Medick, and J. Schlumbohm, eds., *Industrialization before Industrialization: Rural Industry in the Genesis of Capitalism*, Cambridge, 1981.

Kuwabara, J., "P'u shou-keng . . . A General Sketch of the Trade of the Arabs in China during the T'ang and Sung Eras", *Memoirs of the Research Department of the Toyo Bunko*, vol. 7, 1935, 1–104.

Lach, D.F., *Asia in the Making of Europe*, vol. I, Chicago, Ill., 1965.

Lane, F.C., *Venice and History: The Collected Papers of Frederick C. Lane*, Baltimore, Md, 1966.

Lassner, J., *The Shaping of Abbasid Rule*, Princeton, NJ, 1980.

The Topography of Baghdad in the Early Middle Ages, Detroit, Ill., 1970.

Lattimore, O., *The Desert Road to Turkestan*, London, 1928.

Inner Asian Frontiers of China, Boston, Mass., 1940; repr. 1962.

Le Strange, G., *The Lands of the Eastern Caliphate*, Cambridge, 1905.

Leur, J.V. van, *Indonesian Trade and Society: Essays in Asian Social and Economic History*, The Hague, 1955.

Lewis, A., "Maritime Skills in the Indian ocean 1368–1500", *Journal of the Economic and Social History of the Orient*, vol. 16, 1973, 238–64.

Little, J.H., "The House of Jagatseth", *Bengal Past and Present*, vol. 20, 1920, 111–200; vol. 22, 1921, 1–119.

Lombard, M., *The Golden Age of Islam*, Amsterdam, 1975.

Lopez, R.S., "China Silk in Europe in the Yuan Period", *Journal of the American Oriental Society*, vol. 72, 1952, 72–6.

"Du Marche temporaire à la colonie permanente: L'évolution de la politique commerciale au moyen âge", *Annales: économies, sociétés, et civilisations*, vol. 4, 1949, 389–405.

Magalhães-Godinho, V., *L'Économie de l'empire portugais aux XVᵉ et XVIᵉ siècles*, Paris, 1969.

Marshall, P.J., *East Indian Fortunes: The British in Bengal in the Eighteenth Century*, Oxford, 1976.

Meilink-Roelofsz, M.A.P., *Asian Trade and European Influence in the Indonesian Archipelago between 1500 and about 1630*, The Hague, 1962.

Meillassoux, C., ed., *The Development of Indigenous Trade and Markets in West Africa*, London, 1971.

Mingana, A., *Sources syriaques*, Leipzig, 1907–8.

Miquel, A., "Origine et carte des mers dans la géographie arabe aux approches de l'an mil", *Annales: économies, sociétés, civilisations*, vol. 35, 1980, 452–61.

Mollat, M., ed., *Sociétés et compagnies de commerce en Orient et dans l'Océan indien*, Paris, 1970.

Moreland, W.H., "The Ships of the Arabian Sea about A.D. 1500", *Journal of the Royal Asiatic Society*, part 1, 1939, 65–74; part 2, 1939, 173–90.

Needham, J., *Clerks and Craftsmen in China and the West*, Cambridge, 1970.

Özbaran, S., "The Ottoman Turks and the Portuguese in the Persian Gulf, 1534–1581", *Journal of Asian History*, vol. 6, 1972, 45–87.

Pearson, M.N., *Merchants and Rulers in Gujarat: The Response to the Portuguese in the Sixteenth Century*, Berkeley, Los Angeles, and London, 1976.

Pellat, C., "India and Indians as Seen by an Arab Writer of the 3rd/9th Century – Al-Djahiz", in K.S. Lal, ed., *Studies in Asian History: Proceedings of the Asian History Congress 1961*, New Delhi, 1969.

Perlin, F., "Proto-Industrialization and Pre-Colonial South Asia", *Past and Present*, no. 98, 1983, 30–95.

Polyani, K., "Ports of Trade in Early Societies", *Journal of Economic History*, vol. 23, 1963, 30–45.

"Traders and Trade", in Sabloff and Lamberg-Karlovsky, eds., *Ancient Civilization and Trade*.

C.M. Arnesberg and H.W. Pearson, eds., *Trade and Markets in the Early Empires*, New York, 1957.

Pope, J.A., *Chinese Porcelain from the Ardebil Shrine*, Washington, DC, 1956.

Pryor, J.H., "The Origins of the Commenda Contract", *Speculum*, vol. 52, 1977, 5–37.

Qaisar, A.J., "Merchant Shipping in India during the Seventeenth Century", in *Medieval India: A Miscellany*, Centre of Advanced Studies, Department of History, Aligarh Muslim University, vol. 2, Delhi, 1970, 195–220.

"Shipbuilding in India during the Seventeenth Century", *Indian Economic and Social History Review*, vol. 5, 1968, 149–70.

Raychaudhuri, T., and I. Habib, eds., *The Cambridge Economic History of India, Vol. I: c. 1200–c. 1750*, Cambridge, 1982.

Reischauer, E.O., "Notes on T'ang Dynasty Sea Routes", *Harvard Journal of Asiatic Studies*, vol. 5, 1940–1, 142–64.

Renfrew, C., "Trade as Action at a Distance: Questions of Integration and Communication", in Sabloff and Lamberg-Karlovsky, eds., *Ancient Civilization and Trade*.

Richard, J., *Orient et occident au moyen âge: Contactes et relations (XII*ᵉ*–XV*ᵉ* siècle)*, London, 1976.

Richards, D.S., ed., *Islam and the Trade of Asia: A Colloquium*, Oxford, 1970.

Rossabi, M., "Ming China and Turfan 1406–1517", *Central Asiatic Journal*, vol. 16, 1972, 206–25.

"The Tea and Horse Trade with Inner Asia during the Ming", *Journal of Asian History*, vol. 4, 1970, 136–42.

Rostovtzeff, M., *Caravan Cities: Petra and Jerash, Palmyra and Dura*, Oxford, 1932.

The Social and Economic History of the Roman Empire, 2nd edn rev. P.M. Fraser, 2 vols., Oxford, 1979.

Salmon, C., and D. Lombard, "Un Vaisseau du XIIIème s. retrouvé avec sa cargaison dans la rade de 'Zaitun' ", *Archipel*, vol. 18, 1979, 57–67.

Sastri, K.A. Nilakanta, "A Tamil Merchant-Guild in Sumatra", and other essays in his *South India and South-East Asia: Studies in their History and Culture*, Mysore, 1978.

Schafer, E.H., *The Golden Peaches of Samarkand: A Study of T'ang Exotics*, Berkeley and Los Angeles, 1963.

Schrieke, B.J.O., *Indonesian Sociological Studies*, 2 vols., The Hague, 1955.

Schurhammer, G., *Francis Xavier*, 4 vols., Rome, 1973–80.

Serjeant, R.B., *The Portuguese off the South Arabian Coast*, Oxford, 1963.

ed., *The Islamic City*, Paris, 1980.

Shaban, M.A., *Islamic History A.D. 750–1055*, Cambridge, 1976.

Shboul, A.M.H., *Al-Mas'udi & His World: A Muslim Humanist and his Interest in Non-Muslims*, London, 1979.

Simkin, C.G.F., *The Traditional Trade of Asia*, London, 1968.

Siroux, M., "Les Caravanserais routiers safavids", *Iranian Studies*, vol. 7, 1974, 348–75.

So Kwan-wai, *Japanese Piracy in Ming China during the 16th Century*, East Lansing, Mich., 1975.

La Société Jean Bodin, *Les Grandes Escales*, 2 vols., Brussels, 1972.

Spencer, J.E., *Junks of Central China*, College Station, Tex., 1976.

Steensgaard, N., *Carracks, Caravans, and Companies: The Structural Crisis in the European–Asian Trade in the Early 17th Century*, Copenhagen, 1972.

Stern, S.M., "Ramisht of Siraf, a Merchant Millionaire of the Twelfth Century", *Journal of the Royal Asiatic Society*, 1967, 10–14.

Stillman, N.A., "The Eleventh Century Merchant House of Ibn 'Awkal: A Geniza Study", *Journal of the Economic and Social History of the Orient*, vol. 16, 1973, 15–88.

Tibbets, G.R., *Arab Navigation in the Indian Ocean before the Coming of the Portuguese*, London, 1971.

    "Early Muslim Traders in South-East Asia", *Journal of the Malayan Branch of the Royal Asiatic Society*, vol. 30, 1957, 1–45.

Udovitch, A.L., "Credit as a Means of Investment in Medieval Islamic Trade", *Journal of the American Oriental Society*, vol. 87, 1967, 260–4.

    "Formalism and Informalism in the Social and Economic Institutions of the Medieval Islamic World": *see under* Banani and Vryonis, eds., *Individualism and Conformity*.

    ed., *The Islamic Middle East, 700–1900: Studies in Economic and Social History*, Princeton, NJ, 1981.

Vaglieri, L. Veccia, "Dumat al-Jandal", article in the *Encyclopaedia of Islam*, new edn., Leiden, 1960– .

Villiers, A., *Sons of Sinbad*, London, 1969.

Wallerstein, I., *Modern World-System: Capitalist Agriculture and the Origins of the European World-Economy in the Sixteenth Century*, New York, 1974.

Watanabe, M.S., "Causality and Time": *see under* Fraser and Lawrence, eds., *The Study of Time II*.

Watson, A.M., *Agricultural Innovation in the Early Islamic World: The Diffusion of Crops and Farming Techniques, 700–1100*, Cambridge, 1983.

Watt, W.M., *Muhammad at Mecca*, London, 1953.

    Muhammad at Medina, London, 1956.

Weinstein, D., *Ambassador from Venice: Pietro Pasqualigo in Lisbon 1501*, Minneapolis, Minn., 1960.

Wheatley, P., "Geographical Notes on Some Commodities Involved in Sung Maritime Trade", *Journal of the Malayan Branch of the Royal Asiatic Society*, vol. 32, 1959, 5–140.

    The Golden Khersonese: Studies in the Historical Geography of the Malaya Peninsula before A.D. 1500, Kuala Lumpur, 1961.

Wiet, G., "Les Marchands d'épices sous les sultans mamlouks", *Cahiers d'Histoire Égyptienne*, vol. 8, 1955, 81–147.

Wilkinson, J.C., "Bayasirah and Bayadir", *Arabian Studies*, vol. 1, 1974, 75–85.

Will, Pierre-Étienne, *Bureaucratie et famine en Chine au 18ᵉ siècle*, Paris, 1980.

Winstedt, R., and P.E. Josselin, "The Maritime Laws of Malacca", *Journal of the Malayan Branch of the Royal Asiatic Society*, vol. 29, 1956, 22–59.

Wolf, E.R., "The Social Organization of Mecca and the Origins of Islam", *South Western Journal of Anthropology*, vol. 7, 1951, 329–56.

Wolters, O.W., *Early Indonesian Commerce: A Study of the Origins of Srivijaya*, New York, 1967.

Index

WITHDRAWN
BY
WILLIAMSBURG REGIONAL LIBRARY

1364752R00151

Made in the USA
San Bernardino, CA
13 December 2012